how to write
REPORTS •
PAPERS •
THESES •
ARTICLES •

by john p. riebel

New York

Illustrated by ELIZABETH RIEBEL SEVISON

Fourth Printing, 1978

Published by ARCO PUBLISHING COMPANY, INC.,
219 Park Avenue South, New York, N.Y. 10003.

Second Edition, copyright © 1972 by Arco Publishing Company, Inc.
First Edition, copyright © 1962 by John P. Riebel.
All rights reserved.

No part of this book may be reproduced, by any means,
without permission in writing from the publisher,
except by a reviewer.

Cloth Edition: ISBN 0-668-02392-9
Paper Edition: ISBN 0-668-02391-0
Library of Congress Catalog Card Number: 73-125893

Printed in the United States of America

PREFACE TO THE SECOND EDITION

The first twenty-four pages of this book are the actual text I used when I taught report writing at California State Polytechnic College in San Luis Obispo. The balance of this book is supplementary material which consists of what college students should know, but which I have found that they, most unfortunately, did not. The division of words into those which name, act, modify, or connect is, as far as I can determine, unique. The line charts in this book are a very effective way of teaching students the complicated relationships between words and the ways they can vary in usage within English syntax.

For several years, I had the writing of this book under consideration, but I kept putting it off because I was not able to come up with an outline that suited my purpose. Then one day while I was reviewing an article I had written for *Refrigerating Engineering*, I realized that that article contained the very outline I had been seeking. Once I had the outline, the rest was easy, for I had already compiled a large collection of 3" x 5" cards which I had cataloged carefully. I had started to collect these notes while I was teaching at General Motors Institute in Flint, Michigan, and I had added to them at Cal Poly, where I read thousands of reports and letters, many of which provided me with valuable notes for my collection.

Now, some hints on how to use this book in the most effective way, either as a teacher or as a person who wishes to learn to write more effectively. First, grammar consists simply of the accepted rules for good, clear, concise, and correct writing, nothing more. If you hope to learn to write well, you *must* know the rules of good writing, which have evolved throughout the ages during which English grammar has been in use. Just imagine the chaos that would result if football, the dominant game today, or basketball, or any other game, were played by teams that made up the rules as they went along and changed them at will, with no two sets of rules alike, and if every player did whatever he pleased! Grammar *wasn't* devised by fiendish English teachers to torture poor innocent students; rather, it is an accretion of rules which started thousands of years ago, probably with Aristotle, which he carefully detailed in his famous *Rhetoric*. This accretion has been added to, refined, and modified over the centuries to fit the needs of the time. One such rule has been changed during the reader's lifetime: the use of *like* as a conjunction and as a preposition—in the famous, or infamous if you wish, "Winstons taste good *like* a cigarette should." Regardless of whether you agree with this usage (and I don't), this change will inevitably become accepted usage in modern grammar. Actually, this is something we should, in all probability, be happy about, since it shows us that grammar is not merely a set of frozen rules, but rather that these rules are flexible enough to change with the changing times.

Therefore, we can see that grammar is simply an aggregation of the rules of good writing, which has been established not by teachers or by a committee, but by those writers whose work is accepted as good. When I was going through DuPont Manual Training High School in Louisville, Kentucky, many years ago, I despised grammar, and this dislike stayed with me throughout my years of college, at the University of Kentucky, where I earned a B.S. in Chemical Engineering. At that time, I had no desire to become a teacher, much less a teacher of English. But over the next few years, I drifted into the study of English, which I subsequently taught at such schools as Georgia Tech, the University of Illinois, General Motors Institute, and Cal Poly, among others.

Punctuation is another bugaboo which haunts and frightens most people until they realize that punctuation is simply gestures in writing. When you speak, you gesticulate with your body, your arms, hands, eyes, and so forth. So it is with punctuation; you gesture with the use of the appropriate punctuation mark. No really new mark of punctuation has come into use for hundreds of years. In fact, we have lost one that, years ago, was very important: the inverted P (¶), which was used in printed works to indicate the beginning of a new paragraph. Today, the beginning of a new paragraph is signified by indentation or by an extra line in letters written in the National Office Management Association (simplified block flush-left) style. But it is important to remember that punctuation is based on its utility; that is, its usefulness in preventing misreading; it is not used simply because it is esthetic or beautiful. No one in his right mind has ever raved over the beauty of the placement of a comma, or said how dashing a dash is, or in what a magnificent way a semicolon has been used. But many a person has had cause to regret the careless or incorrect use of a comma. (See "Punctuation" pages 52-58.)

Over the years, such refinements as parallelism and word order have been added to English syntax (the arrangement and interrelation of words in phrases and sentences) to help us communicate our thoughts clearly, correctly, and concisely.

As Dr. Samuel Johnson, who in the middle of the eighteenth century compiled our first English dictionary, so aptly said: "Words, sir, are the dress of thought." They are the tools of thought, the building materials out of which our thoughts are created. Try sometime to think about something without also thinking of the words which name or describe your thoughts. It just can't be done. We think in words. We also communicate by means of words, and the more words (vocabulary) we have, the more likely we are to be able to communicate our thoughts clearly, correctly, and concisely.

Words alone, however, are *not* the only language we have. There is the language of the chemist, who immediately recognizes *NaCl* as common salt or

$C_{12}H_{22}O_{11}$ as the most popular sweetener we know, sugar. Then there is the language of the mathematician, the physicist, and the artist who uses form, color, and texture to communicate his thoughts to others. There is also the language of the radio ham, whose argot is wholly unintelligible to the uninitiated. Each different profession soon acquires a vocabulary of its own. And the centennial celebration of the birthday of Beethoven, one of the world's greatest composers, who spoke the language that is universally recognized as music, has just recently passed.

I very vividly recall being invited to a two-week conference at Claremont College, where Jacques Reuff, then chief justice of the European Coal and Steel Community, lectured, along with Dr. Milton Friedman. I sat through Dr. Reuff's lectures in a blue funk, because all he seemed to talk about was contravertibility and incontravertibility, and I was too bashful to ask what those terms meant—simply a matter of my being ignorant of the vocabulary of economics.

The first thing a student must do when he takes a new course is learn the language that his instructor is going to use in teaching that course. Dr. Whitson, head of the math department at Cal Poly, is the only instructor I know who makes a practice of writing every new word he uses on the blackboard and explaining its meaning to his students, a practice which every *good* teacher should adopt. I did it myself, and I have done it in this text. (See "A Glossary of Grammatical Terms," pages 43-51.)

This book also includes the most complete discussion that I have seen of vagueness, ambiguity, and lack of clarity. When I took freshman English, my instructors told me that there were many causes of vagueness, but they never mentioned more than one or two. For this reason, I decided to find all the causes I could, give examples of each, and then show how to turn obscurity into clarity. I found forty-seven causes, and even then, I've probably missed some. If so, I'll add them in subsequent editions. But you must remember that what may seem clear to you may be vague and muddy to the person who will read what you have written. You must be certain that there is only one possible interpretation of what you have written, especially in a letter or a report, which are two specific forms of *factual* writing, as opposed to fictional or imaginative writing, with which this book does not deal.

Over the past fifty years, letter-writing has made tremendous strides, not only in form, but also in language; consequently, the section on word pests has been included in this book. Letters of today don't look like the letters of yesteryear, and why should they? After all, we have discarded many of the styles of fifty years ago, and we don't still ride around in the same kinds of vehicles. Even automobiles have changed, so it is only natural that our letters should change in form and language.

Finally, there is that most invaluable portion of the book that is known as the "Appendix," which contains some very useful articles that back up the points I have made in the text. Read each one carefully and thoughtfully, and believe what you read. Then, try to put the points they cover into practice in your own writing. You'll be much the wiser and far more likely to get ahead, no matter what your profession.

Now, I'd like to close this brief heart-to-heart talk with you with what I consider to be the three most important elements in success, which is something my students have always asked me about:

1. Learn to get along with all kinds of people, devils as well as angels. You'll meet and have to work with both kinds. Sometimes they'll be your superiors, immediate or distant. Unless you can do this, your chances of making a success of yourself are minus zero.

2. Learn all you can about your major subject, even though you'll never be able to learn everything there is to know. The deeper you dig, the broader you become, the more quickly you'll see the relationship between your immediate interest and other subjects. Join several professional organizations in your major field of interest. As a member, you will receive their publications, which you should read and study. Take notes, and keep a file on what you have read. Also keep a bibliography of books and articles on your subject—in short, an up-to-date bibliography for ready reference. Go to as many regional meetings and conventions as you can afford. Pick the brains of anyone you meet who can teach you something worthwhile. This applies especially to your teachers. Also pick teachers rather than courses. A good teacher is a joy forever. I have had teachers from whom I have taken four, five, and even six courses, with very little repetition.

3. Learn to communicate your thoughts clearly, correctly, and concisely. You may have the greatest idea in the world, something truly world-shaking, but if you can't get it out of your brain and into someone else's, this great idea won't be worth a damn. That's where the study of this book *can* and *will* help you immeasurably, if only you will *read* and *believe* and *practice* what you learn. I do in everything I write, and I write voluminously.

And now I'd like to quote something from General Electric's "You and Tomorrow...".

TO UNDERSTAND AND BE UNDERSTOOD: A good education provides the tools for understanding. The first and most important of these tools is language for communication. It may surprise you that we've begun by putting the need to study English first rather than stressing science or mathematics. After all, our business is primarily concerned with science and the useful application of technological developments. Nevertheless, we are convinced that no matter what your career, a command of the English language is the most important skill you can acquire. Learning rules of grammar and acquiring the abilities to write effectively and to read effectively are vital. This background provides the skill to express yourself in speaking and writing and to extract maximum meaning from the spoken and written words of others. This process is called communication. In today's world, and even more so in tomorrow's, the person who cannot communicate clearly labors under a tremendous handicap. The young engineer, for example, might have his most brilliant idea rejected if he is unable to explain its significance to others. In addition, he will be unable to keep up with advances in his own field if he cannot get the facts from the flood of technical information available to him. Think of any career you like: teacher, engineer, actor, salesman, auditor, lawyer, physician, news reporter. Is there one in which you won't have to communicate effectively with others in order to perform successfully?

General Electric goes on to talk about the language of the universe, Science and the Scientific Age, The Technician and Engineering, Fitting the Pieces Together, Language for Tomorrow, and Tomorrow Begins Today. Write to General Electric, Schnectady, New York, and ask for a free copy of "You and Tomorrow." They'll be glad to send it to you. I would like to take this opportunity to express my deepest thanks to this great company for their interest in language communication.

Remember always that nobody was born a good writer of anything, especially not of reports and letters. Good writers are made through their diligent application of the late, great Winston Churchill's "blood, sweat, and tears." Nothing good is ever just written; it is rewritten again and again until it says exactly what the writer means. This is the fourth writing of this preface, and I'm sure that if I had time to rewrite it again, it would be even better.

I have now come to the end of my preaching. In fact, I was supposed to become a preacher, but ended up as a teacher. There is not a great difference between the two; simply substitute *t* for *pr* and you have it. As an old preacher-teacher, I urge you to read this book carefully and thoroughly, and to believe what you read—not because I wrote it, but because it's true. It is the result of the experience of a lifetime spent in studying the problems of communication. Don't worry if what you write isn't perfect. No matter how often you rewrite it, there'll always be something you'd like to change. After all, people *are* human, and human beings are fallible; yet, we can still strive for perfection.

Even the immortal Abraham Lincoln was not satisfied with the first draft of his famous *Gettysburg Address*, which was not really written on the back of an envelope while he was on the train carrying him to that famous battlefield, as is commonly believed. Actually, there are four different copies of this work, each in Lincoln's own handwriting. Each is slightly different. "According to an Associated Press story dated Chicago, November 11, 1950, Lincoln carefully wrote his first draft several days before he left Washington. He wrote the second draft at the house of David Wills in Gettysburg on the morning of the dedication. This draft, according to the Associated Press story, was the paper Lincoln held in his hand when he spoke. But Lincoln was a perfectionist, as you must try to be. He knew that only by carefully revising could he improve his address. As a result . . . Lincoln wrote in his own hand no less than five versions. On November 19, 1950—the day on which the address was "fourscore and ten years old," the Chicago Historical Society displayed these five copies in Lincoln's own handwriting. . . . According to Paul Angle, a noted Lincoln authority . . . one purpose of the exhibit is to show the public that Lincoln did not deliver this speech spontaneously with little or no preparation, as is commonly believed. . . . These revisions, along with occasional crossed-out and changed words, are further evidence of the care that Lincoln took with the address that is a treasured part of the American Heritage."[1]

JOHN P. RIEBEL

[1] Riebel, John P. *Successful Business Letters,* ARCO Publishing Company, Inc., New York, 1971, pp. 40-41.

FOREWORD

I thought I could do no better than to let you read word for word the fine letter Mr. Shippam wrote in answer to my query about helpful hints for budding technical writers. Read what he has to say, take it to heart, and believe it with all the power of your mind. What he has written could be a perfect abstract of the contents of this manual!

MISSILE & SPACE SYSTEMS DIVISION
DOUGLAS AIRCRAFT COMPANY, INC
SANTA MONICA, CALIFORNIA

A2-260-S/SPEC-C-319
Issued: 6-14-

Professor John P. Riebel
Department of English
California State Polytechnic College
San Luis Obispo, California

Dear Professor Riebel:

Your intriguing letter of 7 June tempts us to reply at some length: we are as much interested in the education and training of writers as you are. It occurred to us that if we gave you a few ideas concerning our needs, demands, expectations, and disappointments, you might pass them on to your students for their edification and assistance.

We discourage our people from calling themselves "technical writers". It is of prime importance that they be writers - masters of an exacting craft with an ancient and honorable history. Many so-called technical writers are neither technically inclined nor writers: they tend to season their rather indifferent prose with the bits of jargon they have picked up here and there, and sometimes they do not even know the basic techniques of their own would-be profession. Our writers must understand what they are writing about, whether they have had any scientific or engineering training or not, and must be able to change their frames of reference from one discipline to another without the necessity of extensive research - for which there is never time.

As for their product - technical reports and specifications are bought and paid for by governmental procuring activities and may cost them $25,000 to $50,000. The writing must be a clear, concise presentation of facts, test results, progress, or study recommendations. The reader need not be intrigued into continuing his reading of the document.

We enjoyed the collection of data on letter-writing which you enclosed with your letter, and realize that, of course, this is not the kind of style you would advocate for your writing students. It is obviously intended for direct-mail advertising and related uses. We could not possibly use any such approach in a contractually required document. Even in proposals in which we are trying to sell a design or win a contract award, we stay away from "tricky" writing because it might distract the reader from points we are trying to

Professor John P. Riebel　　　　　　　　　　A2-260-S/SPEC-C-319
　　　　　　　　　　　　　　　　　　　　　　Issued: 6-14-
　　　　　　　　　　　　　　　　　　　　　　Page 2

make: soundness of design, quality of product, reliability of system, ease of maintenance, etc. Since our readers are busy, serious-minded people who are also essentially conservative, they would be more likely annoyed and irritated by a "breezy" approach than by a more traditional one. This is not to say that we think that good writing needs to be dull; on the contrary, we believe that dull writing (cliché-ridden, ungrammatical, verbose) is essentially bad.

The technically educated person, no matter what his occupational assignment, will always be faced with the necessity for expressing himself in writing: to set forth design parameters, to describe scopes of work, to detail steps of test procedures, to report test results, to procure parts from suppliers, report results of business trips, record conference decisions, etc.

The Defense Department is our largest customer for engineering services. It sets forth the way it wants specifications prepared in Standardization Manual M-205 (_Military Outline of Form and Instructions for the Preparation of Specifications_) issued by the Office of the Assistant Secretary of Defense (Supply/Logistics), Washington 25, D. C.

Although most companies normally have their own style manuals, a good basic guideline for a student who contemplates writing the kind of document we have described is the _Government Printing Office Style Manual_, which is issued by the Superintendent of Documents, USGPO, Washington 25, D. C. You are no doubt quite familiar with this book. Our own standard for spelling, usage, and abbreviations is the latest edition of Webster's _Unabridged International Dictionary_.

Engineers-turned-writers seem to have more difficulty with the organization of a paper than with any other single aspect of writing. There is not always time to rewrite a rough draft of a 50-page document; besides, when the organization is faulty, it is usually easier to scrap the original and start over. Outlines are important.

Technical terminology does not pose many problems: everyday English does. We suggest to trainees and others (we conduct an occasional writing workshop) that a long word should never be used for its length alone, nor a short word simply for its brevity, but that the exact word should be used. If a technical word expresses the idea better than any other, so much the better; but it should never be worked in as an ornament for an otherwise undistinguished piece of writing.

Professor John P. Riebel

A2-260-S/SPEC-C-319
Issued: 6-14-
Page 3

Beginners' documents are sometimes not only undistinguished, but indistinct. They are filled with fuzzy thinking, garbled diction, ambiguities and illogicalities. For all our insistence upon the conventional use of punctuation, spelling, grammar, and syntax, we object to the application of rigid rules when common sense and the occasion demand some relaxation. Above all, the student should cultivate a sense of humor, or a sense of the ridiculous, and an ability to see that something he has written may sound nonsensical or worse when read with an inflection which he did not intend.

Applicants for our writing groups are screened in several ways. They are given a test by our Personnel Department, and two further tests by us. The latter consist of a 500-word essay and an editing test designed to discover the applicant's depth of knowledge of punctuation, grammar, and vocabulary, and his ability to penetrate gobbledygook. As a matter of interest, we usually find that Liberal Arts majors (not necessarily English majors), who have been exposed to the sciences, or who have had some technical training, make the best writers. They seem to be more adaptable than the average engineer. We would certainly not turn down an engineer with a decided flair for writing - but these are rare birds, indeed.

We hope that this letter is helpful - it is almost impossible to treat the subject and give satisfactory answers to your questions in much less than the space we have used. If we can be of further service, we'll be happy to hear from you. We certainly hope that you will steer your promising graduates in our direction: the course you teach should save us a great deal of training time.

Very truly yours,

MISSILE & SPACE SYSTEMS DIVISION
Douglas Aircraft Company, Inc.

D. R. Shippam
Chief, Specifications Section
Space Systems

Preface

Prepared as a practical guide for anyone who wants to learn how to improve his writing, especially reports, papers, articles, theses, and technical writing, this manual is the result of twenty-five years of studying and teaching clear, correct, concise writing. It can be used as a basic text in any practical-writing course, or it can be used as a handbook by any person interested in improving his ability to communicate through the written word.

This manual is divided into various sections: the text proper, consisting essentially of the instructional material given in English 301, Report Writing, at California State Polytechnic College in San Luis Obispo; a handbook of composition, consisting of a brief review of the important principles of grammar and punctuation, as well as some troublesome problems in composition, such as vagueness, word order, parallelism, etc., a list of words frequently misspelled, a glossary of words and phrases often misused and often confused, accepted standard abbreviations, an outline of the principles of modern business letter writing and various types of letters which college students are frequently required to write; and finally a list of selected readings taken from magazines, style manuals, brochures, etc. so that the reader may see at first hand the importance people in business and industry attach to clear, correct, concise writing.

It is a pleasure to acknowledge with deep gratitude the following for their gracious permission to reprint here their valuable contributions:

Michael Flagg, Editor, for "Make It Simple!" reprinted from Vol. 45, No. 3, *California Safety News,* September 1962.

Edwin A. Locke, Jr., for "What Price Verbal Incompetence?" *Harvard Alumni Bulletin,* copyright 1962, Harvard Bulletin Inc.

Robert T. Hamlett, Vice-President, Sperry Gyroscope, for "Suggestions for the Preparation of Technical Papers," reprinted from the *Proceedings of the I. R. E.,* Vol. 38, No. 3, March, 1950; and "Technical Writing Grows into a New Profession; Publications Engineering," reprinted from the September-October, 1952 *Sperry Engineering Review.*

Dr. Leon R. Hay and *Advanced Management-Office Executive* for permission to reproduce Dr. Hay's excellent article, "Managing Words," from the June, 1962, issue of this magazine.

Dr. Robert Hay, Southern Technical Institute, Marietta, Georgia, for "What is Technical Writing?" first printed in the April, 1961, *Word Studies.* Reprinted through the permission of both Dr. Hay and the G. &. C. Merriam Company, Springfield, Massachusetts, publishers of Webster's New Collegiate Dictionary.

Ben Hummel, Executive Editor, for permission to reprint James W. Souther's "Applying the Engineering Method to Report Writing," Copyright 1952 (December) by *Machine Design.*

Richard M. Koff, Senior Associate Editor, for "8 Steps to Better Engineering Writing," Copyright 1959 by McGraw-Hill Publishing Co., Inc., in *Product Engineering.*

The G. & C. Merriam Company, Springfield, Massachusetts, for permission to reprint their proofreader's marks and several definitions from their *New Collegiate Dictionary.*

Larry Pathe, Editorial Specialist, Flight Propulsion Division, General Electric, Cincinnati Division, for the entire section pages I-1 to I-18 from his excellent *GE Style Manual.*

D. R. Shippam, Chief, Specifications Section, Missile & Space Systems Division, Douglas Aircraft Company, Inc., Santa Monica, California for permission to reproduce as the "Foreword" of this manual his informative letter of June 14, 1962.

Dr. Charles L. Tutt, Jr., of General Motors Institute, Flint, Michigan, for "Preparation and Evaluation of an Industrial Report," first published in *The General Motors Engineering Journal,* July-August-September, 1957.

There were many other excellent articles which could have—and possibly should have—been added to this distinguished list of eloquent voices exhorting and pleading with young men and women to mend their communications fences if they want to get ahead in their chosen professions. For all whose worthy contributions had to be omitted, my sincerest apologies. To those who so graciously and generously permitted me to use their contributions, my deepest thanks.

Remember, your instructor is not alone when he urges you to learn to communicate your thoughts clearly, correctly, concisely! He is indeed in most distinguished company!

Table of Contents

HOW TO WRITE TECHNICAL REPORTS, PAPERS, ARTICLES AND THESES

INTRODUCTION	1
Kinds of Thinking	1
Four Objectives	1
Definition	1
I. FACTUAL INFORMATION	1
Definition of a Fact	1
Sources of Facts	1
The Library	1
Note Taking	4
Bibliography	4
Footnotes	6
References	7
Bibliography—Table of References	7
II. ORGANIZATION	8
Facts vs. Organization	8
Definition, Requirements of a Good Outline	9
Types of Outlines, Methods of Outlining	9
Helpful Hints for Outlining	9
Need for Organization	10
Special Types of Organization	11
Types of Technical and/or Business Reports	11
III. PRESENTATION	13
The Parts of a Formal Report	13
Prefatory, Cover, Title Page	13
Letter of Authorization, Letter of Transmittal	13
Table of Contents	15
Table of Illustrations, Abstract, Text, Arrangement	15
Numbering of Pages	19
Spacing, Illustrations or Graphic Aids	19
Appendix	20
IV. LANGUAGE	21
V. TIME—TIMING	21
VI. YOUR READER-AUDIENCE	22
Conclusion	23
Helpful Hints for Writing and Speaking	23
Appendix	23
A Table of References	23

Table of Contents

GRAMMAR
THE PARTS OF SPEECH 25
Naming Words, Acting Words 25
Qualifying or Modifying Words 25
Connecting or Linking Words 25
A Brief Outline of the Parts of Speech
    and Essential Grammar, Number 27
Possession or Ownership, Agreement 28
Reference of Pronouns 31
Point of View 34
Verb Chart 36
Principal Parts of Irregular Verbs 37
Qualifying Words (Chart of) 39
A Table of Connectives 40
Groups of Words (Chart of) 41
Units of Thought 42
A Glossary of Grammatical Terms 43

PUNCTUATION
PUNCTUATION SIMPLIFIED 52
The Comma 53
The Semicolon, The Colon, The Dash 54
The Period, The Question Mark 55
    Five Ways of Asking Direct Questions 55
The Exclamation Point, The Hyphen 55
The Apostrophe, Parentheses 56
Brackets, Double Quotation Marks 57
Italics 57
Capitalization 58
The Punctuation of Compound Sentences 58

PARAGRAPHING
PARAGRAPHING 61
Special Types or Kinds of Paragraphs 62

SPECIAL PROBLEMS IN COMPOSITION
Ambiguity, Confusion, Lack of Clarity, Vagueness 63
Awkwardness 73
Choppy, Stringy Sentences 74
    Awkward Sentences 75

Table of Contents

    Parallel Construction 76
    Proofread 77
    Say it Simply! 77
    Word Order 78
    Wordiness and Unnecessary Repetition 80

VOCABULARY

    Some Words Frequently Misspelled by Technical Writers   82
    Prefixes and Suffixes
        Every Technical Writer Should Know 84
    Additional Prefixes and Suffixes 85
    A Glossary of Words Frequently Confused 86
    A Glossary of Incorrect Usage 90

LETTER WRITING

10 POINTERS
FOR WRITING LETTERS THAT GET RESULTS 92
   1. A Letter Takes the Place of a Personal Visit 92
   2. Put Yourself in Your Reader's Place 93
   3. Think in Terms of Your Reader—Not of Yourself 94
   4. Forget the Tired Words of the Dear, Dead Past 94
       If We Talked the Way We Write Letters 95
       Tired Words vs. Strong Words 95
   5. Plan our Letters Before You Start to Write Them 96
   6. Get Off to a Flying Start—and End with a Bang! 98
   7. Accentuate the Positive—Eliminate the Negative 99
   8. Put Smiles into Every Letter You Write 100
       Here Are Some Letters That Scowl at the Reader 101
   9. A Soft Answer Turneth Away Wrath 102
  10. Every Letter Is a Sales Letter 102
       The Parts of a Business Letter 103

TYPES OF BUSINESS LETTERS TECHNICAL
STUDENTS SHOULD KNOW HOW TO WRITE 104
   1. Inquiries and Requests for Information 104
   2. Replies to Inquiries and Requests for Information ...106
   3. Orders 106
   4. Acknowledgement 107
   5. Invitation 107
   6. Accepting an Invitation 107
   7. Refusing an Invitation 107
   8. Introduction 108

Table of Contents

    9. Recommendation,   10. Acceptance 108
  11. Resignation,   12. Request for an Appointment 109
   3. Apology,   14. Follow-up 109
  15. Good Will 109
  16. Thanks,   17. Credit 110
  18. Complaint and Request for Adjustment 111
  19. Regret,   20. Credit,   21. Report 113
Rules for Typing Letters 115
Some Legal Aspects of Business Letter Writing 116
    Application to Collection Letters 117
    Application to Credit Letters 117
    Legal Rights in Business Letters 118
    The Moral 118
Word Pests That Infest Business Letters 118
    Pestifori Vagii 119
    Pestifori Inaccuratii 119
    Pestifori Supercillii 119
    Pestifori Triteii 120
    Pestifori Verbosii 120
    Pestifori Frigidii 120
    Pestifori Pompousii 121
    Pestifori Antiquatii 121

APPENDIX—SELECTED READING

HOW TO WRITE TECHNICAL REPORTS, PAPERS, ARTICLES, AND THESES

Introduction

Kinds of Thinking

According to James Harvey Robinson, there are **four** kinds of thinking:

1. *Reverie or Day Dreaming*—Everyone indulges in this kind of thinking at some time, but it should be kept under control.
2. *Practical Decision-making*—This type is necessary in the everyday conduct of life itself.
3. *Argument*—Today we would call this type of thinking "discussion" rather than argument. At some time, everyone feels the need to defend his ideas, beliefs, opinions, actions, etc.
4. *Creative Thinking*—This is the highest type of thinking, for it is done with a definite purpose in mind: the satisfactory resolution of some problem. Often this type is called "constructive thinking." It may involve the creation of completely new ideas, or it may consist of rearranging old ones into new forms, such as is usually done in the writing of technical reports, research papers, technical articles for periodicals, or theses.

Four Objectives

In order for your thoughts to be useful to others, **you** must communicate them in either writing or **speaking**. In either case, you will be using words. If **you** will learn by heart the following four objectives for better communication, you can't help doing **a better** job of writing or speaking clearly, correctly, concisely:

1. Select, arrange, and develop related main thoughts, usually only a few.
2. Use words that are fresh and that fit the context (meaning) accurately.
3. Write sentences that are clear and flexible—not monotonous.
4. Write simply, naturally, interestingly—sometimes conversationally.

Definition

Now let's define—that is, set limits to—good **factual** writing. A good report, paper, article, or thesis consists of (1) factual information (2) organized **and** (3) presented, within the prescribed (4) time **limit**, in (5) clear, correct, coherent language so that **its** contents may be communicated as quickly and accurately as possible to (6) its reader-audience.

This kind of practical writing involves six distinct elements: factual information, organization or outlining, language, time-timing, presentation, and a reader **audience**.

I. Factual Information

"As soon as you move one step up from the bottom, your effectiveness depends on your ability to reach others through the spoken or written word. And the further away your job is from manual labor, the larger the organization of which you are an employee, the more important it will be that you know how to convey your thoughts in writing or speaking."
Peter Drucker

Factual writing—reports, articles, term papers, theses—differ from other types of writing—stories, novels, plays, poems, anecdotes—in that its primary purpose is to instruct someone, not to amuse him. For that reason, factual writing has a very definite purpose in mind. It is never written for the sheer fun of writing. No one writes a report, etc. just for the heck of it: he does it because someone has requested it. This fact gives special emphasis and importance to the reader-audience, who must always be kept in mind.

Definition of a Fact

A fact is something that can be verified—that is, detected by one or more of your five senses. Here are some facts: Oxygen is an odorless, colorless gas; the earth is round; Lincoln was assassinated; the dog is hungry.

Sources of Facts

Your facts will come from a wide variety of sources:

1. *Your personal experiences*—things you have learned by doing, observed, seen, experienced, suffered, etc.
2. *The experience of others*—things you have learned or observed from your parents, relatives, friends, teachers, supervisors, fellow workers, etc.
3. *The experiences of others—requested*—interviews, questionnaires, letters.
4. *The experiences of others—published*—books of all kinds (texts, encyclopedias, dictionaries, etc.), articles in journals and magazines, various kinds of manuals (owner, operator, service, etc.), film, filmstrips, radio and TV programs, tape recordings, records, etc. *ad infinitum*. This category includes any information (facts) which can be reproduced in multiple copies, such as mimeographing, rexographing, etc.

The Library

A library is your principal source of information, whether it be the college library, the city or the county library, the libraries of various departments or instructors, your own personal library, etc. And to be able to use any library to its maximum value, you should know the following keys:

The Floor Plan

The first thing to do is to learn your way around a library. Know where to locate the various parts, and where to go for the various services a library offers. A floor plan is valuable in helping you find your way around any library.

The Card Catalog

Every college or public library—and many private ones, too—has a card catalog to provide you the address of every book which the library owns and has cataloged.

There are three common ways of cataloging books in a library: alphabetically (which is used so seldom that this method will be ignored here), the Dewey-Decimal System, and the Library of Congress Classification.

The Dewey-Decimal System

Propounded in 1876 by Melville Dewey, the Dewey-Decimal system still remains as the most commonly used method of classifying books in American libraries. The ten categories which Dewey proposed are as follows:

000	General Works	500	Natural Science
100	Philosophy	600	Useful Arts
200	Religion	700	Fine Arts
300	Sociology	800	Literature
400	Philology	900	History

The Library of Congress System

Although well adapted to classifying knowledge in Dewey's time almost 100 years ago, the Dewey-Decimal System is woefully inadequate today, especially in the Natural Science and Useful Arts sections. For that reason, another system was devised about 1923 by W. C. Berwick Sayers as a result of his work as lecturer on classification at the University of London School of Librarianship. The original "outline" or classification was propounded about the turn of the century, but it did not get into its present form until the second decade of this century. Known as the Library of Congress Classification, here are the categories used:

A. General Works. Polygraphy.
B. Philosophy. Religion.
C. History—Auxiliary Sciences.
D. History and Topography (except America).
E-F. America.
G. Geography. Anthropology. Sports.
H. Social Sciences.
J. Political Sciences.
K. Law.
L. Education.
M. Music.
N. Fine Arts.
P. Language and Literature.
PN. Literary History and Literature. General Works.
Q. Science. General.
R. Medicine.
S. Agriculture, Plant and Animal Industry.
T. Technology.
U. Military Science.
V. Naval Science.
Z. Bibliography and Library Science.

The Documents Index or Catalog

Another kind of catalog available to readers in all college and many public libraries is the one that classifies government documents—federal, state, county, municipal, sometimes even foreign. The cataloging of these documents is quite complicated, and the reader is urged to ask the cooperation of a librarian in locating any document wanted. However, like the books listed in the card catalog, each entry may have three cards: an author, a title, and a subject card. Once you have found the document you want, ask the documents librarian to locate it for you.

The Periodical Indexes and Abstracts

The card catalog and the documents index are valuable for finding separate publications in the library—books, manuals, etc. Articles in magazines, however, pose a different problem. It would be impossible to index or catalog every item or article in every periodical publication which any library takes.

Fortunately, this is not necessary, since information about articles in periodical publications (magazines, journals, etc.) is given in the various indexes and abstracts which every large library has available. Here is a brief—*and probably incomplete*—list of indexes, abstracts, and other books in the Walter Dexter Memorial Library at California State Polytechnic College in San Luis Obispo:

Indexes
Aero Engineering Index
Agricultural Index
Applied Science & Technology
Biographic Index
Biography Index
Education Index
Electronic Engineering Master Index
Engineering Index
Poole's Index

Abstracts
Biological Abstracts
Chemical Abstracts
Dairy Science Abstracts
Electrical Engineering
Physics Abstracts
Psychological Abstracts
Refrigeration Abstracts

Others
Bibliography of Agriculture
Facts on File

Public Affairs Information Service
Readers' Guide to Periodical Literature
Zoological Record

Here are some others not in the Cal Poly Library:
Indexes
Bibliographic Index

Abstracts
Animal Breeding Abstracts
Abstracts of Bacteriology
Botanical Abstracts
British Abstracts
Ceramic Abstracts
Engineering Abstracts
Field Crop Abstracts
Forestry Abstracts
Geological Abstracts
Geophysical Abstracts
Horticultural Abstracts
Meteorological Abstracts and Bibliography
Nuclear Science Abstracts
Science Abstracts

Others
Mathematical Reviews
U. S. D. A.'s *Experiment Station Record*
U. S. D. A.'s *Index to Technical Bulletins*
Dalton's *Sources of Engineering Information*
Collison's *Bibliographies*
Holmstrom's *Records and Research in Engineering and Industrial Science*
U. S. Government Publications: *Monthly Catalog*
U. S. Government Research: *Research Reports*
Subject Index of Government Publications

Vertical File Service Catalog
U. S. D. A.'s *Bibliography of Agriculture*
ASTIA's *Technical Abstracts Bulletin* (TAB)

Encyclopedias

Although not too useful for college-level students and those beyond, the encyclopedias should not be overlooked. They do provide a key to general information not current—that is, past. Here are some encyclopedias that you will find in almost any library: *The Americana, The Britannica, The World, Collier's, Encyclopedia of American Associations, Elsevier's Encyclopedia of Organic Chemistry, Encyclopedia of Chemical Technology,* N. W. Ayres & Son's *Directory of Newspapers & Periodicals.*

Dictionaries of Words

The unabridged dictionaries, *Webster's International,* Third Edition; Funk & Wagnalls *New Standard;* the *Oxford* (sometimes called the *New English*), and many others (especially foreign dictionaries), are useful when information about words is needed. There are also many abridged dictionaries and dictionaries of synonyms, antonyms, etc.: *Webster's New Collegiate,* the *Desk Standard,* the *American College, World Webster, Roget's Thesaurus,* Soule's *Dictionary of Synonyms, Webster's Dictionary of Synonyms,* and many others, all of great value.

Here are some miscellaneous dictionaries you should know about: *Chambers' Technical Dictionary, Engineering Terminology, Dictionary of Scientific and Technical Terms, A Dictionary of the Sciences, Dictionary of Electronic Terms, A Dictionary of Dairying,* Crispin's *Dictionary of Technical Terms,* Henderson's *Dictionary of Scientific Terms.*

Of People

Information about people, living as well as dead, may be obtained from the many biographical dictionaries in the library: the various *Who's Who* books, *Current Biography, Dictionary of National Biography* (for Englishmen), *Dictionary of American Biography, American Men of Science, National Academy of Science,* etc.

Other Reference Works

Some other valuable reference works available in almost every college library include *Thomas' Register of American Manufacturers, Moody's Industrials, Moody's Transportation, Agricultural Yearbooks, Yearbook of the United Nations, Standard Advertising Register,* and many others.

Handbooks

Among the most useful books in any library are the many types and kinds of handbooks, in which you can find almost any kind of facts needed. Here is just a small list of the various ones in the Walter Dexter Library:

Accountant's Handbook
American Electrician's Handbook
Chemical Engineer's Handbook
Chemical Rubber Handbook
Civil Engineering Handbook
CPA Handbook
Electronic Engineer's Reference Book
Food Industries Manual
Government Printing Office Style Manual
Handbook of Physics
Handbook of Plastics
Industrial Electronics Handbook
Mechanical Engineering Handbook
NAB Engineering Handbook
Plant Engineering Handbook
Production Handbook
Purchasing Handbook
Radio Engineer's Handbook
Radio Handbook

Here are two bibliographical cards made out correctly, one for a book, the other for an article in a magazine. On each side is an explanation of the entry on the card:

Author's name	Riebel, John P. 37	Bibliographical Key Number
Title (underlined)	How to Write SUCCESSFUL BUSINESS LETTERS in 15 Days	
Publisher	Prentice-Hall, Inc.	
Place of publ.	Englewood Cliffs, New Jersey	
	651.7	Dewey Decimal Call Number
Library	Cal Poly R 548	
	HF 5726 R52	Lib. of Congress

Figure 1. A Bibliography Card for a Book

Author's name	Riebel, John P. 36	Bibliography Key Number
Title in quotes	"How to Write LETTERS THAT GET RESULTS"	
Title of magazine underlined	The American Salesman	
Vol. and No.	Vol. 1, No. 9	
Date	May, 1956	
inclusive pages	pp. 50-61	
Library	Cal Poly	(No call Number)

Figure 2. A Bibliography Card for an Article

Note Taking

If your bibliographical cards are not numbered with a key number, then each time you take a note from any source, you will have to copy the complete bibliographical information given in the card in Figure 1, except, of course, the library and the call number. When dozens of notes are taken, this can become quite a chore.

If, however, you use a different key number for each bibliographical reference, then all you have to do when taking a note is to write in the upper right-hand corner the appropriate key number. That can save you a lot of writing.

Bibliography

The first thing to do after you have chosen your topic is to make a list or bibliography of sources of information on your subject: books, manuals, pamphlets, articles, etc. You will find it far more satisfactory to make such a list on cards, 3 x 5, 4 x 6, or whatever size you wish, putting the following bibliographical information on the card, ONLY ONE ENTRY TO A CARD:

1. The author's name (if given)—last name first, first name, middle name. Since some books (manuals, booklets, and even articles do not use an author's name, then start with the title.
2. The title of the work. If the work is a separate publication (book, handbook, manual, booklet, dictionary, etc.), the title should be underlined once. This is the printer's cue to put these words in italic type. If the work is not a separate publication but an article in a journal or magazine, a chapter in a book, a section in a handbook, then put double quotation marks

around the title. (See Figures 1 and 2 on the facing page.)
3. If the book has gone into several editions, indicate this in parentheses immediately following the underlined title.

For a book:
4. The name of the publisher.
5. The place of publication.
6. The date of publication.

For an article:
4. The title of the magazine or journal.
5. The volume and the number.
6. The date of the magazine.
7. The inclusive pages on which the article appeared.

In Figure 3 we have a note card that is a direct quotation from the source. Quotation marks are necessary. This is not true of the note card in Figure 4, because this is a paraphrase of the information between pages 40 and 57 of the source.

Topic

> 35
> Routine Business Letters
> "No matter what kind of letter you write, treat it as a unique opportunity to spend a few moments of your busy day with your customer-friend. Inquiries, replies, acknowledgements too often are considered as merely 'routine'. This should not be!"
>
> p. 61

Key Number

A direct quotation from this source.

page

Figure 3. A Note Card (quotation)

Topic

> 36
> Letter Planning
> Successful business letters just don't happen—they are carefully planned according to this formula:
> A I D C A + C S P = O. K. This means: Attract your reader's favorable attention, arouse his Interest, make him Desire (want) to do what you ask. Convince him he ought to do it, and then you'll get the Action you want. Add a Central Selling Point and you'll have a successful letter—one that will get results.
>
> pp. 40-57

Key Number

a paraphrase of the information or substance in this reference.

inclusive pages

Figure 4. A Note Card (citation)

Be sure to indicate with double quotation marks ("...") that the material has been quoted or borrowed word for word from some source. When you do this, change any double quotes within this passage to single quotes ('...'), as in Figure 3.

Here are four good reasons why you may want to quote rather than paraphrase:
1. The original working cannot be improved upon.

2. The passage is too well known for you to tamper with.
3. You want an apt quotation to lend the force of an authority to your writing.
4. You want to use the exact wording of two or more authorities or sources to show a divergence of opinions.

NOTE: There are several ways in which a direct quotation may be used in the body of your report itself:

1. It may be included as a part of your text itself, either part of a sentence or as a separate sentence or two itself:

    Time taken to recopy a report is time well spent, for it most certainly is true that "sloppiness is sure to give your reader a negative, unfavorable impression." (35:14).

2. It may be included along with your text as a separate paragraph or as a series of separate paragraphs. In both (1) and (2) above, the quotation is double spaced, as is the rest of the paragraph. The text of all reports should be double spaced:

    "You've probably heard it said that letter writers are born. 'Tain't so—don't you believe a word of it! Good letter writers are MADE. They learn their art hard way: by writing, rewriting, and then rewriting again and again until they learn to say exactly what they mean—and, more important, mean what they say.

    "You can do that, too, if you will lend me your eyes and if you will believe with all your heart what is said here." (38:19)

NOTE: For continuous paragraphs that are quoted, use quotation marks at the beginning of each consecutive paragraph, and at the end of the final one only. After the quotation marks, put your reference.

3. Sometimes you will want to make your quotation a separate entry, not as an actual part of your text body. Under this circumstance, indent your entire quotation 5 spaces (plus 2 extra for paragraph indentions) and single space, as shown here:

    Every business letter you write has two separate functions to perform:

    1. It must *communicate* clearly, concisely, and courteously your thoughts.
    2. It must *create an impression*—and a favorable one—on your reader.

    In some respects, the second function is more important than the first. (34-46)

Note that when you use this method, omit quotation marks entirely. And now to sum up some pointers on note taking:

1. Use 3 x 5 cards, which are inexpensive but still large enough to hold a great deal of information. If two or more are required, they can be stapled or clipped together.
2. Take ONLY ONE NOTE to a card—only one topic. If in doubt, use two separate cards.
3. Indicate the topic when you make the note. You can easily change it, if necessary, and it will help immeasurably when you start organizing your material.
4. Be sure to give adequate bibliographical information if you do not use the "Key Number" system.
5. Put within quotation marks *all* direct quotations.
6. Put on the card the page number of the source. You may want to go back and get additional information, and you'll need it in giving credit.

Footnotes

Uses

Footnotes are used at the bottom of the page to

1. Acknowledge borrowing from other writers.
2. Substantiate a statement not generally accepted as true, or one that is not common knowledge.
3. Amplify points which cannot conveniently be discussed in the text itself.
4. Refer the reader to other parts of the report, paper, thesis, etc.
5. Define technical terms used in the text.
6. Refer to personal letters, interviews, lectures, films and filmstrips, etc. not listable in your bibliography (which includes printed sources only).

NOTE: Whatever is put in a footnote could have been put in parentheses in the body of your report.

Here are some pointers that will help you use footnotes more correctly:

1. Number footnotes consecutively throughout your report, etc., starting with 1.
2. Put the index or reference number immediately after the passage to which it refers, and slightly above the line.
3. Group footnotes at the bottom of the page. Be sure to leave ample room for them, so that they are not crowded.
4. Use a solid line 15 spaces* to separate your last line of text from your first footnote.
5. If you use reference numbers (See page 7), do not use numbers for footnotes. Instead, use an

---

*This is about an inch and a half.

asterisk (*) or a double asterisk (**) as in No. 4.
6. Indent the first line of each footnote 5 spaces, but bring the second and all succeeding lines in the same footnote out to the paragraph margin.
7. Single space the material within each footnote.
8. Double space between footnotes.

Kinds (for Published Material)

Footnotes vary in kind from the shortest possible footnote, the author's last name, and the page from which this material was taken, to the most complete, which is really the complete bibliographical enter PLUS the page number. Here is what the various footnotes mean:

[1]Riebel, p. 65. (Only one Riebel and only one entry by him.)

[2]John P. Riebel, p. 65. (Two different Riebels whose writings were used.)

[3]Riebel, "The Art of Talking by Mail," p. 36. (Several references by only one Riebel.)

[4]John P. Riebel, "Do Your Letters Date You?" p. 42. (Two different Riebels and at least two references by John P.)

[5]Riebel and Rogers, p. 24. (An entry by two authors.)

[6]John P. Riebel, *How You Can Write Better Letters.* The Economics Press, Inc. Montclair, New Jersey, 1957, p. 16. (A complete footnote, differing from the bibliographical entry only in that in the footnote the author's name is not written last name first.)

NOTE No. 1: There are various ways of punctuating a complete footnote, and various arrangements of information within the footnote. All of them are acceptable. The important thing is to adopt a standard way and use it consistently.

NOTE No. 2: Formerly, before shortened footnotes became common and before the latest scientific method called "referencing" became standard, various Latin abbreviations—*ibid., op. cit.,* and *loc. cit.*—were used extensively to save time and work. However, according to one of the latest handbooks, the use of these abbreviations in modern documentation is being discouraged.* Briefly, here is what each one means:

Ibid. means "in the same place" and is used to indicate that this reference comes from exactly the same source as the one immediately before. If it comes from the same page, no page number is necessary. If it is from a different page, then the page number must be given.

Op. cit. must be used with the author's name. This means that this reference comes from the same source as that listed for the author previously. *Op. cit.* must be followed by a page number. *Op. cit.* is used only for a book or other "work" previously cited.

Loc. cit. refers to some article or document previously cited. It, too, must be preceded by the author's name and followed by a page number.

NOTE No. 3: End notes—footnotes placed at the end of a chapter, section, or even report, etc.—are seldom used today.

References

The most recent and, by all odds, the most satisfactory way of acknowledging borrowings from others is called "References." Basically, references consist of two numbers within parentheses placed immediately after the material used. (See the three paragraphs used on page 6.) The first number refers the reader to the similarly numbered entry in what is usually called a "Table of References" or "List of References." The second number indicates the page, just as in a footnote.

Bibliography—Table of References

Bibliography

A bibliography is a formal list of published works consulted in the preparation of a report, paper, article, or thesis. Everything you have honestly consulted—not merely opened and briefly glanced at—should be listed ALPHABETICALLY!

Extensive bibliographies may be divided into "Books," "Articles," "Documents," "Pamphlets," "Manuals," etc. This is not necessary for a short piece of work. Also, it may be desirable to annotate your bibliography—that is, to comment briefly on each entry so as to give the reader the benefit of your findings about each entry. Although very helpful, this type of bibliography is, unfortunately, seldom used in technical writing.

The same information given on your bibliography card is necessary in your bibliographical entry. However, instead of listing each item in order, as on your card, the information is written continuously, as follows, with the first line overhanging the others by five spaces. For example:

Riebel, John P., *How to Write SUCCESSFUL BUSINESS LETTERS in 15 Days.* Prentice-Hall, Inc., Englewood Cliffs, New Jersey, 1953.

Here's another way of writing it, equally correct:

Riebel, John P., *How to Write SUCCESSFUL BUSINESS LETTERS in 15 Days.* Englewood Cliffs, New Jersey: Prentice-Hall, Inc., 1953.

If there are several editions, this is usually indicated in parentheses immediately after the title:

---

*Robert M. Gorrell and Charlton Laird, *Modern English Handbook,* Prentice-Hall, Inc., Englewood Cliffs, New Jersey, 1962, p. 569.

Riebel, John P. and Rogers, Edward P., *Six Steps to More Successful Job Application* (Revised and Enlarged), Blake Printery, San Luis Obispo, California, 1957.

For an article in a magazine, here's how the entry will look:

Riebel, John P., "5 Pointers for Writing STAR REPORTS," *Printer's Ink,* Vol. 247, No. 11, June 11, 1954, pp. 33-34.

NOTE: The numeral 5 was used here because that is the way it was given in the magazine. Normally, we do not start sentences with numerals.

If there is no author listed for the article, then start with the title in quotes:

"Is Anyone Listening?" *Fortune Magazine,* September 1950, pp. 77-83 ff.

NOTE: The entries for articles, chapters from books, sections from handbooks, etc. must include the inclusive page numbers.

Table of References

A table of references, sometimes called a list of references or simply references, differs from a bibliography in only one respect: the entries in a table of references MUST BE NUMBERED, because these numbers are an integral part of the documentation of that source. The first number inside the parentheses refers to the number of the item in the table of references; the second number refers to the page number in that reference. For example, on page 8, the reference (35:14) means: See reference No. 38 in the table of references, and on page 14 you'll find this quotation.

Referencing is much quicker and more satisfactory than footnoting. It's also much easier when you are typing your own material, for you don't have to worry about leaving enough margin at the bottom of the page for a footnote.

One more point: the practice of labeling an article without a designated author as "Anonymous" is an affectation rapidly dying out. Obviously, if there is no author given it must have been written by someone unknown. Besides, a series of "anonymuses" in a bibliography or table of references means absolutely nothing. It's the title that counts.

When you alphabetize the article by its title, use only the first letter of the first important word—that is, omit the articles "the," "a," and "an."

Here are some bibliographical entries that might seem difficult but really aren't. Simply give as much information as possible so that your reader can obtain a copy of this entry, if he wishes it. After all, you are making your bibliography or table of references for his benefit, not for your own.

Better Letters—A monthly service for people who handle business correspondence (edited by John P. Riebel), The Economics Press, Inc., Montclair, New Jersey, Issue No. 101, 1958.

"Medicine," *The Encyclopedia Americana Annual for 1952,* Americana Corporation, New York, pp. 441 ff.

Patterson, Frank A. and Patterson, Frank A., Jr., *Customer Relations and Sales Methods That Sell,* Patterson Sales Clinic, Bethesda, Maryland, and Phoenix, Arizona. (No date—price $1.00)

Practical English and the Command of Words (A personal development service for adults). The Better Speech Institute of America, Westminster Building, Chicago 3, Illinois, 1955.

Riebel, John P., "Word Pests That Infest Modern Business Letters." A talk given before the Pest Control Operators of California, Inc., at California State Polytechnic College, Pomona, December 12, 1958. (Available in reprint form from the author by writing to John P. Riebel, California State Polytechnic College, San Luis Obispo.)

Braun, Carl F., *Corporate Correspondence* (A group of letters to an industrial organization), C. F. Braun & Co., Alhambra, California, 1948.

How the Wheels Revolve (Second Printing). Department of Public Relations, General Motors Corporation, Detroit 2, Michigan, 1952.

Riebel, John P., *Correspondencia Commercial en 15 Dias,* Editorial Labor, S. A., Barcelona, Spain, 1959.

II. Organization

". . . men and women, whatever their job or profession, are willing to begin and stay with an article only if it is well written."

Dwight Van Avery

Unorganized facts are often useless. They're like piles of lumber, bricks, etc.—useless until someone organizes them into a structure. Outlining is the process of organizing or classifying miscellaneous and sometimes heterogeneous facts into a unified, coherent piece of writing called a report, paper, article, or thesis.

Facts vs. Organization

Which comes first, factual information or organization—the data or the outline? That's hard to say. You must have some facts or data before you can start to organize it. Conversely, you have to have some plan of attack or outline before you dare to start taking a great many notes, or else you may be doing a lot of work for nothing.

The truth probably is that both probably evolve about the same time in your mind. But what is more important is how you can use these two all-important elements of successful writing, facts plus organization, work together to make your writing easier and more fruitful.

Definition

An outline is a logical classification or grouping of thoughts into main classes and sub classes according to some plan of organization. It's a means of ordering your information about a particular subject.

An outline is like a living thing: it begins with a seed or germ of an idea; it grows and develops until it is fully blown; and then it comes to an ending, which we call the table of contents. Believe it or not, your final outline of your writing *is* your table of contents, which is not written or made up until the report, etc., has been completed. And as a living, growing "thing," an outline may be changed as often as necessary.

Requirements of a Good Outline

In order for an outline to be considered good or satisfactory, it must meet certain requirements:

1. It must be complete—or as complete as time will permit. Everything necessary must be included.
2. It must be consistent—that is, it must maintain the same point of view throughout.
3. It must be discreet—that is, a fact must be assigned to only one class or position in the outline.
4. It must be useful and usable.

Types of Outlines

There are three kinds or types of outlines:

1. The topical or word-phrase outline (the kind most often used, from the preliminary to the final table of contents) uses only words or phrases, not sentences. The only exception is a question, which cannot be stated or asked in any other way.
2. The sentence outline, in which each heading is a complete sentence, is too cumbersome and should be avoided. A lawyer's brief is in complete sentences, but an outline for a piece of technical writing is not a brief.
3. The paragraph outline is one composed of sentences grouped into paragraphs. In technical writing, this kind of outline is called an abstract. (See page 15.)

Methods of Outlining

There are a number of acceptable ways of outlining or organizing your material. Some are quite simple and direct, others complicated and clumsy. All, however, use the principle of main headings or divisions, subheadings, sub-subheadings, etc. All the main heads are of equal importance; all the subheads are of equal importance; and so on.

One popular or conventional method is to use numbers and letters to designate the degree of subdivision. For example:

  I. *(First main head or division)*
     A. *(First subhead or subdivision)*
        1. *(First sub-subhead or sub-subdivision)*
           a. *(First sub-sub-subhead or division)*
              (1) *(First sub-sub-sub-subhead or division)*
                  (a) *(First sub-sub-sub-sub-subhead)*
                  (a) *(Second sub-sub-sub-sub-subhead)*
              (2) *(Second sub-sub-sub-subhead)*
           b. *(Second sub-sub-subhead)*
        2. *(Second sub-subhead)*
     B. *(Second subhead)*
 II. *(Second main head)*

Many pieces of technical writing, however, do not use the Roman and Arabic numerals, or the capital or lower-case letters of the alphabet. The equality and the degree of subordination is represented by the indention or lack of it:

It should be noted here that in technical writing, unless the piece is very long and complicated, these two sections — sub-sub-sub-subheads and sub-sub-sub-sub-subheads are very seldom used.

A third style of outlining is the decimal, which has come into limited general use. It is especially valuable in military and other government writing, which must maintain an exact degree of uniformity from one publication to another, such as in manuals, etc.

This type is usually too cumbersome for student reports, papers, articles, and theses. However, to make this manual complete, here is the decimal style of outlining:

  1.000000   (First Main Head)
     1.1000   (First Subhead)
       1.1100   (First Sub-subhead)
         1.1110   (First Sub-sub-subhead)
         1.1120   (Second Sub-sub-subhead)
       1.1120   (Second Sub-subhead)
     1.2000   (Second Subhead)
  2.000000   (Second Main Head)

Helpful Hints for Outlining

1. Unless you have a good psychological reason, don't use single headings. Logically you can't

divide something into itself and nothing: you must have at least two parts, or else there is no division, merely restatement.
2. Always use the same margin or indention for headings of equal importance.
3. Be consistent. Don't mix your outline methods or styles.
4. Start each division with a capital letter.
5. Use periods after all numerals and letters.
6. Don't use punctuation after the entries in a topical outline unless it is a question.
7. Change your outline as often as you need to. There's nothing sacred about an outline, and it's much easier to change your outline than to rewrite an entire report, paper, etc.
8. The more thought you give to outlining—that is, ORGANIZING your facts—the easier it will be to do your writing.

Here are some typical outlines which have become crystallized—that is, fixed—as tables of contents of reports or papers:

1. A simple, uncluttered outline on the topic of the Ludlow Typograph:
   History of the Ludlow
   The Ludlow system
   A description of the Ludlow
   The uses of Ludlow material in the printing industry
   A comparison of Ludlow slugs with foundry type
   The steps in the operation of the Ludlow
   The required maintenance of the Ludlow

2. An outline with major headings and subheadings on the methods of grafting:
   Introduction to Grafting
     Origin
     Definition of technical terms
     Common rules to follow
     Limits to grafting
   Inarching
     Purpose
     Methods
   Scion Grafting
     Whip
     Crown
     Bridge
     Veneer
   Budding
     Shield
     Patch
   Conclusion

3. A more detailed outline on the topic of The Common Market:
   Introduction
     Setting
     Participants
   Development
     Coal and steel treaty
     Radical concept
     Common needs
   Rome treaty
     Provisions
     Complete integration
   The Common Market Today
     Progress
       Ready acceptance
       Success
     Policies
   The United States and The Common Market
   Conclusion

4. An outline on the topic of color separation and masking for photochemical reproduction showing the typical designation for headings, subheads, etc.:
   I. Introduction
      A. What a mask is
      B. Why masks are used
      C. How masking corrects color reproduction
   II. How to do transparency masking
      A. The alphabet method of masking transparencies
      B. How to do it
         1. Prepare the step tablet
         2. Prepare the transparency
         3. Make the masks
         4. Make the separation negatives
         5. Make the positive
   III. Other methods of separation
      A. Masking for reflection copy
         1. The magenta masking method
         2. The two-stage masking method
      B. The Fairchild Scan-A-Color

Need for Organization

Almost 24 centuries ago, Aristotle said that every piece of rhetoric (by which he meant speaking and writing) should have a beginning, a middle, and an ending. These words are still true today. They mean that a good piece of writing MUST BE ORGANIZED so that it begins, proceeds, and then ends—not just stops.

It will come as no surprise to you, then, that every piece of technical writing has these three parts, a beginning, a middle or body, and an ending. So let's look for a few moments at each of these parts:

1. *Introduction*

Not every report, article, etc. needs to have an introduction—that is, needs to be "introduced." Sometimes this can easily be done in your opening sentence or opening paragraph. At other times a special "introduction" is needed. Only you as the writer can determine whether you need a special introduction, whether your reader can profit by being properly "introduced" to your topic. If so, by all means use an introduction. If not, then omit it.

2. *Middle or Body*

The most important part of your writing is, of course, the text or body itself, which must logically (or chronologically) be developed from the first main point through the last one until your discussion is completed. To do this, you need a carefully-thought-out outline. However, it must not be so rigid that it cannot be changed at a moment's notice. In other words, it must be flexible.

Every outline is merely tentative, working, or preliminary until your writing has been completed. Then it becomes your table of contents—your final, unchangeable outline.

NOTE: In any piece of technical writing, it is good practice for you to scatter your table of contents throughout your body or text in the form of main and subheads. This will aid your reader immeasurably in his effort to follow your changes in the direction of your thought.

3. *Ending*

Carefully planned technical writing doesn't just stop—IT ENDS! And your ending must be carefully planned so that your reader will accept it as your final word. And you will do this if you use one of these endings:

a. *Conclusion:* Use a conclusion ONLY if you actually come to some conclusion based on your findings.

b. *Recommendation:* Use this type only if you actually have something to recommend.

c. *Summary:* Use this ending to summarize your findings.

d. *Terminating:* Use a terminating ending to stop a written presentation by letting the reader know that that's all, there's no more to come. Use this type when you don't conclude, recommend, or summarize.

e. *Non-terminating:* Sometimes you do not wish to end or terminate your material, as in a series of progress reports. In that case, use a non-terminating ending that lets your reader know that you are through for the time being, but that more will come later.

Special Types of Organization

Some companies use special types of organizations which have proved valuable and/or economical. For instance, General Motors Research likes this type of organization:

    Foreword
    Conclusions [Placed up front to save the reading time of high-salaried executives]
    Recommendations
    Discussion
    Tables, Photographs, Drawings, and Curves
    General Data Required

North American Aviation's Missile and Control Equipment Operation at Downey, California, prefers this organization:

    Cover
    Title Page
    Foreword
    Abstract
    Summary (Optional)
    Contents
    Tables
    Illustrations
    Introduction
    Body
    Appendices
    Nomenclature
    References
    Distribution List
    Index (Optional)

Robert T. Hamlett, formerly Director of Sperry Gyroscope's vast technical writing department and now Vice President in Charge of Technical Personnel at Great Neck, New York, offers the following outline in his excellent "SUGGESTIONS FOR THE PREPARATION of Technical Papers":

    The Outline
    The Introduction
    The Main Body of the Text
    The Conclusions
    Illustrations and Lantern Slides [Films, filmstrips, slides, etc.]
    Bibliography

R. K. Anderson of the Process Engineering Sub-Section, Design Section, Engineering Department, Hanford Works at Richland, Washington, suggests this organization:

    Title and Introduction
    Purpose
    Summary and Conclusions
    Recommendations
    Discussion
    Appendices and Bibliography
    Charts, Graphs, Diagrams, and Illustrations.

Obviously, there is no one form of organization or outline that is right and all the others wrong. Each type of organization used does the best job for the person using it. So regardless of the type of writing you are doing, the important thing to remember is to have some definite organization or outline that will get you started, let you proceed, and then bring you to a safe, satisfactory ending.

Types of Technical and/or Business Reports

Here are ten common types or kinds of business and technical reports commonly written today:

1. Progress
2. Recommendation
3. Investigation
4. Analysis
5. Stockholders'
6. Test-Inspection

A Report on

Hansen's Disease

Submitted to

Mr. John P. Riebel

Submitted by

Jeannie A. Ziegler

May 14, 19

Figure 5. A Typical, Properly-spaced Title Page

7. Technical Inquiry
8. Specifications—Bids
9. Memorandum
10. Letter

No elaboration will be made on any of these types of reports, since I believe that once you know the elements of a good, complete, concise report, you will be able to write any type by simply applying these elements thoughtfully, carefully, conscientiously to the kind you are to do.

III. Presentation

"At the last meeting of our Association, representatives of all the major companies complained about the way their younger men were putting down their words—and futures—on paper. Can't someone tell us what to do?"

Dwight Van Avery

To be usable, facts must not only be organized, but also be presented. Presentation consists of putting the right things in the right places, where the reader can easily find and read them. So let's look at the parts of a formal report.

NOTE: Every possible part of a formal report will be discussed. If necessary, however, you can omit one or more of them if they are not required in the report you are asked to write.

The Parts of a Formal Report

Every formal report, like many informal ones, consists of three distinct parts: (1) the prefatory material, (2) the text or body proper, and (3) the appended material. Each part will be discussed in detail.

Prefatory

The prefatory parts of a formal report, paper, thesis, or article may consist of all of the following parts—but some of them may not be used, depending on the desires or needs of your reader.

Cover

Every formal piece of writing should be enclosed in some permanent binding on which are lettered the following information:

The Title of Your Report (Underlined)

Your Name

The Date the Report Is Due

NOTE: There are three places where you put the date the report is due: on your cover, on your title page, and in your letter of transmittal.

Title Page

Usually the first thing your reader sees when he opens the report is the title page, which should list the following things: the title of the report (underlined), the words "Submitted to" and the name of the reader, the words "Submitted by" and your name, and the date your report is due—or submitted.

On the facing page is a sample title page. Note well that the title seems off center. This is true of all pages of your report, for you must allow $3/4$" for binding. The center line of your report is slightly less than 4" from the right-hand edge of the page.

Letter of Authorization

Although seldom used within an organization, the letter of authorization is a common instrument for authorizing or requesting someone to prepare the report. Remember, no one writes a report or thesis just for the fun of doing so. You write a report because your instructor says you must if you want to get credit for his course!

The following will show you the legal importance of a letter of authorization:

Over 20 years ago, the Division of Highways of the state of Michigan authorized, by letter, a private engineering company in Lansing to investigate the possibilities of putting a bridge across the Straits of Mackinac. This letter authorized the company to spend up to, but not more than, $250,000. In short, this letter was as good as a post-dated check for a quarter of a million dollars—good after the survey had been made. This letter could have been presented in court as a legally-binding contract, if this had been necessary. It wasn't.

Letter of Transmittal

The conventional method of transmitting the report from the writer to the reader, usually the one who authorized the investigation or the report, is called the letter of transmittal, which should include five distinct points:

1. The idea of transmitting something, the report: The attached report . . . , or This report . . . or The accompanying report . . . ,
   The title of your report: entitled ....,
   Purpose of your report: has been prepared for.

2. The scope or limitations of your report: This report is limited to . . . It does not include . . .

3. Acknowledgements to others for their assistance in helping you with this report. Omit printed material: I am especially grateful to Mr. Gene Rittenhouse, our Cal Poly Placement Officer, for his help in obtaining information which otherwise would not have been available to me.

On the following page is Fig. 6, a typical letter of transmittal properly spaced and numbered—with a lower-case Roman numeral ii centered at the bottom of the page.

738 Pacific Street
San Luis Obispo, California
August 15, 19

Mr. John P. Riebel
California State Polytechnic College
San Luis Obispo, California

Dear Mr. Riebel:

    I am submitting this report, <u>Basic Concepts in Chemical Treatments of Replanted Soils</u>, as partial fulfillment of the requirements for the successful completion of Report Writing. My report was written to be presented at an undergraduate seminar.

    The purpose is to point out the problems, the causes, and some proposed answers to the increasing need for correction of replant maladies. The report is by no means detailed, since the subject is very broad. However, it does give a general discussion of the basic concepts.

    I am deeply indebted to you, Mr. Riebel, for your allowance of personal time and assistance in showing me the proper form for writing this report. I must also acknowledge Dr. W.A. Kreutzer for the assistance he has given me in the gathering of information for this report.

Sincerely yours,

Ray Wisnom

Ray Wisnom

ii

Figure 6. A Typical Letter of Transmittal Properly Spaced and Paged

Table of Contents

The final topical outline of your report becomes your table of contents, which is prepared for the sole benefit of your reader. YOU don't need an outline, for you wrote the report. But your reader needs to know what to look for and how to find his way through your material.

NOTE: Throughout your report or paper you should scatter your table of contents in the form of main heads, subheads, etc. at the appropriate places. When you do this, you must not change the wording in any way. In other words, the wording of each heading in your table of contents must be the same as that in your text.

Table of Illustrations

If you use illustrations, list them in a table of illustrations so that your reader will know, first, that your material is illustrated, and second, where to find them.

Your table of illustrations may include any charts, tables, or graphs used if they are short, or you may use separate tables on separate pages. On the facing page is Figure 7, a typical table of contents.

Abstract

An abstract of your report is actually a sentence-paragraph outline—a miniature or postage-stamp report containing only the high points. A technical abstract is the information boiled down to the bare essentials. Few people can read intelligently an outline, which consists of only words or phrases. However, when these words and phrases are put into sentences and paragraphed, they usually become quite intelligible.

With this in mind, the simplest way to write an abstract of your report is to take your table of contents and put each heading into a sentence; then paragraph your sentences. Ergo, your abstract!

Let's try it to see. In the left-hand column is the outline or table of contents of a report given exactly as it was written. In the right-hand column is an abstract which the author of this report wrote FROM THIS TABLE OF CONTENTS! Note how difficult the table of contents is to understand, but how easy it is to follow the sentences in the abstract:

Table of Contents

Introduction

Airborne Particulate matter

Atmospheric Air Cleaners
    Viscous-Impingement-Type
    Moving-Curtain-Viscous
    Dry-Air
    Charged-Medium Electronic
    Air Cleaner

Air-Cleaner Performance and Testing

Conclusion

Appendix
    References

Abstract

Dust particles are harmful not only to membranes of the nose, but to critical manufacturing processes as well. Therefore it is desirable to reduce the concentration of physical impurities by air-cleaning methods. The air filter is just such a device for removing contaminants from the atmosphere.

Atmospheric particles range in size from less than 0.01 micron to ones caught by a flyscreen. This wide range makes it impossible to design a universally applicable filter.

Cleaning devices for atmospheric air are classified according to the principle involved. The viscous-impingement filter consists of a medium treated with oil or grease. The moving-curtain filter consists of a series of plates attached to a pair of chains, forming a curtain, which is revolved (by means of an electric motor) through an oil bath. The dry-air filter, made of wool felt or other similar material, has a high lint-holding capacity. The charged-medium electronic air cleaner, with a 12,000-volt charged gridwork, has the highest efficiency.

The effectiveness of air cleaners is determined by the weight method and the dust-spot test.

Each filter has certain advantages that others do not. Because air cleaning is a continuous process, operating costs, predicated life, and efficiency are more important than initial cost.

Text

Arrangement

Here are some important pointers that will help you do a better job of arranging your technical material so that your presentation will be correct, coherent, consistent:

1. Use a good grade of 8½"x11" white bond paper, preferably 20 pound weight, never less than 16 lb. DON'T USE ONION SKIN OR OTHER LIGHT, TRANSPARENT PAPER!

2. Neatly and carefully type every piece of technical writing—and be sure to proofread it before you hand it in.

3. Use only black or dark-blue inks. AVOID RED, GREEN, PURPLE, OR OTHER LURID COLORS.

Table of Contents

Definition	1
History	2
Biblical References	2
Dispersion	2
Clinical Description	3
Etiology	4
The Bacillus	4
Source of Infection	5
Mode of Transmission	5
Insect Vectors	6
Incubation Period	6
Pathology	8
Lepromatous	8
Tuberculoid	8
Polyneuritis	9
Diagnosis	11
Immunology	13
Treatment	14
Control	15
Summary	16
Appendix	17
References	18

iii

Figure 7. Table of Contents

4. Write on only one side of the page except for illustrations placed on pages facing a page of text.

5. Use adequate but not overly-generous margins. Left-hand margins of 1¾" to 2" will provide the extra paper necessary to bind your report in a cover. Your right-hand margin should be at least 1", top margin at least 1½", and bottom margin at least 1". The margin used on page 14 is good.

6. Keep the same paragraph margins throughout your report except—

   a. When you tabulate, indent 5 spaces on the left and try not to go closer than 1½" from the right-hand edge of your page. Also single space within each item tabulated, but double space between items, as in this tabulation.

   b. When you use a quotation not as part of your text but as a separate entry, indent five spaces (plus an extra three if your quotation starts a paragraph), and make the ends of your lines at least five spaces shorter than your regular line endings. For example:

   > A Word to New Subscribers:
   >
   > Welcome aboard—it's good to have you with us!
   >
   > BETTER LETTERS has already helped thousands of people write better letters and reports. We guarantee it can do the same for you. All it takes is one thing: your active cooperation.
   >
   > BETTER LETTERS isn't like a pill or a shot of penicillin. "Taking it" won't do you a bit of good—you have to "use it." It's a tool, not a painless panacea for all writing ills.
   >
   > Our editors have broken the art of good writing into small, easily-digested portions. Each bulletin (there are two every month) presents a limited number of ideas—the number you can put into practice and make your own before receiving the next issue.
   >
   > If you use BETTER LETTERS, if you try to master and apply the ideas it presents, you'll find it an immensely valuable service. Most subscribers notice an improvement in their writing even within the space of a few months. In terms of practical training value, it's a rare bargain. We don't know any way that you can buy equal results for the same amount of money—or a lot more.
   >
   > Please cooperate—we want you to get your money's worth. Nothing delights us more than satisfied customers, the kind who send us comments like those reproduced on the back of this letter. (52)
   >
   > NOTE: When you use this method of quoting, do not use quotation marks. The extra indention and single spacing are sufficient to set these words off as quoted material. However, a number indicating either a footnote or a reference must be used, as in the example just given.

7. Never put anything in your margins except page numbers.

8. Put the title of your report on the first page of the body. It might be added here that the title should appear in only four different places:

   a. On the cover
   b. On the title page
   c. In the letter of transmittal
   d. On page 1 of the body of your report.

   DO NOT USE IT ANYWHERE ELSE!

9. Underline once (which means to italicize to a printer) the title in each of these four places.

10. Scatter throughout your report your table of contents as main and subheadings. They correspond to the headlines and subheadlines in a newspaper story, and materially help your reader find his way through your writing.

11. Do not change in any way the wording of your table of contents headings when you use them as main and subheads.

12. Underline once for emphasis all headings and subheadings in the body of your report.

13. Put each heading, etc. on a separate line to make it stand out clearly and boldly.

14. Start all main headings in the center of the page and put your page number in the center at the bottom.
    On page 1, center your title about 2½" down from the top (See Figure 8 facing this page).

15. Start on separate lines all subheadings (underlined once) in the left-hand margin (See Figure 8).

16. Start on separate lines all sub-subheadings (underlined once) five spaces in from the left-hand margin.

17. Start each additional subheading five more spaces in from the margin, on a separate line. Also underline.

18. If your table of contents uses numerals and letters, you must use them in the text of your report or paper; if not, don't use them in the body. BE CONSISTENT!

19. Put all headings, main or sub, on separate lines for emphasis, and underline each one once.

<u>Labor Unions in Agriculture</u>

<u>Labor Problems</u>

<u>Distribution of Labor</u>

    One of the most important factors in the labor dispute today is that of labor distribution in the various states. Growers throughout the United States have looked for various solutions to fill their need for labor. Included are the Bracero Program and also ones that deal with the exchange of laborers from Japan and the Philippines.

<u>Areas</u>

    One might look at the agricultural map and see why there is such an acute problem concerning labor at the right place and at the right time. Areas such as Oregon, Washington, Idaho, and Arizona are those hardest hit for an immediate solution.

    As far as labor activity is concerned, California has caught the full force of the attack. Since California is one of the most productive states in the nation, it also has the most pressing labor requirements throughout the entire year.

    Most of the facts, arguments, and debates revolve around court decisions that have been made in cases tried in various California courts.

1

Figure 8. A Typical First Page With Subheadings

Numbering of Pages

1. Number each page in the prefatory part—letter of transmittal, table of contents, table of illustrations, and abstract—in the center of the lower margin with lower-case Roman numerals.

    NOTE: The title page, obviously, is page i, but no number is actually placed on the title page. Allow for it, however.

2. The first page of the text or body and each page that starts a main heading should be numbered in the center of the lower margin.
3. All pages which contain full-page illustrations are also numbered in the center of the bottom margin.
4. The fronts of all facing-page illustrations should also be numbered in the center of the bottom margin.
5. All other pages in the body of the report should be numbered in the upper right-hand margin about ½" down and 1" from the margin.
6. All pages in the appendix should be numbered in the center of the bottom margin.
7. The appendix should be separated from the text by a page on which the word *"Appendix"* has been written about ⅓ of the way down the page. Although this page is given the next consecutive number after the last page in the text, no number is put on this page.
8. The prefatory portions of the report are numbered as in lower-case Roman numerals, and the body and appendix are numbered in Arabic numerals, consecutively from beginning to end.

Spacing

In writing your material, always remember to give it "eye appeal"—make it nice to look at and easy to read. Do this and your reader will read your material much more favorably. Spacing is an important element in eye appeal.

1. Use adequate margins: at least 1½" from the top, 1" from the bottom, and 1½" on the left and 1¼" on the right side of your page.
2. Single space the following portions of your material:
    a. Within the paragraphs of your letter of transmittal
    b. The second and any following lines of an entry in your table of contents, table of illustrations, subheading, etc. requiring more than one line
    c. The second and subsequent lines in a footnote, bibliography, table of references
    d. The second and subsequent lines in a quotation placed in the text as is the one on page 6 of this manual.
    e. The second and subsequent lines in a tabulation

3. Double space the following parts of your writing:
    a. The main text of your paper, report, etc.
    b. Between the page number in the upper right-hand corner and the first line of the text
    c. Between the paragraphs in your letter of transmittal
    d. Between the subheadings and the next line of the text; between the sub-subheading and and the next line of text; etc.
    e. Between items in a tabulation, as well as between the line introducing the tabulation and the last line and the next line of text or the next heading
    f. Between the words introducing an inserted quotation (See page 17) and the quotation proper
    g. Between the paragraphs within an inserted quotation
    h. Between the entries in a table of contents, a bibliography, a table of references, a glossary, or any similar listing
    i. Between the last line of text and the first footnote. NOTE: Draw a line 15 spaces or 1½" long between this last line of text and the first footnote
    j. Between footnote entries
3. Triple space between these parts:
    a. Between the title and your first main heading (centered) on page 1
    b. Between each main heading and either the first subheading or the first line of the text, if no subheading is used
    c. Between the words, *"Abstract," "Table of Contents," "Table of Illustrations," "Bibliography,"* and *"Table of References"* and whatever follows
    d. Between the last line of a section and the heading for the next section. THE TEXT OF ALL REPORTS, PAPERS, ARTICLES, THESES *MUST BE DOUBLE SPACED!*

Illustrations or Graphic Aids

Someone once said, "A good illustration is worth a thousand words." How right he was, especially for technical reports, papers, articles, and theses. The judicious use of illustrative material—drawings, sketches, pictures, maps, tables, charts, etc—can help immeasurably to get your point across and keep the number of words down.

Obviously, not all reports require illustrations—for example, the sample report, *Intestacy and Wills,* by Julie Holmquist. In this kind of report, graphic aids would be completely superfluous. About the only illustrative material that might be desirable would be a sample will, and that probably would be put in the appendix.

However, when illustrations or graphic aids *are* used, whether in the body or text itself or in the appendix, each one should be given a figure number and a caption. Also, if it is used in the text, it should be referred to as such. No illustration should be used in the text without specific reference to the figure.

There are six different ways in which illustrations can be used to advantage in technical writing:

1. *Frontispiece*—Occasionally the writer of a report or paper wants to use a preliminary illustration so as to set the mood of the writing. He may do this by using a frontispiece inside the front cover and before the title page; or he may put the illustration between the abstract and page 1 of the paper. This method will not be illustrated here.

2. *Partial Page*—Some illustrations are so small, yet important, that they must be included in the writing. In these cases they can be put on part of the page, with text above, below, or on either side, whichever way seems the best.

3. *Full Page*—This method is probably the one most frequently used. The illustration may be placed in a cello cover, if desirable. Full page illustrations are paged at the bottom, center.

4. *Facing Page*—Sometimes it is highly desirable for the reader to look at an illustration while he is reading the text. This is especially true of a complicated figure with numbered parts mentioned in the text. A most satisfactory way of handling such illustrations is to place them on the back of the preceding page with the illustration actually facing the discussion. Since reports are written on one side of the page only, the front of the sheet with a facing page on the back should contain the following information:

    The figure number
    The caption
    (Facing page....)

5. *Appended*—Occasionally you will have graphic material that is an integral part of your report as a whole—something you want included between the covers—but is apart from the understanding of the text itself. Under this circumstance the best place to put it is in your appendix. (Sometimes no figure numbers are necessary for these illustrations.) All pages in the appendix should be paged at the bottom center.

6. *Inside either the front or the back cover*—Occasionally it is advisable to glue a small envelope or pocket to either the inside front or the inside back cover. This pocket can hold scales or other things which can be taken out and used by the reader in different parts of the report. Although not used very often, this is an excellent means of handling some graphic aids.

There are several important details which you should observe when using graphic material in your report:

1. All drawings should be done in ink—india ink, preferably.
2. Each illustration must have a figure or table number and a caption.
3. Each illustration should be referred to in the text by figure, table, chart, etc.
4. Full-page illustrations that must be put vertically on the page (that is, across the 11" side of your page, rather than across the 8½" side) must be put in so that the bottom of the illustration, together with the figure number and caption, are to the right of the page. In other words, the reader may easily see and study these illustrations by turning his left wrist 90° clockwise.
5. Illustrative material must not be larger than 8½"x11" unless it has been folded. If it protrudes beyond the pages, it will get dogeared and torn.
6. Whatever illustrative material not absolutely necessary to an understanding of the text should be placed in the appendix.
7. A frontispiece carries no page number. All full-page illustrations are paged at the bottom center. For facing pages, the page number is centered at the bottom of the front page—no number is used on the side showing the illustrations. All partial-page illustrations except those on pages which start main divisions are paged at the top right-hand corner.
8. Illustrations borrowed from printed sources must be credited to those sources with either footnotes or reference numbers (unless the source is actually printed on the illustration itself.
9. The word "Figure" may be capitalized or not, and it may also be abbreviated. But BE CONSISTENT in your use of this word.
10. Figures, graphs, drawings, diagrams, photographs, maps, etc. are referred to as "figures" and are numbered with consecutive Arabic numerals.
11. Tables and charts are usually referred to by capital Roman numerals.

Appendix

Whatever is a part of the report as a whole—that is, within the covers of the report—but not a part of the text proper should be put in the appendix. The first entry in the Appendix should be your bibliography or table of references, if you used printed sources. After that put the items in the order in which they are or could be referred to in the text proper. Remember, not every reports needs to have an appendix, however. If you need one, use it. If not, don't.

IV. Language

"If an engineer, for example, is testing an insulating material and it chars and smells like burned string beans, we can think of no reason why he should not say so.

Dwight Van Avery

The reader of your report will, in a large measure, determine the language you use in your report, paper, article, or thesis, particularly the degree of technicality. Although fairly obvious, this point is often overlooked by technical writers, even experienced ones. No matter how excellent your drawings or sketches, how complete your formulas or equations, how attractive and eye-catching your other visual aids, language is still the backbone of your writing.

Language is your prime medium of communication. Before you can hope to be understood, your factual information must be translated into words and word combinations which will create in your reader's mind pictures, concepts, ideas that he can visualize and understand.

If your reader understands what you have written, he will know what you are talking about, and that will please him. He may not agree with you, but at least he will understand what you have said. Your language must "make sense" to him.

Putting it bluntly, that means following the accepted rules of clear, correct writing. Grammatical errors, mistakes in punctuation, vagueness, omission of important sentence elements, fragments or incomplete thoughts, jumbled and fused sentences, muddled thinking, monstrously long paragraphs—none of them will help you communicate—that is, get your points across to—with your patient, long-suffering reader.

"Oh," you say, "I'll have a secretary to correct my mistakes in composition." In the vernacular, my answer is a long, loud, "Oh yeah?" That's what you think. And even if you do have a secretary, how will you know that she can catch all of your boo-boos unless you know what constitutes good writing?

If you want any further proof on the importance of correct English in technical writing, just look at page 6 of *General Electric's Answer to FOUR WHY'S:*

> The top engineer upstairs is on the telephone. He said to us: "Right before my eyes is a brief report made out by one of our young engineers. I have to guess what the fellow is driving at. I'm no English shark, but I find myself getting a little angry when I see four sentences tied together into one with commas. He has *principal* for *principle,* and he has also misspelled Cincinnati. What if some of this fellow's bad English gets into the hands of our customers?"

That is not an English teacher talking. It's the representative of one of America's largest companies, General Electric!

Unless you write correctly, you can't write clearly. And clarity is the first requirement of any piece of technical writing. Although he lived several centuries before the birth of engineering, scientific, industrial, and business writing, John Dryden the poet once said that the first aim of any writer is to be understood.

Robert Louis Stevenson said something similar when he admonished authors not merely to write so that they could be understood, but so that they could not possibly be misunderstood. There in a few brief words you have the secret of good, forceful, successful technical writing: WRITE SO THAT YOU CANNOT POSSIBLY BE MISUNDERSTOOD! Do that and you will truly communicate with your reader.

V. Time-Timing

". . . in neither your writing nor speaking can you conceal your inadequacies."

Dwight Van Avery

The temporal or time element plays an important part in report writing. A recommendation report on the proposed purchase of a particular machine turned in a week or even a day after the decision has to be made as to whether to purchase this machine is time and effort—yes, MONEY—wasted.

Every day people hand in reports AFTER THEY ARE DUE—reports so badly timed that they miss the boat and consequently are worthless. One hour late may be as bad as a month. The report is unnecessary in either case. So if you want your report to be of maximum value to your reader, time it so that it arrived in his hands or on his desk WHEN IT IS DUE, or even before.

Now let's talk a bit about that other element of the time element, the time you have in which to prepare your report. When you are asked to do a report, you can make it as long and as complete as you have time in which to do the work. For example, if you are asked to do a report on something you have been working on for some time and you are given only an hour, obviously you'll have to get things together in a hurry. However, if you are given a day, a week, or even longer, your report can and should be progressively more complete, thorough, detailed.

The best possible advice that you can get is to do the best job you can under or within the time limits assigned you. You can't be expected to prepare a 100-page paper or treatise in a few hours or even a day. Conversely, it shouldn't take you days or weeks to write a simple report of only a few hundred words.

Here, for example, is a complete, concise progress report on the events that took place over about 48 hours. It doesn't tell everything these two men did—but it does tell the comptroller enough so that when Mr. Schredder calls on July 25, Mr. Conover will have all the details necessary to say, "We'll take it at the price Stevens offered."

July 24, 19xx

To: Mr. R. C. Conover, Comptroller
Los Angeles Office

From: L. M. Stevens, Chief Engineer,
Southern Division

SUBJECT: Equipment offered for sale at the Tom Jones Mine, Blankville, Arizona.

Ben Taylor and I drove to Needles Thursday evening, July 18, proceeded to Blankville Friday morning to inspect the mining and milling equipment at the Tom Jones Mine, and returned to Glendale Saturday morning.

The only equipment that appeared to be in first-class condition was three Allis-Chalmers ball mills with drives, feeders, etc. The mills are driven through herringbone gears by direct-connected, slow-speed electric motors. The ball mills are 6'x6', 5'x5', and 5'x6'. The 6'x6' mill appeared to be in the best condition, and was located in a position where removal from the plant would not be extremely difficult.

The J. J. Sugarman Company, liquidators, has reduced the price on this mill from $16,000 to $9,000. We offered $7,500 for the 6'x6' mill complete with motor, starters, apronfeeder, and miscellaneous spare parts loaded on our truck at the mill site.

Mr. Irving Schredder, the Sugarman Company representative, is to call you July 25 with their decision relative to acceptance of our offer.

VI. Your Reader-Audience

"We know because we rub shoulders with people, at work and in the community, that a solid background in English is prerequisite to happiness and well being. Without a reasonably good command of English—as a means of communication—and without knowledge of what the best minds of all times have put into print, we are not educated for personal happiness, apart from the job, or for personal success in the exciting business of making a living."

Dwight Van Avery

Maybe you've wondered why I put your reader-audience in the middle of the technical-writing star. That's exactly where he belongs! He's the center of attraction in whatever piece of writing you do: report, thesis, article, paper, letter.

It might be said that the pointers of the star are centripetal—center seeking. Everything you have written and done had him in mind—or it certainly should have. You wrote the report for him—most likely because he requested it, not because you wanted to. So DO NOT IGNORE YOUR READER! The fact that your report was written for one reader only —or for a very limited audience if you must present your report orally—accounts for the chief difference between a report and some of the other forms of practical writing.

So remember this above all: YOUR REPORT IS WRITTEN FOR ONE PERSON ONLY, your instructor, your boss, your supervisor, whoever he might be. It is he who must read and understand (and evaluate, too) this report and your findings, and the methods you use to arrive at those findings.

In order to make a favorable impression you must express yourself clearly, correctly, concisely. Your reader may get from dozens of others reports similar to the one you are doing for him. Often, as in large industries, the only way that the man on top (the president of the company) knows what's going on is through series of reports which filter up to him from the lowest level. And if this is any consolation, this top man on the totem pole must, in turn, make a report himself to the stockholders of his organization, or to his board of directors!

But you may be very sure that the report which the president makes to the board of directors or to the stockholders and the report which he receives from those under him are two entirely different documents. And rightly so, for they are aimed at two entirely different audiences or readers. Your report is written for your supervisor, and is in the technical jargon of your field—language which he will understand, language which he expects to hear from you. He in turn will write his report for his superior in language the superior will understand. And so it goes up the ladder to the top man.

But the top man's report is written for non-technical directors, or even less technically minded stockholders, who want to know in simple five-and-ten-cent words just what the organization has been doing, what money it has made (or lost), what its prospects are, etc. In short, he wants to know what the chances are for continued prosperity of the business!

As you have seen in L. M. Stevens' excellent letter-report, many routine business letters are actually miniature reports. As you will see later when we discuss the problem of paragraphing, a letter written by the late B. F. Cake, Vice President in Charge of Labor Relations and Personnel for Gladding, McBean & Co., is actually a concise, complete, correct report on an accident witnessed by Mr. Cake.

Conclusion:

Helpful Hints for Writing and Speaking

"We hope it has occurred to you that English extends beyond a single classroom; that your success or failure in your other classrooms is largely due to your ability to read, to understand, to speak, and to write. English is just as all-embracing in a business organization. Whether we are at drafting board, desk, machine, or calling on customers, we are involved more or less in communication."

Dwight Van Avery

Here are 10 tips for doing better technical writing:
1. Have a definite point and come to it quickly.
2. Write simply, naturally, correctly, clearly, concisely, coherently.
3. Use short sentences, but don't make your writing choppy, jerky.
4. Don't be afraid to paragraph for a change in the direction of your thought.
5. Link your thoughts with suitable connectives.
6. Make your writing long enough to do the job, but short enough to be interesting.
7. Be sure YOU understand what you're trying to say before you tell it to someone else.
8. Give your reader ALL the information he NEEDS to know, no more.
9. Don't try to tell everything you know. You'll only bore him.
10. Use whatever illustrations you need to help you get your points across.

And if you must present your material orally, the following 10 tips will help you do a better job:
1. Know what you want to say, say it, then sit down.
2. Remember your time limit and STAY WITHIN IT. Stop before your time has run out.
3. Speak out clearly, boldly. Don't mumble, whisper, or shout.
4. Be cheerful, natural, friendly, even humorous if you wish—that's being human.
5. Allow time for questions. Audience participation is always welcome.
6. Don't read your material. You wrote it. It's yours. Rehearse it beforehand.
7. Look at your audience and punctuate your remarks with facial and body gestures.
8. Try not to be scared. Be confident and your audience will take you for an expert.
9. Don't talk too rapidly or hurry to get through. But don't dawdle along, either.
10. Be natural and human, and use your pauses forcefully, effectively to let your major points soak in!

Appendix

A Table of References

"As you move up the success ladder, what you write and what you say will determine in part your rate of climb. It is neither too early nor too late to become practiced in the art of communication; certainly not too late to accumulate background through reading experiences . . ."

Dwight Van Avery

1. Aurner, Robert R., *Effective Communication in Business* (Third Edition), South-Western Publishing Company, Cincinnati, 1950.
2. Braun, Carl F., *Corporate Correspondence,* C. F. Braun & Co., Alhambra, California, 1948.
3. Braun, Carl F., *Letter-Writing in Action,* C. F. Braun &. Co., Alhambra, California, 1948.
4. Braun, Carl F., *Presentation for Engineers,* C. F. Braun &. Co., Alhambra, California, 1949.
5. Brown, Stanley M. and Doris, Lillian, *Business Executive's Handbook* (Third Edition), Prentice-Hall, Inc., New York, 1947.
6. Buckley, Earl A., *How to Write Better Business Letters* (Fourth Edition), McGraw-Hill Book Company, Inc., New York, 1957.
7. *Business Letters That Click* (Compiled by the editors of Printers' Ink and Leading Contributors), Funk and Wagnalls Company, New York, 1948.
8. Crouch, W. George and Zettler, Robert L., *A Guide to Technical Writing* (Second Edition), The Ronald Press Company, New York, 1954.
9. Douglass, Paul, *Communication Through Reports,* Prentice-Hall, Inc., Englewood Cliffs, New Jersey, 1957.
10. Flesch, Rudolph, *The Art of Plain Talk,* Harper & Brothers, New York, 1946.
11. Flesch, Rudolph, *The Art of Readable Writing,* Harper & Brothers, New York, 1949.
12. Frailey, L. E. "Cy", *Handbook of Business Letters,* Prentice-Hall, Inc., New York, 1948.
13. Frailey, L. E. "Cy", *Smooth Sailing Letters,* Prentice-Hall, Inc., New York, 1938.
14. Gaum, Carl G., Graves, Harold F., and Hoffman, Lyne S. S., *Report Writing* (Third Edition), Prentice-Hall, Inc., New York, 1950.
15. *GE's Answer to the Four Why's,* General Electric Company, Schenectady, New York (No date).
16. Gorrell, Robert M. and Laird, Charlton, *Modern English Handbook* (Third Edition), Prentice-Hall, Inc., Englewood Cliffs, New Jersey, 1962.
17. Harwell, George C., *Technical Communication,* The Macmillan Company, New York, 1960.

18. Hayakawa, S. I., *Language in Thought and Action,* Harcourt, Brace and Company, New York, 1949.
19. Holmquist, Julie, *Intestacy and Wills* (A student report written for English 301, Report Writing), California State Polytechnic College, San Luis Obispo, May, 1962.
20. Howell, A. C., *Handbook of English in Engineering Usage* (Second Edition), John Wiley & Sons, Inc., New York, 1940.
21. Janis, J. Harold, *Business Communication Reader,* Harper & Brothers, New York, 1958.
22. Leggett, Glenn, Mead, David C., and Charvat, William, *Handbook for Writers,* Prentice-Hall, Inc., New York, 1951.
23. Linton, Calvin D., *How to Write Reports* (Text Edition), Harper & Brothers, New York, 1954.
24. Marder, Daniel, *The Craft of Technical Writing,* The Macmillan Company, New York, 1960.
25. Menning, J. H. and Wilkinson, C. W., *Writing Business Letters,* Richard D. Irwin, Inc., Homewood, Illinois, 1955.
26. Mills, Gordon H. and Walter, John A., *Technical Writing* (Revised), Holt, Rinehart and Winston, New York, 1962.
27. Mitchell, John *Handbook of Technical Communication,* Wadsworth Publishing Company, Inc., Belmont, California, 1962.
28. Nauheim, Ferd, *Business Letters That Turn Inquiries into Sales,* Prentice-Hall, Inc., Englewood Cliffs, New Jersey, 1957.
29. Perrin, Porter G., *Writer's Guide and Index to English,* Scott, Foresman and Company, New York 1965.
30. Perry, Sherman, *Let's Write Good Letters,* The American Rolling Mills Company, Middletown, Ohio, 1942.
31. Phillips, David C., *Oral Communication in Business,* McGraw-Hill Book Company, New York, 1955.
32. *Outline of the Library of Congress Classification* (Revised and enlarged edition of "Outline Scheme of Classes"), Library of Congress Processing Department, Washington, D. C., 1942 (Reprinted 1961).
33. Rathbone, Robert R. and Stone, James B., *A Writer's Guide for Engineers and Scientists,* Prentice-Hall, Inc., Englewood Cliffs, New Jersey, 1962.
34. Riebel, John P., "The Art of Talking by Mail," Rough Notes, April, 1957, pp. 36, 46, 48.
35. Riebel, John P. "How to Write Letters That Get Results," *The American Salesman,* Vol. 1, No. 9, May, 1956, pp. 50-61.
36. Riebel, John P., *Ten Commandments for WRITING LETTERS THAT GET RESULTS,* Printers' Ink Books, New London, Connecticut, 1957.
37. Riebel, John P., *How to Write SUCCESSFUL BUSINESS LETTERS in 15 Days,* Prentice Hall, Inc., Englewood Cliffs, New Jersey, 1953.
38. Riebel, John P., "10 Pointers for Writing Better Letters," Pacific Coast Nurseryman, Vol 16, No. 7, July 1957, pp. 19, 30-33, 44-45.
39. Robinson, James Harvey, "On Various Kinds of Thinking," *The Mind in the Making,* Harper & Brothers, New York, 1921.
40. Schultz, Howard and Webster, Robert G., *Technical Report Writing,* David McKay Company, Inc., New York, 1962.
41. Schulte, William M. and Steinberg, Erwin R., *Communication in Business and Industry,* Holt, Rinehart and Winston, Inc., New York, 1960.
42. Shindle, Norman G., *Clear Writing for Easy Reading,* McGraw-Hill Book Company, Inc., New York, 1951.
43. Thomas, J. D., *Composition for Technical Students,* Charles Scribner's Sons, New York, 1949.
44. Ulman, Joseph N. Jr., *Technical Reporting,* Henry Holt and Company, New York, 1952.
45. *Webster's New Collegiate Dictionary,* G. & C. Merriam Co., Publishers, Springfield, Massachusetts, 1949.
46. Weisman, Herman M., *Basic Technical Writing,* Charles H. Merrill Books, Inc., Columbus, Ohio, 1962.
47. Wellborn, G. P., Green, L. B., and Nall, K. A., *Technical Writing,* Houghton Mifflin Company, Boston, 1961.
48. Weseen, Maurice H., *Crowell's Dictionary of English Grammar,* Thomas Y. Crowell Company, New York, 1928.
49. Wicker, C. V., and Albrecht, W. P., *The American Technical Writer,* American Book Company, New York, 1960.
50. Wilkinson, C. W., Menning, J. H., and Anderson, C. R., *Writing for Business* (Revised Edition), Richard D. Irwin, Inc., Homewood, Ill., 1955.
51. Williams, Cecil B. and Ball, John, *Effective Business Writing* (Second Edition), The Ronald Press Company, New York, 1953.
52. *A Word to New Subscribers,* The Economics Press, Inc., Montclair, New Jersey (no date).
53. Zall, Paul M., *Elements of Technical Report Writing,* Harper & Brothers, New York, 1962.
54. "Writing Star Reports," *Refrigerating Engineering,* Vol. 62, No. 11, November, 1954, pp. 49-50; 90, 92.

GRAMMAR
The Parts of Speech

"When you are applying for a job, personnel men will wonder what you got out of your college education if it doesn't show in your English."

                                            Anonymous

Probably the best way of studying the various parts of speech important to technical writers is to examine them functionally to see just what they are supposed to do. For that reason this division is not the usual one of nouns, pronouns, etc., but rather one based upon the function that each part of speech has to perform:

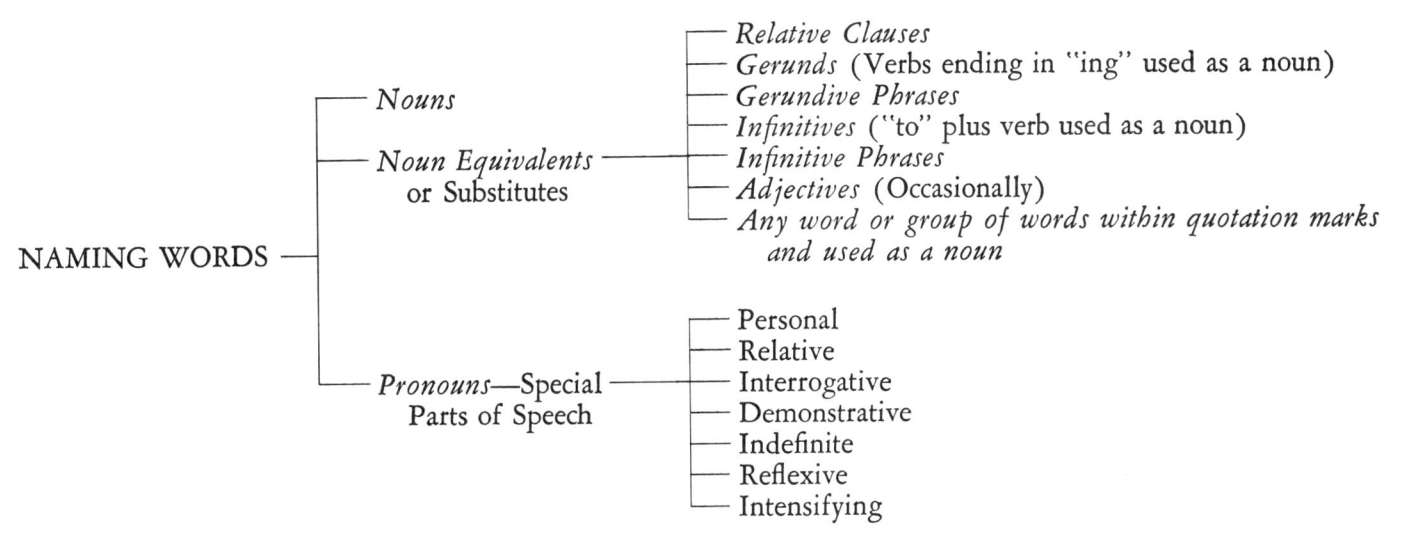

NAMING WORDS
- *Nouns*
- *Noun Equivalents or Substitutes*
  - Relative Clauses
  - Gerunds (Verbs ending in "ing" used as a noun)
  - Gerundive Phrases
  - Infinitives ("to" plus verb used as a noun)
  - Infinitive Phrases
  - Adjectives (Occasionally)
  - Any word or group of words within quotation marks and used as a noun
- *Pronouns*—Special Parts of Speech
  - Personal
  - Relative
  - Interrogative
  - Demonstrative
  - Indefinite
  - Reflexive
  - Intensifying

ACTING WORDS—*Verbs* only—Occasionally some noun will be used as a verb to indicate action—such as, "to broadcast"—but only a verb (a word indicating action) can substitute for a verb.

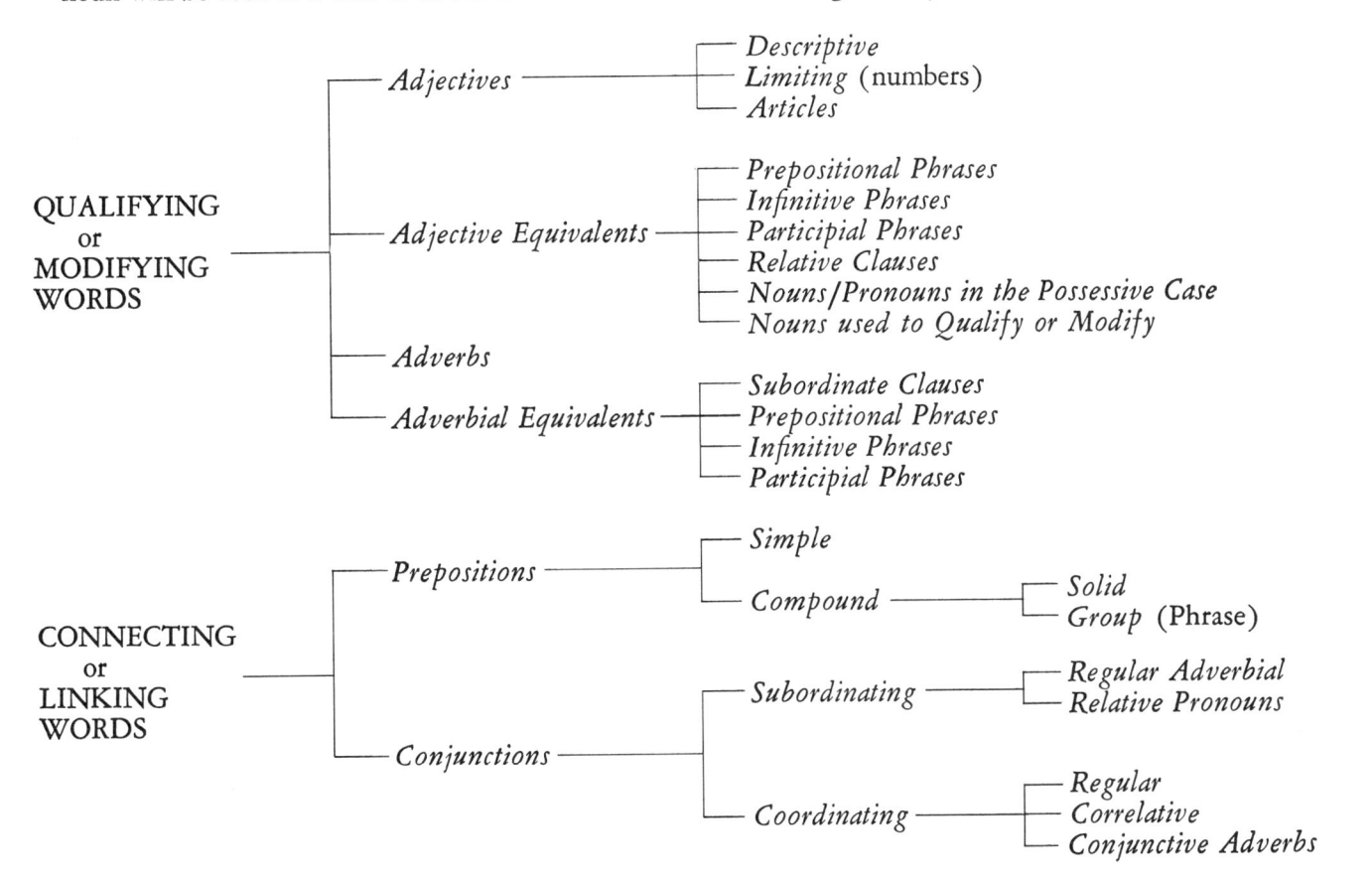

QUALIFYING or MODIFYING WORDS
- *Adjectives*
  - Descriptive
  - Limiting (numbers)
  - Articles
- *Adjective Equivalents*
  - Prepositional Phrases
  - Infinitive Phrases
  - Participial Phrases
  - Relative Clauses
  - Nouns/Pronouns in the Possessive Case
  - Nouns used to Qualify or Modify
- *Adverbs*
- *Adverbial Equivalents*
  - Subordinate Clauses
  - Prepositional Phrases
  - Infinitive Phrases
  - Participial Phrases

CONNECTING or LINKING WORDS
- *Prepositions*
  - Simple
  - Compound
    - Solid
    - Group (Phrase)
- *Conjunctions*
  - Subordinating
    - Regular Adverbial
    - Relative Pronouns
  - Coordinating
    - Regular
    - Correlative
    - Conjunctive Adverbs

NOTE: There is one part of speech which will be ignored here, INTERJECTIONS, since these words express emotion, which has little or no place in technical writing.

NAMING WORDS

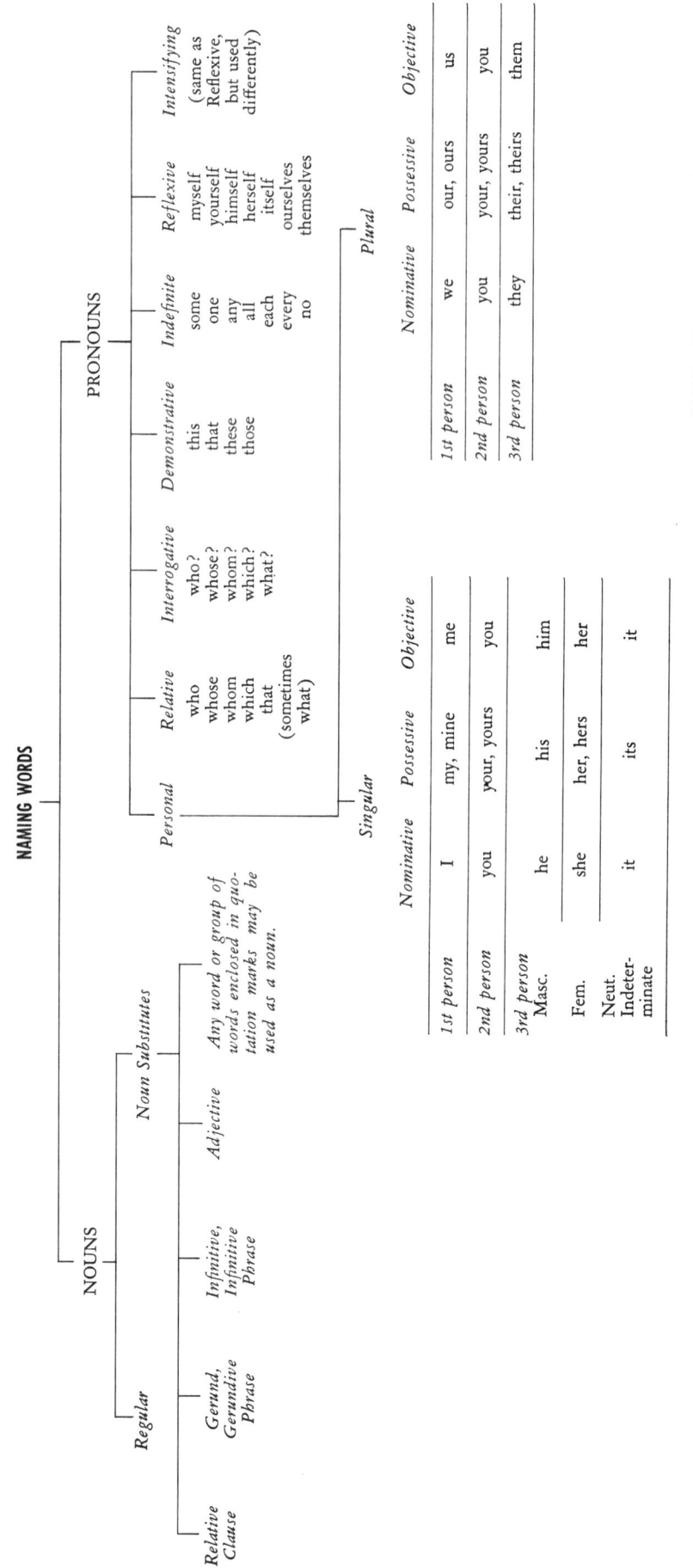

NOUNS

- **Regular**
- **Noun Substitutes**
  - *Relative Clause*
  - *Gerund, Gerundive Phrase*
  - *Infinitive, Infinitive Phrase*
  - *Adjective*
  - *Any word or group of words enclosed in quotation marks may be used as a noun.*

PRONOUNS

Personal	Relative	Interrogative	Demonstrative	Indefinite	Reflexive	Intensifying
	who	who?	this	some	myself	(same as Reflexive, but used differently)
	whose	whose?	that	one	yourself	
	whom	whom?	these	any	himself	
	which	which?	those	all	herself	
	that	what?		each	itself	
	(sometimes what)			every	ourselves	
				no	themselves	

Singular

	Nominative	Possessive	Objective
1st person	I	my, mine	me
2nd person	you	your, yours	you
3rd person Masc.	he	his	him
Fem.	she	her, hers	her
Neut. Indeterminate	it	its	it

Plural

	Nominative	Possessive	Objective
1st person	we	our, ours	us
2nd person	you	your, yours	you
3rd person	they	their, theirs	them

NOTE: The two pronouns that give us the most trouble are *its* and *their*.

its = singular possessive pronoun
it's = a contraction of "it is."
their = plural possession pronoun
there = an adverb of place.

GRAMMAR

A BRIEF OUTLINE OF THE PARTS OF SPEECH AND ESSENTIAL GRAMMAR

The writer of technical, industrial, business, and other reports and papers must know how to use skillfully four kinds of words: Naming, acting, qualifying or modifying, and linking or connecting. The following pages will discuss briefly each type of word, the parts of speech included in this classification, and some grammatical pitfalls into which technical writers so often fall.

Naming Words—Words which name persons, places, things, or actions:

A. *Nouns*—a noun names a person, place, or thing sometimes an action:

1. *Classification:* Nouns may be classified in several ways:
   Common (hat, school, woman, etc.) or
   Proper (Stetson, Cal Poly, Lucy Lee)
   Simple (road, air, company) or
   Compound (railroad, airplane, General Motors Corporation, father-in-law)
   Concrete (tree, gun, book, man, or
   Abstract (love, hatred, learning, schooling)
   Collective (army, company, set of tools, group, etc.)

2. *Properties or Qualities*
   Number—how many: singular (one), plural (more than one)
   Person—who is talking or being talked to or of: first (noun in direct address: *John, please take this to the dump.*); second (noun in apposition with the pronoun "you": I ask you, *John,* what you did with the answers.); third (person, place, or thing spoken of or about: *Cal Poly* is the *nickname* of our *college.*)

   NOTE: Probably 99% of all nouns used are in the third person.

   Gender—Nouns have three genders: Masculine (David), Feminine (Elizabeth), and Neuter: house, school.

3. *Uses or Case*
   Nouns have three uses, usually referred to as "case"
   Nominative Case—A noun used as the subject of a verb: *Reports* are a specialized form of the entire field of technical writing.
   Objective Case—A noun used as the object of a verb, of a preposition, or of a verbal (See page 30), or as the subject of a verbal:
   Underline the *title* of a *report.*
   Possessive Case—A noun used as an adjective to indicate ownership: A *man's* ability to express himself in writing and in speaking are considered by Peter Drucker to be the most important skills he can possess.

NUMBER

Every noun in the English language is either SINGULAR or PLURAL. Here's how the PLURAL forms of English nouns are formed:

1. Most nouns simply add *s* to the singular form: book—books, chair—chairs.
2. Nouns ending in an *s, x, z,* or *sh* sound add *es:* box—boxes, class—classes, lunch—lunches, buzz—buzzes.
3. Nouns ending in *y* preceded by a consonant change *y* to *i* and add *es:* baby—babies,
4. Nouns ending in *y* preceded by a vowel simply add *s:* bay—bays, valley—valleys.
5. Some singular nouns ending in *f* change the *f* to *v* and add *es:* half—halves, knife—knives.
6. Most nouns ending in *o* preceded by a consonant add only *s:* lasso—lassos.
7. Some, however, form their plural by adding *es:* negro—negroes, echo—echoes.
8. All nouns ending in *o* preceded by a vowel add *s* only: studio—studios, ratio—ratios.
9. A few singular nouns form their plural by adding *en* or *ren:* ox—oxen, child—children.
10. Some form the plural with a vowel change: man—men, foot—feet, mouse—mice.
11. A few nouns have the same form for both singular and plural: corn, wheat, sheep, deer, series, species, rye, Chinese, salmon, Japanese.
12. A few nouns are plural in spelling but singular in meaning: mathematics, physics, news, economics, United States.
13. Some are seldom if ever used in the singular: clothes, goods, scissors, riches, suds, shears, trousers, proceeds, statistics, cattle, ashes, eaves, premises, athletics.
14. The plurals of letters and figures are formed by adding *'s:* x—x's, 4—4's, ab—ab's.
15. Some foreign words retain their foreign plurals: basis—bases, thesis—theses, analysis—analyses, crisis—crises, phenomenon—phenomena, curriculum—curricula, datum—data, stratum—strata, nucleus—nuclei, stimulus—stimuli, criterion—criteria.

    NOTE: A few have two plural forms, one foreign and the other English: medium—media, mediums; formula—formulae, formulas; curriculum—curricula, curriculums.

16. A few English nouns have two plurals with different meanings: index—indexes, indices; cloth—cloths, clothes; fish—fishes, fish.
17. Compound nouns may also have plural forms: Solid compounds pluralize the last element: policemen, baseballs. Hyphenated or separate

compounds pluralize the most important element: fathers-in-law, step-brothers, editors-in-chief, textbooks, Knights Templars, menservants, courtsmartial.
18. Some titles also have plurals: Mr.—Messrs., the two Captain Whites, Miss—Misses, Mrs.—Mesdames, the Doctors Harper, Generals Eisenhower and MacArthur.
19. Sometimes the singular form is used to form the plural. When this is done, the words are hyphenated: a ten-foot wall, a two-week layoff, a two-gun cowboy.

POSSESSION OR OWNERSHIP

Sometimes nouns (and pronouns, too) indicate possession or ownership. Whereas the pronouns have special forms to indicate this relationship—my, mine, your, yours, his, her, hers, its, our, ours, their, theirs, whose—nouns must form their possessive case by adding an apostrophe and sometimes an *s*. For example:

"John's brother" means "a brother of John."
"one week's vacation" means "a vacation of one week."
"The Joneses' house" means "the house owned by the Joneses" (plural).
"Procter and Gamble's contest" means "a contest sponsored by Procter and Gable."

Perhaps the following chart will show graphically the difference between plurals and possessives:

No Ownership Involved:
  Singular (one)
    John is here.
    Give it to *John*.
  Plural (more than one)
    The two *Johns* went along for the ride.
Possession or Ownership:
    John's car was stolen. (singular)
    The two *Johns'* cars were stolen. (plural)

1. Most singular and plural nouns not ending in *s* form their possessives by adding *'s*: man's, student's, girl's, men's.
2. Nouns ending in an *s* sound add only the *'*: Moses', Lazarus'.
3. Plural nouns ending in *s* add only the *'*: days', instructors', officers'.
4. Most proper names that end in *s*, whether they are one syllable or two, add simply *'*: Adams', Dickens', Charles', Massachusetts', United States'.
5. Nouns with the same form in the plural as in the singular simply add apostrophe to either singular or plural form: sheep', salmon', deer'.
6. Compound nouns add *'s* to the last element: General Motors Corporation's, AT&T's, Cal Poly's, San Luis Obispo's.
7. Joint ownership is indicated by adding the *'s* to the last member: Crawford and Zimmerman's store, David and Penny's bicycle.
8. The *'s* is used to indicate measures of time and distance: an hour's ride, a day's pay.

NOTE: Be sure to distinguish between the PLURAL (more than one) and the POSSESSIVE (indicating ownership).
NOTE: Do not use the possessive to attribute ownership to something inanimate:
  NOT: the table's top, changes in the steel's structure, the wire's resistance.
  BUT: the top of the table, changes in the structure of the steel, the resistance of the wire.
PLURAL indicates MORE THAN ONE. POSSESSION indicates OWNERSHIP. Plurals may show possession if they indicate ownership.

AGREEMENT

Between the subject of a verb and that verb there exists a relationship called "agreement," which means that if the subject is singular, the verb must also be singular, or if the subject is plural, the verb must be plural. This relationship may be explained as follows:

1. *A singular subject requires a singular verb—*
   NOT: Research have determined by experiment that . . .
   BUT: Research has determined . . .
2. *A plural subject requires a plural verb—*
   NOT: The outside ways is for the carriage to slide back and forth on.
   BUT: The carriage slides back and forth on the outside ways.
3. *If the subject is compound, the verb must be plural—*
   NOT: Enlarging and reducing is done on a pantograph.
   BUT: Enlarging and reducing are done . . .
4. *Words, phrases, or clauses that are inserted between the subject and its verb do not affect the agreement of the subject and its verb—*
   NOT: The use of sulphur and organic accelerators have made continuous vulcanization possible.
   BUT: The use of . . . has made . . .
5. *Only the subject of the sentence, not the predicate nominative, determines the number of the verb—*
   NOT: Carelessness, neglect, and indifference to tools is a common fault . . .
   BUT: Carelessness, neglect, and indifference to tools are common faults . . .
   NOT: The equipment used are four Hobart 100-ampere welding machines and two Lincolns.
   BUT: The equipment used is four . . . Or: Four Hobart and two Lincoln welding machines are used.

GRAMMAR

PAGE 29

6. *An inversion of the normal word order does not affect the number of the verb—*

    NOT: Immediately above the benches are placed a row of lights.

    BUT: Immediately above the benches is placed a row of lights. (A row of lights is . . .)

7. *Collective nouns are usually singular in number, for most of them have plural forms—*

    NOT: A set of standard tools are included with each machine.

    BUT: A set of standard tools is included . . .

    Right: The jury gives its verdict. (The jury acts as one person)

    Right: The jury take their seats. (Each one takes his own seat)

    Better: The jurymen take their seats.

8. *Such borrowed words as "data," "phenomena," and others are plural in form, not singular—*the singular forms are "datum," "Phenomenon," etc.

    NOT: This phenomena is known as filament image.

    BUT: This phenomenon is known as filament image.

    NOT: The data was completed.

    BUT: The data were completed. Or, if you don't like this wording: The information was completed.

9. *Two singular subjects connected by "or" do not take a plural subject:*

    The chuck or fixture to hold the pumps is mounted on . . .

    However, if one or the other subject is plural, then we have a different problem. In that case, the verb agrees with the noun closest to it. Here are two sentences that will help you determine which verb form to use:

    Singular subject or plural subjects require plural verb.

    Plural subject or singular subject requires singular verb.

    For example:

    Any dust or chips that might remain are blown off with compressed air.

    Any chips or dust that might remain is blown off with compressed air.

10. *If the noun is plural or compound in form but singular in meaning, the verb must also be singular—*

    NOT: The first iron works in New York were set up at Ancram Creek.

    BUT: The first iron works in New York was set up at Ancram Creek.

    NOT: Mathematics are a difficult subject for some people.

    BUT: Mathematics is a difficult subject for some people.

11. *Such words or phrases as "plus," "in addition to," "as well as," "with," "together with," etc. do not make a singular subject plural—*

    NOT: On the radial drill, the diameter of the column, as well as the radial swing of the head, are important.

    BUT: On the radial drill, the diameter . . . , as well as . . . , is important.

    NOT: The combination of mechanical fitness along with an artistic appeal have made the modern automobile what it is today.

    BUT: The combination . . . has made . . .

12. *An adjective, whether it be an article, a limiting adjective, or a pronoun, must agree with the noun it modifies—*

    NOT: This phenomena are known as filament image.

    BUT: This phenomenon is known as filament image.

    NOT: It is a new product and an interesting subjects.

    BUT: It is a new product and an interesting subject.

    NOT: The motor blocks are lying on their side throughout assembly.

    BUT: The motor blocks are lying on their sides throughout assembly.

    NOT: Workmen frequently carry their badge on their hat band.

    BUT: Workmen frequently carry their badges on their hat bands.

    NOT: In these studies, a chemically-defined media . . .

    BUT: In these studies, a chemically-defined medium was . . .

B. *Noun Substitutes* (Other than Pronouns)— Often words other than nouns, or groups of words used as units of thought (phrases or clauses), are used to name things:

   1. *Gerunds*—Verbs ending chiefly in "ing" but occasionally in "ed," etc. A gerund is a verb form (See page 36) which, in technical writing, is often used as a noun. In fact, this use often obscures the fact that such words as *writing, reading, talking, singing, thinking, cutting, boring, reaming, facing, turning,* etc. *ad infinitum* originated in verb forms. We think of them as nouns—and as nouns they name actions, not things.

   2. *Gerundive phrases*—Gerunds with their modifying words, as in the phrases italicized in the following sentences:

Applying chemicals to crops by aircraft has become a very important business in California, as elsewhere.

He was addicted to *drinking whenever he watched TV.*

The audience was wildly enthusiastic about *his playing the piano.*

The audience applauded *his playing.*

The officials began *investigating the accident.*

3. *Infinitives*—"To" plus the simple form of the verb—always used as some other part of speech (noun, adjective, adverb), but never as a verb itself:
   He wanted *to talk.*
   To think is the first step in learning *to communicate creatively.*

4. *Infinitive Phrases*—Like gerunds, infinitives retain some of the characteristics of verbs —that is, they can take subjects, and be modified by adverbs, as in the sentence given above. Here are some more examples of infinitive phrases used as nouns:
   The Blank Company proved *to be the most selective.*
   To complete a formal training program is often the first important step up the ladder of success.

5. *Relative Clauses*—A relative clause—one introduced by a relative pronoun—is often used as the subject of a verb, its object, or the object of a pronoun:

Whatever special training you get on the job is important.

The company to choose is the one that will give you *whatever training you need to do your best work on your job.*

Once you get on the payroll, it is usually easy to get transferred to *whatever department you think you can best work in.*

REMEMBER: A NOUN SUBSTITUTE TAKES THE PLACE OF A NOUN—that is, of ONE word only. Therefore it must be considered as a unit in a sentence. All the words used in that phrase or clause have special relationships ONLY TO THE OTHER WORDS WITHIN THE UNIT ITSELF. THEY ARE NOT RELATED DIRECTLY TO ANY WORD OR WORDS OUTSIDE THE UNIT PHRASE OR CLAUSE. In short, they are like subassemblies, to be considered as separate units in and of themselves.

C. *Pronouns*—Pronouns are a special kind of noun substitute considered a separate part of speech.

1. *Classification or Kinds*—There are 8 kinds of pronouns, but only the first five classifications are of vital importance. You should, however, know the others and be able to use them correctly:

   a. *Personal*—The most commonly used type of pronouns. Here is a table showing all the personal pronouns and their various forms and uses:

Table I. Number

	Singular			*Plural*		
	Nominative	Possessive	Objective	Nominative	Possessive	Objective
1st person	I	my, mine	me	we	our, ours	us
2nd person	you	your, yours	you	you	your, yours	you
3rd person—Masc.	he	his	him	they	their, theirs	them
Fem.	she	her, hers	her			
Neut.	it	its	it			

NOTE: The only relative pronouns that give students difficulty are "who" and "whom" and their derivatives, "whoever" and "whomever." Here is an infallible rule to follow:

If the pronoun is the subject of a verb, always use "who":

Who went with you? He asked *who was to blame for the accident. Whoever gave you that idea* was crazy. He asked the same question of *whoever came to the door.*

If the pronoun is the object of a verb or of a preposition, always use "whom":

Whom did you go with? He wanted to know *whom I had talked to.* He said for me to give the report to *whomever I saw first.*

b. *Relative*—pronouns used to relate their clauses (of which they are a part) with some other word in the sentence. The relative pronouns and their uses are given in Table II:

Table II. Relative Pronouns

	Nominative	*Possessive*	*Objective*
Persons only	who	whose	whom
Persons or things that (what)	....	....
Things only	which	....	....

GRAMMAR PAGE 31

c. *Interrogative*—Pronouns used to ask questions (See page 26). The interrogative pronouns are exactly the same as the relative pronouns except that "what" is used instead of "that":
Who gave you this information? Whose report do you have? Whom did you meet at the office? What do you want? Which did you select?

d. *Demonstrative*—The demonstrative pronouns point out persons or things: They always refer to nouns called their "antecedents", which usually should be given in the sentence:

	Near	Far
Singular	this	that
Plural	these	those

NOTE: Avoid the careless use of both "this" and "these":

NOT: I have had one full year of bacteriology. These courses . . .

BUT: I have had one full year of bacteriology, including such courses as . . .

NOT: As the turret moves in at the end of its stroke, the apron hits a collar. *This* opens the valve and starts . . .

BUT: *This action* opens the valve and starts . . .

NOT: Laminated plastics are what might be called "reinforced plastics." This process has been known for years . . .

BUT: The process of making these plastics has been known . . .

e. *Indefinite*—

Some indefinite pronouns are always singular: each, any, either, neither, no and their combination with one, body, and thing: anyone, anybody, anything, etc.

Some indefinite pronouns are always plural: others, ones, several, many, few, both.

A few may be either singular or plural, depending on the noun to which they refer: some, all, such.

NOTE: Watch the agreement of your pronoun with its antecedent:

NOT: Each of the eight machines have one operator.

BUT: Each of the eight machines has one operator.

f. *Reflexive*—Reflexive pronouns reflect the action back upon the antecedent: John bought himself a tie (that means John bought for himself a tie.)

g. *Intensifying*—These pronouns strengthen or intensify the action. Like the reflexive, they also end in "self" or "selves" for the plural form:

The president himself [no one else—no substitute] spoke to us.

h. *Reciprocal*—

Each other—refers to two only: They hated each other intensely.

One another—refers to more than two: The men comforted one another while the rescuers were digging for them.

2. *Properties or Qualities:*

Number—how many: singular (one) or plural (more than one) See Table I, page 30.

Person—the speaker (first person: I), the person spoken to (second person: you), and the person spoken of or about (third person: he, she, it, they).

Use or Case:

Nominative—subject of a verb: I, we, you, he, she, it, they, who, which.

Possessive—Ownership: my mine, our, ours, you, yours, his, her, hers, its, their, theirs, whose.

Objective—Object of a verb or of a preposition: me, us, him, whom, which.

Gender—like nouns, pronouns have three genders:

Masculine—he, his, him

Feminine—she, her, hers

Neuter—it, its (sometimes "it" is *indeterminate*: The baby lost its rattle.

NOTE: The gender of other pronouns depends on the gender of the noun to which it refers.

REFERENCE OF PRONOUNS

Every pronoun refers to some noun known as its "antecedent." Therefore, between each pronoun and its antecedent there is a definite relationship known as agreement-reference. Since this relationship is often complex, it will be explained in simple steps.

I. POINT OF VIEW:

1. Each pronoun agrees with its antecedent in three ways:

a. NUMBER—A singular pronoun must refer to a singular antecedent:

NOT: Round *files* are generally single cut and are usually tapered for the last third of *its* length.

BUT: Round *files* are . . . last third of *their* lengths. Or: A round *file* is . . . last third of *its* length.

b. PERSON—A shift in the person (first, speaker; second, person spoken to; third, person spoken of or about) can be confusing:

NOT: This idea of attending Cal Poly and paying your way through by working on a project appealed to me.

BUT: This idea . . . paying my way . . . appealed to me.

c. GENDER—Since the problem of gender or sex seldom arises in a technical report, article, pa-

per, or thesis, this point is not too important here. However, here is an example:
"John lost her tool kit" means that John lost the tool kit belonging to some girl. If he had lost his own, he would have written: "John lost his tool kit."

2. Although the pronoun and its antecedent do not need to agree in case (the use of the word in the sentence), sometimes an awkward situation arises when the antecedent of the pronoun is in the possessive case:

NOT: I finally reached the boss' office. He was a man of about 50.

BUT: I finally reached the office of the boss, a man of about 50.

3. There are two special pronouns which you must constantly look out for: *its* and *their:*

ITS is the possessive personal pronoun: The report and its parts.

IT'S is a contraction of IT IS: IT'S well known that Cal Poly has the best . . .

THEIR is the plural possessive pronoun: The men and THEIR wives went along.

THERE is an adverb of place: Put it down over THERE. THERE is also used to open some sentences: THERE is a rumor to the effect that . . . Or: There are three ways of doing this problem.

THEY'RE is a contraction of THEY ARE: They're going along with us tonight.

II. REFERENCE-AGREEMENT:

4. As with nouns, the pronoun subject must agree with its verb in number and person: a singular pronoun takes a singular verb, a plural pronoun a plural verb. Personal pronouns seldom give us any trouble in this respect. Relative pronouns, however, often do, for relative pronouns have a double function to perform:

A relative pronoun must agree in number and person with its antecedent;

A relative pronoun which is the subject of a verb must agree with that verb.

NOT: The machinery that were needed . . .

BUT: The machinery that was needed . . .

NOT: The machine has two heads which enables it to take two cuts . . .

BUT: The machine has two heads which enable . . .

5. The demonstrative pronouns—this, that, these, those—are sometimes called demonstrative adjectives. They, too, must agree with the nouns that are their antecedents. *This* and *that* are singular; *these* and *those* are plural:

NOT: This *is* but a few examples of the application of physics . . .

BUT: These are but a few examples of . . .

NOT: These procedure prevents any waste of material.

BUT: These procedures prevent any . . .

The demonstrative pronoun should refer to some specific antecedent, not loosely to the sentence as a whole:

NOT: As the turret moves in at the end of its stroke, the apron hits a collar. THIS opens the valve that starts the reverse movement of the apron.

BUT: As the turret . . . hits a collar. THIS action [movement] opens . . .

The demonstrative is often used incorrectly when the writer shifts his point of view, as in the following sentence:

NOT: Laminated plastics are what might be called "reinforced" plastics. This process has been known for years. (The writer suddenly shifts from the final product, "laminated plastics," to the process of making them.)

BUT: Laminated plastics . . . The process of making these plastics . . .

6. Certain indefinite pronouns are always singular: EACH, ANY, OTHER, EITHER, NEITHER, NO ONE, NONE, and their combination with ONE, BODY, THING.

Others are always plural: OTHERS, ONES, SEVERAL, MANY, FEW, BOTH.

A few may be either singular or plural: SOME, ALL, SUCH:

Some members were present at the meeting.

Some of the book is good, some is worthless.

All were getting ready to leave the office when I came in.

All is fair in love and in war.

WRONG: Each of the eight machines have one operator. (RIGHT: Each . . . has . . .)

WRONG: None of these suggestions are suitable. (RIGHT: None . . . is suitable.)

III. VAGUE REFERENCE
OF PERSONAL PRONOUNS:

7. Such pronouns as IT, THEY, THEIR, and others MUST HAVE ANTECEDENTS DEFINITELY EXPRESSED WITHIN THE SENTENCE ITSELF, or in the previous sentence. Also, the pronoun must refer unmistakably to ONLY ONE ANTECEDENT:

NOT: To move the locator, the operator must use a lead hammer and pound it in place.

BUT: The operator uses a lead hammer to pound the locator in place.

NOT: When holes are drilled, they have burrs on the inside, and they are taken off with a hand grinder.

BUT: When the holes are drilled, the burrs formed . . . are taken off with . . .

GRAMMAR

NOT: All the operations are done automatically and most of them have built-in engines.
BUT: All the operations are done on automatics, most of which have built-in engines.

8. Relative pronouns must have some definite antecedent and must not refer to the entire preceding thought:
NOT: The sharp edge is taken off from around the hole, which finished the operation.
BUT: Taking the sharp edge from around the hole finished the operation.
NOT: Wrong materials and methods were used, which resulted in failure.
BUT: The failure resulted from the use of wrong materials and methods.

IV. VAGUE REFERENCE
DUE TO MISPLACED MODIFIERS
(MISPLACED RELATIVE CLAUSES)

9. A relative clause must stand as close to the word it modifies as possible:
NOT: I have selected five items from your catalog which I wish to purchase.
BUT: I have selected from your catalog five items which I wish to purchase.
OR: From your catalog I have selected five items which I wish to purchase.
NOT: Chipping is a process of removing metal that is not widely used today.
BUT: Today, chipping is not a widely used process for removing metal.
NOT: There is a nurse in each plant who administers first aid.
BUT: Each plant has a nurse who administers first aid.

V. REFERENCE OF THE EXPLETIVE

10. Sometimes it is desirable or even necessary to begin sentences with expletives, IT or THERE, which then become subjects of the verbs of these sentences. The expletive IT seldom gives us any difficulty, since it is always singular. The expletive THERE, however, often does cause trouble, for THERE may be either singular (There is a right way to do everything), or it may be plural (There are several ways of expressing an idea correctly.)

Now there is a very easy way to determine whether you should write "There is" or "There are." Check the number of the first noun or pronoun immediately following the verb. If this noun is singular, THERE is singular; if it is plural, THERE is plural:
CORRECT: There is a *thread* for every purpose.
There are thirteen *cams* on the shaft.
There are no written *record and* loss of *time*.
NOTE: Avoid the too frequent use of the expletive:
AWKWARD: Before the purchase of the $15,000 machine, it required ten men to do the work that one man can easily do now.
BETTER: Before . . . , ten men were required . . .
AWKWARD: There are four brake cylinders mounted on each truck frame.
BETTER: Four brake cylinders are mounted on each truck frame.

PAGE 33

VI. REFLEXIVE
AND INTENSIFYING PRONOUNS:

11. Reflexive and intensifying pronouns, each ending in "self", should be used only to reflect the action back upon the antecedent, or to intensify the action:
RIGHT: I bought myself a new car yesterday.
The foreman himself was unable to operate the new machine.
NOTE: DON'T USE THESE PRONOUNS INDISCRIMINATELY WHEN ORDINARY PERSONAL PRONOUNS SHOULD BE USED:
NOT: My father and myself spent a good deal of time fishing.
BUT: My father and I spent . . .
NOT: If only one light is used, the rest of the room will be dark and the reader will tire his eyes trying to adjust themselves to the change in the light.
BUT: . . . trying to adjust them to . . .

12. BE SURE TO GET THE RIGHT REFLEXIVE FORM FOR EACH PRONOUN:

I—myself   we—ourselves   you—yourself
you—yourselves   he—himself   she—herself
it—itself   they—themselves

NOTE: There are no such forms as hisself, theirself, theirselves.

13. Be sure to have the reflexive agree in number with its antecedent:
NOT: Everyone likes to have fun, enjoy themselves, and laugh.
BUT: Everyone likes to have fun, enjoy himself, and laugh.

VII. SAME, SAID, and SUCH:

14. Modern usage does not sanction the use of SAME, SAID, SUCH, THE SAME as pronouns. Use instead such pronouns, as THIS, THAT, IT, THEY, THEM:
STILTED, POMPOUS, and OLD-FASHIONED
Kindly be informed that we have received yours of June 23rd re the starting switch and the noise in the gear box of your Acme Streamline Mixer, and have forwarded the SAME to our service department in Fresno for further action.
COURTEOUS and NATURAL
Thank you for your letter of June 23 about the starter-switch trouble and the noise in the gear box of your Acme Streamline Mixer. You will soon

hear from our service department in Fresno, to whom your letter has been referred.

AWKWARD

I have purposely omitted any reference to the diamond wheel as I was unable to obtain any information on SAME.

BETTER

... to obtain any information about it.

VAGUE

I have worked under two of the three men whose names are given as references, and have obtained permission to use them AS SUCH.

BETTER

I have worked under two of the three men whose names are listed. All have given me permission to use their names as references.

VERY BAD

SAID addition was made late in 1961.

CORRECT

This addition...

15. Do not use SUCH THAT for SO THAT, or SUCH ... SO AS for SUCH ... AS:

NOT: The stock room of the service department is situated such that material received on the docks can be handled conveniently.

BUT: ... is situated so that the material ...

NOT: The copper must be placed in such a position over the joint so that the solder will flow into the seam, and not merely along the outer edge.

BUT: ... in such a position over the joint that the solder will flow ...

POINT OF VIEW

Every finite verb—one that can take a subject and make a complete statement—is limited in five respects: *number, person, tense, voice,* and *mood.* When you write a report, you deliberately choose to write in a certain number, usually singular; most often in the third person; and in the past tense, since this is the most logical: your report is written *after* you have completed your investigation, etc. As to voice, choose the active voice whenever possible, and your mood is usually indicative—that is, simple statement of fact.

These five elements—number, person, tense, voice, mood—constitute your POINT OF VIEW. Once you have selected your point of view, do not shift it without giving the reader adequate warning. Your reader must be prepared for this shift. He must not be taken by surprise.

A. *NUMBER*—a shift in number, especially within the same sentence, may become awkward or confusing, as in the following sentences:

NOT: All Cyclone furnaces are equipped with a Lindberg Automatic Control. (Sounds as if they have to share one among them.)

BUT: Each Cyclone furnace is equipped with a Lindberg ... Or: All Cyclone furnaces are equipped with ... controls.

NOT: Van Dykes are a brown print.

BUT: A Van Dyke is a brown print. Van Dykes are brown prints.

NOT: The dies are put on hydraulic presses. The press exerts a pressure ...

BUT: The dies are put on ... presses, each of which exerts a pressure ...

B. *PERSON*—Most reports are written in the third person singular unless for some good reason the first or second persons are used, as in letter reports. Any unexpected shift of person is likely to be confusing to your reader:

NOT: It has been proved that in order to maintain your health, one must select the proper amount of food.

BUT: It has been proved that the proper amount of food is necessary for good health.

NOT: If you are starting an economy drive, time will be well spent if the foreman will talk to his men, telling them what he is trying to do, thereby winning their cooperation.

BUT: If you are ..., ... if you will ..., telling them what you are trying to do, ... Or: If an economy drive is started, time will be well spent if ...

NOT: In this present day, there is hardly anywhere you can go without some sort of casting being present. Automobiles, airplanes, trains, ships, and some toys have cast construction. We are now able to cast almost any metal.

BUT: Today there is hardly any place we can go without finding castings being used—for example, in automobiles, airplanes, trains, even toys. Almost any metal can now be cast into various shapes.

C. *TENSE*—Sometimes it is necessary to shift the tense or time of the action. When this is done, the reader must not be taken by surprise or confused:

NOT: Since I use the heat treat code every day but was not familiar with heat treating, I felt that a simple definition of the term and the process will be valuable to me. (How muddled can you get!)

BUT: Since I used the heat treat code every day but was not familiar with heat treating, I felt that a simple definition of terms would be valuable to me.

NOT: The simplest form of lubricating appliance, a survival of machinery practice, is that in which the oil is carried in a tank or cup placed higher than the point to which it is applied. The oil is then delivered to the bearing points in drops through the action of gravity.

With a device of this sort, it was frequently necessary to manipulate the adjustments that control the feed because of the changes that occurred in the temperature. If the supply of oil was regulated in cold weather, the oil would flow too freely when the temperature increased.

The gravity oiler is found only on the earliest of automobile engines, but it is still used to some extent on stationary appliances and marine engines which demand constant attention.

BUT: Change all the verbs to either the past tense (was) or to the present tense (is) and this confusion will be eliminated.

D. *VOICE*—Most reports are written in the active voice—the subject does the acting. However, sometimes it is necessary to shift into the passive. If so, the reader must be prepared for this shift in point of view:

NOT: One will soon automatically raise or lower the chisel, as required, and thus the knack of chipping is acquired.

BUT: One will, . . . , and thus acquire the knack of chipping.

NOT: The workman takes the Request for Repairs to a timekeeper, and here the time for the start of the repair is recorded.

BUT: The workman takes . . . timekeeper, who records the time . . .

E. *MOOD*—One of the most annoying shifts in point of view is from the indicative mood (simple statement of fact) into the imperative (command). Actually, this is a double shift—in person as well as in mood:

NOT: The floor should be as nearly level as possible. All parts should be well fitted and should run smoothly. BE sure that the machine is well oiled. It is also advisable not to do heavy work on it.

BUT: The floor should be as nearly level as possible, and all parts should fit well and run smoothly. The machine should be well oiled. Heavy work should not be done on it.

NOT: In selecting one's soldering paste, get one that is non-corrosive.

BUT: A non-corrosive soldering paste should be selected.

NOT: The Multilith 1250 should be oiled daily or at regular intervals. The best procedure to follow in oiling the press is the diagram supplied by the manufacturer. Always start in the same place and work around the press. By doing this, it is not likely that you will miss any vital part. It is also good to carry a rag to wipe up any excess oil.

BUT: The Multilith 1250 should be oiled daily, or at regular intervals, following the directions supplied by the manufacturer. It is best always to start in the same place and work around the press so that no vital part will be missed. It is also good to carry a rag to wipe up any excess oil that might spill.

NOTE: Wherever possible, avoid the weak, awkward possessive voice. Instead, use the strong active voice:

NOT: From one to three parts of water may be used by the operator to dilute the mixture.

BUT: The operator may use from one to three parts of water to dilute the mixture.

NOT: Your kind communication was received by me today, for which I thank you.

BUT: Thanks for your welcome letter today.

OR: I appreciate your letter which arrived today.

NOT: A new procedure for inspecting the parts was suggested by the gang leader in Department 16.

BUT: The gang leader in Department 16 suggested a new procedure for inspecting parts.

VERB CHART

Finite (Limited by) { number, person, tense, voice, mood }

Non-finite (Unlimited)

Transitive (Takes an object)

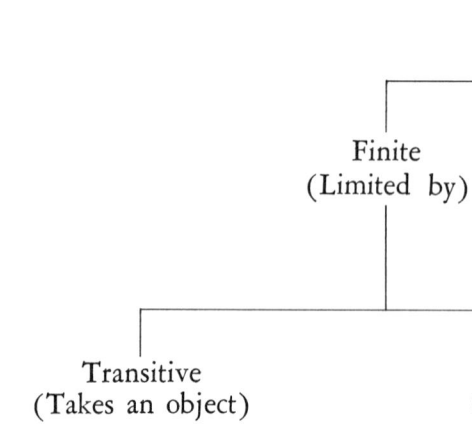

I *smoke* cigars.

The champion *knocked* the contender out in the eleventh round.

Gladding, McBean & Co. *manufactures* a variety of tile products.

Jones *thinks* that we should consolidate.

Note: In a transitive verb, the thought is not completed until the object is given:

I hit ..... The question immediately is: What? The answer may be "ball," "car," "bully," "jack pot," or one of a thousand things.

Since transitive verbs take objects, they are used to make specific statements, since the action started by the subject is completed and centered upon the object.

Intransitive (Does not take an object)

Regular (Takes no object)

I *smoke*.

I *smoke* once in a while.

I *knocked* on the door, but no one responded.

Jones *thinks* too much for his own good.

Note: Intransitive verbs express general statements, not specific ones. The action ends with the verb and is not centered upon an object, which receives the action of a transitive verb.

Any good dictionary will indicate that many verbs can be used intransitively and transitively, as with *smoke, knocked,* and *thinks*. Under certain conditions, a verb requires an object to complete its meaning; under other circumstances, no object is necessary. Both forms for the same verb may be perfectly correct.

Copulative (Requires a subjunctive complement: noun or adjective)

The following verbs are the chief copulas: All forms of the verb "to be"—such as am, are, is, was, were, has been, could have been, etc.—and seem, feel, look, appear, become, taste, smell, and make when these verbs do not express action, but a condition or state of being:

I *am* happy.
Mr. Jones *was* our president.
They *could have been* our men.
Smith *has been* very ill lately.
Jane *was* my friend.
It *seems* warm in here.
Do you *feel* well?
Johnny *looks* good to me.
The prisoner *appears* confident.
Mr. Brown *became* our leader.
This milk *tastes* sweet.
That flower *smells* like a rose and *looks* like a lily.
Joe *makes* a good employee.

1. *Infinitive*—"to" plus verb (Never used as a verb, but as one of three parts of speech):

   a. *Noun: To think* is difficult. She wanted *to walk*.

   b. *Adjective:* All that many displaced persons want is food *to eat* [or *to be eaten*].

   c. *Adverb:* He longed *to be heard*.

2. *Participle*-verb ending in "ing," "ed," "en," "ne," etc. (Never used as a verb itself but either as a helping verb or as an *adjective*.)

   a. *Present Participle*—ending in "ing,"—helps form the progressive form of the verb: I *am leaving* tonight.

   b. *Past Participle*—ending usually in "ed," but also in "en," "ne," and other special forms—is used with a limited (regular) verb to form the passive voice: I *am beaten*. He *has been defeated*. By the time you came, that damage *will have been repaired*.

   c. Both present and past participles may be used as adjectives to modify or qualify nouns: (1) The *following* section is a history of Gladding, McBean & Co. (2) Our Company manufactures many *specialized* products.

   d. Occasionally a participle can be used as an adverb: He came *running*.

3. *Gerund*—a verb ending in "ing," "ed," "en," "ne"—is used as a noun: *Manufacturing* beautiful tile is our specialty.

GRAMMAR

Principal Parts of Irregular Verbs

PRESENT	PAST	PAST PARTICIPLE	PRESENT	PAST	PAST PARTICIPLE
abide	abode	abode	feed	fed	fed
am, are, is	was, were	been	feel	felt	felt
arise	arose	arisen	fight	fought	fought
awake	awoke, awaked	awaked	find	found	found
bear	bore	borne, born[1]	flee	fled	fled
beat	beat	beaten	fling	flung	flung
beget	begot	begotten	fly	flew	flown
begin	began	begun	forbear	forbore	forborne
behold	beheld	beheld	forget	forgot	forgotten
bend	bent	bent	forsake	forsook	forsaken
bereave	bereft, bereaved	bereft, bereaved	freeze	froze	frozen
beseech	besought	besought	freight	freighted	freighted, fraught, (*fig.*)
bet	bet	bet			
bid (command)	bade, bid	bidden, bid	get	got	got, gotten (*adj.*)
bid (money)	bid	bid	gird	girded, girt	girded, girt
bind	bound	bound	give	gave	given
bite	bit	bitten	go	went	gone
bleed	bled	bled	grave	graved	graved, graven
bless	blessed, blest	blessed, blest	grind	ground	ground
blow	blew	blown	grow	grew	grown
break	broke	broken	hang	hung, hanged[2]	hung, hanged[2]
breed	bred	bred	have	had	had
bring	brought	brought	hear	heard	heard
build	built	built	heave	hove, heaved	hove, heaved
burn	burned, burnt	burned, burnt	hew	hewed	hewn
burst	burst	burst	hide	hid	hidden
buy	bought	bought	hit	hit	hit
can	could	——	hold	held	held
cast	cast	cast	hurt	hurt	hurt
catch	caught	caught	keep	kept	kept
chide	chid, chided	chidden, chid	kneel	kneeled, knelt	kneeled, knelt
choose	chose	chosen	knit	knit, knitted	knit, knitted
cling	clung	clung	know	knew	known
clothe	clothed, clad	clothed, clad	lay	laid	laid
come	came	come	lead	led	led
cost	cost	cost	lean	leaned, leant	leaned, leant
creep	crept	crept	leap	leaped, lept	leaped, lept
crow	crowed, crew	crowed, crown	learn	learned, learnt	learned, learnt
curse	curse, curst	curse, curst	leave	left	left
cut	cut	cut	lend	lent	lent
dare	dared, durst	dared, durst	let	let	let
deal	dealt	dealt	lie (recline)	lay	lain
dig	dug	dug	lie (tell untruth)	lied	lied
dive	dived, dove	dived	light	lighted or lit	lighted or lit
do	did	done	load	loaded	loaded, laden (*adj.*)
draw	drew	drawn			
dream	dreamed, dreamt	dreamed, dreamt	lose	lost	lost
dress	dressed, drest	dressed, drest	make	made	made
drink	drank	drunk, (drunken, *adj.*)	may	might	——
			mean	meant	meant
drive	drove	driven	meet	met	met
dwell	dwelt	dwelt	mow	mowed	mowed, mown
eat	ate	eaten	must	——	——
engrave	engraved	engraved, engraven	pay	paid	paid
			pen (enclose)	penned, pent	penned, pent
fall	fell	fallen	prove	proved	proved

PRESENT	PAST	PAST PARTICIPLE	PRESENT	PAST	PAST PARTICIPLE
put	put	put	stave	stove, staved	stove, staved
quit	quitted, quit	quitted, quit	stay	stayed, staid	stayed, staid
read	read	read	steal	stole	stolen
reeve	rove, reeved	rove, reeved	stick	stuck	stuck
rend	rent	rent	sting	stung	stung
rid	rid	rid	stink	stank, stunk	stunk
ride	rode	ridden	strew	strewed	strewn
ring	rang	rung	stride	strode	stridden
rise	rose	risen	strike	struck	struck (stricken, *adj.*)[3]
run	ran	run			
say	said	said	string	strung	strung
see	saw	seen	strive	strove	striven
seek	sought	sought	swear	swore	sworn
seethe (intransitive)	seethed	seethed	sweat	sweated, swet	sweated, swet
			sweep	swept	swept
sell	sold	sold	swell	swelled	swelled, swollen
send	sent	sent	swim	swam	swum
set	set	set	swing	swung	swung
sew	sewed	sewed, sewn	take	took	taken
shake	shook	shaken	teach	taught	taught
shall	should	——	tear	tore	torn
shape	shaped	shaped, shapen	tell	told	told
shave	shaved	shaved, (shaven, *adj.*)	think	thought	thought
			thrive	throve, thrived	thriven, thrived
shear	sheared, shore	sheared, shorn	throw	threw	thrown
shed	shed	shed	thrust	thrust	thrust
shine	shone	shone	tread	trod	trodden, trod
shoe	shod	shod	wake	woke, waked	woke, waked
shoot	shot	shot	wax (grow)	waxed	waxed, waxen
show	showed	shown	wear	wore	worn
shred	shredded, shred	shredded, shred	weave	wove	woven
shrink	shrank	shrunk (shrunken, *adj.*)	wed	wedded	wedded, wed
			weep	wept	wept
shut	shut	shut	wet	wet	wet
sing	sang	sung	will	would	——
sink	sank	sunk	win	won	won
sit	sat	sat	wind	wound	wound
slay	slew	slain	work	worked, wrought[4]	worked, wrought[4]
sleep	slept	slept	wring	wrung	wrung
slide	slid	slid, slidden	write	wrote	written
sling	slung	slung			
slink	slunk	slunk	broadcast	broadcast(ed)	broadcast(ed)
slit	slit	slit	telecast	telecast(ed)	telecast(ed)
smell	smelled, smelt	smelled, smelt			
smite	smote	smitten			
sow	sowed	sowed, sown			
speak	spoke	spoken			
speed	sped, speeded	sped, speeded			
spell	spelled, spelt	spelled, spelt			
spend	spent	spent			
spill	spilled, spilt	spilled, spilt			
spin	spun	spun			
spit	spit, spat	spit, spat			
split	split	split			
spoil	spoiled, spoilt	spoiled, spoilt			
spread	spread	spread			
spring	sprang	sprung			
stand	stood	stood			

[1] *Born,* only in the sense of "born into the world."
[2] *Hanged,* only of execution by hanging; *hung* not so used.
[3] *Stricken,* also used as a participle in a figurative sense.
[4] Modern adjective form.

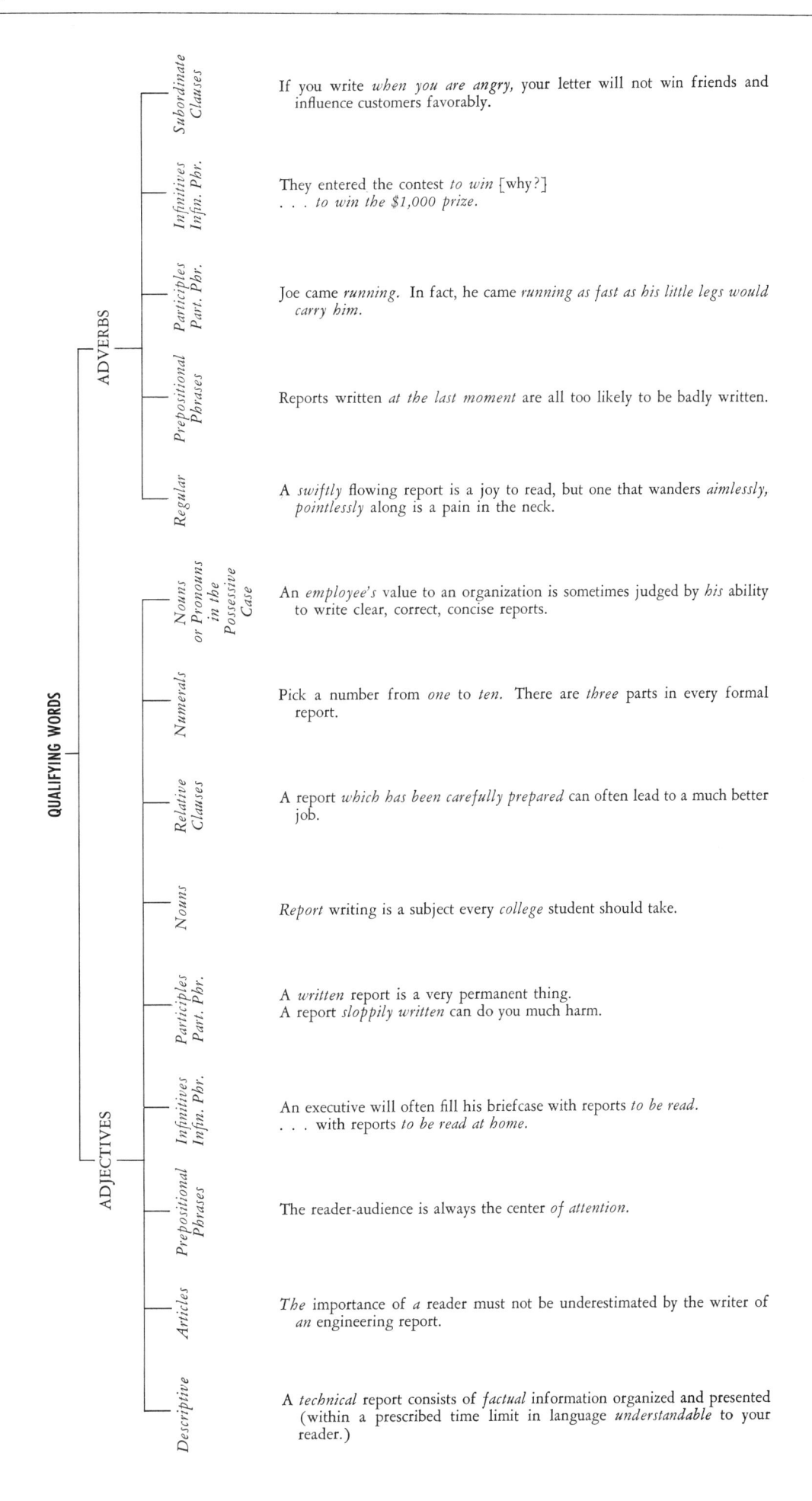

GRAMMAR

QUALIFYING WORDS

ADVERBS

Subordinate Clauses
If you write *when you are angry*, your letter will not win friends and influence customers favorably.

Infinitives / Infin. Phr.
They entered the contest *to win*. [why?]
. . . *to win the $1,000 prize*.

Participles / Part. Phr.
Joe came *running*. In fact, he came *running as fast as his little legs would carry him*.

Prepositional Phrases
Reports written *at the last moment* are all too likely to be badly written.

Regular
A *swiftly* flowing report is a joy to read, but one that wanders *aimlessly, pointlessly* along is a pain in the neck.

ADJECTIVES

Nouns or Pronouns in the Possessive Case
An *employee's* value to an organization is sometimes judged by *his* ability to write clear, correct, concise reports.

Numerals
Pick a number from *one* to *ten*. There are *three* parts in every formal report.

Relative Clauses
A report *which has been carefully prepared* can often lead to a much better job.

Nouns
Report writing is a subject every *college* student should take.

Participles / Part. Phr.
A *written* report is a very permanent thing.
A report *sloppily written* can do you much harm.

Infinitives / Infin. Phr.
An executive will often fill his briefcase with reports *to be read*.
. . . with reports *to be read at home*.

Prepositional Phrases
The reader-audience is always the center *of attention*.

Articles
The importance of *a* reader must not be underestimated by the writer of *an* engineering report.

Descriptive
A *technical* report consists of *factual* information organized *and* presented (within a prescribed time limit in language *understandable* to your reader.)

PAGE 39

A TABLE OF CONNECTIVES

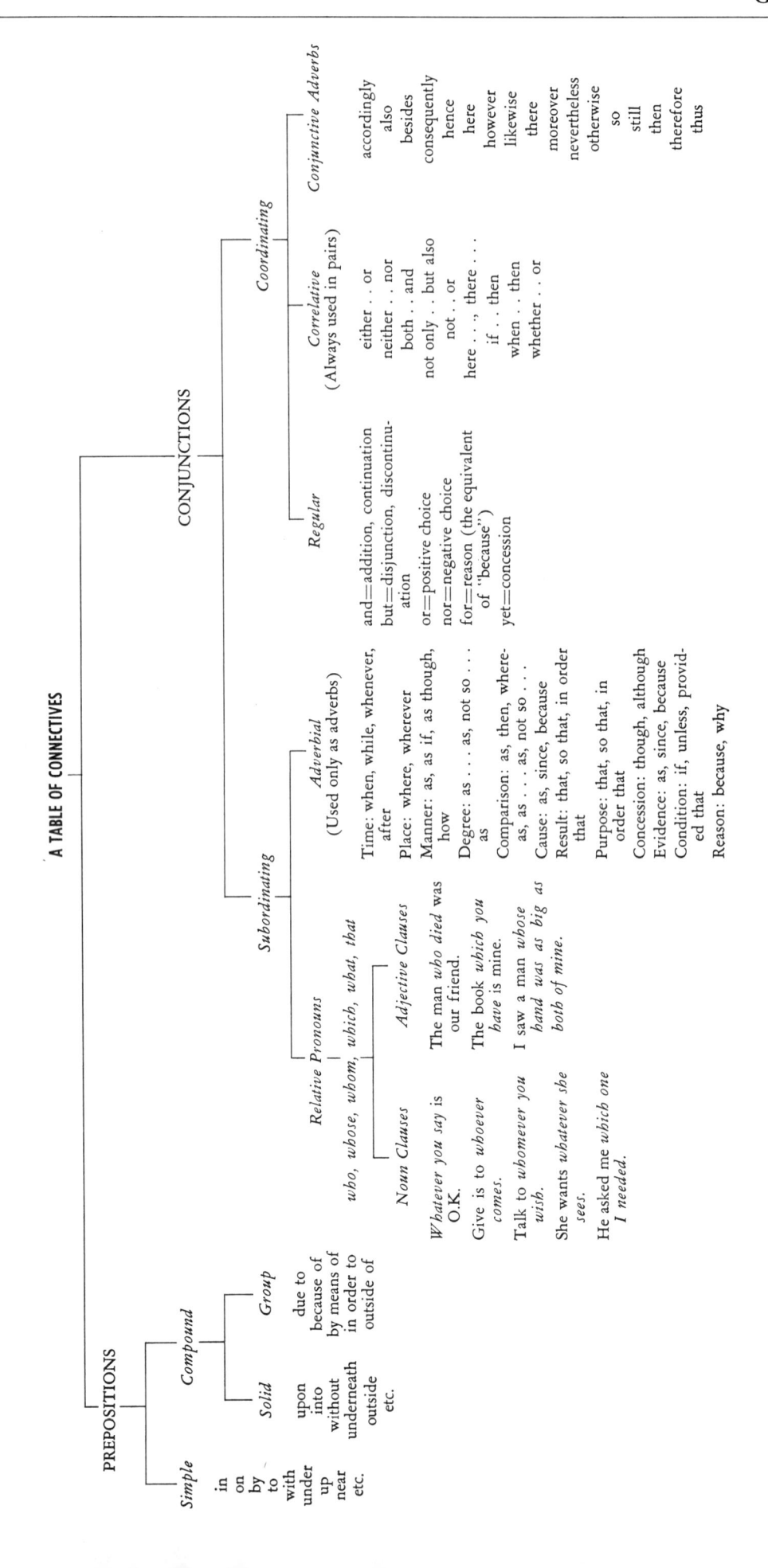

PREPOSITIONS

Simple
in
on
by
to
with
under
up
near
etc.

Compound

Solid
upon
into
without
underneath
outside
etc.

Group
due to
because of
by means of
in order to
outside of

CONJUNCTIONS

Subordinating

Relative Pronouns
who, whose, whom, which, what, that

Noun Clauses
Whatever you say is O.K.
Give is to whoever comes.
Talk to whomever you wish.
She wants whatever she sees.
He asked me which one I needed.

Adjective Clauses
The man who died was our friend.
The book which you have is mine.
I saw a man whose hand was as big as both of mine.

Adverbial (Used only as adverbs)
Time: when, while, whenever, after
Place: where, wherever
Manner: as, as if, as though, how
Degree: as . . . as, not so . . . as
Comparison: as, then, whereas, as . . . as, not so . . .
Cause: as, since, because
Result: that, so that, in order that
Purpose: that, so that, in order that
Concession: though, although
Evidence: as, since, because
Condition: if, unless, provided that
Reason: because, why

Coordinating

Regular
and=addition, continuation
but=disjunction, discontinuation
or=positive choice
nor=negative choice
for=reason (the equivalent of "because")
yet=concession

Correlative (Always used in pairs)
either . . or
neither . . nor
both . . and
not only . . but also
not . . or
here . . ., there . . .
if . . then
when . . then
whether . . or

Conjunctive Adverbs
accordingly
also
besides
consequently
hence
here
however
likewise
there
moreover
nevertheless
otherwise
so
still
then
therefore
thus

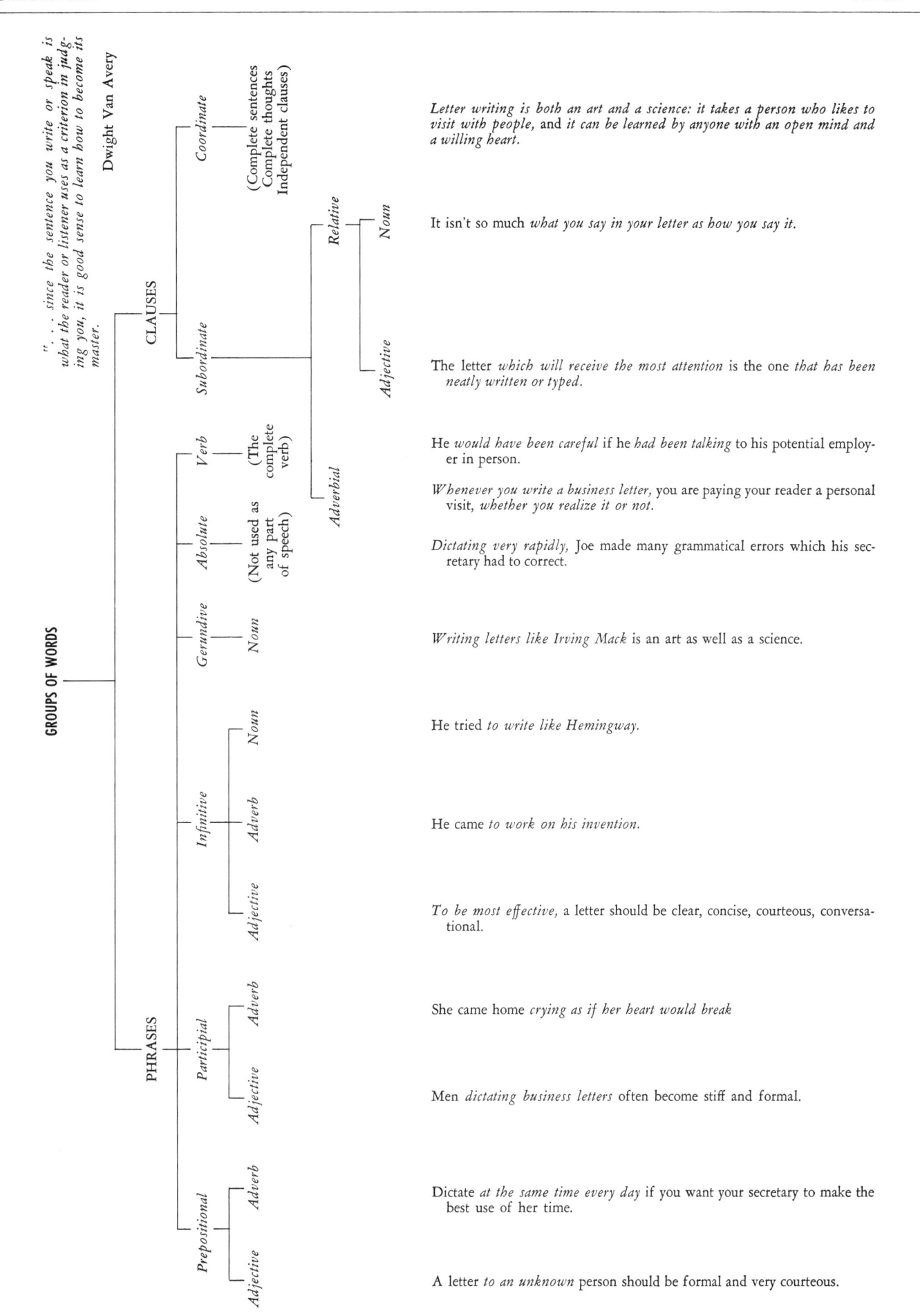

GRAMMAR

"... since the sentence you write or speak is what the reader or listener uses as a criterion in judging you, it is good sense to learn how to become its master.

Dwight Van Avery

GROUPS OF WORDS

CLAUSES
- Coordinate (Complete sentences, Complete thoughts, Independent clauses)
- Subordinate
  - Relative
    - Noun
    - Adjective
  - Adverbial

PHRASES
- Verb (The complete verb)
- Absolute (Not used as any part of speech)
- Gerundive — Noun
- Infinitive
  - Noun
  - Adverb
  - Adjective
- Participial
  - Adverb
  - Adjective
- Prepositional
  - Adverb
  - Adjective

Letter writing is both an art and a science: it takes a person who likes to visit with people, and *it can be learned by anyone with an open mind and a willing heart.*

It isn't so much *what you say in your letter* as *how you say it.*

The letter *which will receive the most attention* is the one *that has been neatly written or typed.*

He *would have been careful* if he *had been talking* to his potential employer in person.

Whenever you write a business letter, you are paying your reader a personal visit, *whether you realize it or not.*

Dictating very rapidly, Joe made many grammatical errors which his secretary had to correct.

Writing letters like Irving Mack is an art as well as a science.

He tried *to write like Hemingway.*

He came *to work on his invention.*

To be most effective, a letter should be clear, concise, courteous, conversational.

She came home *crying as if her heart would break*

Men *dictating business letters* often become stiff and formal.

Dictate *at the same time every day* if you want your secretary to make the best use of her time.

A letter *to an unknown* person should be formal and very courteous.

PAGE 41

UNITS OF THOUGHT

Obviously, this inverted triangle could be extended indefinitely . . .

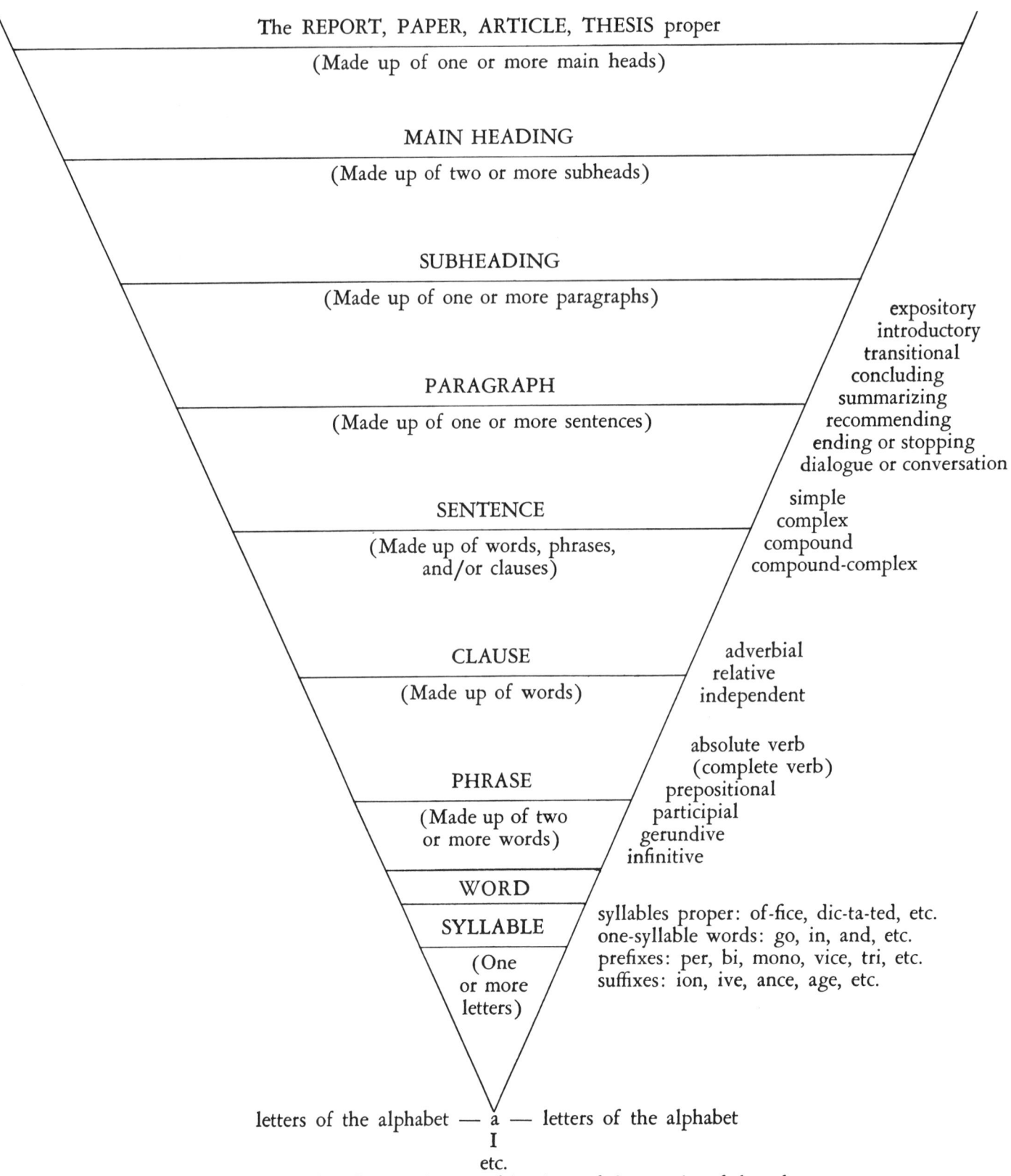

The REPORT, PAPER, ARTICLE, THESIS proper
(Made up of one or more main heads)

MAIN HEADING
(Made up of two or more subheads)

SUBHEADING
(Made up of one or more paragraphs)

PARAGRAPH
(Made up of one or more sentences)

- expository
- introductory
- transitional
- concluding
- summarizing
- recommending
- ending or stopping
- dialogue or conversation

SENTENCE
(Made up of words, phrases, and/or clauses)

- simple
- complex
- compound
- compound-complex

CLAUSE
(Made up of words)

- adverbial
- relative
- independent

PHRASE
(Made up of two or more words)

- absolute verb (complete verb)
- prepositional
- participial
- gerundive
- infinitive

WORD

SYLLABLE
(One or more letters)

- syllables proper: of-fice, dic-ta-ted, etc.
- one-syllable words: go, in, and, etc.
- prefixes: per, bi, mono, vice, tri, etc.
- suffixes: ion, ive, ance, age, etc.

letters of the alphabet — a — letters of the alphabet
I
etc.

All writing is based on various combinations of these units of thought.

PAGE 42

A Glossary of Grammatical Terms

Abstract—A report, article, paper, or thesis boiled down to its minimum essentials, but written in the same language and from the same point of view as the original writing.

Accusative—A Latin noun case indicating the direct object of a verb: He hit *me*.

Adjective—A part of speech which modifies or changes the meaning of a noun or pronoun.

Adjective equivalent—A word, phrase, or clause used as an adjective to modify or qualify the meaning of a noun or pronoun.

Adverb—A part of speech that modifies or changes the meaning of a verb, adjective, or other adverb. Many adverbs end in "ly": *Swiftly, largely, apparently,* etc.

Agreement—There are two aspects of agreement. (1) The subject and its verb must agree in number and in person: a singular subject requires a singular verb; a plural or compound subject requires a plural verb: "Jane is here" and "Jane and Joan are here." (2) An adjective or pronoun and the noun it modifies must agree in number: NOT: *These kind of pencils are used,* BUT: *This kind of pencil is used,* or *These kinds of pencils are used.*

Antecedent—The noun to which a pronoun refers. Every pronoun has a definite antecedent with which it agrees in number, person, and gender: *John* lost *his* hat.

Antonym—A word of opposite meaning, such as *good—bad, rectify—justify, tall—short, include—exclude, life—death, powerful—powerless.*

Apostrophe—A mark of punctuation indicating an omission: *it's* (it is), *we've* (we have), *o'clock* (of the clock). Often the apostrophe is used to indicate the omission of the genetive (possessive) *e: girl's* (girles), *man's* (mannes), etc.

Appended material—Anything added after the body or text has been completed.

Appendix—That part of a report, paper, article, or thesis which is added after the text. Thus it becomes a part of the report as a whole, but apart from the text proper.

Appositive—A word, phrase, or clause used to explain a substantive. It means exactly the same as the word it explains, and has the same grammatical relationship to the rest of the sentence: My brother *Joe* came home. Give it to us, *Bill and me.* Our college, *yours and mine,* has achieved a high standard of excellence. The theory *that all men are equal* is basic to our democratic way of life.

Article—A special adjective used to point out or identify. We have two articles: *the* is the definite article; *a*, along with its variant *an*, is the indefinite article. NOTE: Be careful when you use *a* or *an*. Before a word beginning with a vowel, always use *an* except with words that begin with *un*: *a unit, a union, a university,* etc.; *an excellent record, an interest in, an apple.* NOTE: Use *an* also before words which start with a silent *h: an hour, an heir,* but *a house, a hat,* etc.

Use *an* before all other words starting with vowels. NOT: *a engineer,* but *an engineer; not a artist, an key, an carload,* but an artist, a key, a carload.

Argumentation—Often called simply "argument." This is one of the so-called "four forms of discourse," the others being description, narration, and exposition. Argument, persuasion, debate, etc. are concerned with convincing the mind of someone else and persuading him to act as you wish.

Auxiliary—A "helping" verb used with other verbs to form different tenses, voices, or moods. Here are some auxiliary verbs: all forms of the verb *be, do, have, can, may, must, could, shall, should, will, would, ought.* All but *to be, to do,* and *to have* are called *modal auxiliaries* and cannot be used by themselves with subjects to make complete sentences: "I must" is incomplete without "go," "talk," etc.

Bibliography—An alphabetized list of printed sources of information used in preparing a report, paper, article, or thesis. ONLY PRINTED SOURCES ARE LISTED! Interviews, questionnaires, and all other sources of factual information must be listed elsewhere. (See "Table of References" on page 7.)

Cacophony—Discordant and disagreeable sounds, especially when produced orally. Harsh sounds. The opposite of euphony. Here's a good example of cacophonious writing: It will be very much appreciated if you will send me . . . SAY: I'll very much appreciate your sending me . . .

Case—Case denotes the use of a noun or pronoun in a sentence. A word in the *nominative case* is always the subject of a verb. The *possessive case* denotes ownership and is used as an adjective: *John's* report—*his* paper. A noun or pronoun in the *objective case* is the (direct or indirect) object of a verb, a preposition, or a gerundive. (See page 27.)

Citation—Any information taken from some printed source but not directly quoted. Sometimes called a paraphrase. (See page 5.)

Classification—That form of technical writing which divides information into groups or classes, such as the Dewey-Decimal System of Classification of library books, or the Periodic Table of the Elements.

Clause—A group of related words which has both a subject and a finite verb. There are two types of clauses: Main or independent, and subordinate or dependent. (See page 41.)

Coherence—The "clinging together" of like thoughts so that there is a smooth flow of ideas from one to the next. Incoherence is the result of fuzzy thinking, and leads inevitably to confusion.

Collective noun—a noun that represents not one but a number of things used as a unit: *army, college, set* (of tools), *suite* (of rooms), etc. Collective nouns also have plural forms: *armies, colleges, sets, suites,* etc.

Comma fault—The error made by combining two complete thoughts into a compound sentence by using no connective and only a comma.

Comparison—Adjectives and adverbs may be compared: positive, comparative, and superlative. For example, *good, better, best;* or *slow, slower, slowest.* Some, however, prefix the words "more" and "most" to the positive: wonderful, more wonderful, most wonderful. Sometimes "inferior comparison" is used to indicate diminishing qualities: *little, less, least; bad, worse, worst;* or *good, less good, least good.*
NOTE: Use the comparative degree when referring to ONLY TWO: Joe is *better* than his brother Walter. Sam is the *best* one in the class [more than two.]

Comparison-Contrast—Although antonyms, comparison and contrast are often used when describing something. Comparison shows its similarities with something familiar, and comparison shows its differences.

Compound words—Two or more words combined into one. Compound words are of three kinds: *solid*—schoolhouse, watertower, baseball, etc.; *hyphenated*—an air-conditioning system, an out-of-the-way place; and *separated*—California State Polytechnic College, General Motors Corporation.

Complement—Any noun or adjective used to complete the meaning of a verb is called a "complement." There are actually two kinds of complements: predicate adjectives (Reports are *useful*) and predicate nominatives: A report can be a very useful *document*.

Concrete—As opposed to abstract, concrete words actually say something that can be detected by one or more of the five senses. Use specific, concrete words rather than vague, abstract ones.

Conjunction—A connective which connects words in a sentence. *Coordinating conjunctions* connect two grammatical equals, whether they be words, phrases, or clauses. *Subordinating conjunctions* connect their clauses with the verb in a sentence.

Conjunctive adverb—Although primarily an adverb, a few special adverbs have conjunctive or linking qualities when they stand between two independent clauses. The major conjunctive adverbs are *then, thus, therefore, moreover, consequently, however, accordingly, here, there, also, besides.*

Connectives—Words whose primary use or function is to connect or link groups of thoughts. In English, connectives are divided into prepositions and conjunctions. (See page 40.)

Consonant—The consonants in our alphabet are as follows: *b, c, d, f, g, h, j, k, l, m, n, p, q, r, s, t, v, w, x, z. Y* is usually a consonant, but it may occasionally be a vowel replacing *i.*

Coordination—Making things equal grammatically, as in compound sentences. *Coordination* is the opposite of *subordination*, which means making things unequal grammatically.

Copulative verb—A verb that links its subject with either a predicate noun or a predicate adjective. It is one which does not indicate action, but rather condition or state of being. The common copulative verbs are all forms of the verb *to be*, and such verbs as *seem, look, appear, taste, smell, become, feel,* etc. when they express a condition, as in "She *seemed* afraid," "I *feel* bad about that," "He became our first president," etc. (See page 36.)

Co-relative—A pair of conjunctions which co-relate two ideas: *both . . . and, either . . . or, the one . . . the other, neither . . . nor, the former . . . the latter,* etc.

Cover—Anything used to enclose a report, paper, article, or thesis.

Dangling phrase—A verbal phrase which modifies or qualifies a word that it logically cannot, as in "When only six years old, my father took me to to the zoo."

Dangling modifier—Any word, phrase, or clause that modifiies the wrong word.

Dative—The older term for what we now call the indirect object of a verb. It is in the objective case. Today the same form is used for both the accusative and the dative cases. He gave *me* a car.

Definition—A setting of limits to something, usually a word or group of words. In technical writing, definition is an important way of communicating information. (See page 1.)

Demonstrative pronoun—There are four demonstrative pronouns: *this* (singular, nearby), *that* (singular, farther away), *these* (plural, nearby), and *those* (plural, farther away).

Description—One of the four forms of discourse which concentrates on spatial arrangement—how things look as arranged in space: size, color, shape, etc.

Descriptive Adjective—As opposed to a limiting adjective, a descriptive adjective gives information which appeals to one or more of the five senses: sight, sound, taste, smell, and touch: *big, tall, loud, sweet, pungent, soft,* etc.

Diction—The technical term for the language used, the wording, the vocabulary.

Documentation—The act of giving written credit for material or information borrowed. This may be done through the use of footnotes or through references. (See pages 3-8 for a complete explanation.)

Elegant variation—Blowing up something common and simple until it becomes pompous, oratorical, bloated: "The voluminousness of the inadequacies in the description of the manufacture of the connecting rod renders that description prohibitive," means, simply: "There's too much involved in the manufacture of the connecting rod to describe it in a report."

Ellipsis—An omission of certain words which can readily be supplied by the reader or listener.

Elliptical construction—An incomplete construction which, nevertheless, the reader or listener can understand, as in conversation. Also "I am taller than you" means "I am taller than *you are tall.*"

Emphasis—Putting the words in such a position that they will receive the proper stress, and not burying them in the sentence or paragraph where they are likely to be passed over in haste. The beginning and the ending of a sentence and of a paragraph are usually the most emphatic places. Also in a letter.

Euphony—The opposite of cacophony, euphony means pleasing or agreeable in sound. Any easy-to-read expression is likely to be euphonious in technical writing, although euphony more often refers to poetry and poetic or rhythmic prose.

Expletive—A word that is used to begin or start a thought. "It" and "There" are expletives: *"It* is a fact that . . ." (*It* gives us no difficulty because *it* is always singular; however, *there* may be singular or plural, depending on the number of the noun that immediately follows the verb: *"There is a rumor* to the effect that . . ." "Rumor" is singular —so is "there." *"There are* several *ways* of . . ." "Ways" is plural—so is "there." Although expletives are commonly used, avoid using them too often.

Exposition—Another of the four forms of discourse, *exposition* is concerned with the clear, logical explanation of facts as contrasted with the special spatial arrangement used in description and the time sequence followed in narrative. And it usually is content with explaining something rather than trying to persuade, as in argumentation.

Fact—Something that can be proved or detected by one of the five senses.

Factual writing—Any form of writing which is concerned primarily with factual information rather than the imagination or fiction.

Figurative language—Seldom used in technical writing. Similes and metaphors are used occasionally in the practical forms of writing. (See pages 50, and 47.)

Finite verbs—Verbs which take subjects and are limited in five respects—number, person, tense, voice, and mood (See pages 36, 37, 38)—are called "finite" verbs. The other kind of verbs, nonfinite or infinite—infinitives, participles, gerunds—may take subjects, but they cannot be used as the subjects of independent clauses. (See pages 36, 39, 40.)

Flow of thought—When the first main point leads directly and inevitably into the second, the second directly into the third, and so on through a piece of writing, this material is said to have "flow of thought," or coherence.

Footnote—A note or comment placed at the bottom or "foot" of the page. Sometimes these notes are are placed at the end of a section or chapter or even pages. Then they are called "end notes."

Foreword—Sometimes, as in this manual, someone else will make a comment either on the book itself or, as in Mr. Shippam's letter, on the subject. When this comment is published before the text itself, it is called a *foreword*.

Fragment—A *fragment* is a half-baked idea, an incomplete thought cut off from the sentence to which it belongs. Although used occasionally in imaginative writing—poems, novels, stories, plays, etc.—a fragment must be avoided at all costs in practical writing because it is vague, ambiguous, not clear.

Gender—The sex of a person or animal is called the *gender*. In English we have four genders: *Masculine* for anything male, *feminine* for anything female, *indeterminate* for anything which is either masculine or female but cannot be seen or determined at a glance, and *neuter* for everything neither masculine nor feminine. The pronoun *it* refers to either indeterminate or neuter gender.

Genitive—The older term for what we now call the possessive case. All nouns in the genitive case MUST HAVE AN APOSTROPHE! Most pronouns in the genitive case have special forms for this case. Indefinite pronouns are an exception. (See page 28.)

Gerund—A verbal—a non-finite verb form—used as a noun equivalent: *Running* is good exercise.

Gerundive phrase—A gerund plus all its modifiers used as a noun equivalent: *Writing under pressure* often produces careless errors and seldom anything worth while.

Hackneyed—Any word, phrase, or clause that has been overworked until it becomes trite, stale, moth-eaten, and moss-covered is *hackneyed*. (See list of hackneyed expressions at the conclusion of the section of letter writing.

Homograph—Two or more words with identical spelling, but different meanings, and usually different pronunciations: *lead* (verb) and *lead* (a metal); *bear* (animal) and *bear* (to carry).

Homonym—Two or more words pronounced alike but used differently: *right* (correct), *wright* (one who, as in millwright, shipwright), *write* (to make marks indicating letters, words, etc.), *rite* (a solemn, formal ceremony, as the burial rite, the marriage rite, etc.).

Hyperbole—A rhetorical figure of speech that is an obvious exaggeration: "A mountain filled with uranium." Exaggerations like this are to be avoided in technical writing.

Hyphenation—The act of dividing a word into its syllables, especially at the end of a line. Also used to indicate the compounding of words into an attributive compound adjective, as in *an air-conditioning system.*

Hypothesis—A proposed explanation of some occurrence before actual proof has been obtained. For example, 40 years ago chemists spoke of Avagadro's Hypothesis (that equal volumes of different gasses under the same conditions of temperature and pressure would have the same number of molecules). Today this is called Avagadro's Law.

Identifying pronoun—the only *identifying pronoun* in the English language is *the same,* and this form is not recommended today. Instead, the demonstrative pronoun is generally used. NOT: *The same* can be said of Joe. BUT: *This* can also be said of Joe.

Idiom—The use of words and the form of speech peculiar to a certain language, and often incapable of being interpreted literally. For example, the idiomatic expression "to wait on" means "to serve," but the expression "to wait for" means "to await."

Illogical comparison—When members of the same class are compared, we must use some restricting form, usually "other." It is illogical to say that report writing is more important than any form of practical writing, since report writing itself is a form of practical writing. In other words, we are saying it is more important than itself! We must add the word *other:* ". . . more important than any *other* form of practical writing." This, of course, is debatable!

Imaginative writing—Writing that is done for pleasure rather than for instruction is sometimes called imaginative writing: poetry, short stories, novels, plays, etc.

Indefinite pronouns—Pronouns which often do not have any specified antecedent but refer usually to people in general: *one, some, all, any, each,* and their combinations with *body, thing,* etc. (See pages 31 and 32.)

Infinitive—An infinitive usually consists of "to" plus the root form of the verb as in "to run," etc. Sometimes the infinitive is used without the sign, as in "A good education helped him *reach* his goal in life." Infinitives have four uses, two of them as substantives (noun equivalents):

1. As a noun substitute: *To write* was his major objective.
2. As an adjective: The food *to be eaten* was placed on a separate table.
3. As an adverb: He came *to visit* his brother.
4. As a predicate complement: He is *to become* our next president.

Informative writing—As contrasted with imaginative or literary writing, *informative writing* is concerned primarily with teaching, instructing, communicating ideas, as in technical writing, reports, papers, articles, theses, letters.

Intensifying pronouns—Pronouns ending in "self" or "selves" which intensify the action for the purposes of emphasis are called *intensifying pronouns:* The King *himself* spoke to the group. These pronouns are to be used sparingly.

Interrogative adverbs—Some adverbs ask questions: how? when? where? why? When they do, they are known as interrogative adverbs.

Interrogative pronouns—Pronouns which ask questions: who? whose? whom? what? which? Actually, there are five ways of asking questions:

1. Inverted sentence order: *Are you* going?
2. Interrogative pronoun: *Who* is going?
3. Interrogative adverb: *When* are you going? How . . ? Why . . ? Where . . ?
4. Modal auxiliary: *Can* you go? *May* you go? *Will* you go?
5. Normal work order with voice raised at the end: *You are* going?

Intransitive—A verb that is *intransitive* cannot or does not take an object: I *smoke.* I *smoke* occasionally. I *feel* sorry for them. Copulative verbs (those that express a condition or state of being) are always intransitive: I *feel* bad about having to do that. She *looks* beautiful. He *is* tired.

Inverted sentence word order—Most sentences use the normal word order: subject, predicate or verb, complement/object. Some, however, use the inverted word order. Most questions use the inverted word order. However, occasionally a declarative sentence will use the inverted order: Along the ceiling *are ten rows* of lights.

Jargon—The language of any trade, profession, sport, etc. which usually is not understood by the average person. Jargon is puffed-up, windy, wordy, verbose language full of unnecessary words: "The answer to the question under consideration is in the negative" means, simply, "NO!"

Letter of authorization—A letter written by the person asking someone to do something or make an investigation and authorizing him to expend the time, money, and effort to make this investigation and report on it. Although seldom used or required, the technical report writer should know the function of the letter of authorization.

Letter of transmittal—The device by which a report writer transmits his report to the person who requested it. This letter may be used at any time, but it is necessary when the writer does not deliver his report in person. (See page 13.)

Limiting adjective—Generally considered to be all adjectives that answer the questions *who? what?* and *which?* This includes all pronominal adjectives and numerals, as well as the definite and indefinite articles *the, a, an.*

Logic—This term usually indicates what might be called good sense. When a passage just doesn't make sense, it is called illogical.

Logical opposite—An antonym is a word of opposite meaning, but some words do not have antonyms, such as *perfect, round, square,* etc. These words also do not admit of comparison. However, every word has a logical opposite: *perfect—not perfect, round—not round, square—not square*. The logical opposite of any word can be made by putting "not" before that word. This may or may not be a synonym of an antonym of that word.

Loose sentence—a *loose sentence* is one in which the construction is such that the sentence can be stopped, grammatically, before it actually ends. In other words, the dependent or subordinate element, which is not restrictive, comes at the end of the sentence: Don't be afraid to change jobs. On the other hand, don't be a grasshopper, *who is long on distance but heck on direction!* Other types of sentences from the viewpoint of construction are "periodic" and "semi-periodic." (See pages 48 and 50.)

Metaphor—A figure of speech in which one thing is called by the name of another, or is said to possess the qualities of another: "He is a lion" is a metaphor, but "He is like a lion" is a simile.

Modifier—A word which changes the meaning of another word; a qualifying word. Adjectives and adverbs are modifiers. Adjectives modify or qualify nouns and, occasionally, pronouns: No *private* enterprise can long survive if it doesn't show a profit. Adverbs modify verbs, adjectives, or other adverbs:"... can *long* survive ..." If you *really* want that job, ...

Mood—Indicates the manner in which the action is conceived by the mind of the reader. There are three moods for English verbs: (1) The *indicative mood,* which is used when expressing a fact, as "It is hot in this room"; (2) The *subjunctive mood,* which is used when expressing a wish a statement contrary to fact, such as "I wish I were wealthy," or "If I were wealthy, I would take a trip around the world"; and (3) the *imperative mood,* which is used to express a command, such as "Stand up!" "Don't do that!" etc.

Narration—One of the four forms of discourse. Narration concerned with time sequence: story, novel, chronology, biography, autobiography, process exposition, procedure, etc.

Nominative—Words in the nominative case are subjects of verbs. Therefore the word *nominative* indicates the "subject of a verb."

Non-finite verb—A non-finite verb is often called a verbal: infinitive, gerund, participle. Non-finite verbs have some but not all the limitations that finite or limited verbs have. For instance, a *past* participle, a *present* participle, a *passive* infinitive.

Non-restrictive modifiers — Any modifier — word, phrase, or clause—which is not essential or absolutely necessary is said to be non-restrictive: There are, *however,* many other ways of doing this experiment: He said, *on the contrary,* that this method that we are using is the safest; but I can, *if you wish,* try one or two or three others. Non-restrictive modifiers are usually punctuated with a comma or a pair of commas, depending on where they come in the sentence. Restrictive modifiers are NEVER punctuated.

Normal word order—Most declarative and imperative sentences use the normal word order: subject, verb, complement or object: A letter (1) may be (2) a report (3).

Noun—A part of speech that names a person, place, or thing. It may be the subject of a verb (A *report* may be . . .), or the direct object of a verb (He gave his *report* to his supervisor), or the indirect object of a verb (He gave his *report* a quick once-over before handing it in), or as an adjective to modify a noun (*Report* writing is important to all engineers). There are also other less important uses of nouns.

Number—Indicates how many are involved. In English there are only two numbers: Singular, which indicates only one, and plural, which indicates more than one.

Objective case—A naming word in the objective case is either the direct object or the indirect object of a verb: "He gave his *report* a quick *once-over* before handing it in." Nouns or pronouns which are the subjects of verbals or the objects of verbals are also in the objective case: "I believed *him* to be the *leader* of the gang of thieves."

Outline—Any plan or organization of material. An outline is to the writer of a report what a blueprint is to a machinist or builder, an itinerary to a traveler, an agenda to a committee chairman, a table of contents to a book or report, etc. In fact, the outline, which can be changed as many times as necessary, becomes fixed or crystallized in the table of contents of a report, thesis, article, or paper. The table of contents is the final, unchangeable outline of the work.

Paragraph—The paragraph is the unit of thought, whereas the sentence is the unit of writing. We think in paragraphs, but when we write down our thoughts, we use sentences. NOTE: Make your paragraphs short without making them choppy.

Parallel construction—The casting of similar thoughts or ideas into similar forms is called parallel construction, or parallelism. (See page 76.)

Paraphrase—When you borrow material from someone else but don't quote that individual, you paraphrase his—that is, you put his thoughts into your own words. This is also called a "citation." Both a direct quotation and a citation must be documented—that is, either footnoted or indicated by a reference number. (See page 5.)

Participle—A non-finite or infinite verb form. The present participle is a verb ending in *ing: ending, drilling, acting,* etc. The past participle of regular or weak verbs always ends in *ed: walked, talked, shouted.* The past participle of strong or irregular verbs may end in *en: been;* or in *ne: gone;* or in *d: laid;* or in *t: knelt.* Participles are either used as other parts of speech—as adjectives or as adverbs; or they are used with finite verbs to form (1) the progressive form of the verb: "I *am going* to New York tomorrow," or (2) with some form of the verb *to be* to form the passive voice: "I *am defeated.*" "I *have been elected.*" "I *could have been elected.*" (See pages 36-38.)

Participial phrase—Since a participle is still a verb form, it has many of the characteristics of a verb. For example, it can have a subject or an object, or be modified by an adverb or adverbial substitute. All these modifiers taken with the participle will form the complete participial phrase, which is italicized in the following sentence: *Uncle George's playing the piano with his feet while he blew a trumpet with one hand and banged the drums with the other* amused everyone in the room except his wife, Aunt Susie.

Period fault—A serious sentence error because it indicates that the writer still does not know whether he has written a sentence, or what a sentence is. Specifically, the period fault consists of cutting off with a period a phrase or clause which really belongs to the sentence. This may be done in two ways: (1) cutting off the fragment before the true sentence starts (Being pressed for time. We hurried along). or (2) cutting off the fragment after the sentence has been written (We hurried along. Being pressed for time.). The easiest way to correct a period fault is to make a comma out of the period and change the second capital into a lower-case letter.

Periodic sentence—A sentence in which the thought is not completed until the last word has been read or spoken—until the reader reaches the period, in other words: "After the 5 o'clock whistle had blown, the men who were on the first shift went home." Not until we read the word "home" do we know the full meaning of this thought. Periodic sentences are just the opposite of loose sentences. Here's how this same sentence would look written in the loose form: The men who were on the first shift went home after the 5 o'clock whistle had blown.

Person—Every noun, pronoun, and finite verb has that quality or property known as "person," which indicates the speaker (first), the person spoken to (second) and the person spoken of or about (third). Subjects must agree with their verbs in both number (how many) and person (who is speaking or acting?). The irregular but most commonly used verb "to be" illustrates this better than any other

	Singular	*Plural*
First person	I am	we are
Second person	you are	you are
Third person	man, he, she, it is	men, they are

Personal pronouns—Among the 500 most frequently used verbs in the English language. Here is a table showing the correct form for each of the personal pronouns in their four important relationships: number, person, case, and gender:

	Singular			*Plural*		
	Nominative	Possessive	Objective	Nominative	Possessive	Objective
1st person	I	my, mine	me	we	our, ours	us
2nd person	you	your, yours	you	you	your, yours	you
3rd person *Masculine*	he	his	him			
Feminine	she	her, hers	her	they	their, theirs	them
Neuter-Indeterminate	it	its	it			

NOTE: There are two forms for some of the personal pronouns in the possessive case. The first form *(my, our, your, her, their, his, its)* should be used when a noun immediately follows the pronoun: This is *my* book. The second form should be used ONLY when the noun does not immediately follow the pronoun: The book is *mine (yours, his, hers, its, ours, theirs).*

NOTE ALSO: Among these 30 personal pronouns are two of the most frequently confused and misspelled words: *its* and *their: its* with *it's* and *their* with *there*. These pairs are true homonyms—that is, there is no difference in pronunciation between *its* and *it's,* or between *their* and *there.* BUT there are very marked differences in spelling and in meaning! *Its* is the third person singular possessive pronoun. *It's* is a contraction of two words: *it* and *is: it is. Their* is the third person plural personal pronoun. *There* is either an adverb of place (Put it over *there.*) or an expletive (*There* is a rumor . . . or *There* are some things . . .)

Personification—Seldom used in technical writing, personification means attributing human characteristics or traits to lower animals, inanimate objects, or even abstract ideas: Death is The Grim Reaper.

Phrase—A phrase is a related group of words that, taken as a unit, is used as a part of speech. Prepositional phrases may be used as adjectives or adverbs. Participial phrases are used as adjectives or adverbs. Gerundive phrases are always used as nouns. Infinitive phrases may be used as nouns, adjectives, or adverbs. Absolute phrases have no grammatical relation with the rest of the sentence, but are logically related in an adverbial sense. That is, the absolute phrase may be changed into an adverbial subordinate clause: "Dinner being ready, we sat down to eat" or "Because dinner was ready, we sat down to eat." The complete verb is often referred to as a "verb phrase": "have been," "had been elected," "could have been rewarded." (See page 41.)

Point of view—Every finite verb is limited in five respects, which determine the point of view of the writer or speaker: (1) Number—how many? (2) Person—who is speaking? (3) Tense—the time of the action? (4) Voice—is the subject acting or acted upon? and (5) Mood—what is the manner of the action—simple statement of fact? a condition contrary to fact? or a command or order? (See pages 34-35.)

Possessive case—Nouns and pronouns which indicate or show possession or ownership are always in the possessive case. All nouns in the possessive case MUST HAVE AN APOSTROPHE: "Mr. *Jones*' report," "the report writer's duty to his reader." Most pronouns have their own possessive case form, but a few do not. These pronouns must also use the apostrophe: "Anyone's writing."

Predicate adjective—After a copulative verb—one that indicates a condition or state of being rather than an action (See page 36)—either a predicate adjective or a predicate noun must be used: (1) Predicate adjective: "The report is *excellent*." "The letter was much too *long*." (2) Predicate nominative (or noun): "This report is a *document* that will always be read with interest." "A business letter is a personal *visit* with your reader."

Predicate nominative—See explanation of "Predicate adjective."

Preface—The preface to a book is the place where the author himself talks directly to the reader, telling him the purpose of writing the book, what to find in it, tips on how to get the maximum use out of the book, and acknowledgements to others for their help in preparing the book. In a report, the function of the preface is taken over by the "Letter of Transmittal," which has five functions to perform: (1) to indicate that something is being transmitted (the report itself), (2) to give the title (underlined once) of the report, (3) to tell why the report has been prepared, (4) to indicate the scope and/or limitations of the report, and finally (5) to acknowledge help in the preparation of the report. (See page 13.)

Prefatory material or pages—Everything that comes before page 1 of the text is considered the *prefatory material:* the cover, the title page, the letter of authorization (if one is used), the letter of transmittal, the table of contents (the final outline of the report or thesis), the table of illustrations (if there are any), and the abstract.

Premise—A statement or proposition used as the basis of an argument. It may be used to prove the truth or falsity of a statement, and it may consist of either a truth or an assumption. Premises are used in syllogisms. (See page 51.)

Preposition—A part of speech used to connect or join its object with some other word in the sentence. Therefore a preposition is a connective—the first word in what is called a prepositional phrase. (See page 40.)

Pronoun—A special part of speech that takes the place of a noun. (See pages 25, 26, 30-34.)

Pronominal adjective—A word that is sometimes used as a pronoun, sometimes as an adjective. The major pronominal adjectives are as follows: *each, every, either; this, that, these, those; few, several, many, much; all, none, other, another; any, one, such, some, both; certain, else; first, last, former, latter; neither, own, same; what, whatever, whatsoever; which, whichever.* Some also include the personal and other pronouns used in the possessive case, for they are pronouns used as adjectives: *"His* book," *"my* hat."

Quotation—The exact words of someone else. When a quotation is used, the exact wording must be used, including any misspellings, mispunctuations, etc. Also quotation marks must be put around what has been borrowed, and this material must be documented. (See page 5.)

Reference—(1) In grammar, this means the agreement of a noun and its verb, or the agreement of a pronoun and its antecedent, or the agreement of a limiting adjective (numeral) and its noun.
(2) In technical and other factual writing, it means the source from which information has been obtained.

Reference numbers or referencing—Formerly the most popular and accepted way of giving credit (documenting) the source of borrowed printed information was with footnoted references. Today, however, especially in technical writing, the most popular method of giving credit is through the use of superscript reference numbers, which do not interrupt the flow of thought and make the reader look to the bottom of the page, as with footnotes. (See a full discussion of referencing on page 7.)

Reflexive pronoun—A pronoun ending in "self" or "selves" in which the action is reflected back onto the subject or speaker: "I bought *myself* a new hat." Identical in form to the intensifying pronouns, but different in meaning or function.

Review—As contracted to an abstract, the review is usually done by someone other than the writer. Also the tone and point of view, as well as the language, are different. The abstract is a boiled down report, paper, thesis, etc., using the same point of view and language as in the original. The review, on the contract, tells what the author has done in the paper, etc. There is a similarity between the two, but they are also different in function.

Table of references—Identical to the bibliography except for this important fact: The table of references MUST BE NUMBERED because this number is an integral part of the reference. (See page 7 for a detailed explanation.)

Repetition—One accepted method of emphasizing an idea or thought is through the judicious use of emphasis. This is emphatic repetition—the kind of repetition used between the many parts of this manual to drive home various important points. However, unnecessary repetition can be annoying and sometimes childish: NOT: "One of the main essentials of . . ." BUT: "An essential of . . ." NOT: "Each section of the Parts Book is broken down into its major component parts, and under these parts all the minor parts are listed." BUT: "Each section of the Parts Book is broken down into major components, under which all minor parts are listed."

Restrictive modifier—A modifer that is necessary—that cannot be omitted without destroying the meaning of the sentence—is restrictive. For example, if you read this statement, "Water is unfit to drink," you wouldn't believe it because water is essential to life as we know it. Obviously something necessary has been omitted. This essential word or group of words, when restored, will make the meaning clear: "Water *that is stagnant* is unfit to drink." This we'll accept as true. Therefore the dependent clause "that is stagnant" is a restrictive modifier and MUST NOT BE PUNCTUATED! In fact, no restrictive modifier should be punctuated. Non-restrictive ones should be or may be.

Semi-periodic sentences—A sentence which starts with the main thought, then interrupts it with either a restrictive or a non-restrictive modifier is called a "semi-periodic" sentence. The sentence just given is a good example of this type: it begins with the subject, "A sentence," then is interrupted with a "which" clause, then with a second verb, "interrupts," and finally ends the thought with "is called a 'semi-periodic' sentence."

Sentence—A group of words containing, usually, a subject and a predicate which, taken together, make a grammatically complete, understandable statement. The sentence is our unit of writing, whereas the paragraph is our unit of thinking. We think in groups of thoughts called sentences, but when it comes to writing these thoughts down or speaking them, we must use sentences.

Sentence sense—A person who apparently does not know when he has written a complete thought, or *if* he has written one, is said to lack "sentence sense." Like "driving sense," "sentence sense" is something which can be acquired by diligent effort and careful attention to the rules of correct composition.

Simile—Although not often used in technical writing, a simile is a comparison which uses the preposition "like": The letter of transmittal of a report is like the preface of a book.

Simplicity—Saying something in simple, natural, conversational words is the essence of simplicity. The following passage taken from a student report illustrates a flagrant lack of simplicity: "The voluminousness of the descriptions involved in the manufacture of the connecting rod renders such description prohibitive." A welter of words—as Shakespeare so aptly said: ". . . it is a tale Told by an idiot, full of sound and fury, Signifying nothing." Here's what he meant to write: "There is so much involved in the manufacture of the connecting rod that I can't describe everything." At least that's what I *think* he means!
NOTE: Simplicity does NOT mean childishness. In his greatest passages, Shakespeare was the essence of simplicity. No one could ever accuse him of writing childishly. So with Lincoln or any of the other truly GREAT writers of literature, present and past.

Stereotyped—Anything is stereotyped when, because of its form of language, or both, it has become meaningless. Stereotyped words, phrases, clauses are ones that have become trite, hackneyed, outworn: "we beg to remain," "time is of the essence." "Kindly send," "we feel you," "enclosed please find," "the undersigned," "the writer," "herewith," "your patronage," "at the present writing," etc. Certain parts of business letters have become stereotyped, meaningless: the salutation, the complementary closing, the typed name of the company under the complementary closing, the dictator's and also the typist's initials.

Style—Simply stated, style is the man—the individuality of the writer or speaker as expressed in the words he uses and the way in which he uses them. Simplicity in style is always admirable, for simplicity in writing usually leads to clarity, correctness, and conciseness.

Subordination—One of the two universal principles of living, of art, of music, of writing. The other is coordination. Subordination consists of making one thing dependent upon another, of making one thing unequal, of making one statement inferior. The judicious use of subordination will give smoothness and flow to a passage by putting in an inferior grammatical construction less important thoughts and making the important ones equal, coordinate, or superior.

Superscript number or symbol—The conventional device used in documentation to call the reader's attention to either a footnote or to a reference listed in the Table of References. (See pages 4-8 for a detailed discussion of documentation.)

Syllogism—A logical scheme of reasoning devised by Aristotle consisting of three successive and related propositions called—
Major Premise: All men are mortal.
Minor Premise: John is a man.
Conclusion: Therefore John is mortal.

Synonym—A word which means nearly the same as another word. Actually, no two words mean exactly the same thing, semantically, but for general purposes, two or more words may have very closely-related meanings: *delightful,* may, upon occasion, be synonymous with *delicious, delectable, luscious.* Or *imaginary* may mean *fanciful, visionary, fantastic(al), chimerical, quixotic.* Definition by synonym is quite common, although not too specific: "Steel is an alloy." Most college-level dictionaries not only give synonyms of various words, but also, on occasion, distinguish between various synonyms. The two examples selected, *delightful* and *imaginary,* were taken from *Webster's Dictionary of Synonyms,* pages 234 and 424.

Table of contents—The final outline of a report, thesis, etc., made after the material has been written. After this outline has been made, no more changes may be made in the written material.

Table of illustrations—A preview of what illustrations, if any, are used in this paper. But remember, not all reports need to be illustrated.

Tense—The time of the action. In English we have six tenses, three simple, three perfected. Illogically, we start with the present, jump into the past, and then vault over the present into the future. Here we see how they operate:

	Present	*Past*	*Future*
Simple:	I am . . .	I was . . .	I shall be . . . I will be . . .
Perfected:	I have been	I had been	I will have been I shall have been

NOTE: Simple future is expressed with "shall" in the first person (singular and plural) and "will" in the second and third persons. Determination or promise is expressed with "will" in the first person and "shall" in the second and third persons. When General MacArthur said, "I shall return," he was not making a promise, but in his supreme confidence saying, simply, that he would return one day. He did!

Title page—Every report should have a title page. (See page 13.)

Transitive—In a transitive verb, the action goes from the subject, through the verb, and settles upon the object: I smoke cigars; I hit the ball, etc. (See Intransitive, page 46.)

Trite—A synonym for "hackneyed," "stereotyped," "old fashioned." Here are some trite phrases. "of even date," "at hand," "contents noted," "aforementioned," "in the amount of," "consensus of opinion," "kindly acknowledge," "your esteemed communication," "I beg to remain." Avoid them like the plague!

Unity—The first of that trinity of old but still very important principles of good writing: Unity, coherence, and emphasis. Unity means that everything necessary is there, and that everything there is necessary.

Verb—That part of speech which denotes the action. Without verbs, we could not write sentences or say anything meaningful. There is no substitute for a verb except another verb. (See pages 34-38.)

Voice—Indicates whether the subject acts (active voice) or is acted upon (passive voice). "John hit a car this morning" means that John acted upon the car. "John was hit by a car" means that John was acted upon by a car and, apparently, had nothing to do with the accident. In technical writing, use the ACTIVE VOICE wherever and whenever possible. In other words, prefer the active voice to the passive.

Vowel—In English, we have 5 regular vowels—*a, e, i, o, u*—and one letter that on occasion may be used as a vowel (as a substitute for *i*), *y.*

PUNCTUATION

- **Separating Only**
  - *End-stopped*
    - . Period (Declarative Sentence)
    - ? Question Mark (Interrogative Sentence)
    - ! Exclamation Point (Exclamatory Sentence)
  - *Internal*
    - ; Semicolon
- **Both**
  - - Hyphen
  - : Colon
  - ' Apostrophe
- **Either**
  - , One Comma to separate
  - , , a pair of commas to enclose
  - — One dash to separate
  - — — a pair of dashes to enclose
- **Enclosing Only**
  - ( ) Parentheses
  - [ ] Brackets
  - " " Double quotes
  - ' ' Single quotes
  - (Used ONLY in pairs)

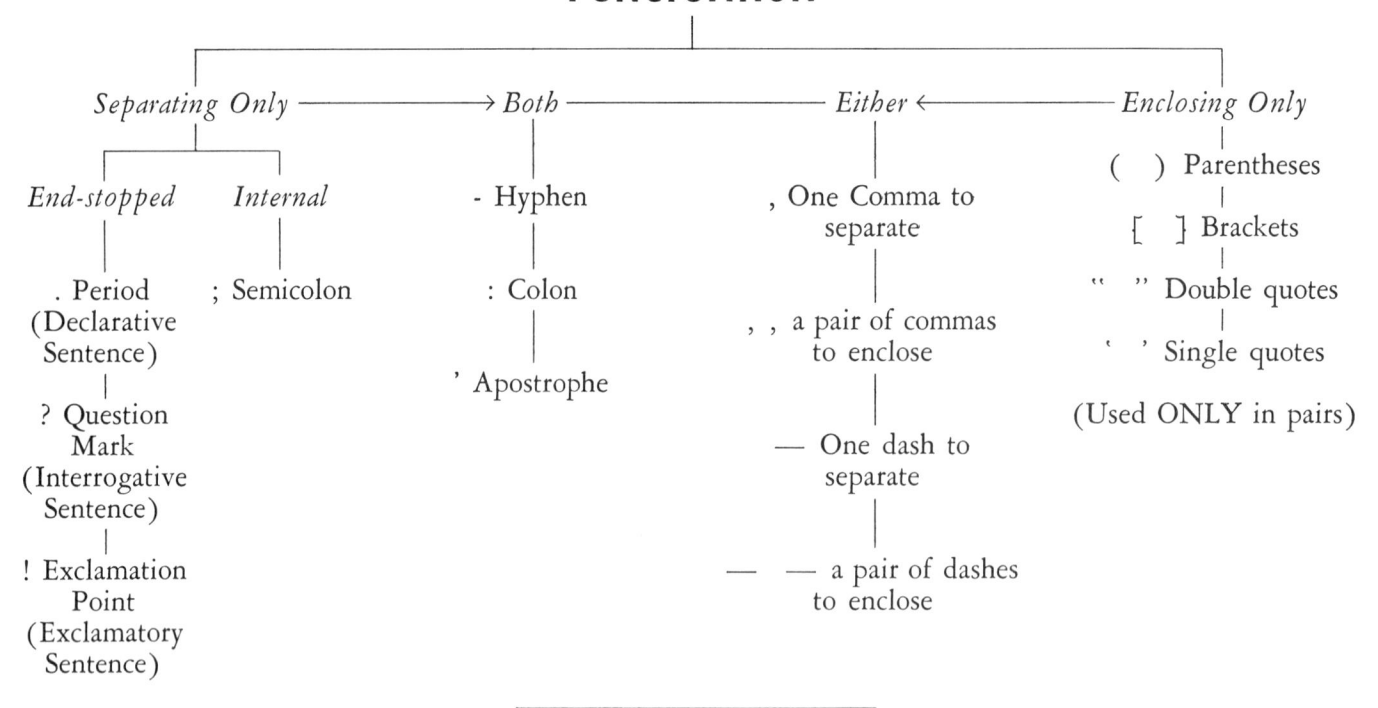

Punctuation

Punctuation Simplified

Punctuation can best be described as GESTURES IN WRITING. When you want to gesticulate to give emphasis or point to your writing, you use one or more of the various marks of punctuation.

The only function of punctuation is to prevent misreading. For example, look at these two sentences and see if you can find any difference between No. 1 and No. 2:

No. 1. Woman without her man would be a savage.

No. 2. Woman without her man would be a savage.

No difference? Right! In both No. 1 and No. 2, the meaning is exactly the same: a woman without her man would be a savage. In other words, the word "woman" is the subject of the verb "would be." Right? Right! Now let's punctuate No. 2:

No. 3. Woman—without her, man would be a savage.

Does that mean the same as No. 1? No indeed. That tells an entirely different story: in this version, "man" without a woman "would be" the savage. This is just the opposite of the original sentence—and all because of a little punctuation mark!

O.K. Maybe you still aren't convinced; so let's try another pair, this time with one punctuated:

No. 4. Jones says his boss is a jackass.

No. 5. Jones, says his boss, is a jackass.

Get the point? And if you want your reader to get your point, punctuate correctly!

Now try finding your way through this mess of words—without punctuation to help:

No. 6. That that is is that that is not is not that that is is not that it it is. O.K. Give up? Want to see these thoughts punctuated? Here you are—

No. 7. That that is, is. That that is not is not that that is. Is not that is? It is!

Take a good look at the comma in the following sentence—it's the most expensive comma in history, that's for sure!

No. 8. All foreign fruit, plants shall enter duty-free for one year.

That little measly comma cost the U.S. Government over $3,000,000—and that's a tidy sum at any time. Many years ago Congress was considering a tariff bill. The clerk in the House copied it exactly as shown. The bill passed both the House and the Senate, and it was signed by the President—but nobody discovered that little comma. Nobody, that is, until some punctuation-smart importer caught it and began importing all kinds of foreign fruit, plants, and fruit-plants.

When the Customs Office charged him duty, he took the case to the courts, which ruled that in this sentence that little comma was the equivalent of an "and" and that the bill actually said that all foreign fruit and all foreign plants should enter the country duty-free! And it had to stand for a full year, too!

Someone really goofed on that one. One can't help wondering how many goofs are committed in technical writing every day—all because the writers didn't bother to learn how to use some simple marks of punctuation!

PAGE 52

PUNCTUATION PAGE 53

O.K., you say, that just doesn't happen in technical writing. It doesn't? Look:

No. 9. The screen is luminescent so when electrons strike the screen light is emitted.

Did you have to back up and re-read that one? If you didn't you are most unusual. You either don't need this course, or it won't do any good, anyhow. Try this one:

No. 10. The screen is luminescent so that when electrons strike the screen, light is emitted.

Here's another that takes pretty careful reading not to be misunderstood:

No. 11. Some plastics are softened by the first application of heat and thereafter are not affected by heat.

Did you get it right the first time? Would a little comma properly placed help any?

No. 12. Some plastics are softened by the first application of heat, and thereafter are not affected by heat.

Was that easier to understand? You see, misreading because of lack of punctuation in technical writing does happen, perhaps much oftener than we realize. So learn to use correctly each of the following marks of punctuation and you won't goof in your writing—or speaking, either, for correct reading and speaking depend in a large measure on correct punctuation.

THE COMMA—

Used to indicate a "brief" pause.

A. An introductory word, phrase, or clause is often separated from the rest of the sentence by a comma:
   1. First, the report should be carefully planned before you start writing.
   2. Of course, this makes you think before you write.
   3. If you want to be sure of doing the right thing, make a brief outline first.

B. An inserted or parenthetical (that is, unnecessary or not restrictive) word, phrase, or clause is enclosed between two commas within the sentence itself:
   1. Some report writers, however, prefer to use a detailed outline.
   2. There are, to be sure, a number of ways of using an outline to advantage.
   3. Any outline, you may be sure, can help you do a better job of organizing your thoughts into a clear, coherent form.

C. Words, phrases, or clauses in series are usually punctuated:
   1. The report was long, dull, uninteresting.
   2. It was revised so that it was short, lively, and informative.
   3. The report was written by three different sets of writers: Jones and Bell, Johnson and Anderson, and Dr. Grant himself.
   4. In recent years, engineers have become better acquainted with the technique used in the correct application of Carboloy tools, and are arriving at the correct method much faster by information gathered through their experience and from the data furnished by the Carboloy manufacturers.
   5. The oils are tested for specific gravity, flash and fire points, viscosity, cloud and pour tests, and carbon.

NOTE: Here are some of the conventional uses of the comma:
   a. Between the day of the month and the year—and after the year, if the sentence continues: She was born May 4, 1910, in Kansas.
   b. Between the city and the state—and after the state, if the sentence continues: Ellinwood, Kansas, was her birthplace.
   c. After the complimentary closing in a business letter:
      Sincerely yours,   Cordially yours,
           Yours truly,
   d. Between the day of the week and the date: Saturday, July 2.

CAUTION: If you are in doubt about using a comma, don't. Today the tendency is to use only as much punctuation as is necessary to make your meaning clear. If there is no brief pause, don't punctuate. Even if you do pause briefly to catch your breath, don't punctuate unless you could actually stop your sentence and start a new one. Here are several misuses of the comma you MUST AVOID:

NEVER SEPARATE THE SUBJECT OF YOUR SENTENCE FROM ITS VERB BY A SINGLE MARK OF PUNCTUATION, OR THE VERB FROM ITS OBJECT OR ITS COMPLEMENT BY A SINGLE MARK:

WRONG: The report, which I am writing is on the population explosion.

BUT: The report which I am writing is on the population explosion.

NOT: Outlining is, simply organizing your thoughts on paper.

BUT: Outlining is simply organizing your thoughts on paper. *Or* Outlining is, simply, organizing your thoughts on paper.

NOT: Every formal report should have, a letter of transmittal.

BUT: Every formal report should have a letter of transmittal.

A good rule to remember is never to use a single comma unless it separates an introductory word, clause, or phrase, or a terminating (ending) one which could be omitted from the sentence.

THE SEMICOLON—

Used to indicate a longer pause, but not a full stop. There are four well-defined uses of the semicolon:

A. Between the parts of a compound sentence connected by a regular coordinating conjunction (and, but, or, nor, for, yet), a semicolon is used if either or both of the sentences contain commas:

1. An informal report, which may be in the form of a memorandum or letter, does not need a letter of transmittal; but a formal report should have one.

NOTE: Sometimes the parts of a compound predicate are separated by a semicolon if each one is long and punctuated with commas:
"It is neither too early nor too late to become practiced in the art of communication; certainly not too late to accumulate background through reading experiences . . ." (From Dwight Van Avery's "Why Study ENGLISH?" page 9.)

B. Between the parts of a compound sentence connected by a conjunctive adverb (so, then, thus, therefore, moreover, consequently, accordingly, however, here, there, also, besides, etc.), a semicolon MUST BE USED:

1. The report must be as concise as possible; however, nothing essential to a complete understanding of the contents may be omitted.

C. Between the parts of a compound sentence without any connective, a semicolon MUST BE USED:

1. A technical report may be very formal; it also may be quite informal.

D. Between the parts of long, parallel groups of words—phrases or clauses—a semicolon should be used to give proper emphasis to each part, and also to prevent misreading. To prove my point, read first the following sentence punctuated only with commas; then read it properly punctuated with both commas and semicolons:

NOT: The standard tapers are as follows: Morse, which has a taper of 0.600 to 0.630 inches per foot, Browne and Sharp, 0.500 inches per foot except Number 10, which has 0.5161, milling machine, 3½ inches per foot, Jarno, 0.60 inches per foot, Briggs Pipe, 0.750 inches per foot, and Pratt and Whitney, ½ inch per foot, or 0.0208 inches per inch.

BUT: The standard tapers are as follows: Morse, which has a taper of 0.600 to 0.630 inches per foot; Browne and Sharp, 0.500 inches per foot except Number 10, which has 0.5161; milling machine, 3½ inches per foot; Jarno, 0.60 inches per foot; Briggs Pipe, 0.750 inches per foot; and Pratt and Whitney, ½ inch per foot, or 0.0208 inches per foot.

The use of semicolons gives greater pause or emphasis to each type of thread.

THE COLON—

A mark of expectation equivalent to the equal sign (=) in mathematics. Again there are four well-defined uses of the colon:

A. The colon is used to introduce a formal series of words, phrases, clauses:

1. Every report should have three parts: an introduction or beginning, a middle or body, and an ending or closing.

2. Your letter of transmittal should do five things: indicate that something (your report) is being transmitted, give the title of your report, give the reason why you are writing it, indicate the scope and/or limitations of your report, and finally acknowledge your borrowings.

B. A colon may be used to separate the parts of a compound sentence when the first leg is a general statement and the second one is a specific explanation of the first:

1. One thing is certain: Your advancement will depend in a large measure on your ability to communicate your thoughts clearly, correctly, concisely in writing, as well as in speaking.

C. A colon is used to introduce a formal quotation or question when the word "said" is not used.

D. A colon has certain standard, conventional uses:

1. After the salutation of a business letter:
Dear Mr. James: Gentlemen:

2. Between the hour and the minute, and between the minute and second in expressions of time: He ran the mile in 3:58. Come at 4:15 tomorrow afternoon.

3. Between major and minor items in what is considered a unit of thought, as in this expression: Your assignment for tomorrow is I: 3-6, 9-12; II: 1-4, 8-10; and III: 1-10.

THE DASH—

Used singly to separate and in pairs to enclose. The dash is a much stronger mark than the comma, but not as separative as parentheses. Again there are four distinct uses of the dash:

A. A dash indicates an addition to the thought presented—an afterthought:

1. A business letter takes the place of a personal visit—it is YOU on paper.

B. Dashes may be used to replace commas when enclosing or separating material which has been punctuated with commas already:

1. Every form of language communication—memos, letters, reports, speeches, oral presentations, etc.—is important in your struggle for success.

C. In a sentence containing a group of words introduced by "that is," a dash or pair of dashes will give greater emphasis than a comma or commas:

1. In technical writing, abbreviations are permis-

PUNCTUATION

sible if they are standard—that is, approved by the American Standards Association.

D. Occasionally a sentence will begin with a series of words or phrases, all of which are referred to in the main clause by such words as "these," "all," "each," etc. Under these circumstances a dash is used:
1. Commas, semicolons, dashes, colons, quotation marks, etc.—each mark has a meaning and a use of its own!

NOTE: I have purposely omitted one use of the dash which has no application in technical writing: A dash is the conventional literary mark to indicate a sudden break in thought, as in conversation.

THE PERIOD—

Used chiefly as the principal end-stopped mark of punctuation:

A. The period is used to end a declarative sentence—one that makes a statement:
1. Dwight Van Avery of General Electric agrees with Peter Drucker that "the ability to express ideas in writing and speaking heads the list of requirements for success."
2. A period should be used after each standard abbreviation (except, of course, most of the ones approved by the American Standards Association).
3. Although the standard abbreviations—Mr., Mrs., Dr.—are still used today, modern business letter writing practice does not approve of the following: St. for Street, Ave. for Avenue, Jan. for January, Ky. for Kentucky, Co. for Company (unless, of course, this spelling is a part of the legal name of that organization: Gladding, McBean & Co., & for and, etc.
4. Use dots (three or four spaced periods) to indicate an omission in a quoted passage: ". . . you will often have to make a choice between two contradictory so-called facts. . . . Then you'll have to choose the most plausible —the one your reader is most likely to accept as a fact. Likewise, your conclusion or recommendations, if you have come to any, must be the logical result or outgrowth of the factual evidence you have presented. . . ."

NOTE: For inserting some of your own comments into a quotation, see Brackets.

THE QUESTION MARK—

Used exclusively to end an interrogative sentence:

A. Every direct question must end with a question mark:
1. In "Why Study English?" Dwight Van Avery asks the top engineer upstairs: "After all, English is almost as important as math in our business, isn't it?"

NOTE: For the top engineer's answer, see The Exclamation Point, A.

B. Sometimes a series of short interrogatives may be punctuated as follows:
1. How much English have you had—104? 105? 219? 301?

C. A question mark in parentheses may be used to indicate the writer's uncertainty about a date, fact, name, etc.:
1. In 1921 (?), the late E. P. Corbett wrote three famous collection letters that set a new pattern for all future writers trying to collect just obligations.

NOTE: DO NOT USE A QUESTION MARK IN PARENTHESES TO INDICATE SARCASM OR IRONY!

NOTE: There are five ways of asking questions:
1. Inverted sentence structure: Are you going?
2. Interrogative pronoun: Who is going?
3. Interrogative adverb. Where are you going?
4. Modal auxiliary: Can you go? Will you go?
5. Normal word order: You are going?

THE EXCLAMATION POINT—

Seldom used in technical writing:

A. Although technical writing is not usually given to the strong emotion required for the use of the exclamation point, it can on occasion be used to advantage, as in the top engineer's reply to Van Avery's question in The Question Mark, A, 1: "Change the word 'almost' to 'just', and, brother, you've said a mouthful!"

THE HYPHEN—

Used primarily to separate words into their syllables, as at the end of a line. It is also used to form compound adjectives:

A. The hyphen is the conventional mark of punctuation used at the end of a line to indicate that the word is continued on the next line:
1. Although any word may be divided between syllables, it is inadvisable and considered incorrect to hyphenate in either of these two ways:

    a-   heat-   slow-
  bove   ed   ly

NOTE: Here are some illustrations of incorrect hyphenation taken from student reports, papers, letters, etc.:

WRONG

exchan-ge	you-ng	suppl-ying	me-tal
structu-re	hydroxi-de		necess-ary
satisfact-ory	distribu-ting		meta-llic

INADVISABLE

| probabil-ity | a-bility | unfortunate-ly | |
| de-signed | buy-er | Pacif-ic | offer-ed |

2. It is inadvisable to double hyphenate:
un-equal-ed
3. It is not good practice to hyphenate consecutive lines:
. . . automobiles, electrical appliances, musical instruments, and sporting goods; or luxuries, such as jewelry, and furs to wholesale to other merchants and the general consuming public.
Merchant salesmen restrict their efforts to limited numbers of wholesalers and retailers . . .
4. Sometimes two words are joined into a temporary compound attributive adjective:
a one-room grammar school
a one-way single-spool open-center valve
a 220-volt single-phase 3-wire AC circuit
for north- and south-bound traffic
a five- or ten-point bonus
a one-quart can
compound-complex sentence
low-cost methods
continuous-tone copy
green-and-yellow blood
a single-revolution press
plate-making equipment
the cross-sectional area
the one-inch-bore hydraulic cylinder
twenty-six cents
a heavy-gauge stamped-steel housing

THE APOSTROPHE—

Used to show an omission. Most of the time, this omission is of the genetive "e" indicating possession.

A. The apostrophe is generally used to indicate possession or ownership. Here are some rules that will help you avoid making errors in the use of this important mark of punctuation:
1. Most singular nouns form their possessive case by adding simply *'s:*
day—day's   girl—girl's   mother—mother's
man—man's
2. Nouns of one syllable ending in *s* or an *s* sound (x, z) add *apostrophe (')* only:
Max—Max'   Jess—Jess'   Liz—Liz'
Bess—Bess'
3. Proper nouns ending in an *s* sound, simply add the apostrophe:
Metz—Metz'   Adams—Adams'   Lomex—Lomex'
4. Plural nouns ending in *s* add only the apostrophe: girls—girls'   farmers—farmers'
colleges—colleges'
5. Plural nouns not ending in an *s* sound add *'s:*
men—men's   mice—mice's   children—children's
6. Nouns with the same form in the plural as in singular add *'s* to form the possessive case of either singular or plural:
salmon—salmon's   sheep—sheep's   deer—deer's
7. Compound nouns add the *'s* to the last element of the compound:
Cal Poly—Cal Poly's
brother-in-law—brother-in-law's
the two Cal Poly's campuses
brothers-in-law's   Knight-Templar—Knights Templar's   court martial—courts martial's decision
8. Joint ownership is indicated by attaching the *'s* to the last member:
Crawford and Zimmerman's store
David and Penny's bicycle
9. The *'s* is used to indicate time, distance, etc.:
an hour's ride   a two-week's vacation
a month's pay   a stone's throw
NOTE: DON'T USE THE POSSESSIVE CASE INDISCRIMINATELY—don't attribute ownership to something inanimate and not personified:
NOT: the table's top   the steel's structure
the wire's size
BUT: The top of the table   the structure of the steel   the size of the wire
B. The apostrophe is also used to show the omission of one or more letters in a word, as in such contractions as:
can't   didn't   he's   it's   you're   '62
o'clock   you're   don't
NOTE: You must distinguish between it's and its: *it's* is a contraction of *it is*. *Its* is the singular possessive pronoun.
C. The possessive personal pronouns NEVER take an apostrophe—they have their own special possessive form: my, mine, you, yours, his, her, hers, its, our, ours, their, theirs.
NOTE: There is a vast difference between these two words:
Their is possessive plural. *They're* is a contraction of *they are*. *There* is an adverb.
Whose is the possessive relative pronoun. *Who's* is a contraction of *who is*.
D. The apostrophe is also used to form the plural of figures, letters, symbols, and words referred to as words:
Dot your *i's* and cross your *t's*. The Great Depression of the 1930's. He made all B's. Do not use the ampersand (&) for your and's.

PARENTHESES—

Used to enclose something not a grammatical part of the sentence.

A. Parentheses are often used in technical writing to indicate an enumeration:
The parts of a formal report include (1) the

prefatory parts, (2) the body, and (3) the appendix.
B. Parentheses, never used singly but always in pairs, may be used to include in the text something that could have been put in a footnote:
>Essential oils (volatile hydrocarbons derived from plant products) are also important to the flavor industry.
>The lithographer's press (See Figure 1) is used to . . . .
C. Parentheses are used to enclose reference numbers. (See pages 7ff.)

BRACKETS—

Used by a writer to add something to or comment upon a quotation within the quotation itself:
>Since brackets are used so seldom, they do not appear on any standard typewriter keyboard, but must be drawn in by the typist.

DOUBLE QUOTATION MARKS—

Used in the United States to indicate borrowing from some other writer.
A. Double quotation marks are used to enclose a direct quotation:
>"The top engineer upstairs is on the telephone. He says to us: 'Right before me is a brief report made by one of our young engineers. I have to guess what the fellow is driving at. I'm no English shark, but I find myself getting a little angry when I see four sentences tied together with commas. He has *principal* for *principle,* and he has also misspelled *accommodate* and Cincinnati. What if some of this fellow's bad English gets into the hands of our customers?'"
B. The titles of articles in magazines, of chapter headings, etc. are put in double quotation marks:
>"Why Study English?" is one of a series of worth while articles published by General Electric under the title *General Electric's Answer to Four Why's.*
C. Naturally, quotation marks are used to indicate conversation, as indicated in the quotation in A above. Technical writing, however, seldom uses conversation. Here is an example of a direct quotation and the same material rewritten as an indirect quotation:
>According to John P. Riebel of the Cal Poly English Department, "The laws and rules of good writing—grammar, spelling, punctuation, sentence structure, word order, position of modifier, paragraphing, etc.—have not been repealed for technical writers! They are simply applied in toto to another medium of communication and the vocabulary appropriate to this subject matter." (direct quotation)
>Mr. John P. Riebel of the Cal Poly English Department said that . . . (Continue on with the exact same words without quotation marks and it becomes an indirect quotation.)

Quotations may be used in technical reports in several ways:
a. as an integral part of the text itself as shown on page 57.
b. As a separate insertion as shown on page 17. No quotes necessary.
c. As a footnote.

D. Sometimes quotes are used to enclose words used in a special sense:
>Soil penetrometers are hand operated and thus subject to "human" errors.
>The natural control of a pest by predators or competitors is called "biological control."

NOTE: Don't overwork quotation marks, such as by labeling your humor, well-known nicknames, technical words, or slang except when used in formal reports. Quotation marks should not be used for emphasis.

E. Use single quotation marks to enclose a quotation within a quotation:
>"The top engineer is wound up. 'At the last meeting of our Association, representatives of all the major companies complained about the way their younger men were putting down their words—and futures—on paper. Can't someone tell us what to do?'"

ITALICS—

Used chiefly in technical writing to indicate the titles of separate publications. Although not usually considered a mark of punctuation but rather as "mechanics," it seems most appropriate to discuss italics here.

A. Italicize—that is, underline once—the titles of separate publications: reports, books, magazines, manuals, brochures, government documents, dictionaries, encyclopedias, etc.:
>*Mosquito Control Programs   Six Steps to More Successful Job Application   Refrigerating Engineer   General Electric's Answer to Four Why's   Guide Letters   American College Dictionary   Encyclopedia Americana*

B. Foreign words and phrases are italicized:
>*semper fidelis   e pluribus unum   auf wiedersehn   adios   au revoir*

C. Words, letters, or figures used or mentioned as such are usually italicized:
>Dot your *i*'s and cross your *t*'s.
>There is no *cow* in Moscow.
>Before decimals in technical reports, always use a *0*.

D. Although not often used in technical writing, the titles of movies, works of art, ships, aircraft, pullman cars, etc. should be italicized:

The Mona Lisa, Gone With the Wind, The Columbine, The Mt. Washington, The Queen Mary, Nobody Writes Letters Anymore, Writing Better Business Letters.

E. The Latin names of plants, bacteria, etc. are italicized:

Culex pipiens carries a minute worm which cause filariasis. The viruses encephalitis (sleeping sickness) are transmitted by *Culex tarsalis.*

CAPITALIZATION—

Used to distinguish proper nouns from common nouns. While we're at it, we might as well talk a bit about capitalization and how it is used in reports, articles, theses, and term papers:

A. Capitalize all proper names, derivatives of proper names, and their abbreviations:

California State Polytechnic College   Cal Poly   Engineering Division   Printing Department   English 301   Republican Party   Biblical   Negro   Memorial Day   December 31   Sunday   World War II   God   Southern California

B. In titles of reports, papers, etc., capitalize the first letter of the first word, and the first letter of each important word thereafter:

Mosquito Control Programs   Ten Commandments for Writing Letters That Get Results
"*Five Pointers for Writing Star Reports*"
Artificial Food Flavorings

C. Capitalize the first letter of each title preceding a person's name:

President Julian A. McPhee   Dr. Dale Andrews   Dean Harold Hayes   Mr. Mead Johnson   Miss Joan Johnston   Mrs. Elizabeth Anderson   Professor Jefferson   Associate Professor Lebeir   Instructor Orlovich

D. Capitalize the pronoun I.

E. Capitalize the first word in every sentence.

*   *   *

"*I'm no English shark, but I find myself getting a little angry when I see four sentences tied together with commas.*"

Dwight Van Avery

The Punctuation of Compound Sentences

There are two incorrect ways of punctuating compound sentences:

1. *Comma Fault:* "Technical writing" is a term that is used to refer to many forms of practical writing, report writing is a specialized form of technical writing.

2. *Run-on or Fused Sentence* (a Comma Fault without the comma): Technical writing is any kind of factual writing that is "technical" to a particular subject it can be done by engineers or by cooks.

There are several ways of correcting both comma faults and run-on sentences: with the use of stronger punctuation, with the use of connectives, or with the use of both.

Here are seven legitimate ways of joining two complete thoughts into one sentence (called a compound sentence):

1. With the coordinating conjunction "and" (only "and" can be used):

    I signed up for report writing and my friend took letter writing.

2. With any coordinating conjunction ("and," "but," "for," "or," "nor," "yet").

    Joe wanted to take technical writing, but he couldn't work it into his schedule.

3. With a semicolon and a coordinating conjunction, especially if one or both parts of the compound sentence are punctuated with commas:

    There are many ways of writing reports that do the job well, and every one is correct; but in this course you will learn how to write a standard, formal report form which is used by one large corporation in the United States.

4. With a semicolon when no coordinating or other conjunction is used:

    Some reports are formal; others are informal.

5. With a semicolon when the two parts are connected by a conjunctive adverb:

    Not every report required an appendix; however, it is a convenient place in which to put everything a part of the report as a whole, but apart from the body itself.

6. With a colon when the second part of the compound sentence is a direct explanation of the first part:

    One thing is certain: your ability to write clear, concise, correct reports will determine in a large measure how rapidly you climb the ladder of success.

7. With a dash to represent an afterthought:

    A report may be quite informal—that is, it may be in memo or letter form if this fits the occasion.

*   *   *

Sentences

Frequently you hear the complaint that English sentence structure (syntax) is so restricted that it doesn't compare with Latin syntax. Granted, English sentence structure is not as flexible as Latin sentence structure, but it is not true that a person needs to be hampered by English syntax in writing or speaking. Those who make this complaint just have not yet discovered how flexible English sentences can be. This same English sentence structure was used by such great English writers as Chaucer, Shakespeare, Milton, Marlowe, Ben Jonson, Addison, Swift, Thackery, Dr. Samuel Johnson, and Hemingway, to mention only a few. *They* didn't feel cramped or constrained because they couldn't use Latin syntax. Actually, if one has a thought worth expressing, he can express it adequately, even beautifully, by using modern English sentence structure. Let's look at some of the many types of English sentences at your command:

SIMPLE SENTENCES—

Only one complete thought, which can be represented by the figure *1*. Unfortunately, we associate the word "simple" with simple-mindedness. This is far from the truth of the matter, for a simple sentence may contain any number of words and phrases, just so long as it has only one verb. Here are a number of simple sentences, listed in order of their complexity, with the least-complicated first:

1. *One subject and one verb only:* It rained today.
2. *Two or more subjects with only one verb:* The rain and the wind were intense.
3. *One subject with two or more verbs:* The Colts ran and passed at will.
4. *Two or more subjects with two or more verbs:* The Colts and the Raiders will pass and run frequently today.
5. *The addition of one or more phrases (prepositional) to either the subject or the predicate, or to both:* The Rams of Los Angeles lost four consecutive games.

An infinite number of examples of the addition of one or more phrases to either the subject or the predicate or to both could be given, which shows that even in the most elemental sentence form there can be great variety, especially when one considers the numerous kinds of phrases—prepositional, infinitive, gerundive, participial, absolute—which can be added. (See "Groups of Words," page 41.)

COMPLEX SENTENCES—

A complex sentence consists of one complete thought plus part of another thought; yet it never contains two complete sentences. This can be represented by the symbol 1+: The + part may be a relative clause or an adverbial clause. (See "Groups of Words," page 41.) The following is an example of a complex sentence:

One simple sentence plus a relative clause: All the men who were dressed in white were doctors.

"Who were dressed in white" is a relative clause that modifies or qualifies the men who were doctors.

Now, let's see this written as a simple sentence (the first two examples below) and as a complex sentence (the third example below):

1. *Simple sentence with a prepositional phrase:* The men in white were doctors.
2. *Simple sentence with a participial phrase:* The men dressed in white were doctors.
3. *Complex sentence (simple sentence plus a relative clause):* The men who were dressed in white were doctors.

Each of these sentences has exactly the same meaning, yet each has been written in a different way, depending on the way the author wanted to express the thought. This gives variety, which someone has called the spice of life. One may add as many adverbial and relative clauses as one desires, and the result will still be a complex sentence, so long as one does not add another simple sentence, which would result in two complete thoughts within the same sentence.

COMPOUND SENTENCES—

A fragmentary sentence may occur by itself, or it may be cut off from the parent sentence by means of a period, in which case the sentence is said to contain "a period fault." First, let's examine a sentence fragment closely: *Reclining on the side of a steep hill.* Immediately, the reader asks "What or who is reclining on the side of a steep hill?" One just has to guess at the answer. This usage is often permissible, even desirable, in imaginary writing, where the author isn't really concerned whether the reader gets the full meaning of each sentence, but is rather concerned about communicating a mood or feeling. In fact, dialogue in stories, novels, and plays consists mostly of sentence fragments, just as in the case in our everyday conversation. However, in factual writing, such as reports or letters, or in technical writing, fragments are absolutely tabu. In such writing, the meaning must be crystal clear. One time, I almost lost my eyesight because I was using a chemical process from a text which had been inaccurately translated from the German. I finally had to go back to the original German text and retranslate it. Then, and only then, was I able to find the error in the translated version. But let's get back to the original fragment. By attaching a sentence to this fragment, one can make sense out of what was nonsense:

1. *"Reclining on the side of a steep hill, we could overlook the entire city."*
2. *"Some steers were reclining on the side of a steep hill."*
3. *"We found the missing steers reclining on the side of a steep hill."*

Unless you have a very good reason, avoid sentence fragments!

OVERLOADED, RUN-ON, OR
FUSED SENTENCES—

Such sentences are also to be avoided in factual writing, for they too are confusing, and they cause the reader to waste time deciphering them. Factual writing is based on facts which can be verified; imaginative writing may, but need not, be based on facts. It's usually easy to correct a comma fault, for instead of a comma, one can simply use a period, a semicolon, or some other mark of punctuation. (See page 58.) Don't think that this is everything that can be said about English sentences. It isn't, and I admit this cheerfully. But I hope that I have at least awakened in you a greater appreciation of English syntax, which can be defined as "the arrangement and interrelationship of words in phrases and sentences."

NOTES

Paragraphing

"Your survival, too, as the adult you are aiming to be, depends upon your ability, desire, and courage to put your best foot forward in a world that will judge you by your words as well as your actions."

Dwight Van Avery

Originally, paragraphing was a matter of punctuation rather than of mechanics. The paragraph symbol, ¶, at one time was the strongest mark of punctuation used. But over the years paragraphing came to be more a matter of mechanics and organization of material than simply of punctuation.

Today we consider the sentence a unit of writing, and the paragraph the unit of thinking. In other words, when we think, we think in clusters of ideas, not in single or separate ideas. But when we write down our thoughts, we still write them one idea at a time.

For that reason today we paragraph not only for a change in thought, but for a change in the direction of the thought. For example, here is a letter report dealing with an automobile accident. How would you like to keep in mind everything with the first sentence to the last, as you are supposed to do with the material within a paragraph?

> Dear Mr. Masters:
> I am glad to send you, as you asked in your letter of April 3, my version of the accident that happened at North Broad and Channing Streets last Thursday evening at 6:45. Shortly after the traffic light had turned green for north- and south-bound cars—I presume eight or nine cars had crossed the intersection—an old woman started to cross Broad Street from the northeast corner. As nearly as I could see she walked into the side of a south-bound car a little ahead of me and just to my right, and was knocked down. I stopped my car and went to her. When I reached her, she was unconscious, but regained consciousness by the time I lifted her into my car. With Officer Johnson, No. 949, who was handling traffic at the corner, I drove her to the Emergency Ward of the Alport Hospital. When we got there, she was conscious, though somewhat dazed and bleeding slightly from a cut on her head. Shortly after we reached the hospital, the man whose car was directly involved in the accident arrived and gave his name and address to Officer Johnson. I hope that these details will give you the information you want. At all events, it is as complete a version of the accident as I can give.
> Very truly yours,

Whew! What a welter of words to have to keep in mind! Now this is really an excellent letter report: it's factual, concise, accurate, complete. But few readers would care to try to keep in mind everything from the beginning to the end. And there's no reason to do so, for there are definite changes in the direction of the thought. You have probably noticed them as you read the paragraphs.

For example, there's no mistaking the introductory paragraph, or the paragraph that ends the report. And the second paragraph is also quite well defined. So there we have a good starter:

P1—*Introduction*—
> I am glad to send you, as you asked in your letter of April 3, my version of the accident that happened at North Broad and Channing Streets last Thursday evening at 6:45.

P2—*What happened*
> Shortly after the traffic light had turned green for north- and south-bound cars—I presume eight or nine cars had crossed the intersection—an old woman started to cross Broad Street from the northeast corner. As nearly as I could see, she walked into the side of a south-bound car a little ahead of me and just to my right, and was knocked down.

P3—*What I did*
> I stopped my car and went to her. When I reached her, she was unconscious, but regained consciousness by the time I lifted her into my car. With Officer Johnson, No. 949, who was handling traffic at the corner, I drove her to the Emergency Ward of the Alport Hospital.

P4—*At the hospital*
> When we got there, she was conscious, though somewhat dazed and bleeding slightly from a cut on her head. Shortly after we reached the hospital, the man whose car was directly involved in the accident arrived and gave his name and address to Officer Johnson.

P5—*Ending*
> I hope that these details will give you the information you want. At all events, it is as complete a version of the accident as I can give.

Yes, it is possible to write this letter report in six paragraphs—that is, to make paragraphs 3 and 4 into three. And who is to say this would be wrong? The one thing we *do* know is that this report MUST BE PARAGRAPHED FOR EASY, QUICK UNDERSTANDING.

The second fault to avoid is overparagraphing—that is, making each sentence into a separate paragraph. This is just as bad as underparagraphing:

> As you know, I am currently doing research on my project for Report Writing, English 301.
> The subject I have chosen is color, with the main topic relating to psychology and color.
> I have decided on *The Psychological Effect of Color in the Business Office* for the title of my report.
> To date, I have made a list of a number of periodi-

cal references by checking with the *Business Periodical Index* in the Cal Poly Library.

I have also acquired a few books on the subject.

I plan to see various paint shops, office buildings, architects and the Building Coordinator of Cal Poly for additional material to be used in my report.

I will be in touch with you during the remainder of this quarter to keep you informed of my progress.

This letter report is not only badly paragraphed, but wordy. The revision corrects both of these faults:

The title of my project for report writing, English 301, is *The Psychological Effect of Color in the Business Office.*

I have listed a number of periodical references by checking the *Business Periodical Index* in the Cal Poly Library. Also I have obtained a number of books on the subject. I plan to see various paint shops and office buildings, and to talk with some architects and Mr.   , the Building Coordinator at Cal Poly.

You may be sure that I'll keep you informed as to my progress throughout the quarter, Mr. Riebel.

No one can tell you how long a good paragraph should be. It should be long enough to do the job intended, but short enough to be interesting. Vary your paragraph lengths—some short, some long, some medium length. Remember, paragraph for eye appeal: long, unbroken blocks of type are forbidding, and short, choppy paragraphs make your writing jerky.

Now let's see if we can formulate some principles that will help you do a more satisfactory job of paragraphing your technical writing:

1. Make your paragraphs as short as possible without making them choppy.
2. Be sure that each paragraph presents one important idea in the chain of facts that will interest your reader and convince him that you know what you're talking about.
3. Put each important thought into a separate paragraph unless the two ideas are so closely related that they cannot logically be separated.
4. See that the facts in each paragraph are presented in a unified, coherent, emphatic arrangement. Do not smother an important idea in the middle of a paragraph; put it at the beginning or at the ending, the two most emphatic positions.
5. Develop the thought in each paragraph with one or more of these methods:
    a. Statement and restatement—repetition of facts, points, ideas, etc.
    b. Division and/or explanation, logical sequence.
    c. Definition of the subject for further development.
    d. The use of particulars and details, examples, instances, etc.
    e. Comparison and contrast, analogy, similarity, difference, etc.
    f. From general to particular, or particular to general.
    g. Cause to effect or effect to cause; purpose to result or result to purpose.
    h. Origin, history, background, substantiating facts, etc.
    i. Chronology, narrative, history, story, anecdote, time sequence.
    j. Description—spatial arrangement of things.
    k. Reasons or proof.
    l. The use of quotation, statement of authority, testimonial, etc.
    m. The use of any other means of developing an an idea or thought.
6. Link the ideas within each paragraph (and one paragraph with another) by means of—
    a. Connectives—conjunctions, prepositions, linking words or phrases, such as first, second, then, next, thereafter, lastly, hence, finally, etc.
    b. Repetition—either the same word, phrase, or clause, or a synonym.
    c. Pronouns—personal, demonstrative, relative, identifying, etc.
7. See that there is continuity or flow of thought from one paragraph to another, a definite progression of the thought from the beginning to the ending of your writing.

Special Types or Kinds of Paragraphs

1. *Introductory*—May be used anywhere in your writing to introduce a new line or thought.
2. *Transitional*—Used to bridge the gap between two divergent lines of thought.
3. *Concluding, Summarizing, Recommending*—Used to end a piece of technical writing that comes to a conclusion, a summary, or a recommendation.
4. *Terminating*—One that is used simply to bring your writing to a simple, safe stop which is neither a conclusion, a summary, or a recommendation. Not all writing requires one of the latter three endings, but every piece should draw to a close in such a way the reader will know that that's all, there is no more!

SPECIAL PROBLEMS IN COMPOSITION

Ambiguity, Confusion, Lack of Clarity, Vagueness

"The top engineer upstairs is on the telephone. He says to us: 'Right before my eyes is a brief report made out by one of our young engineers. I have to guess what the fellow is driving at'."

Dwight Van Avery

John Dryden, the Seventeenth Century English poet, once said: "The first duty of the writer is to be understood." How true that was in his day, nearly 300 years ago! How much more true it is today in this time of technical writing! If your reader doesn't understand you, then you had better just keep quiet and not waste your time and his.

Vagueness in writing may be caused from a number of things, or from a combination of them. Here are examples of the major causes of vagueness in technical writing:

1. Vagueness is often caused by the use of the wrong word:

    NOT: If this is not the manual you want, please let us know and we will justify our error. (Stuff it down your throat, in other words!)

    BUT: . . . we will rectify our error. (That's better, much, much better.)

    NOT: I'm saving my money to buy a candied camera. (Sweet of him, isn't it?)

    BUT: I'm saving my money to buy a candid camera.

    NOT: Sodium chloride is so plentiful in sea water that there is one chlorine ion and one sodium ion for every 100 molecules of water; next ranges magnesium with one magnesium ion for every 1000 molecules of water.

    BUT: . . . ; next comes magnesium, with . . . every 1,000 molecules of water.

    NOT: The first lettuce was packed in wooden crates. (How does he know for sure?)

    BUT: Lettuce was packed first in wooden crates. (Sounds better, eh?)

    NOT: California farmers also threat the workers with respect . . . (How's that?)

    BUT: California farmers also treat the workers with respect. (Now I understand.)

2. Misspelling is often the cause of ambiguity, vagueness:

    NOT: Attach to the headstall is the bit. (Sounds as if this is to be a command.)

    BUT: Attached to the headstall is the bit.

    NOT: Sometimes it is necessary to divide a sentence into its subject, its predicate, and its compliment. (Praise?)

    BUT: Sometimes it is necessary to . . . , and its complement.

    NOT: Your presents will always be welcomed at our meeting, Mr. McPhee. (Gimmee?)

    BUT: Your presence will . . .

    NOT: May 28 will be one of my bussiest days. (On a kissing spree, eh?)

    BUT: May 28 . . . one of my busiest days. (I'll buy this version.)

    NOT: I went to see Mr. Perello and ask him . . . (Watch this common misspelling.)

    BUT: I went . . . and asked him for . . . (Don't forget that "ed" on the past tense.)

    NOT: A map showing the location of the Crops House will be attacted.

    BUT: A map . . . will be attached.

    NOT: With a little service given free know, there is a good chance you'll be back when you need new or recapped tires.

    BUT: With a little service given free now, . . .

    NOT: Both supply and demand register an affect on the price. ("Affect" is not a noun.)

    BUT: Both supply and demand register an effect on price. Or: Both supply and demand affect the price.

    NOT: This tool is used to scrap the surface. (Junk it?)

    BUT: This tool is used to scrape the surface.

3. The excessive use of jargon inevitably leads to vagueness:

    NOT: I have had some management experience in the agricultural field.

    BUT: I have had some management experience in agriculture. OR: I have had some agricultural-management experience.

    NOT: The sales field was well represented by courses.

    BUT: Sales courses were well represented. OR: There were many sales courses.

    NOT: I feel you will be interested in knowing . . . (Keep your hands to yourself.)

    BUT: I'm sure you will be interested in knowing . . .

4. Awkward wording leads to confusion and ambiguity:

    NOT: One of your refrigerators in your store is what my husband and I have been looking for for the past month. (How's that? I'm confused.)

    BUT: For the past month, my husband and I have

been looking at one of the refrigerators in your store.

NOT: He sawed the limb he was sitting on off. (What!)

BUT: He sawed off the limb he was sitting on.

NOT: This constitutes the last operation and the finished product is ready . . .

BUT: This constitutes the last operation before the finished product . . .

NOT: The depth of hardness varies with the time from 0.003 to 0.030 of an inch.

BUT: The depth of hardness varies from 0.003 to 0.030 inches, depending on the length of time the part is in the carburizing furnace.

NOT: A great deal of skill in the judgment of the operator is depended upon when he attempts to straighten the shaft. (How's that—come again.)

BUT: (Just how would YOU attempt to clarify this mess of words and have them make some semblance of sense? I give up!)

5. Unidiomatic expressions often cause confusion:

NOT: I would like to refer a Mr. White to one of these openings.

BUT: I would like to recommend Mr. White for one of these openings.

NOT: By the enclosed data sheet you can see . . .

BUT: From the enclosed data sheet . . .

NOT: Enclose please find a copy of my resume. (Why make your reader hunt?)

BUT: Enclosed is a copy . . .

NOT: Unemployment and welfare benefits discourage these people to go to work.

BUT: . . . discourage these people from going to work.

NOT: The inspiration to writing this report came from . . .

BUT: The inspiration to write this report came from . . .

6. The use of non-technical language can sometimes be confusing:

NOT: This pathetic first shipment of lettuce was . . . (Poor little lettuce!)

BUT: This small first shipment of lettuce . . .

NOT: The tunnel will have a first cost of . . .

BUT: The tunnel will have an initial cost of . . .

NOT: Joe Blow is wonderfully well qualified for this position.

BUT: Joe Blow is exceptionally well qualified . . .

7. Pompousness or lack of simplicity often can cause ambiguity:

NOT: A goodly portion of the hundreds of young men who are affiliated with the automobile study functions of our clubs have requested that literature with concern of your training program should be filed in our reference libraries. Factitive to association with our accrescent clubs, most of the boys have thought very seriously of entering into some phase of the automotive industry as a means of life sustentation and luxury provision. (Do you really know what he's trying to say?)

BUT: Many of the young men interested in the automobile-study functions of our club would like to have in our libraries information about your training program. Most of them have thought seriously of working in some automobile plant.

NOT: Because managements negotiating committee had a very important story to relate to the Union, and inasmuch as the International Union was very apparently and obviously delaying approval of the local Union proposal, and finally because the existing contract was due to expire of June 30th, managements committee took the initiative and called the meeting. (54 words.)

BUT: The Management Committee called the meeting because it had an important story to tell the Union, because the International was obviously delaying the approval of the local's proposal, and because the existing contract was to expire on June 30. (Only 39 words.)

8. Muddled, fuzzy thinking leads inevitably to vagueness, ambiguity:

NOT: Mr. Hook, at the time of the accident was driving his car, a 1957 Ford sedan was reported by the police to be in a normal condition.

BUT: At the time of the accident, Mr. Hook, who was driving his 1957 Ford, was reported to have been in a normal condition.

NOT: If a good salesman does not receive recognition and promotion in his own company, competitors are aware of his ability and are slow to make him good offers.

BUT: . . . , competitors, who are aware of his ability, are not slow to make him good offers.

NOT: It is found that even in humans say which suffer with paralysis can regain the use of their injured areas if the stimuli is sufficient.

BUT: Even human beings who suffer paralysis can regain the use of the injured areas if the stimulus is sufficient.

NOT: The crate was lined with heavy waterproof paper, and three layers of heads placed between each layer. Usually these layers would contain 16, 20 or 25 heads corresponding to four, five or six dozen crate.

BUT: . . . , and three layers of heads were

placed between each layer. Usually these layers contained 16, 20, or 25 heads. (Even the student himself didn't know what he meant by "corresponding to four, five or six dozen crate"!)

NOT: The overdeveloped areas, are removing water at a rate that greatly exceeds the rate of replenishment. This is what leads to the salt water intrusion as these areas keep drilling deeper and deeper till they hit salt water. (This sounds as if they were intent on hitting salt water and kept drilling for it!)

BUT: The overdeveloped areas are removing . . . This leads to salt-water intrusion, for ranchers in these areas keep drilling deeper and deeper. Inevitably they hit salt water.

9. Inconsistency in wording can be confusing to your reader:

NOT: The 6 oz. and smaller potatoes are put into the ten-pound cellophane bags. The 10 lb. cellophane bags are put into a master paper container.

BUT: The 6 oz. and smaller potatoes are put into the 10-lb. cellophane bags, which in turn are put into master paper containers.

NOT: Four months ago my wife and I purchased a color General Electric TV from your store situated on 1301 Monterey Street. The set has been working very good in the last twelve months, but since two weeks ago we are having trouble with the picture. (Get what he's driving at? I don't!)

BUT: Four months ago my wife and I bought from your Monterey Street store a General Electric color TV, which has given us very good service. However, two weeks ago we started having trouble with the picture.

10. Ungramatical constructions are very likely to be vague and confusing:

NOT: The total delivery of water from the San Joaquin Division would be around 8,165,000 acre-feet per season to the San Joaquin Valley and the Central Coastal Area, and would also transport around 9,100,000 acre-feet to the Buena Vista Forebay.

BUT: The total delivery of water from the San Joaquin Division would be about 8,165,000 acre-feet per season to the San Joaquin Valley and the Central Coastal Area, and about 9,100,000 acre-feet to . . .

NOT: I work there till the present time.

BUT: I worked there until the present. Or: . . . until now.

NOT: The most important point in safety is never hold anything being drilled with the hands. (No foolin'!)

BUT: The most important point in safety is never to hold in your hands anything being drilled.

11. Illogical comparison is certain to be confusing and vague:

NOT: The wages the Braceros earn and take back to Mexico makes up the third largest source of income. (Of whom?)

BUT: The wages the Braceros earn and take back with them constitute Mexico's third largest source of income.

NOT: This study was made to determine how the hydraulic pruner costs compared with the pneumatic models. (You can't compare costs with models!)

BUT: This study was made to compare the cost of the hydraulic pruner with those of the pneumatic models.

NOT: As the years pass, I believe there will be a greater demand for all kinds of cooperatives, as well as in agriculture.

BUT: As the . . . all kinds of cooperatives, as well as agricultural.

12. Faulty reference of the pronoun usually causes vagueness:

NOT: Lettuce-packing machines were an attempt to bring some of the advantages of the packing shed to the field. They were popular for a brief period. When a law was passed prohibiting the use of Mexican Nationals on machines, they were forced to use a more costly source of labor. (What—the machines?)

BUT: Lettuce-packing machines . . . prohibiting the use of Mexican Nationals on machines, the packers were forced to use . . . (Sounds logical.)

NOT: To a supervisor trying to teach a female worker how to pound aluminum rivets: I'll position the rivet. When I nod my head, you hit it with this lead hammer. (She did! He went to the hospital!)

BUT: When I nod my head, you hit the rivet with this lead hammer. (Better? Right!)

NOT: Maximum size of a job on a platen press is about 5,000 copies. They are limited to a maximum sheet size of 12"x18". (What? the copies?)

BUT: A maximum of about 5,000 copies can be handled in one job on a platen press, which will print a sheet no larger than 12"x18".

13. An unwarranted shift in point of view is sure to be confusing, vague:

NOT: The principle of the rotary press allows printing with each revolution of the cylinder because there is no type bed. These presses can be run at high speeds with extremely fine register. The form of the rotary press consists of a curved plate which is mounted on a rotary press.

BUT: . . . This press can be run . . .

NOT: The use of the Multilith 1250 Duplicator has even spread to the commercial printer. They have found that . . .

BUT: . . . to the commercial printer, who has found that . . .

NOT: In selecting one's soldering paste, be sure to get one that is non-corrosive.

BUT: A non-corrosive soldering paste should be selected.

14. Vagueness is often caused by faulty word order in a sentence:

NOT: Eli Whitney did not gain fame or wealth from his cotton gin, but he did make a fortune by manufacturing rifles for the army that had interchangeable parts. (What kind of army would it be if it didn't!)

BUT: Eli Whitney did not gain . . . by manufacturing for the army rifles that had interchangeable parts. (Sounds much better, doesn't it?)

NOT: The Pipe Shop is provided with the necessary material and equipment to be able to repair any trouble that may happen quickly and accurately. (No foolin'!).

BUT: The Pipe Shop is . . . to repair quickly and accurately any trouble . . .

NOT: I am submitting the following report which describes the procedure followed in conducting a point usage test, for your approval.

BUT: For your approval, I am . . . a point-usage test.

NOT: In the case of magnetos, efficiency and successful operation are both determined by the quality of the magnets.

BUT: The quality of the magnets determines both the efficient and the successful operation of the magnetos.

NOT: The raw ingredients which are used in synthetic resin manufacture are all obtained from natural products.

BUT: All the raw ingredients used in the manufacture of synthetic resins are obtained from natural products.

15. Vagueness often results from misplaced modifiers:

NOT: the power truck multiplies the capacity of the workman who is pushing a hand truck by many times. (Poor fellow. He should get a horse!)

BUT: The power truck multiples by many times the capacity of . . .

NOT: The two lines show the difference in visibility, head room, foot room, and any other increase or decrease in dimensions at a glance. (Watch where you glance!)

BUT: The two lines show at a glance the difference in . . . (Better? Certainly!)

16. Dangling phrases are almost always vague:

NOT: When only six years old, my father took me to the zoo. (My, my! I don't believe it!)

BUT: When I was only six, my father took me to the zoo. (This I'll buy.)

NOT: The air is discharged by means of exhaust vents in the roof hatches after passing through the radiators. (Amazing! Unbelievable!)

BUT: After passing through the radiators, the air is discharged by means of exhaust vents in the roof hatches. (Sounds plausible, eh?)

17. Dangling thoughts lead inevitably to vagueness, confusion, ambiguity:

NOT: With exposure to light a chemical reaction results, which when fixed by washing gives a blue color.

BUT: When the paper is exposed to strong light, a chemical reaction results. Then when the paper is washed in water, the paper turns blue.

NOT: As the presiding officer of a meeting, it is well to keep in mind that you are not in the position of an instructor, a speaker, a director, or a boss.

BUT: You must keep in mind that when you are presiding at a meeting, you are not in the position of . . .

18. Illogical or awkward coordination is often confusing:

NOT: Most of the details can be figured from a print which is drawn to scale and various charts and printed material.

BUT: Most of the details can be figured out from a print drawn to scale and from various charts and printed material.

NOT: After the polishing operation is completed the temporary hinges are removed and put on in the body shop to facilitate handling of the body during various stages of its assembly, and they may be used over again.

BUT: After the polishing operation, the temporary hinges put on in the Body Shop to help handle the body during the various stages of assembly are removed so that they may be used again.

19. Stringy sentences frequently contribute to vagueness:

NOT: Last Thursday I visited the Cal Poly library and looked at several reports which had

SPECIAL PROBLEMS IN COMPOSITION

been written as partial requirement for this course and they greatly helped me to guide me as to the correct form that should be followed.

BUT: Last Thursday . . . reports written as partial fulfillment of this course. These reports helped me greatly to understand the proper form to be used.

NOT: Some of the dangers are spilled gasoline, oil, and other lubricants, along with poor light, dirty floors, and poor heating and ventilating systems which are very necessary to the workers health.

BUT: Some of the dangers are . . . systems, which are detrimental to the workers' health.

NOT: The tubes are inspected for cracks, and, if any of the tubes are cracked, they must be replaced as a cracked tube causes backfiring which may result in serious damage to the heater.

BUT: The tubes are inspected and any cracked one removed because they cause backfiring, which may result in serious damage to the heater.

20. Wordiness or excessive repetition can easily lead to ambiguity and confusion:

NOT: The tap must be run at a slow speed when tapping. (When else, pray?)

BUT: The tap must be run at a slow speed.

NOT: Because Department 124 does much original work and cannot have smooth regular work of a production line, the work is more costly than production work.

BUT: The work done in Department 124 is more costly because of the original work which cannot be done on a production line.

NOT: The South Coast is an extremely dry area and the need for imported water is great. An example that typifies this statement is the . . .

BUT: . . . An example is the . . .

NOT: It is because of the fact that heat is created or generated when gasses are compressed that there is no need of an ignition system for the operation of a diesel engine.

BUT: Because heat is created when gasses are compressed, there is no need of . . .

NOT: A cutter is selected which will produce the the radius which is specified for the part.

BUT: A cutter is selected to produce the radius specified for the part.

21. Vagueness is occasionally caused by faulty parallelism:

NOT: Posters should be printed to remind workers of the dangers of doing their work improperly, and also showing the correct and safest way of doing it.

BUT: Posters should be printed to remind . . . , and also to show the correct . . .

NOT: Boilers supply steam for heating the building and to the paint ovens.

BUT: Boilers supply steam for heating the building and the paint ovens.

NOT: The grinding cutter spindle must run free but the bearing fitting snug so as to eliminate end-play and chatter.

BUT: The grinding-cutter spindle must run free, but the bearing fitting must be snug so as to eliminate end play and chatter.

NOT: The toolhead may be turned at an angle by the loosening of two binding bolts, swiveling the head, and then the tightening of the bolts.

BUT: The toolhead may . . . angle by loosening two binding bolts, swiveling the head, and then tightening the bolts.

NOT: If the cut is shallow, the material soft, or a fine finish is desired, the fine-tooth cutter should be used.

BUT: If the cut is shallow and the material soft, or if a fine finish is needed, the . . .

NOT: Punches are held in punch holders by set screws, riveting, and by flanges on the shanks.

BUT: Punches . . . by set screws, rivets, and flanges on the shanks.

NOT: The work is either laid directly on the table or is rested on parallels.

BUT: The work is either laid directly on the table or rested on parallels.

22. Carelessness inevitably leads to vagueness and confusion:

NOT: This is a vasx network of conkuits, canals, an improvd river chanels which will covoy the waters if the State to areas of difency.

BUT: This is a vast network of conduits, canals, and improved river channels which will convey the waters of the state to areas of deficiency.

NOT: This makes it possible for all parts of the cortex to preform a habit, so that lesions of equal sizes produce equal loses of habit irrespectively of their locus.

BUT: This makes possible all parts of the cortex performing habitually so that lesions of equal size produce equal losses of habit irrespective of their locus.

23. Omission of necessary words inevitably results in vagueness:

NOT: The San Joaquin River Siphon will deliver the water developed in the North Coastal Area and the Upper Sacramento River Basin and deliver it to the Delta by the Sacramento West Side Canal.

BUT: ... and delivers it to the Delta ...

NOT: When packers were forced to use local labor on their machines instead of the far cheaper Mexican Nationals the industry back ground packing where cheaper source of labor could be legally employed.

BUT: ... the industry turned back to ground packing, where a cheaper ...

NOT: Two men are required to work on the carton assembly operation. Next two men pick up the cartons at the truck side ... (The same two men?)

BUT: ... Next two other men ... (Now I understand who does what.)

NOT: Patents have applied for on the process.

BUT: Patents have been applied for on the process.

NOT: The last operation is on another machine.

BUT: The last operation is done (performed) on another machine.

24. Sentence fragments or incomplete thoughts are assuredly vague and ambiguous:

NOT: More proof to back up this statement of Mexico being put under pressure to shut down the amount of Braceros. (Do you know what he means? I don't.)

BUT: More proof ... the number of Braceros is as follows: ... (? ? ? ?)

NOT: One of the oldest known foods. (What is?)

BUT: Corn is one of the oldest foods known to man.

NOT: Serving the people in the San Luis Obispo area. (Who or what is?)

BUT: This company is serving ...

NOT: The shakedown cruise being soon over.

BUT: The shakedown cruise was soon over.

NOT: To be able to give my children the gifts they want.

BUT: I hope to be able to give ...

25. A fragment cut off from its main sentence is called a "period fault" and is usually confusing as well as annoying to a reader:

NOT: When the bin tags show the parts to be of small number. The Purchasing Department orders more. Thus replacing the old ones.

BUT: When the bin tags show the number of parts to be below the minimum required, the Purchasing Department orders more, thus replenishing the stock.

NOT: Oils are reclaimed by one of two methods. Either by filtration or centrifuging.

BUT: Oils are reclaimed by one of two methods: filtering or centrifuging. Or: Oils are reclaimed by either filtering or centrifuging.

NOT: Dust collecting as it was first practiced was not dust collecting in the true sense of the word. But was accomplished by the use of a fan to blow the dust away from that particular operation.

BUT: (Just change the period to a comma and make "B" lower case.)

26. Comma faults—the error that the "top engineer" at GE complained about—can be very confusing:

NOT: Chromium can be deposited from a simple salt solution, such as chromium chloride or sulfate, however, such methods have never been practiced commercially.

BUT: Chromium can be deposited from a simple solution such as chromium chloride or sulphate; however, such ...

NOT: One type of snap gauge has two sets of points, the outer ones are set at the maximum dimension, and the inner ones are set at the minimum limit.

BUT: One type ... points: the outer ones are set at ....

NOT: The millwrights and pipefitters work throughout the shop, thus most of their tools must be portable.

BUT: Since the millwright ..., most of their tools ...

NOT: In the toolroom steel is treated by the use of heat, the heat is produced by electricity.

BUT: In the toolroom ... use of heat produced by electricity.

NOT: As I entered the Employment Office, I was met by a receptionist, she asked me if I had any references.

BUT: As I entered ... receptionist, who asked if I had any references.

NOT: The grindstone is practically a natural grinding wheel, it is a natural binding together of quartz with a bond of silica.

BUT: The grindstone, a natural grinding wheel, is a natural binding together of quartz with a bond of silica.

NOT: Light is one of mankind's most valuable assets, in fact, without it, man could not long inhabit this earth.

BUT: Without light, one of mankind's most valuable assets, man could not long inhabit this earth.

NOT: There are two operations where the form tool method can be put into practical use, they are in production work and in small taper work.

BUT: There are ... practical use: in production work and in ...

SPECIAL PROBLEMS IN COMPOSITION

NOT: The saddle is formed by the letter H, it rests on the ways.

BUT: The saddle formed by the letter H rests on the ways.

NOT: Approximately 80% of our leather is used for shoes, the rest is used for upholstery, luggage, belting, clothing, and sundry articles.

BUT: Approximately . . . for shoes, the rest being used for . . .

27. An even more confusing sentence occurs when two complete thoughts are fused or run together without the benefit of even a comma:

NOT: The valve springs are first removed then the valves are cleaned.

BUT: The valve springs are first removed; then the valves are cleaned. OR: After the valve springs are removed, the valves are cleaned. OR: The valve springs are first removed, after which the . . .

NOT: In internal grinding the work is held by chucks, faceplates, or fixtures the right one to use is usually determined by the job itself.

BUT: In internal grinding . . . or fixtures. The right one to use . . .

NOT: The atmosphere of the furnace is hydrogen this prevents oxidation of the tungsten.

BUT: The atmosphere . . . hydrogen, which prevents . . .

28. Incorrect punctuation or a lack of it often causes vagueness:

NOT: Testing the last operation is done on an ordinary bench. (Ever test an operation?)

BUT: Testing, the last operation, is done on . . .

MUCH BETTER: The last operation, testing, is done on . . .

NOT: However the casting is heated to a temperature below the melting point of the metal and then allowed to cool. (Sounds as if "In whatever manner . . .")

BUT: However, the casting is heated . . .

NOT: By 1912 2000 spark plugs were being turned out daily.

BUT: By 1912, 2,000 spark plugs were being turned out daily.

NOT: When burned wood resolves itself mostly into ammonia gas and carbon beads the residue.

BUT: When burned, wood resolves itself mostly into ammonia gas and carbon beads, the residue.

NOT: Die repair in Department 890 includes tearing down the die replacing worn parts realigning the die grinding and filing rough and battered surfaces and assembling and fitting the die together.

BUT: Die repair in Department 890 includes tearing down the die, replacing worn parts, realigning the die, grinding and filing rough and battered surfaces, and assembling and fitting the die together.

29. Incoherence is always vague, confusing, disconcerting:

NOT: Through the Marine Corps and as a civilian, I have nearly five years in Hawaii, Japan, and Southeast Asia. Talking to local farmers and viewing their farming situations, I have developed a great respect for American agriculture and a desire to help improve it still further.

BUT: (It is very difficult, if not impossible, for me to correct this incoherent shift from Asia to "local farmers," whoever they may be. This paragraph is extremely confusing and ambiguous.)

NOT: The Russians have been recognized as having done some early experimental work in this field [artificial insemination]. Today more than 60% of all dairy cows in Denmark are now being bred artificially.

BUT: (Here, again, it is difficult to see why this writer suddenly shifted from the Russians to Denmark. Obviously a transition is needed, such as: In addition, today more than . . .)

NOT: Bud Antle has developed a harvesting machine which uses the shrinkable film to wrap the individual heads of lettuce. The heads are cut, and all wrapped leaves are removed by the cutter-trimmers. In all other methods of field packing, four wrapper leaves are left on the head. Next the heads are handed to the wrappers, who wrap the lettuce in the film, seal the wrap on a hotplate, and put the wrapped heads in a shrink tunnel, where the film shrinks tightly around each head.

BUT: (The sentence beginning "In all other methods . . ." is obviously an interjection of something extraneous to the main thought of the paragraph. It is, actually, a footnote injected into the paragraph. For this reason this sentence should be put in parentheses to show a break in the main trend of the thought.)

30. Lack of a transitional word, phrase, or clause often causes ambiguity:

NOT: I was so successful in my job that the office manager offered me a better position with a wage increase if I would not return to school that fall. I felt one more year of college was more important and returned to Cal Poly.

BUT: (Use the transitional word "However," at the beginning of the second sentence, and insert the word "so" before the word "returned.")

NOT: Gutenberg did not invent the first movable type. The Koreans did. Gutenberg simply helped the printing industry along. The students at Cal Poly who are enrolled in Printing Engineering and Management are being trained to further the advancement of the most important industry, printing.

BUT: (Add the word "Now" as a transition between the ancient Koreans and Gutenberg, and present-day Cal Poly. In addition, add the word "also" between the parts of the verb "are being trained".)

NOT: I have completed courses in Zoology, Histology, Bacteriology, Chemistry, and Microtechnique. I have had experience typing reports and letters . . .

BUT: I have completed courses in zoology, histology, bacteriology, chemistry, and microtechnique. Also I have had . . . Or: I have also had . . .

31. The use of abbreviations that might not be clear to the reader should be avoided:

NOT: I am a member of the ABWA, the SAE, and the ASEE.

BUT: I am a member of the American Business Writing Association, the Society of Automotive Engineers, and the American Society of Electrical Engineers.

NOTE: If these names are to be used again, their abbreviations should be put in parentheses immediately after they have been written out. Then any succeeding reference may be with these abbreviations.

32. Sometimes the improper hyphenation of words at the end of lines can be confusing:

NOT: After diligently looking for several weeks he was able to buy a better than average used car.

BUT: After . . . to buy a better-than-average used car.

33. Failure to follow standard and accepted forms and writing procedures often causes ambiguity:

NOT: I have taken such courses as:

    Human Relations
    Personnel Administration
    Industrial Relations
    General Psychology

along with my regular Business curriculum courses.

BUT: Along with my regular business courses, I have taken human relations, personnel administration, industrial relations, and general psychology.

NOTE: Believe it or not, the following three-paragraph sentence is given exactly as it was written in a letter which I have in my files. No, the writer did NOT get the interview or the job—obviously!

                          4th December
                            1 9 5 4

TELEGRAM-TRIBUNE
San Luis Obispo
California

   *   Gentlemen:
              In reply to your advertisement for a
NEWSPAPER DISPLAY SALESMAN . .

The writer is now open to consider a new assignment and if the people in your vercinity can be taught to be—"Promotion minded" there is no reason whatever why the

30 YEARS EXPERIENCE IN NEWSPAPER DISPLAY ADVERTISING of the writer can not assist you in obtaining your objective, most of my training was received in New York City from the TIMES, HERALD, WORLD, TRIBUNE, SUN, PRESS, TELEGRAM, but since my return from Europe in 1950 I have been running my own Advertising Agency which has sure kept me very busy as I find by this time it is not a one-man propersition!

And his closing is equally bizarre:

                        . . . , my age is 49 years YOUNG which is better than 19 years OLD!

    With best wishes and compliments of the season, I remain dear Sirs

              Sincerely yours

Here is the opening paragraph of a subheading under the general heading, "Creating an Impression":

Creative

    (Science, engineering, architecture, publishing, art, music and related fields.) For offices engaged in the realm of ideas, a feeling of light, air and space will express the idea of freedom of thought, creativeness and overwhelming imagination. This is done with pale white or off-white walls, light floors, lightweight furniture, accented with dark woods, dark wood paneling and using things of contrast such as stone, brick, and interior planting.

NOTE: This completely floored me. Do you know what he was trying to do or say? Frankly, I don't. Therefore I can't offer a means of correcting this welter of words. In short, I'm really confused!

SPECIAL PROBLEMS IN COMPOSITION

34. Although you may write a complete sentence, sometimes the omission of some important words may create confusion, ambiguity, vagueness:

   NOT: I have made no progress since my last letter to you. (On what?)

   BUT: I have made no progress on my report, *Botulism,* since my last . . .

   NOT: I hope that soon a bolt of lightning will strike with an outstanding title. (Strike what? whom?)

   BUT: I hope that soon I'll come up with a satisfactory title for my report.

   NOT: Mr. Prewett of Hillcrest Fur was interviewed. (Why?)

   BUT: I interviewed Mr. Prewett of Hillcrest Fur Farm on raising chinchillas.

35. Unusual, odd, or illogical sentence constructions inevitably lead to vagueness:

   NOT: By being able to pick your own subject a report can be both informative and interesting.

   BUT: When you can pick your own report subject, your report can be both informative and interesting.

   NOT: If it passes the inspection it is inspected. (Obviously!)

   BUT: After it has been inspected, it is passed on to the shipping department. (Is this what he meant to say? Scratch me!)

   NOT: I appreciate your offer more than enough. (How's that? Come again.)

   BUT: I appreciate your offer very much.

   NOT: Thank you too much. (Wow! I could interpret this several ways, one not good.)

   BUT: Thank you very much.

   NOT: I feel you will be in a position to help me. (Keep your cotton-picking paws to yourself!)

   BUT: I believe you can help me.

   NOT: After a microscopic check, a microscopic check is used. (What for? Why use it twice? I really am confused. I don't know what to do with this jumble of nonsense.)

   NOT: Punctuation is a great helper to the sentence. (No foolin'!)

   BUT: Punctuation is a great help to the reader of of a sentence. (Now I get it.)

   NOT: Therefore, about 100% of reinforcing fabric is this area was being done by Local 790 shops, the remaining 80% by shops under different unions and with wage rates 20¢ per hour less than the existing 790 agreement. (That's what the man wrote, believe it or not!)

   BUT: (How can I correct this bit of illogicality without accurate facts and figures?)

36. Unidiomatic expressions can be confusing:

   NOT: By the enclosed data sheet you can see that . . .

   BUT: From the enclosed data sheet, you . . .

   NOT: Get rid of that greasy cream stuff and get with Vitalis.

   BUT: Get rid of that greasy cream and use Vitalis.

37. The use of non-technical language in a technical paper can often be ambiguous:

   NOT: This pathetic first shipment of lettuce was . . . (poor little lettuce!)

   BUT: This small first shipment of lettuce was the beginning of . . .

38. The use of too highly technical language without due consideration for your reader is bound to be confusing and annoying to him:

   NOT: Acetyl salicyclic acid of efficacious in alleviating the excruciating pains of sundry types of cranial pains.

   BUT: Aspirin is often helpful in curing certain types of headaches.

   NOT: The aridity of the season is deleterious to the crops.

   BUT: The crops are suffering from lack of water.

39. Failure to use enough words often causes vagueness:

   NOT: The depth of hardness varies with the time from .003 to .030 of an inch.

   BUT: The depth of hardness varies from 0.003" to 0.030", depending on the time the part is in the carburizing furnace.

40. Illogical subordination can often be ambiguous:

   NOT: I came to town when I bought a new part for my tractor.

   BUT: When I came to town, I bought a new part for my tractor.

   OR: When I needed a new part for my tractor, I had to come to town.

41. Failure to list or tabulate items can often be confusing to your reader:

   NOT: The procedure used in polishing a car body is very simple. There are just three steps needed to polish a car body. The first step is called the "first cut." This is cutting down of the paint until it is flattened out fairly well. The second step is called the "slush cut." This is the final polish operation in the sense of the word "polish." The third step is a buffing operation which brings out the shine in the paint.

   BUT: The three simple steps used in polishing a car body are as follows:

1. Cutting down the paint until it is fairly well flattened out;
2. Making the "slush cut," the final step in the actual polishing; and
3. Buffing the body to bring out the luster in the paint.

OR: The three simple steps . . . follow: 1. cutting down . . . ; 2. making the . . . ; and 3. buffing . . .

42. Short, choppy, jerky sentences are often confusing and annoying:

NOT: On September 29, 1913, Dr. Rudolph Diesel boarded the cross-channel steamer *Dresden* at Antwerp. It was a clear evening. The water was calm. He had many important papers with him. His health was excellent. He was at the height of his success. Diesel engines were being used more and more. They had made submarines possible. As far as is known, he strolled around the deck in the early evening. He then retired to his cabin. That was the last anyone ever saw of Rudolph Diesel.

BUT: On the clear, calm evening of September 29, 1913, Dr. Rudolph Diesel, who was carrying many important papers, boarded the cross-channel steamer *Dresden* at Antwerp. He was in excellent health and at the height of his career. Diesel engines, which had made submarines possible, were being used everywhere. As far as is known, Dr. Diesel strolled around the deck in the early evening before retiring to his cabin. That was the last anyone saw of him.

43. Failure to paragraph is sure to be annoying, as well as confusing:

NOT: Your letter of November 17 inquiring about the CG-5678 Condenser has been sent to me by Mr. Blain of the Blank Company for possible further attention. The CG-5678 Condenser is a 1000 volt condenser but it is not used directly with the TT-2 system but rather with the testing apparatus that is used in maintaining the system. We have no information available at the present time on the power equipment for the TT-2 but we will have an article in the Laboratories Magazine probably February 1962 covering it. There was a general article on the TT-2 system in the Testing Journal Part II for October which treats of the systems in general and gives some of the information on the power supply. You may have seen this but if not I could arrange to send you a copy. The forthcoming article in the Magazine will describe the various power supplies and auxiliary gas engine-driven generator. If you have any specific questions I could probably answer them for you at once.

BUT: Mr. Blain of the Blank Company has asked me to give you more complete answers to the questions in your recent letter.

The CG-5678 is a 1,000-volt condenser which is not used directly with the TT-2 system, but rather with the testing apparatus used in maintaining this system.

Although we have no available information on the power equipment for the TT-2, we will have an article in the LABORATORIES MAGAZINE, probably in the February, 1962, issue. This article will interest you, for it will describe the various power supplies and also the auxiliary gas-engine-driven generator.

Part II of the TESTING JOURNAL for October, 1961, carried an article on the TT-2 system, which it discussed in general and gave some information on the power supply. If you wish, we'll be glad to send you a copy of this article, Mr. Knesevich.

Whenever you have any specific questions, just drop me a line. I'll try to answer them promptly.

44. Conversely, too frequent (choppy) paragraphing can also be confusing and annoying:

NOT: If you have a tire give out anywhere within five miles of Tire Town, call 3157.

We have full conveniences, a complete store of tires, tubes and accessories.

We have established as a service station for Blank tires. We chose Blanks after several years experience because they prove to be tires that stand up best on our customers cars.

Our garage is the cleanest and most inviting place to leave your car you'll find in the country. It's fireproof, and roomy enough to turn in without danger of bumping.

When your tires need care, just drive up in front an blow your horn. Our men are always at your service.

We maintain a service station for Blank batteries and are equipped to do all kinds of battery overhauling.

Our repair men are experts in all kinds of automobile repairs. You'll find them just as familiar with your car as a doctor is with the ailments of your family.

Take advantage of our service. It will mean a saving to you.

BUT: If you need tire service within five miles of Tire Town, just call 3157. Tires, you know, *are* our business!

Here at Tire Town we are equipped to give you complete tire service from periodic inspections that often prevent tire failure to the installation of a complete set of new tires. Also we can recap or retread your worn tires so that you will get many thousands of miles of safe

SPECIAL PROBLEMS IN COMPOSITION

PAGE 73

driving at a minimum cost. No matter what your tires need, Mr. Roberts, our men are always at your service.

If you have tired tires, come in and re-tire with Blanks, the tires that we found gave our customers the best service for the least amount of money.

P.S. You'll be interested to know, Mr. Roberts, that we can offer you many other automotive services: battery check and overhaul, parking, and expert mechanical work—all at very reasonable prices.

45. Sometimes the use of the passive voice instead of the active can be confusing:
   NOT: The workman takes the request for repairs to the timekeeper, and here the time for the start of the repair is recorded.
   BUT: The workman takes . . . timekeeper, who records the time for . . .
   NOT: One will soon automatically raise or lower the chisel, as needed, and thus the knack of chipping is acquired.
   BUT: One will soon . . . , and thus acquire the knack of chipping.

46. Poor organization of your material inevitably causes vagueness, confusion, ambiguity, and annoyance. So . . . organize your material—that is, outline it—carefully. Time spent in organizing and outlining your material is time well spent, believe me.

47. Inconsistency in headings, capitalization, underlining, etc. can't help making your writing confusing to your reader. You may know what you mean, but your long-suffering reader won't. He's depending on you to do everything you can to guide him safely, swiftly through your maze of thoughts.

* * *

In literary or imaginative writing—and please don't think I have anything against that kind!—if you do not understand everything that Hemingway or Thurber or Faulkner or whoever might be writing has to say, you probably won't lose too much. Maybe the writer didn't quite understand what he was trying to say anyway. And what's the difference?

But in practical writing, reports, business letters, technical articles and manuals, theses, etc.—*the writer must know exactly what thoughts he wants to convey*—and he must get them across clearly, concisely, correctly.

John Dryden, the great 18th Century writer, once said. "The first duty of a writer is to be understood." How true that is today, when countless millions of words are written each month in technical articles, service manuals, reports, theses, business letters, etc.

Two centuries later another great Englishman had this to say: "You must write not so that you can be understood, but so that you can't possibly be misunderstood!" Thus wrote a man who studied to become a lighthouse engineer, but who through destiny became one of the world's greatest short-story writers, Robert Louis Stevenson.

Believe both Dryden and Stevenson. What they said has been, is now, and forever will continue to be true—in both practical as well as imaginative writing. Better advice has never been given. Better advice can never be given! The rest is strictly up to you! So . . .

ALWAYS BE CLEAR!

Awkwardness

"In the very large organization, whether it is the government, the large business corporation, or the Army, this ability to express oneself is perhaps the most important of all the skills a man can possess."

Peter Drucker

Awkward expressions are ones which are grammatically correct but not easily read and understood. An awkward expression cannot be read quickly and smoothly. You have to read it over and over to get the meaning. Try reading this sentence quickly:

I would appreciate it if you would let me know of a date when I may come in.

Now let's rewrite this awkward expression and see how it reads:

I would appreciate your letting me know when I may come in. OR: Will you please let me know when I may come in?

Awkwardness is hard to define grammatically or rhetorically because, usually, the sentence or expression is grammatically correct. But it still doesn't sound "right." Here are some other NOT—BUT examples of awkwardness:

NOT: I would be very grateful to you if you could arrange an interview for me soon.
BUT: May I have an interview soon? OR: . . . at your convenience?
NOT: Ink is forced through the openings in the stencil and is transferred to the sheet.
BUT: Ink forced through the openings in the stencil is transferred to the sheet.
NOT: The last part of a bridle is the chin strap. This can be made of almost anything and is used to keep the bit from sliding back and forth across the mouth.
BUT: The last part of the bridle, the chin strap, can be made of almost anything. It is used to keep the bit . . .
NOT: I am slow in progressing on my report entitled *Radioactivity*.

BUT: I am progressing slowly on my report, *Radioactivity*.
NOT: I am waiting for replies from . . . Until I receive these replies . . .
BUT: I am awaiting replies from . . . Until they come, progress . . .
NOT: These activities, being dull and routine, caused the membership to decline rapidly.
BUT: These dull and routine activities caused the membership to decline rapidly.
NOT: I have found several valuable references both in the college library and in my personal library from which I have gained much information.
BUT: I have gained much information from several valuable references located in both the college library and my own.
NOT: May I introduce you to my qualifications?
BUT: Here are my qualifications for this job.
NOT: For the trucks and cars on premises public liability and property damage is carried.
BUT: Public liability and property damage are carried for . . . on the premises.
NOT: I already have in my possession sufficient materials to . . .
BUT: I have sufficient material to . . .
NOT: My comb is about 8 inches long, made of nylon, and is pink in color.
BUT: My pink nylon comb is about 8" long.
NOT: The drivers and swampers are paid union wages which are listed below. A swamper is one who loads and unloads the trucks.
BUT: The drivers and swampers (who load and unload the trucks) are paid . . .
NOT: I was helped this weekend by Joe Blow. He spoke to me on the original of jazz.
BUT: This weekend Joe Blow gave me some good points on the origin of jazz.
NOT: Little progress was made due to exams and extra-curricular activities.
BUT: I made little progress because of exams and extra-curricular activities.
NOT: On either side of the cerebral cortex there are four lobes. These lobes are only anatomical designations. There is no actual separation between them.
BUT: On each side of the cerebral cortex are four lobes, which are only anatomical designations, for there is no actual separation between them.
NOT: My report has been coming along very well. It is on Agricultural Marketing . . .
BUT: My report, *Agricultural Marketing,* is coming along very well.
NOT: I am an ambitious 21-year-old. I am expecting to graduate in December of 1962.
BUT: I am 21 years old, ambitious, and will graduate in December, 1962.
NOT: A saturable reactor is basically an electrically controlled inductor. It consists of a magnetic core . . .

BUT: A saturable reactor, basically an electrically-controlled inductor, consists of . . .
NOT: This principal was first patented in 1907 and has been used many times.
BUT: This principle, first patented in 1907, has been used many times.
NOT: The Intertype Fotosetter, a cold-type machine, was developed over a decade ago. It composes type, by means of a camera mechanism, upon film.
BUT: The Intertype Fotosetter, a cold-type machine developed over a decade ago, composes type on film by means of a camera mechanism.
NOT: The Intertype mixer principle has also been adopted. The principle provides . . .
BUT: . . . been adopted to provide for the assembly and distribution of the matrices . . .
NOTE: Wherever possible—and it usually is—avoid using the awkward passive voice:
NOT: Last week new library material was consulted for my report . . .
BUT: Last week I consulted new library material for my report . . .
NOT: Satisfactory progress has been made toward the completion of the report for English 301. Bibliography cards have been made and preliminary research has been completed. No unsurmountable difficulties have been encountered thus far.
BUT: I have made satisfactory progress on my English 301 report, with all my bibliography cards and preliminary research completed. I've come across no insurmountable obstacles.
NOT: The topic that has been chosen for my report for your class in Report Writing is the organization and operations of a wholesale produce house. This produce house is located in the Los Angeles City Market.
BUT: For your class in report writing I have decided to write on the organization and operation of a wholesale produce house located in the Los Angeles City Market.
NOTE: Avoid also the awkward, illogical possessive when referring to inanimate things:
NOT: The metal's temperature was . . .
BUT: The temperature of the metal was . . .

Choppy, Stringy Sentences

Two types of sentences the technical writer should avoid are choppy sentences and stringy ones. Of course, no one can say just how long a good sentence should be. It should be long enough to do its job and no longer. If that is one word, fine. Use only one word. If it takes a hundred. O.K. Use a hundred. Now let's look at a few samples of each kind of sentence to avoid:

CHOPPY SENTENCES

NOT: The Carton Department is located in Plant

SPECIAL PROBLEMS IN COMPOSITION

Four. Its purpose is to put small service parts in suitable containers. These containers may be boxes, bags, paper tubing, or brown wrapping paper.

BUT: The purpose of the Carton Department located in Plant Four is to put small service parts in suitable containers: boxes, bags, paper tubing, or brown wrapping paper.

NOT: On September 29, 1913, Dr. Rudolph Diesel boarded the cross-channel steamer *Dresden* at Antwerp. It was a clear evening. The water was calm. He had many important papers with him. His health was excellent. He was at the height of his success. Diesel engines were being used more and more. They had made submarines possible. As far as is known, he strolled around the deck in the early evening. He then retired to his cabin. That was the last anyone saw of Rudolph Diesel.

BUT: On a clear, calm evening of September 29, 1913, Dr. Rudolph Diesel, who was carrying many important papers, boarded the cross channel steamer *Dresden* at Antwerp. He was in excellent health and at the height of his career. Diesel engines, which had made submarines possible, were being used everywhere. As far as is known, he strolled around the deck in the early evening before retiring to his cabin. That was the last anyone saw of Rudolph Diesel.

NOT: Orders originate in the Sales Department. They are checked there for price and then they are sent on to the Order Department.

BUT: Orders originate in the Sales Department, where they are checked for price before being sent on to the Order Department.

NOT: The procedure used in polishing a car body is very simple. There are just three steps needed to polish a car body. The first step is called the first cut. This is the cutting down of the paint until it is flattened out fairly well. The second step is called the slush cut. This is the final polish operation in the sense of the word polish. The third step is a buffing operation which brings out the shine in the paint.

BUT: The three simple steps used in polishing a car body are as follows: 1. cutting down the paint until it is fairly well flattened out; 2. making the slush cut, the final step in the actual polishing operation; and 3. buffing the body to bring out the luster in the paint.

STRINGY SENTENCES

NOT: Buying your own tools will give the student an opportunity to become familiar and used to his own tools and this is important to any trade worker as a trade requires speed and accuracy, and if you are not used to your own tools you are undoubtedly slower and then too is the fact that it gives the student a sense of ownership which builds up his pride and care of his tools is immediately improved.

BUT: Buying your own tools will give you an opportunity to become familiar with them. This is important, for to be good at a trade requires speed and accuracy. If you are not used to your own tools, you will be slow—and probably inaccurate. Also owning your own tools gives you a sense of pride of ownership, and you will certainly take better care of your own tools.

NOT: If a fellow didn't have to put a tool back he might lay it down and thus he stands a chance of getting it lost and also there is a chance that some one else may come along and pick it up.

BUT: If you don't put a tool back immediately, it might get lost or stolen.

NOT: Probably iron's scarcity and difficulty to produce and the demand for its use in tools and implements was the reason for its being valued even more than gold in antiquity.

BUT: In antiquity, iron was valued more than gold because iron was scarce, hard to produce, and useful in making tools and implements.

NOT: The demand for manufactured articles led the craftsman to seek new methods to increase daily production, and jigs, tools, and forms were invented, improved, further developed, and added to in order that metal goods could be produced faster, cheaper, and in greater volume.

BUT: The demand for manufactured articles led to new methods of production. Jigs, tools, and forms were invented, improved, and further developed so that goods could be produced faster and cheaper.

NOT: The conveyor helps move material forward continually and thus speeds up production and yet makes the work easier and faster for the worker.

BUT: The conveyor moves material continuously, speeds up production, and makes it easier for the workman.

NOT: Truck fenders are heavy and more work is done on them and therefore fewer truck fenders are turned out per hour.

BUT: Because truck fenders are heavy and more work is done on them, fewer are turned out each hour.

AWKWARD SENTENCES

NOT: I appreciate the many suggestions I have received from, and admire the high efficiency of, your department.

BUT: I appreciate the many suggestions I have received from the members of your highly efficient department.

NOT: The foreman is generally the person responsible for the necessary instructions in the use of the machinery to the newcomer.

BUT: The foreman is generally responsible for instructing the newcomer in the use of the machines.

NOT: If the curvature is not right, it is easily made right by a series of light blows with a hammer.

BUT: The curvature is easily corrected with a few light blows with a hammer.

NOT: Experiments such as these are what Edison performed.
BUT: Edison performed experiments like these.
NOT: Almost all machine shops of today are possessed of one or more turret lathe.
BUT: Almost every machine shop today has at least one turret lathe.

Parallel Construction

You know what parallel lines are in mechanical drawing and mathematics. Well, the same thing is true for parallel thoughts in writing: two or more—usually three—words, phrases, or clauses that are equal logically and grammatically. They are of equal importance logically—and they must be put in equal or the same grammatical forms. Here are some very commonly recognized examples of parallelism: (The parallel ideas are italicized.)

Life, liberty, and the *pursuit* of happiness.

Government *of the people, by the people,* and *for the people.*

Here are some examples of faulty parallelism with each one written correctly:

NOT: I'm looking forward *to our interview* and *working* for Bank of America.
BUT: I'm looking forward *to our interview* and *to working* for Bank of America.
NOT: The phrase may be used as *an adjective, adverb,* or *a noun.*
BUT: The phrase may be used as *an adjective, an adverb,* or *a noun.*
NOT: My job included *making the semi-monthly payrolls, preparation of monthly statements,* and *the preparation of quarterly reports on payrolls.*
BUT: My job included *making* the semi-monthly payrolls, *preparing* the monthly statements, and *preparing* the quarterly reports on payrolls.
NOT: Color can convey the wrong message; it can have a harmful effect on the morale; it can add to eye strain and fatigue, and can be quite displeasing. NOTE: this is also a good example of failure to use parallel punctuation.
BUT: Color can convey the wrong message, have a harmful effect on employee morale, add to eye strain and fatigue, and be quite displeasing.
NOT: I have made a few changes *where* it was impossible to get enough information or *that* the topic was, in my estimation, too complicated.
BUT: I have made a few changes *where* it was impossible to get enough information, or *where* the topic was too complicated.
NOT: The areas of water deficiency are also having floods which destroy *houses, roads,* and *erode soil.*
BUT: . . . which destroy houses and roads, and erode soil.
NOT: The superheterodyne receiver has been *decreased* in size, *increased* in efficiency, and *has been priced* within the means of almost everyone.
BUT: . . . *decreased* . . . , *increased* . . . , and *priced* within the means . . .
NOT: Knowledge of markets, knowledge of people who comprise the markets is a key to success. (False parallelism as well as disagreement of subject and verb.)
BUT: Knowledge of markets and knowledge of people . . . are the keys to success.

NOT: ONLY—BUT ALSO Parallelism:

NOT: This report will *not only deal* with the effect of soil moisture on the structure of the soil, *but will also deal* with the effect of lime on soil.
BUT: . . . *will not only deal with* . . . , *but also deal with* . . .
OR: will deal not only with . . . , but also with . . .
OR: will deal with not only the effect . . . , but also the effect of lime.
NOT: This condition would not only affect both California and the nation's food supply, but also our economy as well.
BUT: . . . would affect not only . . . , but also our economy.
NOT: *The ad must not only create* a desire for the product, *but it must also describe* in detail the product advertised.
BUT: The ad must *not only create* . . . , *but also describe* . . .

Parallelism in tabulation and listing:

Items in a listing or tabulation MUST BE PUT IN THE SAME GRAMMATICAL FORM!

NOT: 1. The composition of the soil.
2. That the force is a measure of consolidation rather than compaction.
3. That it helps characterize soil structure.
BUT: 1. The compaction of the soil.
2. The consolidation of the soil rather than the compaction.
3. The characterization of the soil structure.
NOT: To make good use of audio-visual materials, the teacher should do the following: (1) careful selection of visual aids, (2) teacher and class preparation of visual aids, (3) plan presentation of these materials, (4) follow-up and application of these materials, and (5) evaluation of the lesson and methods of use.
BUT: To make good use of audio-visual materials, the teacher should (1) carefully select these aids, (2) prepare them with the aid of the class, (3) plan the presentation carefully, (4) follow up and apply these materials, and (5) evaluate the lesson and methods of use.

Here's how parallelism in writing is similar to parallel lines in drawings:

SPECIAL PROBLEMS IN COMPOSITION

The Institute prepared a list of monographs—
- on individual agriculture products,
- on farm credit,
- on co-operatives,
- on marketing of selected commodities,
- on farm household management,
- on the rural exodus, and
- on rural hygiene.

This sentence could also have been written with the word "on" immediately after the word "monographs," and each word-phrase following then becomes the object of this preposition. This method would eliminate the awkward repetition of "on."

Proofread

There's a saying that if a thing is worth doing at all, it is worth doing well. That applies doubled and redoubled to report writing, with a slight variation: if a report is worth writing, it certainly is worth proofreading—CAREFULLY!

Here are some samples of student failure to proofread his paper:

A Platen Press is so designed that the form is placed in a vertical position in the bed of the press.

The automatic presses have feeder and delivery mechanisma that work with suckion to pick up and deliver the sheets of paper. These devises take the place of a pressman because of there speed.

Morale and the will to work are mysterious because their make up has not been scientifically seperated. There is, however a great more nown twent-five years ago.

Morale is defined as an attitude . . . which causes him to eagerly enter into the activities of the group with which he works. . . . If the morale of a personal is high it will usually be found that the willtowork is cooespondingly high.

This is a vast network of conkuits, canals, and improved river chanels which will convoy the waters if the State to areas of defficiencies.

This makes it possible for all parts of the cortex to participate equally in the learning to preform a habit, so that lesions of equal size produce equal loses of habit irrespectively of there locus.

Ther are two basic types of orgainzation in common use today . . .

This, unfortunately, is an exact reproduction of a paper one of my students handed in to me! Do you wonder why I marked it with an S.O.S. in a flag and stopped reading? Oh yes, the S.O.S. means "If I read the rest, it would be the Same, Only Sorrier!" Anyone—instructor, supervisor, executive, etc.—resents being asked to read something this poorly written.

You don't believe me? Let me quote again from Dwight Van Avery's "Why Study ENGLISH?"

"The top engineer is wound up. At the last meeting of our Association, representatives of all the major companies complained about the way their younger men were putting down their words —and futures—on paper."

When you write a report, paper, article, thesis, letter, etc., you don't know who will eventually read it. Maybe the top man on the totem pole will look at it. If he finds all kinds of stupid errors in grammar, spelling, punctuation, etc.; evidence of carelessness and indifference; lack of knowledge of the basic forms of correct writing—if he finds evidence of these things, you may be sure that his opinion of you as a potentially promotable person will drop drastically.

So if you're smart enough to get your degree in engineering, science, mathematics, or any of the other really tough majors, you certainly should be smart enough to realize and appreciate the importance of correct writing and speaking. After all, it's your language—and no matter where you go or what you do, you'll have to use it, day in and day out. So why not learn to use it to your advantage—correctly? After all, it's strictly up to you!

Say It Simply!

Simple English is no one's mother tongue. It has to be worked for.

Jacques Barzon

Technical writing is no place in which to show off your rhetoric. This kind of writing is concerned simply and solely with communicating accurately, correctly, concisely factual information. It is no place for so-called "purple" writing. So, say your piece simply, naturally, concisely and have done with it.

NOT: I have had previous experience affiliated with manual and semi-manual work.
BUT: I have done manual and semi-manual work.
NOT: The pace of expansion of material was retarded during the past week.
BUT: I didn't get much done last week.
NOT: I will endeavor to ascertain from Mr. Jones if someone in the department has the interest in and the information regarding the mountain lion.
BUT: I'll find out if someone in the department is interested in or knows anything about the mountain lion.
NOT: Regarding our discussion in your office, the subject matter of my report will include a presentation of economic conditions in Ghana as they may be related to future investments by North American Corporations.
BUT: My report will include the economic conditions in Ghana as they relate to future investments by North American corporations.

NOT: I wish to discuss with you the ways in which these drawings can be integrated with the report.
BUT: I want to see how these drawings can be used in my report.
NOT: I am sure you will take care of this matter with your usual competence and promptitude.
BUT: I'm sure you'll take care of this matter promptly and efficiently.
NOT: I am writing you concerning my report, *Selling Printing,* and the progress I have made concerning it.
BUT: Here's the progress I've made on my report, *Selling Printing.*

Yes, Say It Simply—BUT NOT CHILDISHLY!

NOT: Now that I have told you about the advantages of artificial insemination, I will tell you about the disadvantages of using it. There are only two of them but I think that they constitute the majority of the main ones.
BUT: Now that you know the advantages of using artificial insemination in breeding cattle, you should know the two main disadvantages of using it.
NOT: You wrote to Mr. Blow on the seventh to thank him for his books. And you very kindly invite him to visit you in San Luis Obispo.

Mr. Blow asks me to thank you for this invitation. But he feels he'll not be able to go. He gave your letter to Mr. Smith and me. The two of us are in the education business, in a way. We deal with training here in the company, and in the employment of your engineering graduates.

BUT: Mr. Blow has asked me to thank you for your enthusiastic comments about his books and for your invitation to see Cal Poly the next time he is in San Luis Obispo.

Although Mr. Blow will not be able to take advantage of your kind invitation to stop off, either Mr. Smith or I will try to see you on one of our trips. The two of us are primarily concerned with employee training and engineering recruitment. We would like very much to know more of the philosophy of education at Cal Poly, Mr. Riebel.

Word Order

The order of the words in an English sentence is usually a simple matter:
Subject + its modifiers, verb + its modifiers, complement + its modifiers.

Sometimes, however, we put a verb modifier—that is, an adverb—at the beginning, especially an adverb of time, as in this sentence:

> Last week, Ed Thompson and I made note cards and a rough outline for our report, *The European Economic Community.*

NOT: I purchased a radio from one of your dealers, Walker's Appliance, on March 2.
BUT: On March 2, I purchased . . .

NOT: Last year at this time I purchased an electric stove.
BUT: This time last year I purchased . . .
NOT: I will have more for you next Monday, Mr. Riebel.
BUT: Next Monday I will have more for you, Mr. Riebel.
NOTE: Always put the modifier as close as possible to the word it modifies:
NOT: This week I plan on finding more material in the Cal Poly Library that should add to the information already compiled for my report.
BUT: This week I plan to find in the Cal Poly Library more material that should add to the information I already have.
NOT: During the Easter holiday I was able to get information for my project, *The Psychological Effects of Color in the Business Office,* from my home town library.
BUT: During the Easter holiday I was able to get from my home-town library information for . . .
NOT: Little progress was made on my topic, What Is Juvenile Delinquency?, last week.
BUT: Last week I made little progress on my report, *What Is Juvenile Delinquency?*
NOT: Quantity and quality both improved in the next few years.
BUT: Both quantity and quality improved . . .
NOT: Some operators are successfully known to use their forefinger to clean up such areas on halftones instead of the red rubber.
BUT: Some operators can use their forefingers instead of the red rubber to clean up such areas on halftones.
NOT: In the *Los Angeles Times* of May 9, you advertised for . . .
BUT: In the May 9 *Los Angeles Times* you advertised for . . .
NOT: I, and many of his other students were inspired to . . .
BUT: Many of his other students and I were inspired to . . .
NOT: The National Civil Service League, in December of 1952, troubled by charges that government administration falls short of private industry in efficiency, decided to find out why and what measures could be taken to rectify any mistakes.
BUT: In December, 1952, The National Civil Service League, troubled by charges that government administration falls short of private industry in efficiency, decided . . .
NOT: Governments, in countries where they can afford it, have established . . .
BUT: In countries where they can afford it, governments have established . . .

One small word that is frequently misplaced in a sentence is "only." Part of the difficulty results from the fact that "only" can be used as either an adverb

SPECIAL PROBLEMS IN COMPOSITION

or an adjective. Here are five sentences each containing the same seven words. The only difference is in the position of "only." No two sentences mean exactly the same thing:

1. ONLY I offered to buy the horse. (No one else offered.)
2. I ONLY offered to buy the horse. (I didn't buy it—I merely offered to.)
3. I offered ONLY to buy the horse. (I didn't offer to take it home, feed it, ride it.)
4. I offered to buy ONLY the horse. (I didn't want the saddle, the wagon, the colt.)
5. I offered to buy the ONLY horse. (There was only one and I offered to buy it.)

Now look closely at each of the following "NOT" sentences and see why the word ONLY is out of place:

NOT: I have only talked to him once.
BUT: I talked to him ONLY once.
NOT: This report is only intended to give the basic operations . . .
BUT: This report is intended to give ONLY the basic operations . . .
NOT: These costs can only be reduced if . . .
BUT: These costs can be reduced ONLY if . . .
NOT: Today it is only recovered from the sea as a by-product.
BUT: Today it is recovered from the sea ONLY as a by-product.
NOT: Some foods can only be eaten on certain days.
BUT: Some foods can be eaten ONLY on certain days.
NOT: Veterans should only be given five year rights.
BUT: Veterans should be given ONLY five-year rights.
NOT: The operator only has to load the camera, press a button, and remove the picture.
BUT: The operator has ONLY to load . . .
NOT: It can only operate the power supply . . .
BUT: It can operate ONLY the power supply . . .

Watch also the position of the word "above":

NOT: I can be reached at the above address.
BUT: I can be reached at the address above.
NOT: The above definitions are shown in graphical form in Figure 2.
BUT: The definitions above are shown in . . .
NOT: I was able to purchase the above mentioned parts.
BUT: I was able to purchase the parts mentioned above. OR: . . . these parts . . .
NOT: Several models of each of the above mentioned tractors were studied.
BUT: . . . of each of the tractors mentioned above . . . OR: . . . of these tractors . . .

Watch the position of that little word "not." For example, the expression, "All is not gold that glitters" doesn't mean the same thing as "All that glitters is not gold." The first one means that nothing that glit-

PAGE 79

ters is gold. And this we know isn't true, for gold very definitely glitters in the sunlight.

Here's another sentence in which the word "not" is misplaced:

NOT: All our civil service laws were not enacted at one time, but piecemeal.
BUT: Not all our civil service laws were enacted at one time, but piecemeal.
NOT: I don't think it was right of him to not approve this purchase.
BUT: I think it was wrong of him not to approve this purchase.

Here are some more awkward word orders:

NOT: Student organizations, such as the IE Club can offer much to the individual, through group efforts, toward developing his own ability to take part in all levels of our democratic self-government.
BUT: Such student organizations as the IE Club can, through group efforts, offer . . .
NOT: The Executive Committee members must work harmoniously together . . .
BUT: . . . work together harmoniously . . .
NOT: The civil service, as opposed to the civil servant, is not and cannot, really be non-political.
BUT: . . . is not and cannot be really non-political.
NOT: Congress, until recently, has been miserly about financing training programs . . .
BUT: Until recently, Congress has been . . .
NOT: . . . by a method using some other cutting force than human effort.
BUT: . . . by a method using some cutting force other than . . .
NOT: There have been many commercially-built mechanical pruners in the last two decades, and these designs fall into two categories.
BUT: In the last two decades, there have been . . .
NOT: It may be used merely to implant a certain idea in the mind of the recipient which calls for no action . . .
BUT: It may be used . . . of the recipient a certain idea which calls for . . .
NOT: My report is mainly an attempt to examine how I might justify investing as I did to my father.
BUT: . . . how I might justify to my father investing . . .
NOT: I, unfortunately, as the victim of bureaucracy.
BUT: Unfortunately, I am . .
NOT: Salesmen, in many organizations, are given more training and cooperation than . . .
BUT: In many organizations, salesmen are given . . .
NOT: . . . an incentive for similar undertakings by IE Club members in the future.
BUT: . . . for similar undertakings by future IE Club members.
NOT: There was a time when I, upon examining the college catalog for the first time, was quite curious as to . . .
BUT: There was a time when, upon examining the college catalog for the first time, I . . .

Wordiness and Unnecessary Repetition

"Whenever you can shorten a sentence, do. And one always can. The best sentence? The shortest."
Gustave Flaubert

Every time you use unnecessary words or undue repetition, you tend to befuddle your reader and make him do extra work. So say what you have to as simply, naturally, concisely as possible without becoming curt or abrupt.

A. Don't use more words than necessary. In the following sentences, all unnecessary words have lines drawn through them:
   1. ~~Complying with your recent request at hand, you will find~~ attached is a copy of our ~~very latest, up-to-date~~ price list ~~for your perusal~~.
   2. I take taken many courses in ~~the field of~~ labor relations.
   3. ~~It is~~ this end ~~that~~ is threaded.
   4. This report is by no means complete ~~in every detail~~. OR: . . . is not complete.
   5. Whenever we may be of help ~~and assistance to you in any way whatsoever,~~ kindly do not hesitate one moment to write to us~~ immediately ~~and let us know what we may do for you,~~ Mr. Blow.

B. Often sentences beginning with "It is . . .", "There is . . .", "There are . . .", "They are . . .", etc. can be combined with the previous sentence:
   1. There are four lobes of the cerebral cortex on each side of the head. They are the temporal, occipital, frontal, and parietal lobes.
      Say: On each side of the head are the four lobes of the cerebral cortex: temporal, occipital, frontal, and parietal.
   2. The following final proposal on unresolved items was made by the Union. They were:
      Say: The Union made these final proposals on unresolved items:
   3. ~~There is~~ one other way that the farmer can beat organized labor ~~and that~~ is to move. (NOTE: The relative "that" may also be omitted.)
   4. ~~It was~~ during World War II ~~when~~ welding came into its own. (NOTE: The words "came into its own" are not technically proper for writing. Perhaps "really became important" would be better.)

C. Sometimes a writer is just verbose—a prodigal with words. He has plenty of them in his vocabulary, so he just spews them out on the page:

NOT: This coming week I plan to photograph the Shell Ammonia Plant in Ventura. Pictures of field applications will also be taken.

BUT: This week I plan to photograph the Shell Ammonia Plant in Ventura, as well as field applications.

NOT: Nitrogation has many distinct advantages over the generally used conventional methods of applying fertilizers. One of these advantages of applying fertilizers is the labor that is saved thereby. Whenever a farmer feels the need to irrigate a field, he will find it not much trouble to put a little ammonia into the water he uses for this purpose. This he can readily do by placing a tank near the irrigation system he is using and running a hose into the water to be used for irrigating.

BUT: Nitrogation offers many advantages over conventional methods of applying fertilizers. One is the labor saved. When a farmer has to irrigate, it is not much trouble to put a little ammonia into the the water by placing a tank near the irrigation system and running a hose into the water.

Sometimes we can combine two sentences into one to eliminate needless repetition:

NOT: Although radio receivers vary in size, color, shape, and price, their basic operations are the same. Most radio receivers that are designed for use in the home are technically known as superheterodyne receivers. Prior to the superheterodyne receiver, radio receivers were very crude and imperfect. One of the earliest, and perhaps the best known, was the crystal set. Although the crystal set was a functional receiver, it has many disadvantages. The major disadvantage was that of selectively. Crystal radios were capable of picking up only two or three stations.

BUT: Although radio receivers vary in size, color, shape, and price, their basic operations are the same. Most of them designed for home use are technically known as superheterodyne receivers, prior to which radio receivers were very crude and imperfect. One of the earliest and best known was the crystal set. Although a functional receiver, it had many disadvantages, chiefly that of selectivity. It was capable of picking up only two or three stations.

NOT: Today there are three concepts of color: the psychological concept of color, the physical concept of color, and the chemical concept of color.

BUT: Today there are three concepts of color: the physical, the chemical, and the psychological.

NOT: The bonded parts of the pruner are joined by the oxyacetylene method. This method of welding is used because of the varied thicknesses of the bonded parts.

BUT: The bonded parts of the pruner are joined by oxyacetylene welding because of their varied thicknesses.

NOT: The object that I have pulled out of my pocket is called a toothpick. The toothpick is made of white birch wood and is used for picking the teeth.

BUT: The object I removed from my pocket is a toothpick made of white birch.

SPECIAL PROBLEMS IN COMPOSITION

NOT: I have decided to change the topic of my report to California producer cooperatives. A Study of California Co-ops will be the title.

BUT: I have decided to change the title of my report to *A Study of California Co-ops.*

Avoid needless repetition within the sentence itself:

NOT: Before the first game of basketball was played, Naismith set down a list of 13 rules; twelve of these thirteen rules are still basic rules of the game.

BUT: Before the first game of basketball was played, Naismith formulated 13 rules, 12 of which are still basic to the game.

NOT: Two of the sources which I have found to be extremely informative are *Report to the Public on the Biological Effects of Atomic Radiation* by National Academy of Science, Washington, D.C., Committee on the Biological Effects of Atomic Radiation and *The Biological Effects of Atomic Radiation* by National Academy of Sciences. Washington, D.C.

BUT: Two very informative sources from the National Academy of Sciences, Washington, D.C., are *The Biological Effect of Atomic Radiation* and The Committee of the Biological Effects of Atomic Radiation's *Report on the Biological Effect of Atomic Radiation.*

Avoid undue repetition in tabulations:

NOT: Every industrial plant has to meet five types of cost:

    Plant construction costs
    Opertation labor costs
    Plant maintenance costs
    Raw material costs
    Power costs

Eliminate needless repetition of any kind:

NOT: The information you requested in your letter of January 22 is being sent to you and you should receive it within the next two days.

BUT: The information you requested January 22 should reach you within the next two days.

NOT: My mother has been ill for some time, and a few days ago she was taken to the hospital. I must stay at home and care for the family while my mother is in the hospital.

BUT: Mother has been ill for some time. A few days ago she went to the hospital. I must remain at home to take care of the family while she is away.

NOT: One farmer in Butte County reported that he cut his labor costs in half by the use of a machine to pick his peaches. This machine not only enabled him to cut his labor costs down to half but he also got his crop picked in less time.

BUT: A Butte County farmer reported that he picked his peaches by machine in less time and at half the cost.

NOT: We are fortunate that in this country we have almost unlimited opportunities to associate with those we wish. These opportunities would not exist if it were not for the fact that we have a democratic form of government.

BUT: Fortunately, in this country we can associate with whom we wish because of our democratic form of government.

Don't run on any one word:

NOT: I finally received all of the additional materials that I will need. Unless there are some extreme difficulties I will be able to meet your deadline easily.

BUT: I have received all of the additional material needed. Unless some extreme difficulties arise, I'll be able to meet your deadline.

NOT: I am submitting this report, The Main Uses of Corn in the United States, as partial fulfillment of the requirements for the successful completion of English 301, Report Writing.

The purpose of this report I am writing is to set forth the value and many uses of corn in the United States. This report covers the history, importance, and main uses of corn in the United States. This report excludes information on the production of corn.

I would like to thank Mr. Howard Rhodes and Mrs. William R. Troutner for their lecture notes in my topic of corn and its uses. I would also like to thank Mr. Clinton E. Wilcox for his assistance to me in putting together this report.

I sincerely hope that this report will prove informative to anyone who may read it.

BUT: I am submitting this report, *The Main Uses of Corn in the United States,* as partial fulfillment of the requirements in English 301.

The purpose of my report is to set forth the value and many uses of corn, including the importance, history, and main uses of this grain. Information on corn production is omitted.

Thanks are due to Mr. Howard Rhoads and Mr. William R. Troutner for their lecture notes, as well as to Mr. Clinton E. Wilcox for helping me put this report together.

I sincerely hope that this report will prove interesting and informative.

VOCABULARY

"The top engineer upstairs is on the telephone. He says to us: 'Right before my eyes is a fried report made out by one of our young engineers. I have to guess what the fellow is driving at. I'm no English shark, but I find myself getting a little angry when I see four sentences tied together with commas. He has principle *for* principal, *and he has also misspelled* accommodate *and* Cincinnati. *What if some of this fellow's bad sentences get in the hands of our customers?"*

— Dwight Van Avery

On every campus today, as well as in every office, industry, and business, there are four "gals" that all of us must constantly be on the lookout for: Mis-Spelling, Mis Pronunciation, Mis Understanding, and Mis Use.

Yes, that's a pretty corny way of bringing to your attention the fact that misspelling and mispronunciation almost inevitably lead to misunderstanding and misuse of words. But corny or not, it's true: if you mispronounce a word, you're almost sure to misspell it, and vice versa. And in either case, you will misunderstand its meaning and then misuse this word.

So why not get busy and learn to spell correctly the words in the following list? Remember what some anonymous personnel man once said: "Personnel people wonder what a student got out of his college education if it doesn't show in his English." And, believe it or not, spelling *is* a very important part of English!

Some Words Frequently Misspelled by Technical Writers

absence
accessible
accidentally
accommodate
accustom
ache
acidity
acquainted
acquired
acre
across
adaptation
address
adviser—advisor
aggression
aggressor
airplane—aeroplane
alcohol
allege
all ready
already
all right
although
amateur
analogous
analogy
analysis
analyze
anesthetic—anaesthetic
announcer
annual
answer
antecedent
antiknock
anxiety
apology
apparatus
apparent
appearances
appreciate
Arctic—Antarctic
argue
argument
aroused
article
ascertain
asinine
assassin
association

athlete
athletics
attacked
attendance
attendant
attorney
attractive
audience
autobiography
auxiliary

bachelor
balance
believe
benefited
bibliography
breath—breathe
brilliant
Britain (Great)
Briton (a Britisher)
bulldozer
bunker
bureau
bureaucracy
business

cafe—cafeteria
campus
captain
carburetor—carburettor
carpentry
carriage
casualties
ceiling
center
centigrade
challenger
champagne
chieftain
changeable
characteristic
cigaret—cigarette
coast
cocoa
coercion
collar
collegiate
color
column

combined
coming
commit—committee
comparative
compel—compelled
competitor
complaint
concede
conceive
conscience
   —conscientious
conservation
consistent
constitute
control—controlled
cooperative—
   co-operative—
   cooperation
corrugated
costume
courteous—courtesy
crept
curricular—curriculum
curtain
custom
cylinder—cylindrical

damned
deceive
decide—decision
defendant
deficient
definite—definition
deliver
dependent
descendant
describe—description
despair
develop—development
dexterous—dextrous
diagrammatic
diaphragm
dietitian
dilapidated
diphtheria
dirigible
disappearance
disappointment

disastrous
disciplinary
discretion
disgusted
dispatch
dissipate
distributor
disturbance
divert
divine
division
doctor
dominant
don't
dormitory
dry—drier—driest
dyeing
dying

echo—echoes
ecstasy—ecstasies
eligible—eligibility
electric
eliminated
embarrass
emphasize—emphatic
   —emphatically
encyclopedia
energetic
enforce
engraved
enjoy
environment
equipment—equipped
especially
esthetic—aesthetic
exaggerate
examine—examining
exceed—excessive
excel—excellence
except
exhausted
exhilarating
existence
expeditionary
extracurricular
extravagant
extremely
exuberance

PAGE 82

VOCABULARY

facile—facility
fallacy
familiar
fascination
February
fiery
financier
foggy
forehead
foreign
forfeit
forty-four
frantic—frantically
fulfill—fulfil
fundamental
furniture
futurity

gage—gauge
gelatine—gelatin
general—generally
ghost—ghostlike
grammar—grammatical
gray—grey
gruesome
guarantee
guardian—guard
guerrilla
guide—guidance

handicap—handicapped
hangar
harassed
heavy
height
heinous
highlights
hindrance
horizontal
huge
hurry—hurried
husbandry
hygiene
hypnosis—
  hypnotize—hypnotic
hypocrisy—hypocrite—
  hypocritical
hysterical

illiterate
illogical
imaginary—
  imagination
immediately
implement
impromptu—
  impromptus
inadequate
incessantly
incidentally
incredible—incredibly
independence
indictment
indispensable
initiation
inoculate
intellectual
intelligent
intern—interne
interview
interpretive
intersection
intolerance
inventer—inventor

investigate
irresistible
its—itself
it's—it is

judgment—judge

kidnap—kidnaped
  kidnapped
knowledge
knuckles

laboratory
ladle
legitimate
leisurely
levee
liable
liar
library—librarian
likable
linear
livelihood
loneliness
lunatic

mackerel
magazine
magnificent
maintain—maintenance
manageable
maneuver
manual
manufacturer
mean—meant
mediocre—mediocrity
miniature
misspell—misspelled
mold—mould
mortgage
motto—mottoes—mottos
mountainous
muscle
mysterious

naive
naphtha
necessary—necessarily
Negro—Negroes
neither
nickel
ninety-ninth
noticeable
notoriety

obedience—obey
obligated
obliged
obstacle
occasion—occasionally
occur—occurred—
  occurring
official
oily
omit—omitted—
  omission
oneself
opening
opportunity
optimism—optimistic
organization
origin—originally
outrageous
pay—paid—paying

pamphlet
parallel—paralleled
parameter
participate
particularly
passed—past—pastime
perimeter
permission—permissible
persevere—
  perseverance
persistent
perspiration
persuade—persuasion
Philippines
physician
piano—pianos
pickle
plague—plaguey
playwright
pneumatic
pneumonia
politics
possible—possibility
potato—potatoes
preparation
practical—
  practicability
practice
preceding—precede
preference
prejudice
prevalent—prevail
primitive
privilege
proceed—procedure
program
pronounce—
  pronunciation
propaganda
propeller
protein
provide—providing
psychology—psychotic
  psychoanalysis
publicly
pursue—pursuit

quality—qualitative
quantity—quantitative
quantum
quarantine
quarrel
quay
quiz—quizzes

realize
really
recent
receive—recipient
reclaim—reclamation
recognize—recognition
recommend
re-enter
refer—referred—
  reference
reforestation
regional
relevant
reliable—rely
religious
reminisce
rendezvous
repair
repel—repellent

repetition—repetitious
reservoir
resistance
reverent
restaurant
rhythmical
ridicule—ridiculous

sacrilegious
salary
sandwich
scandalous
scar
scare
scene—scenic
schedule
secretary—secretarial
seize
semester
senator
sensible—sensibility
separate
sergeant
severely—severity
sieve
significance
similar
sincerely—sincerity
siphon
sit—sitting
skeptical
slimy
sluggish
soluble
sophistication
sophomore
speak—speech
specifically
specimen—specimens
specter
spicy—spiciness
sponsor
staccato
story—storey
strength
stretched
structure
studying
subsidize—subsidy
subtle
succeed—success
suction
sulfur—sulphur
superintendent
supersede
suppose
suppress
surprise
susceptible
syllable
symbol
symmetry—
  symmetrical
system

tariff
technical
technique
temperamental
tentative
theater
thorough
though
thousandths

through
today
together
traffic—trafficking
tragedy—tragic
transferred
tremendously
truly
Tuesday
typewriter
typical

tyranny

undoubtedly
unprecedented
until—till
usually
utensil

vacuum
vegetables
vengeance

ventilate—ventilation
vertical
viewpoints
vigilance
villain
visible—visibility
vitamin—vitamine
volume

warfare—warring
weight—weighty

weird
woolen—woolly—wooly
write—writing—written
wrought

yield
you're
your

zoology—zoological

NOTE: There are some minor differences in spelling between the American system and that used in Great Britain, Canada, and other members of the British Commonwealth.

For instance, they spell center and theater "centre" and "theatre." Also they put an extra *u* in "odour," "honour," etc. These spellings, although not standard in the United States, are approved variants of our "odor" and "honor."

Since spelling seems to be a problem with quite a few people, here are some hints that may help you spell more correctly:

1. Most people do not misspell a great many words, but rather misspell a few words frequently.
2. Unfortunately, these few words are usually the most common ones and are used often.
3. It is difficult sometimes to tell if the error is one of spelling or of confusion between a similar-sounding or similarly spelled word.
4. One good way to correct misspelling is to copy down in a small, pocket-size notebook (preferably one that is alphabetized) each word you misspell—but copy the correct spelling!
5. That means you must use your dictionary, and everyone should have at least two dictionaries: a college-level one, such as *Webster's New Collegiate, The World Webster, American College Dictionary,* and *Desk Standard:* and also a small pocket-size dictionary that can be carried around easily.
6. If you are really sincere about learning how to spell correctly—and remember what the anonymous personnel man said: "I wonder what a man got out of his college education if it doesn't show in his English"—here is something else you can do:
   1. The first time you have to look up a word, put a dot out beside it in your dictionary:

   • **ex·trin·sic** \ek-'strin-zik, -'strin(t)-sik\ *adj* [F & LL; F *extrinsèque,* fr. LL *extrinsecus,* fr. L, adv., from without; akin to L *exter* outward and to L *sequi* to follow — more at EXTERIOR, SUE] **1 a** : not forming part of or belonging to a thing : EXTRANEOUS **b** : originating from or on the outside; *esp* : originating outside a part and acting upon the part as a whole **2** : EXTERNAL — **ex·trin·si·cal·ly** \-zi-k(ə-)lē, -si-\ *adv*
   syn EXTRINSIC, EXTRANEOUS, FOREIGN, ALIEN *shared meaning element* : external to a thing, its essential nature, or original character *ant* intrinsic

   2. The second time you look up the word, put a circle around the dot:

   ⊙ **ex·trin·sic** \ek-'strin-zik, -'strin(t)-sik\ *adj* [F & LL; F *extrinsèque,* fr. LL *extrinsecus,* fr. L, adv., from without; akin to L *exter* outward and to L *sequi* to follow — more at EXTERIOR, SUE] **1 a** : not forming part of or belonging to a thing : EXTRANEOUS **b** : originating from or on the outside; *esp* : originating outside a part and acting upon the part as a whole **2** : EXTERNAL — **ex·trin·si·cal·ly** \-zi-k(ə-)lē, -si-\ *adv*
   syn EXTRINSIC, EXTRANEOUS, FOREIGN, ALIEN *shared meaning element* : external to a thing, its essential nature, or original character *ant* intrinsic

   3. The third time you look up the word, put a BIG X through the dot—then GET BUSY AND LEARN TO SPELL THAT WORD. YOU'RE WASTING YOUR TIME LOOKING IT UP!

   ⊗ **ex·trin·sic** \ek-'strin-zik, -'strin(t)-sik\ *adj* [F & LL; F *extrinsèque,* fr. LL *extrinsecus,* fr. L, adv., from without; akin to L *exter* outward and to L *sequi* to follow — more at EXTERIOR, SUE] **1 a** : not forming part of or belonging to a thing : EXTRANEOUS **b** : originating from or on the outside; *esp* : originating outside a part and acting upon the part as a whole **2** : EXTERNAL — **ex·trin·si·cal·ly** \-zi-k(ə-)lē, -si-\ *adv*
   syn EXTRINSIC, EXTRANEOUS, FOREIGN, ALIEN *shared meaning element* : external to a thing, its essential nature, or original character *ant* intrinsic

By permission. From *Webster's New Collegiate Dictionary,* copyright 1961, by G. & C. Merriam Co., Publishers of the Merriam-Webster Dictionaries.

   7. The same scheme is useful in adding to your vocabulary. You can use a different color ink, if you wish, to distinguish between spelling and word building.

Prefixes and Suffixes Every Technical Writer Should Know

1. *Prefixes*—Inseparable:

   a, ab—away from: avert, avocation, abduct, abnormal

   ad, ap, at—to: adjoin, adhere, approach, appear, attract, attain

   ante—before: antedate, antecedent, anteroom

   anti—against, opposed to: anticlimax, antisocial

   co, col, com, con, cor—with, together,: co-exist, co-equal, collateral, colinear, commit, compete, compromise, connect, conduct, correspond

   counter—against, opposed: counteract, counterbalance, counterpart

   de—down, away from: decay, deduct, detour, declivity

   di, dif, dis—away from, not, apart: digest, dilate, dilute, diffuse, diffident, diffraction, disqualify, disapprove, disconnect

   e, ex—out, from: eject, erase, educate, emit, exhale, export, extract *in, im* (before *m* and *p*), *il*, (before *l*), *ir*, *un*—not: innumerable, inorganic, impure, impractical, illogical, illegal, irregular, irrational, unreal

un—not: untrue, unfair, unscrupulous, ungracious

in, im (before *b, m,* and *p*)—in: include, inspect, immerse, import, imprint, imbibe, imbed, immobile

inter—between: interlinear, international, interject

mis—wrongly, badly: misspell, miscalculate, mispronounce

non—not: nonconductor, nonsense, nonresident

per—through: perforate, percolate, percussion, perspire, perform

post—after, behind: postgraduate, postmortem, postpone

pre—before: preform, prearrange, preface, prepare, presuppose

pro—forward: propel, project, produce, protractor

re—again: reorganize, revive, reproduce, reprint, reconstruct

sub—under: subsoil, submarine, subtract, subtitle

trans—across, beyond: transcribe, transmit, transfer, transfuse

vice—instead of: vice-president, viceroy, vice versa, vice-chancellor

2. *Prefixes*—Separable: Many English or borrowed words may be used as prefixes to other words, as well as stand alone. Among the most common are these words:

after, as, at, by, extra, for, forth, in, off, on, out, over, through, to, under, up, with

3. *Suffixes*—Inseparable:

able, ible—capable of being, fit: reliable, honorable, marketable, advisable, avertible

acy, ance—state of being: accuracy, continuance

age—condition, collection of: marriage, foliage

al, eal, ial—relating to, that which: glacial, comical, paternal, historical, architectural, arboreal

an, ane, ean, ian—one who, relating to: Roman, humane, ruffian, protean

ance, ence—state of being: compliance, reliance, diligence, phosphorescence

ant, ent—one who, being: tenant, servant, communicant, dependent, correspondent

ar, er—relating to, like: circular, muscular, dodger

ary—relating to, one who, place where: missionary, infirmary

ate—one who, to make, having the quality of: licentiate, staminate, circulate, prevaricate

cle, cule, kin, ling—diminutive: particle, animacule, lambkin, duckling

eer, ier—one who: engineer, volunteer, gondolier, brigadier

en—to make: toughen, harden, soften, lengthen, deaden, fatten

ence—state of being, quality of: presence, permanence

er, or, ar—one who: robber, gardener, governor, actor, liar

ent—one who: student, equivalent, (See *ant*)

ess, stress—one who (female): goddess, sorceress, laundress, seamstress

ferous—bearing: coniferous

fy, ify—to make: solidity, liquefy, simplify, magnify

ible (see *able*)

ile—relating to, that which: mercantile, fragile

ion—act of, condition: repulsion, revulsion, condition, action

ise, ize—to make: fertilize, immunize, summarize, standardize, sterilize, chastise, disguise

ist—one who: scientist, physicist, chemist, machinist, pacifist, dramatist

ity—state or quality: timidity, liquidity

ive—one who: captive, native

ment—state of, state of being: improvement, adjustment, government, achievement

ness—state or condition: awareness, business, consciousness, happiness, darkness

or, er—one who: assessor, professor, adviser

ory—place where: dormitory, observatory, laboratory, depository

ose, ous—abounding in: glucose, cellulose, verbose, dubious, envious, superstitious

tude—condition, state of being: altitude, multitude, aptitude, gratitude

ure—act or state of, that which: departure, creature, feature

4. *Suffixes*—Separable: As with separable prefixes, many English or borrowed words may also be used as suffixes, as well as separate words:

craft, fare, fold, head, hood, less, man, ship, some, son, ward, wife, wright.

All English words consist of a root—a primitive word form as it existed before the addition of either a prefix or a suffix. If we were limited to root words only, our vocabularies would indeed be small. However, with the addition of prefixes and suffixes, singly or multiply, we can create as many as 650,000 words, some of which you will never even hear of—BUT quite a few of which you should know how to spell and use as well as you know your own name!

Additional Prefixes and Suffixes

5. *Greek Prefixes:*

a, an—no, not: aseptic, anarchy, anemia

amphi—(Latin *ambi*)— about, around, both: ambidextrous, amphitheater, ambiguity

ana—up, against: anatomy, Anabaptist, analysis, anagram

anti—(same as Latin *anti*)—against, opposed, opposite: antidote, antagonist

cata—down: cataclysmic, catalepsy, catapult

dia—through, across: diameter, dialogue, diaphragm

epi—up on: epidemic, epithet, epidermis, ephemeral

hyper—over, extremely: hypersensitive, hypercritical, hyperbola, hyperbole
hydro—water: hydrolysis, hydrogen, hydroplane, hydrometer
hypo—under, in smaller doses: hypodermic, hypoacidity, hypophosphate, hypoeutectic
meta—after, over: metaphysics, metaphor, metamorphosis, metatarsal
para—beside: paraphrase, paraphernalia, paragraph, parallel
peri—around, about: peripheral, periscope, peristyle, perimeter, perigee
pro—before: pronoun, prophet, proboscis, proposal, propellant
syn—together, with: synthesis, sympathy, synthetic, synopsis, syntax

Special prefixes every technical writer should know:
bi, bis, di—twice, doubly, two: biangular, biannual, bi monthly, bifurcate, discuit, bissextile, dichromate, diamine, diandrous, dicuspid
cent—one hundred: centimeter, centigram, centenarian
deca—ten: decagram, December, Decalogue, decapod
hepta—seven: heptahedron, heptameter, heptagon
hexa—six: hexagon, hexameter, hexane
kilo—one thousand: kilogram, kilometer
mil—one-thousandth: milliliter, milligram
mono, mon (before vowels)—alone, single, one: monologue, monolith, monomial, monotone, monastery, monogamy
nono—nine: nonogenarian, November
octo—eight: octogenarian, octopus, October
penta—five: pentagon, Pentatuch, pentameter
quadr—four: quadrangle, quadratic, quadrant, quadrille
sept—seven: Septennial, September
sex—six: sextet, sextant, sexagenarian, sextuplet
tetra—four: tetrachloride, tetrahedron, tetrameter, tetrasyllable, tetraspore
tri—three: triangle, tricycle, trichloride, triad, tricolor

6. *Greek suffixes:*
   itis—accute infection: bronchitis, appendicitis, pneomonitis
   osis—chronic infection: tuberculosis
   oid—in the shape of: rhomboid, ovoid, ellipsoid

7. *Italian suffixes:*
   esque—similar: picturesque, statuesque, picaresque

8. *Anglo-Saxon suffixes:*
   dom—state of: kingdom, boredom, dukedom
   ed—done: finished, walked, talked (All regular past tenses and past participles of the regular or weak verbs)
   en—like: oaken (adjective), brazen
   en—action: harden, stiffen, soften (verb)
   er—that does, one who: baker, tracer, worker
   er—more than: greater, lesser, larger, taller
   ery—place where: bakery, nursery, hatchery
   est—most: greatest, least, largest, tallest
   ful—fullness: grateful, hopeful, vengeful
   head—state of: Godhead, fatherhead
   hood—state of: motherhood, fatherhood, childhood, brotherhood
   ing—act of: singing, writing, doing (all present participles end in "ing")
   less—without: pitiless, merciless, priceless
   ly—like: brotherly, princely, kingly, fatherly
   ness—abstract state of: greatness, holiness
   scape—state of: landscape, seascape
   ship—state of: ownership, lordship
   some—characterized by: winsome, lonesome, handsome, fearsome
   ward, wards—in the direction of: toward, seaward, forward
   ways—in the manner of: sideways, lengthways, crossways
   wise—in the manner of: crosswise, lengthwise, edgewise, sidewise
   y—pertaining to: fussy, rainy, cranky

A Glossary of Words Frequently Confused

"After all, English is almost as important as math in our business, isn't it?"

"The engineer's answer is deliberately emphatic: 'Change the word almost *to* just, *and brother, you've said a mouthful! Tell them that English is important to them—and to us—because very soon their ability to read and to know and to remember what they have read and to speak and to write well, will make all the difference, whether they and we or some other company of their career choice will succeed together'."*

Dwight Van Avery

The first and most important commandment for the technical writer is BE CLEAR. This means that you must be accurate and choose the right word every time. Robert Louis Stevenson said that one should write not so that he can be understood, but that he cannot possibly be misunderstood. How true that is in this day of practical writing: technical, reports, papers, articles, theses, letters!

Here is a partial list of words that some technical writers confuse and misuse:

accept—to receive. Will you *accept* the added responsibility?
except—to exclude. The law will *except* no one, not even Judge Jones.
access—admittance, approach. We have *access* to all documents.
excess—more than enough; too much. Don't do anything to *excess*.
adapt—to make suitable. We will *adapt* the formula to fit our needs.
adept—proficient, skilled. He is *adept* at imitating others.

adopt—to accept, approve. We will *adopt* the name you suggested.

advice—a noun meaning "counsel." I am always glad to give you my *advice*.

advise—a verb meaning "to counsel." I cannot *advise* you what to do.

affect—a verb meaning "to influence." His action does not *affect* me.

effect—a noun meaning "result"; also a verb meaning "to make or create." What will be the *effect* of their actions? We must *effect* a compromise.

aggravate—means "to intensify a condition that already exists." It does not mean to irritate: Not: You *aggravate* me. But: you *irritate* me. Tearing off the bandage *aggravated* his wound.

irritate—means "to annoy." His action certainly *irritates* me.

agriculture—a noun.

agricultural—the adjective form of "agriculture."

among—used when referring to more than two. The three men divided the loot *among* themselves.

between—used when referring to two only: *Between* you and me, . . .

amount—used when referring to things in bulk: A great *amount* of money.

number—used when things can be counted. A *number* of dollars were spent.

Here both are used correctly: The *number* of injuries was great, but the *amount* of injury to any one person was light.

allusion—a reference to something. He constantly made pointed *allusions* to his noble ancestry.

illusion—a deceptive appearance. A mirage in the desert is just an optical *illusion*.

all together—means everything is together. The lost children were found *all together*, huddling in a shallow cave.

altogether—means entirely, wholly. The letter is *altogether* too long and wordy.

alright—there is no such word. The spelling should be *all right*.

all right—means everything is right or O.K. That's *all right* with me.

all ready—means that everything is ready. The children were *all ready* to go camping.

already—means that something has happened previously. They had *already* packed their gear.

angel—a mythical religious creature that flies through the air; a cherub. She is an *angel*.

angle—a geometric figure. A 30° *angle* . . .

accent—the increased force given when pronouncing certain syllables.

ascent—a climbing upwards, as of a mountain.

assent—an agreement or O.K.

bad—an adjective meaning ill, wicked, etc. I feel *bad* about that.

badly—the adverbial form meaning "poorly." Never say "I feel *badly*." This means you have a poor sense of touch. I feel *bad*. He limped *badly*.

balance—incorrect for "remainder" except in a bank *balance*. Say "rest" or "remainder."

remainder—what has been left over after something has been taken away.

berth—a place to sleep, as on a train or ship.

birth—the act of coming into life.

beside—a preposition meaning "at the side of, nearby, next to, etc."

besides—chiefly as adverb meaning "in addition to."

break—a verb meaning "to fracture," or a noun meaning "a fracture."

brake—a device for slowing down or stopping a mechanical device, such as a car.

bridal—pertaining to a bride or marriage.

bridle—a device for guiding and restraining horses.

bus—a large motor car for hauling passengers.

buses—the plural of "bus."

busses—kisses.

can—this word means you are able to do something; you have the strength to do it. I *can* do it.

may—this word means you have someone's permission to do it. *May* I go?

canvas—a rough, strong piece of cloth used to cover things exposed to the elements.

canvass—the act of soliciting or inquiring, as a city-wide *canvass* of voters.

choose—the present tense of the verb meaning "to select." *Choose* whichever book you want.

chose—the past tense of the same verb. Note the change in pronunciation, too. He *chose* to walk.

coarse—rough, crude, as in "coarse" salt.

course—a program of study, as in a "course" in practical writing.

complement—something which "completes" the meaning of something; a necessary adjunct.

compliment—praise.

conscience—that wee inner voice that tells you when you have done something wrong.

conscious—awareness, mentally awake, alive and aware of it. He was *conscious* of her beauty.

corps—a group that works as a unit. The Marine Corps.

corpse—a body after life (consciousness) has passed out of it.

councillor—one who gives advice or help, as a camp councillor.

counselor—a lawyer.

council—a group or assembly called to give advice.

consul—an officer of a foreign country who gives advice about his country: the French consul.

dairy—a place where milk cows are cared for and milked.

diary—a book in which a person writes periodic happenings. Her *diary* created a sensation.

deceased—dead.

diseased—infected with some kind of illness or sickness.

decent—conforming to the proper standards; free from immodesty or obscenity.

descend—a verb meaning "to climb down."
descent—the act of climbing down, as from a mountain.
desert—an arid place. The Anza *desert*.
desert—a verb meaning to abandon.
dessert—a delicacy usually eaten at the end of a meal.
die—to expire or give up life.
dye—to color (verb); a color (noun).
different from—the preferred form to indicate difference: John is *different from* Joe.
different than—not in good use anywhere. British often use "different to."
dining—the act of eating. The present participle of the verb "to dine."
dinning—a loud, unpleasant sound. The present participle of the verb "din."
dual—two, as in "dual" carburetors.
duel—to fight formally, as with swords or pistols.
due to—an adjective prepositional phrase which should never be used at the beginning of an independent clause except when saying: "Due to arrive at noon was the President."
because of—an adverbial compound preposition used to open independent clauses.
NOTE: Here are some good rules to remember:
  NEVER open a main clause with "due to" (except under the conditions previously given). ALWAYS use "because of":
  INCORRECT: *Due to* his illness, John was hospitalized.
  CORRECT: *Because of* his illness, John was hospitalized.
  INCORRECT: He was hit by a car and, due to this accident, he became an invalid.
  CORRECT: . . . and, because of this accident, . . .
  ALWAYS use "due to" under one of these two circumstances:
  1. Immediately after some form of the verb "to be": His illness is due to flu.
  2. Immediately after a noun which the adjective phrase modified: Illness due to flu can be serious.
employ—a verb meaning to hire. I'll *employ* him.
employee—a noun designating the person hired or employed. Every *employee* was loyal.
exceed—to surpass or go beyond. Do not *exceed* the speed limit.
accede—to give in to. The company *acceded* to the demands of the workers.
farther—to go beyond something which can actually be measured. The *farther* I walk, . . .
further—something additional in thought. The *further* they studied the matter, the more convinced they were that the plan would work.
fewer—refers to things that can be counted. I have *fewer* dollars today . . .
less—applies to amount, quantity, degree, value. I have *less* money today . . .
flier—one who flies, as an aviator.

flyer—a variant of "flier."
formally—in an established, customary, or conventional manner. She was dressed *formally*.
formerly—previously. *Formerly* he was chief of this bureau.
good—an adjective often interchangeable with "well," but not in "He writes good." He is *good*.
well—both an adjective and an adverb. He writes *well*.
healthful—conducive to health. *Healthful* foods.
healthy—in a state of health or vigor, as a *healthy* child, tree, situation, etc.
hoard—to store up, amass, conceal.
horde—a loosely organized group.
human—characteristic of people. DO NOT USE as a substitute for "human being."
humane—benevolent, sympathetic.
imply—what a writer or speaker suggests in his language. He *implied* that Joe was evil.
infer—what a reader or listener gets from these words. I *infer* that you mean he is evil.
ingenious—clever, skillful, dexterous.
ingenuous—artless, childlike, sincere, unreserved.
irrelevant—extraneous, not pertinent or applicable.
irreverent—disrespect for what is sacred or reverent.
its—the third person singular possessive personal pronoun. The dog wagged *its* tail.
it's—a contraction of *it* and *is*. *It's* a beautiful day.
later—the comparative form of the adverb "late." It's *later* than you think!
latter—the second of two things just mentioned. Often used with "the former," meaning "the first."
lead—the present tense of the verb meaning "to take away," as *Lead* the children out . . ."
lead—a metallic element, as in *lead* oxide.
led—the past tense of the verb "to lead": The teacher *led* the children away.
lightening—the act of lessening the burden by taking something away to make it less heavy.
lightning—electricity from the sky, especially during a thunderstorm.
lend—a verb meaning to give someone something temporarily. "*Lend* me your watch."
loan—a noun signifying what someone has given temporarily. His *loan* was due today.
loose—something not fastened down tight, as a "*loose*" board.
lose—a verb meaning to misplace something or get rid of it. Did you *lose* your watch?
mantel—the shelf above a fireplace, a beam, etc.
mantle—the cloak or sleeveless garment; something spread over something else.
metal—steel, iron, copper, aluminum, etc. are examples of metals.
mettle—a quality of disposition or temperament, especially as regards honor, etc.
minute—one-sixtieth of an hour; sixty seconds. Accent on first syllable: min′ute.

VOCABULARY

minute—very small. Accent on second syllable: mi-nute'. A *minute* amount of gold.

moral—an adjective meaning right, virtuous. NOT interchangeable with morale. A *moral* code.

morale—a noun meaning a mental state of confidence or hope, especially of a group. A problem of *morale*.

passed—the past tense and also the past participle of the verb "to pass." He *passed* me.

past—a noun meaning what has gone before. In the *past*, he passed everything in sight.

perform—a verb meaning "to do." He will *perform* that operation. NOT the same as "preform."

preform—a verb meaning "to do or make beforehand." The part is *preformed* when we get it.

personal—of or pertaining to a person; one's own. These are his *personal* belongings.

personnel—the collecive name of a body of employees. NOT the same as "personal."

plain—unadorned.

plane—flat, smooth as opposed to curved.

presence—the act, fact, or state of being present or there. Your *presence* is requested.

presents—gifts. Your *presents* are requested by the end of the week.

principal—an adjective (usually) meaning chief: His *principal* objection was to . . .

principle—a noun meaning a general truth. Avagadro's *principle* has now become a law.

probable—an adjective meaning likely to be or become true. The *probable* reason was.

probably—the adverbial form meaning the same. He *probably* went directly to the house.

quite—means "completely, entirely." Erroneously used to mean "somewhat" or "very." *Quite* dead.

quiet—means lack of noise, still. Deep in the cave it was *quite quiet*.

raise—a transitive verb meaning to lift or pick up. Will you *raise* your hands?

rise—an intransitive verb meaning to get up. *Rise* up and walk.

receipt—a written acknowledgement. Here is a *receipt* for your payment.

recipe—a formula used both in cooking and in medicine. The ℞ on a prescription means Recipe: "Take."

respectfully—full of respect for someone. The closing "Respectfully yours," should be used sparingly.

respectively—an adverb meaning as relating to each other. You, Jim, and I, *respectively*, . . .

scar—a mark left from an injury or operation.

scare—a verb meaning to frighten. Don't *scare* me.

shear—to cut off.

sheer—bright, shining; very thin, diaphanous, as *sheer* hosiery.

sight—a spectacular view; the ability to see. Colloquial for "odd," "ludicrous."

site—a location, as in "The *site* chosen presented a magnificent *sight*."

cite—a verb meaning to mention or bring forward as an authority. He *cited* Shakespeare.

sometime—an adverb (written solid) meaning at some unspecified time. Come *sometime*.

some time—in this usage, "some" is an adjective modifying "time." We'll have *some time!*

stationary—permanent, not movable.

stationery—writing paper used especially in business or personal correspondence.

statue—a monument or memorial to someone or something.

stature—height, often used figuratively. He was a man of considerable *stature* in his community.

statute—a law. The *statute* reads as follows: . . .

suit—a noun meaning a man's outer clothes; also a shortening of "lawsuit."

suite—a connected series of things, such as rooms in a hotel, etc. A *suite* of rooms.

than—an adverb of comparison. . . . taller *than* his sister. DO NOT CONFUSE WITH "THEN."

then—an adverb (conjunctive) of time. He stood up; *then* he began to walk slowly . . .

their—the third person plural possessive pronoun. The men waved *their* hats.

there—an adverb of place. Put it over *there*. NOT the same as "their."

they're—a contraction mean "they are." *They're* (they are) coming soon.

therefore—a conjunctive adverb meaning "for that reason." I was late; *therefore* I . . ."

therefor—an adverb with very limited use today. It means "for this, for it."

to—a preposition meaning primarily place, direction, etc. Go *to* town for me, Joe.

too—an abverb meaning also, likewise. I, *too*, will do it. NOT the same as "to."

two—an adjective (numeral) meaning a pair. *Two* things I want you to get for me: . . .

vice—evil in people; also used as a prefix to mean "one who takes the place of" as in vice president.

vise—a fixture for holding wood, metal, etc., while it is being worked on.

wait for—to await. I will *wait for* you at the corner of Marsh and Broad.

wait on—to serve. I shall *wait on* you next.

weather—the atmospheric phenomenon. Everybody talks about the weather, but . . .

whether—a conditional subordinate conjunction. I'll go *whether* you like it or not.

were—the past tense of the verb "to be." Sometimes confused with the adverb "where."

where—an adverb of place. The children *were* playing *where* their mother could see them.

while—during the time that. He died *while* he was asleep. DO NOT use when you mean "although."

although—means "notwithstanding." A conditional or concessional conjunction.

whose—the possessive form of the relative pronoun "who" or of the interrogative "who?"

who's—a contraction of "who is." *Who's* (who is) the mother of the child *whose* hat you found?

A Glossary of Incorrect Usage

". . . if someday your employer finds you wobbly in English, he will be critical of you, not some long-suffering teacher or parent."

Dwight Van Avery

alright—incorrect for all right.

and etc.—incorrect. "etc." alone is correct. Omit "and."

anxious—indicates anxiety and is not a synonym for "concerned" or "eager."

area, case, deal, field, character, nature, etc. — too often used loosely and unnecessarily, as in " I am studying in the field of electronics."

as—should be used to indicate simultaneous action, as in "As he entered the room, the lights burned out." Do not use as a synonym for "since" or "because."

at—unnecessary in such expressions as "Where is he at?"

being as, being as how—incorrect for "since," or "because" as in this sentence: "Being as how the Supreme Court ruled that . . ."

bunch—not to be used when referring to groups of people.

but that, but what—incorrect for that when implying doubt, as in "There is no doubt but that (but what) he is working too hard." Use "that."

can't help but—incorrect for "can't help—ing." Do not say: "I can't help but like him." Instead, say: "I can't help liking him."

can't hardly—a double negative and therefore incorrect in "I can't hardly see it." Instead, say: "I can hardly see it."

a combine—used colloquial for a group that performs together. Should not be used in formal reports, papers, or theses.

complected—incorrect for complectioned.

contact—a word often overworked. "Contact" is primarily a business word and should not be used in formal writing, only in colloquial and letter writing.

continue on—repetitious. The word "on" is unnecessary.

could of, might of—an illiterate corruption of "could have" or "might have."

couple—used loosely in the sense of two. This use is inadvisable in technical writing.

data—a plural often misused as the singular, which is datum. "Data are" is correct.

disregardless—no such form. It is used erroneously for *regardless*.

enthuse—incorrect for "enthusiasm."

equally as—redundant. Both words mean the same. Use only "equally."

expect—misused for "think," "suppose," "believe."

extra—not a synonym for "unusually."

fact (in the *fact* that)—circumlocution. Use "that" alone.

famed—instead, use "famous" or "well known."

feature—not in good use for "to give special prominence to."

fellow—colloquial for a "person."

figure—colloquial when meaning "amount," "price," "sum," or "to understand," "to make out."

fine—should be omitted entirely in most technical writing except when "sharp" is meant.

funny—means "comical," "laughable," NOT "odd," "queer," "unusual."

good and—colloquial as in "good and tired," etc. Avoid using. Instead, use "very," "exceedingly."

guess—colloquial for "believe," "think," "suppose," "expect." Use only when the evidence is slight.

heighth—incorrect spelling—and also pronunciation. Do not use the final "h."

hisself—no such form. Use the proper reflexive or intensifying forms: *myself, yourself, himself, herself, itself, ourselves, themselves*.

in back of—colloquial for "behind."

in regards to—unidiomatic. Use instead "in regard to" or "concerning."

individual—colloquial for "man," woman," "person."

inferior than—never right. Say either "inferior to" or "lower than."

inside of—colloquial when applied to time. Instead, say "within," "in less than," "before the end of." When referring to place, omit the "of."

irregardless—an incorrect and unacceptable form of "regardless."

kind of, sort of—crude and meaningless as an adverb, as in "He is kind of dull." Say: "rather," "somewhat."

kind of a—the "a" is unnecessary in "What kind of man is he?"

line—jargon sadly overworked for "branch of business," etc. Avoid.

loan (verb)—often misused for "lend." "Loan" is a noun. "Lend" is the verb form.

lot—much overworked for "much," "a great deal." Correct when used to refer to a collective group: "That lot brought the highest price."

lots of—colloquial and sadly overworked for "much," "many."

math—colloquial for "mathematics."

most—incorrect for "neatly" or for "more."

muchly—obsolete form of "much."

myself—an intensifying or reflexive form incorrectly used in "Joe and myself went." Instead, say "Joe and I went."

nowheres—vulgar form of "nowhere."

on—(as "on Sunday")—the "on" is unnecessary. He will arrive Sunday.

VOCABULARY

out of—incorrect in "out of doors." Say "outdoors."
over with—colloquial for "over."
party—slang or vulgar when referring to a "person" EXCEPT IN LEGAL DOCUMENTS, where its use is sanctioned, as in "party of the first part," etc.
phase—a variant of "faze," a colloquial expression meaning "disconcert," "perturb."
phenomena—the plural form of "phenomenon." A phenomenon is . . . The phenomena are . . .
phone (up)—colloquial for "telephone."
plan on—the "on" is unnecessary.
plenty—colloquial for "abundant" or "plentiful."
Prof.—Colloquial for Professor.
put across—along with "put in" and "put over," colloquial and to be avoided in formal writing.
quite—incorrect for "rather," "somewhat," "very."
re.—like "in re." a legal Latin phrase meaning "concerning." Should be avoided in modern letters and other forms of practical writing.
reason is because—illogical construction. NOT: The reason is because . . . BUT: The reason is that . . .
regards—correct only in the expression "as regards." Not in "in regards to." Say, instead, "in regard to."
said—in good, established legal usage as a synonym for "aforesaid" or "before mentioned," but not considered good technical usage.
same—often used incorrectly as a pronoun. We have your letter and are answering same. Instead, say "it."
should of—illiterate for "should have."
show up—colloquial for "appear" or "expose."
sign up—the "up" is unnecessary.
situated—often unnecessary, as in "He is situated in San Francisco." Omit "situated."
so—should not be used in formal writing because of its many uses, some inexact. "So" is a colloquial subordinate conjunction for the more exact "so that."
so as—correlative conjunctions correctly used in this sentence. "He left early so as to be there on time."
so . . . as—Used to show negative comparison. "He is not so tall as his brother." To show positive comparison, use, "as . . . as": He is as old as I.
somewheres—a variant of somewhere, but not in good formal usage.
sort of—correct in "this sort of experiment," or "these sorts of experiments."
sort of a—as in "kind of a," omit the "a".
state—quite formal for "say" or "tell" as in "Will you state what you want?"
such—colloquial when used as an intensifying adverb. "That is such a large screen." Omit "such."
suspicion—incorrect when used as a verb. The correct form is "suspect."
that—a relative pronoun which should not be used as an adverb. "That" always introduces restrictive clauses—ones that must not be punctuated with a comma. "The man that I saw was . . ."

that there—a vulgarism for "that"—omit the "there." The same is true of "This here."
these, this—demonstrative pronouns which should not be used without an accompanying noun. NOT: These are . . . or This is . . . BUT: These words are . . . This part is . . .
these kind—ungrammatical for "These kinds." The same is true for "These sort."
thusly—incorrect for "thus."
try and—unidiomatic for "try to."
unique—used incorrectly for "unusual," "rare," etc. Means "only one of a kind."
want for—colloquial for "need." "For" is unnecessary.
where at—the "at" is unnecessary.
and which—an illogical combination. Usually "which" is the word intended. Omit "and."
would of—like "could of," an illiterate expression for "would have."

Obviously, this list is incomplete; otherwise it would require more pages than are in this entire manual. In case of doubt, consult a good dictionary, preferably unabridged, or a good rhetoric textbook.

LETTER WRITING

1. 10 Pointers for Writing Letters That Get Results

The ability to write good letters is an essential part of every business person's equipment. Fortunately, this ability can be learned by study and practice.
　　　　　　　　　　Walter R. Bimson
　　　　　　　　　　Valley National Bank
　　　　　　　　　　Phoenix, Arizona

Here are 10 pointers that will help you write business letters that get results:

1. A letter takes the place of a personal visit. So . . .
2. Put yourself in your reader's place and then write the kind of letter you would like to receive—or the kind you wouldn't resent getting.
3. Think in terms of your reader, not in terms of yourself—in other words, don't get I-trouble or we-writis: use plenty of YOU-words.
4. Forget the tired words of the dear, dead past and use fresh words of everyday conversation.
5. Plan your letters before you start to write them, for business letters are expensive.
6. Get off to a flying start—end with a B-A-N-G!
7. Accentuate the positive—eliminate or at least soft-pedal the negative.
8. Put smiles into every letter you write.
9. A soft answer turneth away wrath.
10. Every letter IS a sales letter.

NEVER FORGET THE CUSTOMER-PUBLIC-HUMAN RELATIONS VALUE OF A GOOD LETTER!

Pointer No. 1: A Letter Takes the Place of a Personal Visit—

A business letter does by mail what you would do in person if time and money permitted. It actually is like paying a visit with your reader by mail.

O.K., what kind of "personal visit" does *this* letter make?

Dear Mr. Doe:

This will acknowledge your letter of Oct. 21st, and we note your request for a copy of Riebel's *How to Write SUCCESSFUL BUSINESS LETTERS in 15 Days* to be sent to Mr. John Dunn, Room 348, Cottage Hospital.

As we do not accept applications for accounts by mail, it will be necessary for you to arrange to call at our Credit Office to file your application in person. The only other alternative would be for us to send out this book to you C.O.D. and you might deliver it to Mr. Dunn yourself.

Should you wish to do this, kindly place your order through our Customer Shopping Service.

Trusting we may have the opportunity to serve you in the near future, we remain,

　　　　　　　　　Yours very truly,

　　　　　　　　　Division Credit Manager

Do you think that this is a pleasant personal visit with this division credit manager?
Let's analyze it and see why it is weak, ineffective, even insulting:

1. *It's cold, formal, unfriendly*—"This will acknowledge . . ." "we not your request . . ." "it will be necessary for you to arrange to call in person."
2. *It's negative, uncooperative, even insulting*—"As we do not accept applications for accounts by mail, . . ." "the only other alternative . . ." "we note your request . . ."
3. *It uses trite, old-fashioned, lifeless language*—the tired words of yesteryear: "Kindly place your order . . ." "Trusting we may have . . ." "we remain."
4. *It was written entirely from the company point of view with a "customer be damned" attitude.*
5. *It does not make the reader want to jump right up and open an account, the action desired.*

The question is this: Could this cranky letter have been written in such a way as to MAKE Doe want to come in and open his account? Definitely YES!

Dear Mr. Doe:

Thank you for your letter of October 21 requesting a copy of Riebel's *How to Write SUCCESSFUL BUSINESS LETTERS in 15 Days* to be sent to Mr. John Dunn, Room 348 Cottage Hospital. I'm glad to do this for you.

Since I know you're eager to have this book sent promptly, I'm asking our Customer Shopping Service to have one delivered tomorrow. And because we don't open charge accounts by mail, one of our drivers will stop by your office tomorrow and collect $5.15, the price of the book plus sales tax. O.K.?

The next time you're in town, Mr. Doe, won't you stop by our Credit Office? We'd like very much to open a charge account for you.

　　　　　　　　　Sincerely yours,

There you have a friendly, conversational, cooperative letter—one sure to win the prospective customer's confidence—and to get him to come in and open his account in person!

LETTER WRITING PAGE 93

Now let's analyze this version:
1. *It's warm, cordial, friendly, straightforward—*"Thank you for . . ." "I'm asking our Customer Shopping Service . . ."
2. *It's positive, cooperative, cheerful—*"Im glad to do this for you." "Since I know you're eager to have this book sent promptly . . ."
3. *It's written in modern, everyday, conversational language—*"I hope you won't mind." ". . . won't you stop by our Credit Office . . ."
4. *It's entirely from the reader's point of view.* Here the reader is KING!
5. *It makes the reader want to come in and open his account so that he can do business with such normal, friendly, cooperative people.*

Note that the revision does not give the reader anything the original refused him.

How's this for a nice, friendly visit with the president of a great company—Mr. W. B. Carpenter, formerly President of DuPont—who takes the time and trouble to welcome a new stockholder. . . .

Mrs. Leona Williston
Bay City, Michigan
Dear Mrs. Williston:

It is a pleasure to welcome you as a stockholder of this company.

Naturally you will be interested in the Company's condition and progress, and in order to keep you informed, quarterly statements of earnings and semi-annual statements of the Company's financial condition will be mailed to you. You will also receive, periodically, letters outlining important activities of the Company.

Your Company's principal activities and products are listed on the following pages of this letter. Its diversified line of products for individual use is described in the enclosed booklet, "Made by du Pont."

The stockholder is not under obligation either to use or to sell his Company's products. It is natural nevertheless for the management to hope that the stockholder, as a partner in the enterprise, will find its products to his liking, that he will wish to buy them for his own use on their merits, and that by example and by appropriate suggestion, he will have opportunity to interest others in their use.

It is inevitable that the cumulative effect of your use of the Company's products and your constructive interest in their use by others will have an appreciable and gratifying effect on its total sales volume with correspondingly favorable effect on the Company's earnings. As a stockholder partner, you will enjoy your proportionate share of benefits accruing from improvement in the Company's prosperity.

Any inquiries or suggestions you may care to make, addressed to the Stockholders' Relations Division, will be given careful attention.

Very truly yours,

Or how about this one for a delightful personal visit with a man I had never met?

TORGESEN
&
CUTCLIFFE
incorporated

31
sixteenth street, n.w.
atlanta 9
georgia
elgin 2609

Mr. John P. Riebel
California State Polytechnic College
San Luis Obispo, California
April 3, 1956

Dear Mr. Riebel:

It was with a great deal of pleasure that I read your letter asking for our folder of 200 sales techniques. You are very welcome to several copies. This folder was designed to be of assistance to those who received it, and if it finds a place in the teaching of your courses, that would indeed be a compliment.

Your name reminded me of the fine book on letter writing which I read while associated with Gladwin Plastics. The effect that this book had on my own letter writing I leave up to you.

Atlanta is reaching the peak of its Springtime beauty right now. As often as one sees this phenomenon of color in pink and white dogwood, red quince, brilliant azaleas, lavender-tinted redbud trees and fresh, green grass, the magic never dulls. It's like a picture of fairyland!

And your erstwhile school, Georgia Tech, has grown beyond recognition. The new sports arena now being built, and the already famous library are really wonders of modern architecture.

I hope you will come back, and when you do, drop in to see us.

Sincerely yours

TORGESEN & CUTCLIFFE, INC.

Harald J. Torgesen

HJT/de

(Typed on executive letterheads—7¼"x10½"—NOMA Simplified form.)

How did you like that delightful personal visit with Mr. Shippam of Douglas in the "Foreword?"

Pointer No. 2: Put Yourself in Your Reader's Place . . .

Since a letter really does take the place of a personal visit, just put yourself in your reader's place. Then write the kind of letter you would like to receive—or at least the kind you wouldn't resent.

How would you like to receive the original letter from that division credit manager? I didn't either—it was addressed to me some 15 years ago. I've never forgotten it—and I never will. I hope you don't either. So when you write letters . . .

Pointer No. 3: Think in Terms of Your Reader—Not of Yourself

When you think of your reader first, you don't catch I-trouble—or we-writis, either.

Although the following letter is friendly, sincere, and helpful, it suffers badly from I-trouble. Each paragraph begins with I; six out of seven sentences begin with I, and there are 15 I-words out of 138—over ten percent. There are only eight YOU-words!

> I am very glad to hear from you and to have your kind reassurance that you will be able to make use of the copies of the September issue of *Blank's Magazine* that I recently sent you.
>
> I am returning your exercises enclosed, and I can sincerely assure you that I am profoundly impressed with them. I wish I knew a publisher who might be interested in doing the sort of workbook which you outlined. I have asked one of our editors who has been with a textbook publishing house, but he could suggest no publisher to ME. I can't help thinking that the *Reader's Digest* might be interested, but I do not know.
>
> I shall be wishing you every success in your project. Please call on ME at any time I can be of assistance to you.

Note how easy it is to rewrite the letters from the YOU point of view:

> Thank YOU for YOUR assurance that YOU will be able to make good use of the copies of the September issue of *Blank's Magazine* recently sent YOU.
>
> YOUR exercises, which are enclosed, really interest me, Mr. Jones. Some publisher would probably be glad to publish the sort of workbook YOU outlined. Unfortunately, neither I nor any one of our editors to whom I spoke about YOUR work knows of any. Perhaps YOU might try the *Reader's Digest*.
>
> May YOU have every success with YOUR project! Please call on me at any time that I can be of help to YOU.

Each paragraph begins with a big YOU, as well as five of the seven sentences. There are eleven YOU-words plus one use of the reader's name in the body of the letter. There are only six I-words in the 99-word revision—39 fewer words than in the original.

The following letter suffers from acute We-writis:

> *We* thank you for your recent inquiry about *our* product and *we* are pleased to send herewith the information requested. *We* trust it will be helpful.

> *Our* building materials are sold by *our* dealers throughout the country. *We* are taking the liberty of notifying *our* nearest dealer of your interest in *our* products.

Revised from the YOU point of view:

> Thank *you* for *your* inquiry about (trade name) products. It is a pleasure to send *you* the information *you* requested. May it be useful to *you* in *your* work.
>
> (Tradename) building materials are sold by (trade-name) dealers throughout the country. Within a few days *you* will hear from Mr. Sam Jones, Manager of the Fresno office. Mr. Jones will be delighted to give *you* whatever additional information *you* may need, Mr. Schrick.

Pointer No. 4: Forget the Tired Words of the Dear, Dead Past . . .

Letters, like people, can have personality, too. You don't believe me? Here's a letter that's completely devoid of personality:

> We beg to thank you for your kind letter of recent date and for the information contained therein. In accordance with your valued wishes, we beg to state your kind order will be shipped at our very earliest convenience.
>
> Thanking you in advance for your valued patronage and hoping to serve you in the very near future, we beg to remain,

That's "rubber stamp" talk—written with a batch of rubber stamps!

> beg to thank you
> your kind letter
> of recent date
> contained therein
> in accordance with
> your valued wishes
> we beg to state
> our very earliest convenience
> thanking you in advance
> your valued patronage
> hoping to serve you
> in the very near future
> we beg to remain

Here's how a good shot of personality could improve this letter and make it sound as if it had been written by a human being, not a robot:

> Thanks for your letter of May 5 and for the information you sent. You will be glad to know that your order will be shipped within a week.
>
> Your orders are always very much appreciated, Mr. Doe.

Let's see why the rewrite is so much better than the original:

1. It's much shorter—37 words *vs.* 61 in the original—a saving of 24 words.

2. It's written entirely from the reader's point of view: five YOU-words and one important use of the reader's name—at the end of the letter, where it counts.
3. It's modern, conversational language—not a sign of rubber-stamp lingo here.
4. It has PERSONALITY—that is, it sounds as if it had been written by a real human being, not a mechanical man.

People just don't talk to each other that way, do they? Of course not. Now let's look at a little farce that Kermit Rolland, formerly of New York Life Insurance Company, wrote. It's entitled—

If We Talked the Way We Write Letters—

Customer: (walking up to counter) Package of cigarettes, please.
Clerk: Your favor received and order duly acknowledged.
Customer: (blankly) Huh?
Clerk: In reply beg to state your request is receiving our immediate attention.
Customer: (with growing bewilderment) What's going on around here?
Clerk: Re product mentioned above, beg to state same is packaged under various different and sundry trade names. If you will be so good as to kindly inform us, at your very earliest convenience, name of brand you contemplate purchasing . . .
Customer: (names his brand)
Clerk: We take pleasure in advising that upon receipt of your remittance in the amount of twenty-five cents, we will forward to you promptly and immediately said merchandise mentioned above.
Customer: (lays a quarter on the counter.)
Clerk: Full requirements having been received, we are pleased to forward at once said merchandise requested by you, and in accepting, with deepest appreciation, your remittance for same.
Customer: (gingerly picks up his package of cigarettes and edges uneasily toward the door.)
Clerk: In conclusion, permit me to say that it is our sincere hope and trust that you will again favor us with your patronage in the near future. (By this time the flabbergasted customer has flown. He's probably looking for the little men in white jackets!) May we also take this occasion to express our deepest appreciation for your kind consideration. We are, dear sir, very truly yours . . .

Absurd, isn't it? And so is this kind of stilted, unnatural, antiquated, old-fashioned, moss-covered, moth-eaten language used in so many of our letters today. You don't believe me? Then just take a long look at a dozen letters you have received recently—or at some you have dictated yourself—and see how modern *your* business letter language really is! Remember—there is no language of business-letter writing other than the conversational language of modern, up-to-date telephone talk.

Here is a good breakdown on the eight major categories of TIRED WORDS:

Tired Words vs. Strong Words

1. *Vague Words:*

NOT: At your earliest convenience, by return mail
BUT: promptly, immediately, at once, within five days, soon, by May 4. (Be specific!)

NOT: of recent date
BUT: of December 31

NOT: We will initiate your shipment soon.
BUT: Your order will be shipped next week.

NOT: I feel you . . .
BUT: I think you . . .

2. *Inaccurate Words:*

NOT: Enclosed please find
BUT: Enclosed is . . . attached is . . .

NOT: Your kind order at hand
BUT: Thanks for your nice order.

NOT: Thank you kindly for your patronage
BUT: Thanks for your order. It's a pleasure to get an order from you.

NOT: We are not in a position to
BUT: We can't

NOT: We take pleasure in
BUT: We are glad to . . . It is a pleasure to . . .

NOT: A self-addressed envelope is enclosed
BUT: The enclosed envelope is for your reply.

3. *Snooty, Supercilious Words:*

NOT: Your letter at hand and contents noted.
BUT: Thanks for your letter of October 1.

NOT: In due course of time
BUT: As soon as we can . . . promptly

NOT: the undersigned; the writer; yours truly
BUT: I or me, whichever the case may be.

NOT: Kindly sign
BUT: Please sign

NOT: with your kind permission
BUT: If I may . . . with your permission

NOT: We trust same is satisfactory
BUT: We hope you will be pleased. We hope this is O.K.

4. *Trite, Hackneyed, Overworked Words:*

NOT: The above mentioned order, parts
BUT: The parts, orders mentioned above . . . these parts, orders

NOT: Aforementioned, aforesaid, herein, hereto, herewith, said
BUT: OMIT. Use only in legal documents, not in letters.

NOT: A party is interested in buying.
BUT: A prospective buyer is interested in.

5. Wordy, Windy Words:

NOT: Inasmuch as
BUT: because . . . since

NOT: at all times
BUT: Always

NOT: relative to
BUT: about

NOT: at this time . . . at the present time . . . at the present writing
BUT: now

NOT: costs the sum of
BUT: costs

NOT: consensus of opinion
BUT: consensus

NOT: first of all
BUT: first

DOUBLING: The requisite steel necessary . . . conclude and end . . . cognizant and aware . . . prime urgency . . . six of one and half a dozen of the other . . . first and foremost . . . sincere and earnest . . . refuse and decline . . . unjust and unfair . . . demand and insist . . . obligation or responsibilities . . . immediately and at once.

6. Cold, Unfriendly Words:

NOT: This will acknowledge your request
BUT: Thanks for your request.

NOT: Your complaint has been received.
BUT: We are sorry to know that . . .

NOT: Kindly acknowledge
BUT: Please let me hear from you.

NOT: Attached hereto kindly find literature covering our pumps.
BUT: Here is the information you wanted about our pumps.

NOT: We have received your inquiry.
BUT: Thanks for your inquiry.

7. Pompous, Bloated, Oratorical Words:

NOT: Kindly be good enough to send me . . .
BUT: Please send me

NOT: Your esteemed communication at hand.
BUT: Thanks for your nice/welcome letter.

NOT: For your perusal
BUT: For you to read

NOT: Pursuant to yours of the 20th
BUT: In reply to your letter of Feb. 2

NOT: This office is in receipt of
BUT: We received . . . Thanks for . . .

NOT: Per your request, we take pleasure in enclosing herewith catalog of products of our manufacture.
BUT: It is a pleasure to enclose a copy of the catalog you requested.

8. Old-Fashioned Words:

NOT: As per your letter of . . .
BUT: In your letter of . . .

NOT: I beg to remain
BUT: (Omit entirely—absolutely unnecessary.)

NOT: Thanking you for your kind attention
BUT: Your prompt attention will be appreciated.

NOT: Hoping to hear from you in the near future, I am . . .
BUT: May I hear from you soon? I hope to hear from you promptly.

NOT: Trusting you will favor us with your order
BUT: I hope you will give us this order. Your order will be filled promptly.

MAGIC WORDS: Please, Thank you, Thanks, It is a pleasure to, Of course we will, We are glad to, You are right, Mr. Doe.

Pointer No. 5: Plan Your Letters Before You Start to Write Them . . .

Forceful business letters aren't accidents—they are very carefully planned. Like all other pieces of GOOD writing, letters have three distinct parts: a BEGINNING, a MIDDLE, and an ENDING. In a carefully planned letter, there can be only one direction to the flow of thought: from beginning to ending.

The formula for a successful business letter, then, is, simply: A I D C A + CSP = OK.
This means . . .

Your BEGINNING must

1. Attract the favorable ATTENTION of your reader
2. Arouse his INTEREST in your message

Your MIDDLE must

3. Quicken his DESIRE so as to make him WANT to do what you want him to
4. Establish CONVICTION by overcoming his sales resistance

Your ENDING must

5. Get the ACTION you want.

This explains the A I D C A portion of the formula. Now what is CSP? It's your

CENTRAL SELLING POINT!

Your CENTRAL SELLING POINT is the real reason why you are writing that letter. Without it, your letter is pointless and doomed to failure. Your CSP may be mentioned in the body of your letter, or it may remain simply understood. But it must be there, either actually or figuratively. Here, for example, are different types of letters and the *central selling points* which motivate them:

LETTER WRITING

Letter Type	Typical Central Selling Point
Application for employment	I'm the one for the job. I'm best qualified. I can make money for you.
Inquiry or Request for Information	It's good business to send me this material (information). Tell me what I need to know and I'll have good will toward your company, organization, etc.
Collection	It's good business to pay your just debts; pay up now and save trouble later on. We've been fair with you — don't you want to be equally fair with us?
Invitation	You'll create a lot of good will by accepting this invitation. We really want you to come.
Complaint	This is something that needs looking into and correcting.
Request for an adjustment	I'm unhappy now, but if you will make an adjustment, I'll feel more kindly toward your company.

The following letter shows the five distinct parts of a letter. In the space provided at the left of the letter, indicate each part: Attention, Interest, Desire, Conviction, Action. Underline once what you think is the central selling point of this letter:

Dear Mr. Jones:

One hundred selected West Coast architects are being invited to a dinner and preview of an exhibit designed to portray Cal Poly's program of architectural education—and YOU are one of those invited.

This is *not* a typical exhibit of student work, but an extensive portrayal of *our* solution to the problem of closing the gap between architectural education and actual practice. We believe that a student's college training should equip him, upon graduation, to be of immediate value to his profession. For this reason the entire presentation will be of vital interest to architects who are constantly confronted with the problem of obtaining properly-trained young men.

The Student Architectural Club at Cal Poly, through its president, Mr. Cletus Fencl, has asked me to send you the attached invitation to attend an informal dinner preceding the exhibits. We believe that the entire two-day program at Cal Poly is so packed with interesting events that you will want to bring your family along to combine a bit of pleasure with the more serious aspects of this important professional problem.

We have been fortunate in obtaining a limited number of hotel reservations. At Poly Royal time, hotel reservations are at a premium. How many would you like us to hold for you, Mr. Jones?

Cordially yours,

If you are starting or initiating the correspondence—

Your OPENING sentence or paragraph should
1. Identify you:
   a. Tell who you are—your name, title, company, etc., *or*
   b. Give your reason for writing this letter, *or*
   c. Mention your point of contact—who suggested you write and why, *or*
2. Identify your letter—what kind it is: application, request, etc., *or*
3. Start right off with your first main point, *or*
4. Open in some way to attract your reader's favorable attention and arouse his interest so as to *make* him want to read the rest of your letter.

The BODY or MIDDLE of your letter should
1. Start with your first main point (unless you opened with it).
2. Present your second main point.
3. Proceed this way until you have completed your presentation.

Your ENDING should be short—one sentence or a short paragraph. It must—
1. Be clear—your reader must know exactly what he is supposed to do.
2. Be courteous—molasses catches more flies than a barrel of vinegar.
3. Be concise—come directly to your point, and then shut up.
4. Be complete—make your ending complete and final, not indefinite.
5. Be modern—avoid like poison old-fashioned endings and incomplete ones!

If you are answering a letter—

Your OPENING sentence or paragraph should
1. Tie in with the letter you are answering, *or*
2. Mention your point of contact, *or*
3. Begin with your first main point.

The BODY or MIDDLE of your letter should
1. Start with your first main point, unless you have already used it.
2. Present your second main point.
3. Present your third main point.

NOTE: After you have started your letter, there is little difference between initiating new correspondence and answering a letter.

Your ending or closing paragraph should be clear, courteous, concise, complete, final, and modern.

There are two types of endings to letters:
1. *Terminating endings* button up the correspondence neatly and surely. The reader does not feel

he has to read further. It's over, finished, kaput! For instance:

> Thank you very much for your nice order, Bill. Your cooperation is most sincerely appreciated, Mr. Brown.

2. *Non-terminating endings* leave the door open for further correspondence, and in some instances require some kind of answer from the reader. Questions and challenging endings are always non-terminating. Here are some examples:

> After you've previewed this film, Don, let me know what you think of it. As soon as you know how long it will take, please let me know. Can you send me any information that will be helpful, Mr. Jones?

Pointer No. 6: Get Off to a Flying Start— and End with a Bang!

The two hardest parts of any letter to write are the opening sentence and the ending. In many ways they are the most important ones, too. Your opening sentence must attract your reader's attention and then arouse his interest. If you fail to do this, your letter will likely end up in File 13—his wastebasket. And your ending must get the action you are going after: his name on the dotted line, an appointment, etc. If your ending is weak, most likely you will fail to get the action you want.

So look to your openings and your closings. And to help you take a better look at them in general, here are some forceful letter beginning:

1. *Begin with the subject of your letter*—The specifications you requested are being mailed today.
2. *Use the YOU point of view*—Your inquiry about prices on blower equipment is very much appreciated, Mr. Roe.
3. *Ask a pertinent question*—Where do we go from here, Mr. Jones?
4. *Accentuate the position*—Modern processes and production are constantly needing more precise control and instrumentation.
5. *Use some kind of "appreciation" opening*—Your courtesy is much appreciated, Bill.

> Thanks for your . . .
> It was nice of you to . . .
> We certainly appreciate . . .
> Thank you for . . .
> I am delighted to receive your . . .
> Your thoughtfulness is . . .

6. *Make a courteous request or command*—May I have a moment of your time, Mr. White!
7. *Give a gift or make an offer*—The attached coupon entitles you to . . .
8. *Use a familiar name as your point of contact*—Bill Jones suggested that I write and ask you if . . .
9. *Use a split opening for eye appeal*—If you want REAL service . . . just call on us!
10. *Use any opening that will capture your reader's attention and arouse his interest in your product or service*—I wish you were just a little closer, Mr. Brown, so that I could drop in to tell you in person about . . .

Next are some weak, spineless, old-fashioned openings you must avoid at all costs:

1. *Don't have I-trouble—or We-writis, either*—I want to thank you for asking for information about OUR products, which I think are the best that money can buy.
   WE wish to thank you for inquiring about OUR products, and in reply WE wish to say WE are happy to send information describing OUR complete line of air conditioners.
2. *Don't beat around the bush—have a point and come to it quickly, courteously*—We have received your postal inquiry of February 2, 1956, asking us to send you our latest catalog on air conditioning equipment, and we are happy to comply. (Silly, isn't is? He knows what he wanted.)
   Instead, say: It is a pleasure to send you our latest catalog on air conditioning equipment, Mr. James.
3. *Don't use hackneyed, old-fashioned expressions*—Pursuant to yours of the 29th inst., beg to state we take the liberty to enclose herewith copy of our latest catalog for your perusal.
   Instead, say: Thanks for your inquiry. Here is your copy of our latest catalog, Mr. Blow.
4. *Don't be curt or abrupt*—Re yrs, enclosed find bulletins and catalog of products.
   Instead, say: We are glad to send you the enclosed catalog and bulletins.
5. *Don't use the weak participial opening*—Answering your inquiry, your order will be shipped January 15. (Who is answering whose inquiry?)
   Instead, say: Your order, Mr. Brown, will be shipped January 15.
6. *Don't use the F.B.I. opening*—This is to inform you that we are happy to send you our latest price list. (Omit those frightening first six words.)
   Instead, say: We are glad to send you our latest price list.
7. *Don't be silly*—We have received your postcard asking for . . . (How could you be answering it if you hadn't received his inquiry? Silly, isn't it?)
   Instead, say: Thanks for your inquiry about . . .

There you have seven types of openings that won't get you off to a flying start. Remember, your opening is the first thing your reader really looks at carefully. Make yours attract his favorable attention!

And after you have finished your message and want to button up your letter, end with a real BANG! Here are eight ways of doing just that:

1. *Ask a pertinent question*—May we hear from you promptly, Mr. Blake?

LETTER WRITING

PAGE 99

2. *End with a statement of fact*—For only $1.00, this booklet is well worth while!
3. *Make a courteous request or command*—Remember, Mr. Helmberg—the pictures you'll enjoy tomorrow must be taken today!
4. *Stress the YOU point of view*—Your cooperation is sincerely appreciated, Bill.
5. *Accentuate the positive*—Mr. Taylor will be glad to give you complete details on all of our products, Mr. Hartmetz.
6. *Use some variation of the appreciation ending*—You may be sure that it will be a pleasure to add your name to our list of satisfied customers, Mr. Dick.

NOTE: Don't open your letter with "Thank you" and also close it with "Thank you."

7. *Close with a strong sales appeal*—Recommend and specify Dux-Sulation for all your heating, ventilating and air-conditioning jobs, Mr. Keeler.
8. *Use any closing that is simple, natural and forceful*—Good luck, Dave!

Here are some endings that you should avoid at all costs:

1. *Don't catch We-writis—or I-trouble, either*—WE trust the literature WE have sent you will be of some help, and WE wish to thank you for your inquiry about OUR products.
   Instead, say: Thanks for your inquiry, Dr. Grant. We hope this literature will be of much help to you in your work.
2. *Don't use the deadly participle*—Awaiting your further commands, we remain,
   Instead, say: May we hear from you soon, Mr. Wurm?
3. *Don't be gruff or curt*—If this doesn't satisfy you, kindly advise.
   Instead, say: If you need more information, call on us.
4. *Avoid, "We remain" or "We are" endings*—With many thanks for your interest, we are,
   Instead, say: Many thanks for your interest, Mr. Crowe.
5. *Don't be stiff or stuffy, pompous, or windy*—We trust this information will prove to be of some assistance to you in your endeavors, and if we can be of further service, kindly advise the undersigned.
   Instead, say: We hope this information will help you in your studies. If you need more, let us know.
6. *Don't beat around the bush and repeat yourself*—As I mentioned previously, we really do appreciate your courtesy to us, and we are very grateful.
   Instead, say: Many thanks for your interest, Mr. Rogers.
7. *Eliminate trite, hackneyed, stock phraseology*—Enclosing check herewith and attaching order hereto, we beg to remain,
   Instead, say: Here's our check, along with a new order.
8. *Soft pedal the negative*—Regretting our inability to serve you this time, we are,
   Instead, say: Perhaps the next time we can send you just what you need.

Remember, your ending is the last really important thing your reader will see in your letter. Last impressions are lasting ones. Make yours well worth remembering!

Pointer No. 7: Accentuate the Positive—Eliminate the Negative

It's just as easy to say your piece positively as it is to say it negatively:

Negative: If you don't pay this bill by June 1, there will be an added penalty.

Positive: Pay this bill by June 1 and there will be no added penalty.

Negative: This report never goes into any phase of the matter in detail, but covers each part briefly.

Positive: This report discusses each part briefly.

Negative: If the enclosed information is not sufficient and you feel you need more, kindly let me know.

Positive: If you need more information, please let me know.

Negative: If it is not your desire to maintain both of your accounts, kindly advise the undersigned and we will be more than happy to transfer the funds in your Dime-a-Check account into your regular account.

Positive: Would you like us to transfer the money in your Dime-a-Check account into your regular account, Mr. Doe?

Negative: Due to the fact that printing charges are exceptionally high, we have no other alternative than to make a slight charge of 50¢ for this manual.

Positive: Although printing charges are quite high, Mr. Jones, you can still get this excellent manual for only 50¢.

Negative: We regret exceedingly that we are not in a position to comply with your kind request regarding a supply of literature as we are in the process of making a revision of all of our published literature, which should be available in the near future.

Positive: All our literature is being revised, Mr. Blow. Just as soon as the printer delivers the new copies, we'll send you some.

Negative: There isn't anything advertised in the A.E.C. that isn't carried or stocked on the West Coast.

Positive: Everything advertised in the A.E.C. is carried or stocked on the West Coast.

NOTE: Every positive statement is not only shorter, but more forceful!

Pointer No. 8: Put Smiles into Every Letter You Write:

Dear Mr. Blank:

Thanks for your letter of August 20. Naturally, we are sorry to know that you have arranged to renew your insurance through a representative whom you have known for many years.

We sincerely appreciate the opportunity of serving you these many years; however, we can understand your desire to consolidate your insurance needs in one agent. You are doing the right thing.

If at any time we can be of service to you, please call on us. In the meantime, best wishes for your good health and contentment in the New Year to come, Mr. Blank.

Sincerely yours,

Dear Mr. Blank:

As you requested, your policy will be terminated as of its expiration date, February 26, 19xx.

I guess we feel like you do when a good student leaves your class at the end of a term. You hate to see him go and you hope that you have done a good job for him while he was in your class. We are sorry to see you go, Mr. Blank, and we hope that we have given you the service you expected.

Please call on us if we can be of help to you in your future insurance needs. It has been a pleasure to know you as a policyholder.

Sincerely yours,

Congratulations, John . . .

You've done it again! Mr. Kennedy sent in the copy of the national magazine, THE REPORTER OF DIRECT MAIL ADVERTISING, which displays your picture so prominently.

The tribute the magazine editor pays you as "a man of letters" is certainly an honor. I was especially pleased to see that Cal Poly's name was also prominently mentioned in the article about you.

Your article, "Salutopenings and Compliendings," was very interesting—but you've got yourself a difficult obstacle to overcome. The habits of writing are so steeped with traditional form that it will take sustained campaigning to break down even a small group of followers who will help you pioneer this modern trend in business letter writing.

But I like pioneers, John, so stick to your guns and don't give up. Cal Poly has a pioneering job to do in selling its "upside down" philosophy of occupational education—and we're not going to let the traditions of hundreds of years of academic formality stand in the path of doing our job the right way.

If I don't adopt your letter-writing ideas, don't feel hurt. You'll just have to remember, John, that it is easier to teach new tricks to a young dog than it is to teach tricks to . . .

An old one,

Dear Mrs. Frederick:

I was very sorry to learn from your letter of May 28 that Mr. Frederick is ill, and I sincerely hope that he will have a rapid recovery.

With respect to the past-due note about which I wrote to him on May 16, just tell him to call at the bank when he is able, and not to make a special trip. Since he may want to renew this note, here is a renewal notice for him to sign and return to me. That will save him a trip to the bank.

Please give Mr. Frederick my best regards and sincere wishes for a speedy recovery.

Sincerely yours,

Dear Mr. Riebel:

What do we say? Why, what else *can* we say to such a letter as yours—what else can we say but "YES!"

And on second thought, just to prove the graciousness with which you have endowed this Company, we will send you not one but TWO copies of our new correspondence handbook.

As you have noted in your letter, this book was prepared for the use of our own people. But we are not prone to play dog in the manger, even to "a rank outsider," when it can serve such a good purpose as outlined for your college letter-writing course. May it serve your purpose well!

Sincerely yours,

Dear Joe:

I haven't forgotten your request of last week. In fact, Dr. Grant and I have been going over your papers and final examination—and we both agree that your failing grade must stand. I couldn't justify making a big protest over the grade I have given you.

But don't lose heart, for Dr. Grant says that preparatory courses do not carry transfer credit. You *will* have the chance of taking a placement test in English when you enter Junior College. So that leaves it pretty much up to you, Joe.

I suggest you get out your high school English books and do some tall and fancy boning up on grammar, punctuation, spelling, sentence structure, etc. Then when you take the placement test, do your best to write clearly, correctly, in complete sentences.

It isn't easy to tell a nice fellow like you that I can not do anything about his low grade, but that's what I have to do. You have my very best wishes for happiness and success in your new college. And when you again get back down in this direction, be sure to look me up.

Cordially yours,

Touche, Warren old man—Touche!

I guess there comes a time in every man's life when the only thing he can do is to honestly apologize in order to live with himself. That I'm doing now.

I'm sincerely sorry for what happened, particularly for my part in this unfortunate incident. I hope you will accept this apology in the spirit in which it is made, and let bygones be bygones.

Regretfully,

Here are Some Letters That SCOWL at the Reader

Dear Mr. Blank:

Thank you for your letter of May 18 in which you enclosed a corrected invoice on the John Doe car which you returned to our dealer in Salinas from Keokuck.

The second paragraph of your letter is what I would term, to say the least, words that were in this particular instance very poorly used, especially that portion which reads: "but apparently it is necessary to make these revisions to keep your good will."

For your information, I seek nothing, nor does anyone have to keep my good will. I am always working for the best interests of my bank.

Regarding the raising of rates for returning automobiles to the State of California from points in the United States, that is a matter we do not care to discuss now.

Sincerely yours,

Why didn't he say:

Dear Mr. Blank:

I'm very sorry that you found it necessary to say what you did, especially when you intimated that it was necessary to make these revisions in order to keep our good will. I am sure that you know, as well as I, that we are naturally working for the best interests of our bank, just as you are for those of your own company.

The matter of raising the rates for returning automobiles to California cannot be discussed at this time, Mr. Blank.

Sincerely yours,

Here's another, curt and cold:

Dear Sir:

Mr. Jones is no longer working for this organization.

Very truly yours,

That, and nothing more. In other words, drop dead! Why didn't he unbend, smile—

I am sorry to have to say that Mr. Jones is no longer working for us. He left a year ago, but we do not have his forwarding address.

or

Although Mr. Jones left us a year ago, his forwarding address is the Blank Company, 150 Center Street, Chicago 11. It is a pleasure to send you this information.

or

It is a pleasure to forward your inquiry to Mr. Jones, who left us about a year ago to accept a very fine position with the Blank Company, 150 Center Street, Chicago 11. Your letter should reach him promptly, Mr. Blow.

Here's a downright brutal turndown:

Dear Sir:

Re your application for employment with this company. Beg to state we have nothing to offer you.

Yours truly,

This kind of answer would have allowed the poor fellow to have saved face:

Dear Mr. Blank:

Thank you for your application of August 30. We are pleased that you are interested in our company. Unfortunately, however, we just don't have any vacancy into which a man with your excellent qualifications would fit now. Write us again in six months if you haven't accepted a permanent position. Who knows what may develop in the meantime, Mr. Blank.

Sincerely yours,

Dear Sir:

We cannot allow your claim No. 6790 for $6.35 and No. 6791 for $10.12, as this merchandise was delivered in January and you should have notified us before this that the breakage was our fault.

It is true that we gave you permission to dump this broken merchandise, but you did not tell us when you reported this breakage that you had received this merchandise in January.

We trust the above will enable you to cancel your claim.

Yours truly,

For a mere $16.47 he insults a good customer and throws his good will to the winds. Here's how he could have turned him down and educated him at the same time:

Dear Mr. Jones:

I am sorry that there has been a misunderstanding about the broken boxes listed on your claims Nos. 6790 and 6791.

When we gave you permission to dump these broken boxes, we did not understand that this breakage had occurred on the January delivery—three months ago. We were under the impression that it had happened on your April shipment. This creates an entirely different situation, Mr. Jones.

As you probably recall, in order to get credit for breakage, you must notify us within 30 days after the delivery of the damaged merchandise. For that reason we cannot allow your claim for this damage.

Thank you for calling this to our attention, for it gives us the opportunity to clear up a point that, unfortunately, is not too clearly understood by some of our good customers.

Sincerely yours,

Let's close this series of unpleasant letters with one that really smiles—

Because illness is never welcome, it would not do for me to "welcome" you to Cottage Hospital, but we do want you to know that you will be among friends during your hospitalization—friends who are doing all they can to speed your recovery. Everyone in the hospital, including those you may never see, is interested in making your stay with us as pleasant as possible.

I hope your stay with us will be a short one and that you will help us to help you by giving us your comments and suggestions, Mr. Appleton.

It's just as easy to put SMILES into your letters—and it will win many more friends for you and your organization!

Pointer No. 9: A Soft Answer Turneth Away Wrath:

It takes two to get into an argument, or to make a fight. So if you want to learn how to win new friends for yourself and influence more favorable old and valued customers for your company, remember that Biblical passage: A soft answer turneth away wrath.

Some years ago a Cal Poly student received from his Congressman, this ill-humored reply to a request for an agricultural yearbook:

Dear Mr. Doakes:

Inasmuch as I have had so many requests for Agricultural Yearbooks from students of your college who should look to their Congressmen from the State and Congressional District in which they or their family are registered voters, and in order to give the legal residents of my District their rightful share of these books, I find it necessary to ask for the registered voting address when I do not find it listed in the Register.

Because of this, may I ask you for the above information, and if you do not know the name of your Congressman I shall refer your request to him for fulfillment. However, if you are a constituent of mine I shall be glad to send the book.

Sincerely,

And speaking of wrath, this student was livid with rage at having received such a cold, unfriendly reply from one who must always consider himself a servant of the people. Little wonder this Congressman decided not to run for reelection the following year. With such an attitude—which was perfectly captured by Steig's famous cartoon of a glum character sitting in a box and saying: "People are no damn good!"—this man had little or no chance of being reelected.

Here's how he could have said his piece in a friendly, cooperative, noninsulting way:

Dear Mr. Doakes:

Thank you for your letter of January 5 requesting an Agricultural Yearbook. I am always glad to send one to students at your fine college.

As you probably know, Congressmen are limited as to the number of Yearbooks they may send out. For that reason we try to send them to the constituents in our own Congressional Districts who may need them.

Since your name doesn't seem to be listed in the current Congressional Register, won't you please send me your voting address, or that of your parents? Just as soon as you do, I'll either send along your copy of the Yearbook or have your own Congressman mail you one.

It was very good of you to write me, Mr. Doakes.

Sincerely,

After all, the tone of the letter depends on the tone of the writer. If he is a friendly person who likes to smile, his letters will usually reflect that attitude—or at least he can easily be taught to write that kind of letter.

Pointer No. 10: Every Letter Is a Sales Letter—

Every letter you write, personal or business, is really a sales letter. You are trying to sell someone on the idea of doing something, usually something favorable to you.

Here, then, are the four things which every letter sells—some only one, some two, others three, and a few all four:

1. *A product*—You have some specific product which you wish to sell: a car, a gun, a horse or bull, your knowledge and potential as a job applicant, etc.

2. *A service*—Sometimes you're trying to sell a service rather than a specific product: radio or TV repair, concrete work, your skill in painting or plastering, or even prompt, efficient service, as in a bank or a dry-cleaning business.

3. *An idea or course of action*—Sometimes you want to "sell" a person on the idea of contributing some money or his services or equipment to a cause; or you want to "sell" a person on the idea of making a long trip to address your club or organization. These and many other instances are selling an idea or course of action. A very good example is writing for information which you want to use in a report or senior project. Yes, college students have occasion to write many such "sales" letters.

4. *Good will*—If you sell nothing else in your letter, you are selling GOOD WILL. The Supreme Court of the United States once gave the best definition of good will that I have ever heard: "Good will is the tendency on the part of the customer to return to the place where he has been well served." Can you think of a better one?

LETTER WRITING

Here's a letter that sells all four, and does a magnificent job, too. It was written by Irving Mack, president of Filkack Trailer Company of Chicago. Mr. Mack is selling (1) a product—a trailer or "commercial" for the Fremont Theatre; (2) a service—quick, courteous service; (3) an idea—that business can be and is friendship, not warfare, and (4) GOOD WILL by the carload! This is a rare example of one man acknowledging with thanks an order he has just filled and in almost the same breath asking for another order. That takes consummate mastery of words —and of good will toward your reader. But let's get to the letter itself (written in 1935!):

Dear Mr. Shaw:

By this time, you have received so many of my flowery acknowledgements that you may think they're just a bunch of "hooey."

But I really believe in the stuff I'm handing out . . . in the firm I represent . . . and in my ability to make you realize that I appreciate your business.

I get real enjoyment out of the work I'm doing . . . I believe in courtesy, kindness, good cheer, friendship, and honest competition . . . and I think there is nothing finer than to have friends who like us well enough to send us their work regularly.

But why say more? If you've read this far, you have probably come to the conclusion that I'm one of the most appreciative fellows in the world.

I only regret that our friendship has been rather one-sided and that you are doing all of the giving and I do all the accepting.

However, I really enjoy writing these letters to you . . . maybe more than you enjoy receiving them . . . So here's hoping I will get a chance very soon again to acknowledge another order from you, Mr. Shaw.

Sincerely yours,

The Parts of a Business Letter

Now that you know the underlying psychology of forceful, friendly, modern business letter writing, let's take a look at the standard parts of a letter.

Every modern business letter has seven parts:

1. The *Heading:* (Try to limit to 3 or 4 lines)
   a. The writer's street address (or post office box and name of school)
   b. City and State
   c. Date
2. The *Inside Address* or the *Introduction:* (Limit to 3 to 5 lines)
   a. Name of the person addressed
      Street address or post office box number
      City and State
   b. Name of the person addressed
      Title or position (if you know it)
      Name of the Company (if any)
      Company address (sometimes not necessary in large companies)
      City and State
   c. Title of person addressed (if you don't know his name)
      Company
      City and State
   d. Name of the Company
      City and State
      Attention of *(the title of the person who is to get your letter)*

NOTE: If you know the exact address of the Company, use it.

3. The *Salutation* and 5. The *Complimentary Close* should harmonize in tone: Here are correct salutations and complimentary closes for individuals and for companies (or organizations):

Individuals
Salutations:
   Dear Mr. Doe: (preferred)
   Dear Sir: (old-fashioned except in 2c)
   Dear Joe: Dear Sally: (for a friendly, personal business letter. Use cautiously)
   Dear Mrs. Doe: (if she is married)
   Dear Miss Doe: (if she is not married)
   Dear Ms. Doe: (if you are not sure, don't know, *or if she prefers this title*)

Complimentary Closings:
   Cordially yours, Sincerely yours,
      (Cordially, or Sincerely, alone may be use if you address the reader by his first name; in this case, it is not good practice to use any of the following closes):
   Yours truly,
   Yours very truly,
   Very truly yours,
   Yours faithfully, (British usage)
   Fraternally yours, (correct for a fraternal organization)
   Faithfully yours, (correct for a fraternal organization)

Companies
Salutations:
   Dear Manager—Professor—Doctor—Order Clerk: (use of job title is preferred)
   Dear Sir or Madam: (for formal correspondence only)
   Gentlemen: (legal salutation)
   Dear Sir: or Sirs: (seldom used except by the British)

Complimentary Closings:
   Sincerely yours,
   Yours sincerely,
   Yours truly,
   Yours very truly,
   Very truly yours,

4. The *Body* of the letter—The main part of any letter, *be sure of that!*
6. Your *Signature*—should be legible, or else your name should be typed.
7. Your typed name 4-5 spaces below your signature.

(1)
```
                    ........................
              ............, ............
                ............, ............
```

(2)
```
............................
............................
............................
......................, ............
```

(3)
```
..................:
```
....   This is the indented style
....   of paragraphing. It is still
....   in good usage in modern
....   business letters.
```
..............................................
```

(4)
```
..............................................
```
....   This is the block style of
....   paragraphing. It also is
....   used in many modern
....   business letters.

....   This is the overhanging
....   style of paragraphing. IT
....   IS SELDOM USED EX-
....   CEPT IN VERY SPE-
....   CIAL TYPES OF BUSI-
....   NESS LETTERS. DO
....   NOT USE IT IN YOUR
....   LETTERS!
```
..............................................
```

(5)
```
                    ...................,
```

(6)
```
                    ..............................
```

(7)
```
                    Your typed name (signature)
```

(1) The Heading
(2) The Inside Address or Introduction
(3) The Salutation
(4) The Body
(5) The Complimentary Closing
(6) The Signature
(7) The typed signature—your name

Jim Randolph's revised order

> R. F. D. No. 4
> Porter's Lake, Iowa
> July 14, 19xx

Miss Elaine Thomas
Marshall Record Shop
443 Oak Street
Elmwood 5, Iowa

Dear Miss Thomas:

Will you please send me the Swing Sisters' recording of "Meet Me at the Corner," "Sad Sally," and "Blue Blues?" These are Regal Record numbers 3890, 3751, and 3808, priced at 85 cents each.

I enclose a money order for $2.55 for the three records. I understand you will pay postage on this order.

I need these records by July 28, and since I have always received prompt and helpful service in the past, I feel sure you can fill this order by this time.

> Sincerely yours,
>
> Jim Randolph

Types of Business Letters Technical Students Should Know How to Write

Here are some types of letters which every technical student should know how to write, for at some time in his career he will surely have occasion to write them:

1. Inquiries and Requests for Information:

Every technical student, and most others, as well, has occasion to write a letter requesting information, sometimes called an inquiry. There is, however, a difference between these two types. For example, an inquiry may consist of merely asking if a company manufactures or handles a certain product, or what it costs, etc.

Here are 10 tips of how you can write more forceful, friendly inquiries:

1. *Tell who you are.* Your reader has the right to know who you are—if you are a student, a business man, a teacher, etc.
2. *Tell why you want this information and what use you will make of it.* Sometimes companies are leery of ulterior motives, and for that reason want to know just what use you will make of this information.
3. *Express willingness to acknowledge credit for information or material given.* This can easily and courteously be done as follows:

Through the courtesy of Gladding, McBean & Co. of Los Angeles, I was able to obtain the following comparisons of the refractory properties of all firebrick manufactured on the Pacific Coast.

This is your way of thanking your source impersonally.

4. *Don't ask for "all the information you have" or for "everything you have."* Such a request is being plain hoggish and often will get you nothing. A former student once wrote to the president of Lufkin Rule Company in Saginaw, Michigan, asking for "all the information you have on precision instruments," believe it or not! The president wrote back, saying that they would be glad to move their files and library down to Flint, but it would be quite costly, and also the company might need them in the meantime. Here is what he should have said in his letter:

Dear Sir:

As a student at General Motors Institute, I am writing a report on precision instruments. Since The Lufkin Rule Company is famous for the fine measuring instruments which you manufacture, could you help me by answering the following questions, if this information is available?

1. What type of steel and/or other metals are used, and why?
2. What special precautions must be used, such as dust and humidity control, etc?
3. How are precision instruments calibrated and tested?

Although I'm interested in all kinds of precision instruments, I am especially eager to have this information about micrometer and vernier calipers, if you can readily obtain it for me.

Since my report is due three weeks from today, I'll appreciate your sending this information by a week from Friday, November 15. All information obtained will be acknowledged, of course. If you wish, I shall be glad to send you a copy of my report.

Sincerely yours,

Here are some things to note about this excellent request for information:

1. The writer identified himself as a student at GMI.
2. He gives a legitimate reason for asking for this information.
3. Twice he gives the reader an "out" if the company doesn't want to give out any information.
4. He tabulates his points, which he has put in the form of polite questions. This makes it easy to answer his points.
5. He asks for information about special precision instruments while indicating an interest in all kinds of them.
6. He indicates when the information must be obtained in order to be of use. This is an excellent idea, but it must be done courteously, politely.
7. He expresses willingness to acknowledge receipt of this information.
8. He expresses a willingness to send the president a copy of his completed report. NOTE: This should be done *only* when writing to one or two, at the most, companies. I once had a student who made this offer when soliciting information on his thesis topic. About 50 replied and asked for copies of his completed thesis! And since some of them were very definitely job prospects, he had to have these copies reproduced at his own expense! In this case he should have offered to send them copies of his conclusions, or recommendations, or a summary, not the entire paper.

5. *Ask specific questions about points you wish cleared up.* Questions are always a good way of riveting the reader's attention, and they are usually easy to answer, often with simply a "yes" or a "no." Phrase your questions short and to the point.

6. *Tabulate your questions or points.* Your reader will like that and be more inclined to answer promptly.

7. *Ask for "available information," or "information that is readily accessible."* Sometimes the information you want is classified or highly confidential. If you ask for it bluntly, you put your reader on the spot: obviously, he can't give it to you and he must turn you down. However, if you ask for information which is available, you give him an easy "out": he can say, "Sorry, this information is not available" and thus save face.

8. *Don't pose as a "big shot" in hopes of getting something you might not get otherwise.* Sure, maybe writing on letterheads you shouldn't use for personal matters, or posing as a "big shot" may help you eight times out of ten. But it's mighty embarrassing when you do get caught—and you WILL one of these days! Of that you may be sure. One of my former students got caught—and was *he* embarrassed!

9. *Offer to return the favor.* Even though there is slight chance of your being able to do so, offer to return the favor: for example, offer to send one person a copy of your report or paper, or if you have written to a number of people, offer to send a summary, or your conclusions or recommendations, any of which can be easily put on one sheet and mimeographed.

10. *Motivate a reply by being clear, concise, courteous.* Remember, your letter requesting information is a sales letter: you're trying to "sell" the reader on going to the trouble and expense of getting this

information for you. And often it does take a lot of time and trouble and cost quite a bit to get the material you want or need. Once it cost Cadillac about $250 to get some information about the order of firing of the cylinders in a 16-cylinder V-8 Cadillac engine!

NOTE: When you write inquiries or requests for information—or any other kind of business letter, for that matter, put into practice the 10 Pointers for Writing Letters That Get Results!

2. Replies to Inquiries and Requests for Information:

Someday you will be on the other side of the desk and have to answer inquiries and requests for information. When you do, remember that your letter takes the place of a personal visit; so put yourself in your reader's place and then write the kind of answer you would like to receive, or wouldn't resent if you can't give the information requested.

Remember this very human quality in everyone: PEOPLE LIKE TO BE TURNED DOWN GENTLY, NOT SLAMMED TO EARTH. So when you refuse a person something, do it courteously, gently, never brutally, as this man did:

Dear Sir:

Mr. Jones is no longer working for this organization.

Yours truly,

In other words, DROP DEAD—or D.D.T.: DROP DEAD TWICE! Why didn't he say:

I'm sorry to have to say that Mr. Jones is no longer working for us. He left about a year ago, but we do not have his forwarding address.

Or:

Mr. Jones left about a year ago. His forwarding address is The Blank Company, 150 Center Lane, Chicago 11. It is a pleasure to send you this information.

Either of these two rewrites will create a lot of good will for your company. And GOOD WILL is the most priceless commodity any company has to offer.

So let's sum up the main points about answering inquiries:

1. If you give something, give it graciously and promptly—get the maximum of good will out of your gift.
2. If you have to refuse, do it gently, courteously. Express regret. Don't start off with your refusal, but gradually work up to it by saying something nice at the outset. Here's the way NOT to grant a request:

Dear Sir:

We cannot grant your claim No. 6790 for $6.35 and No. 6791 for $10.12, as this merchandise was delivered in January and you should have notified us before that the breakage was our fault.

It is true that we gave you permission to dump this broken dinnerware, but you did not tell us when you reported this breakage that you had received this merchandise in January.

We trust the above will enable you to cancel your claims.

Yours truly,

For a lousy $16.47 he insults a good customer and throws away the good will that has been built up over many years. Here's how the writer could have refused these claims and at the same time courteously, considerately educated this customer in company policies:

Dear Mr. Jones:

I am sorry that there has evidently been a misunderstanding about the broken dinnerware listed on your claims No. 6790 and No. 6791.

When we gave you permission to dump this broken dinnerware, we did not understand that this breakage had occurred on the January shipment—over three months ago. We thought that it had happened on your April shipment. This throws an entirely different light upon this matter, Mr. Jones.

As you will probably recall, in order to get credit for breakage, you must notify us within 30 days after the delivery of the damaged merchandise. For that reason we cannot allow your claim for this damage, since 90 days have elapsed since the shipment was made.

Thank you for calling this to our attention, for it gives us the opportunity to clear up a point which, unfortunately, is often overlooked by some of our good customers like you, Mr. Jones.

Sincerely yours,

3. Orders:

When an order blank is used, it is often unnecessary to write a letter. However, if no order blank is available, a letter ordering merchandise must be written. This letter should be complete as to catalog number, quantity, size, color, etc., as well as price per unit and total price. In addition, any special shipping or other instructions should be included:

Gentlemen:

Please send me the following items listed in your 1952-53 General Catalog:

1 Hinged extension sides for pickup truck	No. 87A 7443F	$109.50
1 7-piece micrometer set for mechanics	No. 84A 5075	39.95
1 Power-Kraft metal lathe, 24" between centers	No. 84A 2130R	273.95
1 Heavy-duty high-output piston-type paint sprayer, electrically operated	No. 75A 6435RS	136.95
3 Spray guns at $10.95 each	No. 75A 6402SX	32.85
Total:		$593.20
Sales Tax:		23.73
GRAND TOTAL:		$616.93

Attached is a DO-MRO priority rating under CMP Regulation 5, which is required for purchase of the Power Kraft metal lathe.

Add these items to my regular account, although I may take advantage of your 2% discount for cash within 10 days. Please send the micrometer set by parcel post immediately. The other items can be shipped via Santa Fe or California Motor Express, whichever is cheaper.

Sincerely yours,

4. Acknowledgement:

It's always a courteous gesture to acknowledge a letter, especially an order, even if you are shipping it immediately. You can make this acknowledgement a goodwill letter if you are prompt, sincere, and courteous. It need not be long, as witness this nice acknowledgement:

Many thanks, Asher . . .

Your last order was most welcome. It will be shipped tonight, of that you may be sure. And I'm looking forward to the time when soon again the mailman will walk in with another letter from Asher Shaw—and another order for

Irving Mack

5. Invitation:

When you invite someone to do something—such as to come and speak to the Poly Phase Club or some other organization, on or off campus—you must be complete, sincere, and courteous. Your appeal is a personal one; so you show him what a favor he will be doing you if he will accept. You recognize him as an authority in his field, one who has something worth while to say. But don't put your reader in such a position that he will find it difficult or impossible to refuse, even if it is inconvenient for him to comply. Above all, BE CLEAR, COMPLETE, CONSIDERATE:

Dear Dr. Grant:

You are very cordially invited to attend the Annual County Education Conference on March 6 at the San Luis Obispo Senior High School.

Enclosed is an announcement of the day's program. This is the annual occasion when educators of the county meet with citizens who are interested in education. Of particular interest will be the showing of the motion picture, *Passion for Life*, described in the announcement.

Please use the enclosed post card to request tickets to this film. You can have as many as you wish, without charge, of course, Dr. Grant.

Sincerely yours,

6. Accepting an Invitation:

When you accept an invitation, be sincere and gracious to show that you really appreciate their asking you. It's also a good idea to repeat the conditions of the invitation to let them know you understand them correctly. This applies equally well to any kind of acceptance: to a job, to an assignment, etc.

Dear Mr. Rhodes:

It will be a pleasure to accept your gracious invitation to attend the Annual County Education Conference to be held from 9 a.m. to 4 p.m. on March 6 at the San Luis Obispo Senior High School.

I can use three tickets to the motion picture, *Passion for Life,* described in the announcement. And if I can be of any help in any way, Mr. Rhodes, please let me know.

Sincerely yours,

7. Refusing an Invitation:

When you refuse an invitation, you must be especially tactful. There are "good" reasons, and there are "real" reasons. "Good" reasons are simply plausible excuses for doing or not doing something. "Real" reasons often are hidden from the person himself. For example, you may be invited to a party at the home of a person you just can't stand. Obviously, you refuse. But you are too tactful to tell him why you won't come; so you invent some "good," plausible excuse, such as a previous engagement, a trip out of town, too much homework, etc. *ad nauseum.* But no matter what your reason may be, good or real, you just appear sincere, courteous, regretful. Who knows, someday you may want or need that person's friendship!

Dear Mr. Rhodes:

Thank you very much for your gracious invitation to attend the Annual County Education Conference on March 6. Unfortunately, I have a previous engagement on this day and will not be in the city.

I am very much interested in your program and hope that next year you will keep me in mind and send me another invitation.

Regretfully yours,

8. Introduction:

In a letter of introduction, you are the point of contact between your reader, whom you know, presumably very well, and the person you are introducing, also whom you presumably know very well. You are the go-between between two persons who have mutual interests: social, economic, political, educational, etc. So your letter should be friendly and sincere, but not effusive or flattering. You will naturally say something nice about both your reader and your introducee, but for Pete's sake, don't heap it on! Here's a good example:

Hello, Mr. Otto—

I want you to meet Dr. and Mrs. Stanley Hall, who are in Detroit to pick up their new Fleetwood Cadillac from the factory.

This is the Halls' first visit to Detroit. Since they plan to be there for several days before their car will be ready, I'm sure that you will be able to suggest some major points of interest and, if possible, furnish them a courtesy car until their Fleetwood is ready.

Any courtesies you can give my good friends from Long Beach, Mr. Otto, will be most sincerely appreciated by

John P. Riebel

9. Recommendation:

At some time in your lifetime you will be called upon to recommend someone, a friend or an employee. If your letter is to be worth the writing, it must be clear, honest, sincere. Don't say anything you can't prove, if necessary. Be specific. Don't use vague generalities. Above all, remember that a fair, sincere recommendation is far better than a flattering one. The former will be taken at face value; the latter will be discounted almost 100 per cent. Here's a good example:

Dear Dr. Curtiss:

I am pleased to have the opportunity to recommend John Doe for your 1954 Fellowship-in-business Program. Following your suggested outline, I wish to make the following comments:

1. I have known the applicant for two years as a fellow faculty member at California State Polytechnic College. My work in engineering frequently brings me into close contact with Mr. Doe, who is in our Liberal Arts Division. Our relations have always been very cordial.
2. The candidate's strong points are his powerful drive and determination to do an outstanding teaching job and to make valuable contributions to the field of letter writing in business. He is fortunate in having the necessary natural ability to go along with his zeal. His only weak point is that he can't find enough hours in the day to do the many things he is anxious to accomplish.
3. I rate Mr. Doe's basic intelligence at a very high level. In our doings which involve blending his courses into our engineering program, I have found him very open-minded and cooperative. He has an inquiring mind which has enabled him to study the needs of engineers in language communication and to develop courses to meet those needs. If by research attitude you mean intellectual curiosity and determination to seek the truth, Mr. Doe has an outstanding research attitude.
4. In confidence and respect of students and faculty, Mr. Doe ranks, in my opinion, in the upper twenty per cent of our faculty.
5. It is my understanding that Mr. Doe hopes to make teaching a lifelong career.
6. Mr. Doe has a charming personality and a great respect for the effectiveness of tact and diplomacy.

Thank you for the opportunity to make these comments.
Sincerely yours,
Harold P. Hayes, Dean
Division of Engineering

10. Acceptance:

Whether it be a gift, an appointment, an office in an organization, or something else, a letter of acceptance must ring true—be plausible and sincere. It must leave your reader with the feeling that he has made no mistake in appointing or electing you to this office or position:

Dear Mr. Johnson:

It is a pleasure to accept the appointment as membership chairman of the newly-organized Pozo Chamber of Commerce. You may be sure that I shall see every member of our district personally and impress upon him—or her—the importance of becoming an active member in an organization that has the best interests of the entire district at heart.

I am really proud as well as pleased that you have seen fit to give this important assignment to me, Mr. Johnson.

Cordially yours,

LETTER WRITING

11. Resignation:

One of the hardest letters to have to write is a letter of resignation. But once in a while it is necessary to resign from an office, or even a position. When you do, you are called upon to write a real sales letter because you must be sincere, but firm. Your reasons must be "good" ones; they may not be "real" ones. They must be convincing, and you must show no anger, resentment, or anything that could possibly be used against you. Above all, avoid sarcasm. If you are resigning from a job, don't burn your employment bridges behind you. You just *may* want to accept employment with that organization later:

Dear Mr. Blow:

I am sorry, but I feel that the only fair thing to do is to give you my resignation as manager of your restaurant.

As you know, things have not been going well lately. Some of this very likely was my fault, but much of it was caused by conditions over which I had no control, as you well know. Also it has been impossible for me to forget the unfortunate incident involving Miss White two weeks ago. The strained relations which developed have made it impossible for me to carry out my obligations to you and the other people whom I am supposed to be managing.

When I came here a year and a half ago, I had high hopes of becoming an important part of the fabulous establishment you are creating in this my home town. However, as time goes on, I find that my position is constantly being lessened in importance. So to be fair to both of us, I am resigning so that you may hire someone who, possibly, will not start with as high aspirations as I had.

I am deeply grateful for everything you have done for me, and I wish you only the best of success. My only regret is that when your establishment is completed, I will not be here to share in your justifiable pride of accomplishment, Mr. Blow.

Regretfully yours,

12. Request for an Appointment:

Your letter must "sell" your reader on the advisability of giving you this appointment or interview. Your letter must be clear, specific, courteous, sincere. It should be short and should stress your reason for this request. It is a good idea to suggest an alternative time in case the original one requested is not convenient:

Dear Mr. Downing:

When we corresponded several months ago, you suggested that the next time I came to Fresno I drop in to see you. I'll be in your area for three days next week, beginning Tuesday. May I come to see you one of these days?

I am still very much interested in talking to you about the offer you made me, as I indicated in my last letter. So if you can spare me a few minutes next week, I'll be glad to make my plans accordingly, Mr. Downing.

Sincerely yours,

13. Apology:

One of the hardest things to do is to apologize. But sometimes it's the only thing a person can do and still live with himself, especially if the apology is directed to someone you meet or are associated with frequently. Here is a good example of a letter written by a man who swallowed his pride and did the manly thing by saying "I'm sorry":

Dear Mrs. Sills:

I want you to know how very sorry I am for the misunderstanding of several weeks ago. If I said anything I should not have, please accept my sincerest apology. Nothing was further from my thoughts than to offend or embarrass you, Mrs. Sills.

Regretfully yours,

14. Follow-up:

There's an old saying that if at first you don't succeed, keep on trying. So that is the purpose of your follow-up letter: to let your reader know that you are still very much interested in whatever your original letter was about: an interview, an appointment, some additional material, etc. Here is a good example of an unsolicited follow-up—one written by Mr. Howard L. C. Leslie, Vice President, Value Analysis, Incorporated, Schenectady, New York:

Dear Mr. Wicke:

At a recent forum held at California State Polytechnic College, you expressed further interest in Value Analysis.

The enclosed reprints are being sent at the request of Mr. J. K. Fowlkes, President, who addressed your engineering group. We certainly hope this information will be of interest to you, Mr. Wicke.

Very truly yours,

15. Good Will:

Often quite similar in purpose to the follow-up letter, the good-will letter is written solely for the purpose of promoting good will in the reader-customer. This letter is usually written *after* the customer has made his purchase, but not necessarily. An excellent example of this type is the letter Mr. W. S. Carpenter, retired president of DuPont, wrote to a new stockholder, Mrs. Williston. (See page 93.) Here is another excellent illustration. This letter was written by Mr. Ernest R. Lee, Executive Vice President of the Indianapolis Morris Plan:

The beginning of a new year, Paul,
recalls the activities of the year just past.

The courtesy and service extended to us by you and your associates during 1953 is one of our pleasant recollections. We appreciate having been one of your customers.

We sincerely hope that 1954 will be a year of prosperous opportunities for you.

Please call on us whenever we can help you—or your friends.

Cordially,

This letter, although nearly 10 years old, proves that there is a timelessness to really GOOD letters. They never get out of date. The Irving Mack letter quoted on page 107 is almost 30 years old!

16. Thanks:

Writing a letter of thanks is the simplest and often least expensive—but also most effective—way of showing appreciation. The Immortal Shakespeare hated ingratitude with a vengeance which is best exemplified in this verse:

> Blow, blow, thou winter wind!
> Thou art not so unkind
>   As man's ingratitude.
>
> *As You Like It,* Act II, Line 174

In business, as in social contacts, letters of thanks are very helpful in building that priceless ingredient called GOOD WILL—"the tendency on the part of the customer to return to the place where he has been well served," so pronounced the Supreme Court of the United States. Here is an excellent example straight from the heart of that master letter writer, Irving Mack:

> An orchid to you, Wilfred, for recommending FILMACK to Mr. Fey Rogers of the Appalachian Broadcasting Corporation in your city.
>
> It certainly makes me feel good to know that there are still people in this good old world of ours who will do for their friends favors without being moved by mercenary reasons.
>
> I want you to know that your courtesy is very much appreciated . . . and I hope someday I can reciprocate.
>
> When that opportunity does present itself, need I tell you all you have to do is just command
>
> Irving Mack
>
> for FILMACK CORPORATION

17. Credit:

The word "credit" comes from the Latin *credo,* which means "I believe." That is the essence of credit: belief in the inherent honesty of mankind. It means that some company believes that you will fulfill your obligation as you promised—that is, you will pay your bill as you promised, when it is due. Actually this matter of "credit"—that is, "belief" in you—is manifested in a number of facets of your life, believe it or not:

1. In your college education—you are working for "credits," because you know that if you don't have the right number of them and in the right subjects, you won't graduate. Right? RIGHT!

2. In your religious belief—many faiths have as an integral part of their service a recital of The Creed—which always begins with "I believe in . . ."

3. In business—as the late E. P. Corbett wrote in one of the most famous collection letters ever written, "Business would go to smash if we couldn't depend on the sacredness of a commercial agreement." And when you ask for, receive, and use credit, you are giving your word that you will live up to your agreement—and your word is, or should be, something sacred to you if you ever hope to succeed and not go the way of Billie Sol Estes! So one of the most precious things that a young person can establish is his credit rating. YOU—and *only* YOU—can do that. So guard well your credit rating, for your rating is constantly being reevaluated and based upon your performance. A minor slip or two may be overlooked, but a major breech of trust will continue to have serious repercussions for years and years, maybe for the rest of your business life. When you give credit information, you must give complete and accurate information. This can be done in two ways: by filling out a credit application, and by writing a letter which contains this same information. For example:

> Gentlemen:
>
> I should like to open a charge account at your store. Here are some pertinent credit facts about me:
>
> 1. I have Charga-Plate accounts at the following stores: Macy's, The White House, The Emporium, The City of Paris, The Broadway, and The May Company, as well as at Riley's and Wickenden's in San Luis Obispo.
>
> 2. I have a checking account with the main office of Bank of America in San Luis Obispo.
>
> 3. I also have a savings account at this office.
>
> 4. We are purchasing our home with a Prudential loan, No. 767,907. Aside from the mortgage (about $4,000 on a $25,000 home), we have no other debts.
>
> 5. I am an assistant professor at Blank College, where I have taught for the past 15 years.

6. My gross income for last year was slightly over $23,000.
7. I am married (for 31 years) and have a son 25 and a daughter 24.
8. On the attached sheet is a list of personal and business references to whom you may write for additional information about me.

If you will please send me one of your regular credit blanks I shall be glad to fill it out and send it in promptly. Also I want to purchase one pair of your English-made brown shoes advertised in Sunday's *Examiner,* Style 745, size 7½C, priced at $8.95. I'd very much appreciate your putting aside a pair for me and sending them as soon as my credit has been approved.

Sincerely yours,

Giving false credit information either about yourself or about someone else may involve you in both civil and criminal suits.

18. Complaint and Request for Adjustment:

Although usually considered as the same, complaint and requests for adjustment are two different kinds of letters. You write a complaint when there is an intolerable condition which you want corrected, but about which you do not expect recompense, such as money or replacement of faulty merchandise. For instance:

For the past week, Mr. Hesse,

The doors to Engl 212E have been locked and my 7:30 to 9:00 class has been unable to start on time. Since this is a speech class and the speaking schedules have been made up and are very tight, I hope you will instruct your custodian in this building to be sure to unlock both doors early enough so that we may start promptly at 7:30.

Also there is the problem of ventilation in this room. None of the windows will open. We therefore must keep one or both doors open. This is inadvisable because of the noises in the hall. So your looking into this matter will be very much appreciated by

John P. Riebel
Department of English

A request for adjustment is written when something you purchased is defective and you want it replaced or your money back. The following letter written to the Heath Company about a defective Heathkit is a good example of this type:

Gentlemen:

Recently I purchased a V-5A Vacuum Tube Voltmeter kit and assembled it last week. The instrument works fine electrically, but on any range where the needle moves past the 24-30 volt markings, it sticks. It doesn't appear that the pointer end of the needle is rubbing on the front scale of the meter, but rather that the movement which is attached to the needle is rubbing in the housing at this deflection.

Upon your advice, then, I shall either send the meter from the VTM or the entire VTM to you for repair or replacement.

I like my Heathkit VTM and am eager to put it to use. Since the end of the college year is June 7, after that date I'll be living at my home address in Los Angeles. Enclosed is an airmail envelope. If you will answer promptly, your reply will reach me while I am still at Cal Poly.

Sincerely yours,

There are several important things to note about Earl Weinstein's excellent letter:

1. He is very clear and accurate in describing the difficulty.
2. His explanation is complete.
3. He is courteous and considerate even though he is naturally put out at having received a defective kit.
4. He gives the company two alternatives. In other words, he tells them specifically what he wants in the way of an adjustment.

And since the success of any letter depends upon the results it brings, let's have a look at Mr. G. Krepp's excellent reply to Earl's request for adjustment:

Dear Mr. Weinstein:

We are sorry to learn that you have been inconvenienced by a defective meter movement in your model V-5A VTM. You may be sure that the Heath Company will provide you with the necessary replacement.

You will soon receive a replacement meter movement, and we will appreciate the return of the defective meter at your convenience. Of course, there will be no charge for this service, and we sincerely hope that no further difficulty will develop.

If you have any question about your Heathkit VTM, just write to me.

Sincerely yours,

Mr. Krepp follows the approved plan for answering a request for adjustment: if you grant the request,

1. Do it promptly, in the first sentence.
2. Do it graciously so as to get the maximum good will out of your action.
3. Express sorrow or regret that this thing has happened.
4. After you have let your reader know he will get what he wants, or at least something, explain or go into details about the problem.

REMEMBER: Politeness will get you more than rudeness!

If, however, you cannot make the adjustment requested or cannot give anything, take a little longer:

1. Express sorrow or regret that this problem has arisen.
2. Take each request seriously. Your reader has. Don't be flippant or try to pass it off lightly or humorously. That won't win friends for you.
3. Give a detailed explanation as to the trouble and explain your position and why you can't make the adjustment requested.
4. If possible, offer an alternative suggestion.
5. Close with an appeal for good will and continued business.

Here is the substance of a letter my wife once received from Lane Bryant in reply to a request to exchange a dress she had purchased by mail but was not completely happy with:

Dear Mrs. Riebel:

Thank you for writing us about the dress, Style 64B, which you recently ordered from our Chicago store and which you wish to return for exchange. Every woman who orders a Lane Bryant dress has the satisfaction of knowing that nobody else has ever worn or even tried that dress on. She is the first one to do this. That assured her of receiving dresses fresh from the presser, sealed in cellophane bags.

As you know, we sent you the style and size which you ordered. For that reason we cannot accept the dress for return or for exchange. We sincerely hope that you will be pleased with this dress and that we may have the pleasure of serving you again soon.

Cordially yours,

My wife was so pleased with this reply that, although it refused her request, she wore it and came to like the dress very much. So remember when you write a complaint or request for adjustment, or if you have to answer such a letter, a letter *does* take the place of a personal visit; so put yourself in your reader's place and then write the kind of letter you would like to receive—or at least wouldn't resent. Accentuate the positive and subdue the negative if you can't eliminate it. Put smiles into your letters. Remember, your reader is another human being probably quite like you. Treat him as one and he will like you all the more for your consideration. Remember well these words:

IT ISN'T SO MUCH *WHAT* YOU SAY THAT BLESSES OR BURNS YOU, THAT HELPS OR HURTS YOU, AS HOW YOU SAY IT!

You can say something that isn't so pleasant, but if you smile and act human about it, your reader will accept your decision graciously. What you can give, GIVE GRACIOUSLY, CHEERFULLY, GLADLY. What you refuse, refuse courteously, clearly, logically, considerately.

19. Regret:

Although we don't want to go around being Casper Milquetoasts or Uriah Heeps, there are times when we have to express regret or sorrow that something happened, or maybe didn't happen as expected. Here are some additional words of wisdom:

DON'T BE AFRAID TO SAY "I'M SORRY." Some people have the odd notion that it is unmanly to say "I'm sorry" for something that has happened. Nonsense! That's a foolish, short-sighted attitude. Most people are human. Mistakes will happen. We can't prevent them. But we can do two things: (1) express regret that they did happen, and (2) indicate that we'll try not to let them happen again. Irving Mack does an excellent job of expressing personal regret in the following letter:

I was certainly sorry to learn, Mr. Russell, that you were disappointed in the MAIN ATTRACTION trailer we made for you recently.

There's one thing we at Filmack strive for—that's a customer who is satisfied 100 per cent, whether he spends $2.50, $25.00, or $250.00 for a trailer.

If we in any way slip up on our workmanship or service, we want to be the first ones to know about it, because our work is unconditionally guaranteed.

Will you return the defective trailer so that we can screen it and hold a post mortem to see just where we went wrong? When we see what happened, we'll be happy to remake it and send you a trailer for which neither of us will have to apologize.

Believe me, Mr. Russell, we sincerely regret any inconvenience you may have been caused. I do hope that you will understand it was one of those things that can happen in the best regulated families, of which FILMACK is no exception.

Regretfully,

20. Sympathy:

One of the hardest kind of letter to write is one expressing sympathy for the death of a friend or acquaintance. Perhaps it is better to start out with what NOT TO DO:

1. Don't get sloppy sentimental. Say your piece and have done with.
2. Don't call upon the Deity by saying "It's God's will," etc.

LETTER WRITING

PAGE 113

3. Don't quote poetry.

Now here are several things you should do:
1. Be brief—nobody at such a time wants a long-drawn-out eulogy.
2. Be sincere—this is the wrong time and place to shovel it on.
3. Be specific—say something personal about the deceased.
4. Be helpful—at least offer your services even though there is slight chance that they will be accepted.

Here are two excellent examples written by Mr. Vern Boget, retired vice president in charge of sales at Gladding, McBean & Co. in Los Angeles:

Dear Tom:

There isn't much that anyone can say that will comfort you in your great loss, but I do want you to know that you have our heartfelt sympathy.

I have known and worked with your father over thirty years. He was always grand to me and a bulwark of the business. His passing is a terrific loss to all of us.

Sincerely,

Dear Mrs. Miller:

Although there isn't much that we can say that will be of much comfort to you at a time like this, we at Gladding, McBean want you to know that Walter's passing has made us feel that we have lost a very close friend whom we shall miss very much.

If there is anything we can do to be of help, won't you please let us know?

Sincerely,

21. Report:

Since all good things have to come to an eventual close, I'll end this discussion of types of letters technical writers should know by combining a type of letter, the memo-report, with a style or form of letter writing known as the "inter-organization form."

A memorandum is seldom in full or complete business letter form. It is usually a note, sometimes with a salutation, usually without a complimentary closing, but always with a signature, either complete or simply initials. Some years ago there developed a form or style called the "interorganization," which really should be called the "intraorganization" because it is used almost exclusively within ("intra") an organization itself, such as within the Cal Poly family of campuses—San Luis Obispo, San Dimas, and Kellogg-Voorhis—rather than between ("inter") Cal Poly and the other state colleges, etc. But the term "interorganization" has become so firmly established that, although it is a patent misnomer, nothing I can say or do will change the inevitable. So be it. Here is the kind of letterhead used in such memos and letters:

MEMO

To   Date

From

Subject

Copies To   File No.

CALIFORNIA STATE POLYTECHNIC COLLEGE   •   SAN LUIS OBISPO CAMPUS

Here is one of the finest, most complete yet concise letter reports that I have ever read. To the left is a running explanation of what makes this such an outstanding specimen of technical communication:

(NOTE: Often the writer of an interorganization letter will place his initials either immediately after his name, or under the last word to show that he has read and approved this memo.)

Date: July 24, 19

To: R. C. Conover, Comptroller
Los Angeles Office

The heading

From: L. M. Stevens, Chief Engineer
Southern Division

Subject: EQUIPMENT OFFERED FOR SALE AT THE TOM REED MINE, KINGMAN, ARIZONA.

Who went where, when, how, and what they did.

Ben Taylor and I drove to Needles, Thursday evening, July 19, proceeded to Kingman Friday morning to inspect the mining and milling equipment, and returned to Glendale Saturday morning.

Note that Stevens used the word "appeared" twice. Note also the detail with which he described the mills.

The only equipment that appeared to be in first-class condition was three Allis-Chalmers ball mills with drives, feeders, etc. The mills are driven through herringbone gears by direct-connected, slow-speed electric motors. The ball mills are 6x6, 5x5, and 5x6 feet. The 6x6 foot mill appeared to be in the best condition, and was located in a position where removal from the plant would not be extremely difficult.

He's a good bargainer, too! Note the detailed description of the conditions of this offer!

The J. J. Sugarman Company, liquidators, has reduced the price on the 6x6 foot mill from $16,000 to $9,000. We offered $7,500 for the 6x6 foot mill complete with motor, starters, apronfeeder, and miscellaneous spare parts loaded on our truck at the mill site.

Since Stevens rejected their revised offer to $9,000, his counter-offer must first be checked with the liquidators.

Mr. Irving Schredder, the Sugarman representative, is to call us July 25 with their decision relative to acceptance of our offer.

The memorandum is usually much less formal than the business letter. Also it may be typed or handwritten. There are a few distinguishing features which mark the interoffice memo: all terminal punctuation in the heading is eliminated. There is no indention or salutation and complimentary closing. And the "subject" is often written in all capitals. It is a quick, concise, convenient way of communicating within an organization, office, or college.

Rules for Typing Letters

1. Use only standard typewriting paper, 8½x11, white, a good grade of bond, 16 lb. or 20 lb.
2. There are 10 pica spaces or strokes to an inch, or 95 across the sheet. There are 12 elite spaces or strokes to an inch, or 102 across the sheet.
3. If the left edge of the paper is at 0, the pica center on the 8½" sheet is 42 or 43. The elite center is 51.
4. There are 6 vertical lines per inch, or 66 lines from top to bottom on an 11" side.
5. Single space all letters. Double spacing is seldom used today within paragraphs.
6. Double space between paragraphs, between the last line of the inside address and the salutation, between the salutation and the first line of paragraph 1, and the last line of your last paragraph and your complimentary closing.
7. The space between your heading and the first line of your inside address will depend on the length of your letter.
8. Leave from 4 to 6 spaces for your signature and your typed signature.
9. Always type your signature exactly as you signed your letter to avoid confusion.
10. If a letter has over 300 words, use two pages and follow the rules for a long letter (below). Use letterhead paper for page 1 only; use the same quality and grade of paper for any succeeding pages. Never use letterheads for second or carbon copies. On page 2, type on lines 7, 8, or 9 the name of the addressee, the page number, and the date:

    John P. Riebel   page 2   August 30, 19

11. Set your margins as follows:

Length of Letters		*Length of Line*	*Pica* — *Margins* — *Elite*	
Short:	0-100 words	4" or 40 pica strokes	23 and 63	27 and 75
Medium:	100-200 words	5" or 50 pica strokes	18 and 68	21 and 81
Long:	200-300 words	6" or 60 pica strokes	13 and 73	15 and 87
Very long:	over 300 words	6½" or 65 pica strokes	10 and 75	12 and 90

The right margin release may be set at 63 and the margin release used to complete a word or syllible, or it may be set to ring at 63.

12. Type your heading—SINGLE SPACE:

    1933 San Luis Drive
    San Luis Obispo, California

    (Avoid all but the most necessary abbreviations.)

    August 30, 19

    Put your date on the 12th line from the top except on very short letters. Then use the 14th line. If you use letterheads, put date 2 lines below letterhead.

Type the longest line in your heading first so that it will end at the right-hand margin. DO NOT ABBREVIATE THE NAME OF THE STATE, THE WORDS "STREET, AVENUE, ROAD," etc. NEVER TYPE YOUR NAME IN THE HEADING. Put it under your signature.

13. Type the inside address—usually identical to the address on the envelope:

    Use as few lines as possible, but include everything absolutely necessary, such as the person's title, department, etc. Often this inside address is omitted on letters after the first. It is useful only when further correspondence is necessary.

Words in the body of the letter		*Line from the top on which to begin inside address:*
	Under 50	25 (11 to 13 spaces between the date line on the
Short —	50 - 75	24 the 12th line and the inside address.)
	75 - 100	23
	100 - 125	22 (7 to 10 spaces between the date line on the 12th
Medium —	125 - 150	21 line and the inside address.)
	150 - 175	20
	175 - 200	19
	200 - 225	18 (4 to 6 spaces between the date line on the 12th
Long —	225 - 250	17 line and the inside address.)
	250 - 300	16

Mr. George W. Otto
General Parts & Service Manager
Cadillac Motor Car Division
Detroit 2, Michigan

Set the tabular stop at 5 if you wish to indent your paragraphs, and at 38 (pica) and 46 (elite) for your complimentary closing. However, you need not indent your paragraphs, for many letter writers today do not indent their paragraphs.

14. The envelope:
A No. 6¾ (small): Space down 12 lines and in 2½" (25 pica or 30 elite spaces). You may single or double space, but always block.
A No. 10 (large) Space down 14 lines and in 4" (40 pica or 48 elite spaces).
Your return address in the upper left-hand corner: Space down 2 lines and in 3 spaces. Always single space and block.
To address postal cards: Space down 11 lines and in 2" (20 pica or 24 elite spaces).
Complimentary closing: Begin 5 spaces to left of center (at 38 pica or 46 elite spaces).

Some Legal Aspects of Business Letter Writing

Since engineers and others who do technical writing have to write business letters, it is good to know what legal entanglements one can get into by not knowing at least the basic elements of responsibility attendant upon the writing and use of business letters. Here is a brief but comprehensive outline of these responsibilities:

Civil Responsibility—almost entirely a matter of contracts, agreements enforceable by law. A contract is a promise or agreement between two parties (in the legal sense) to do or to refrain from doing some lawful act.

A. There are two types of written contracts:
  1. "Made in fact" (letters).
  2. "Formally agreed upon" (written and signed).
B. To be valid, contracts must . . .
  1. Have parties capable of contracting:
    a. Be of legal age.
    b. Be of sound mind.
    c. Have unrestricted civil rights—must not be in prison.
  2. Have freedom from coercion.
  3. Have a lawful purpose.
  4. Have sufficient "consideration" (money)—if insufficient consideration is given, it becomes a promise, not a contract.
C. In letters, a contract is made when an offer is accepted:
  1. An offer must be definite as to price, terms, number of items to be sold. (A mere quotation of price, as in a catalog, is not an offer.)
  2. An offer is not effective until it is communicated to the offeree by the offeror or his authorized agent.
  3. An offer must be written, mailed, and received before it can be accepted.
  4. Once the offer is received, it remains open until it . . .
    a. Is withdrawn—the offeror can withdraw his offer at any time prior to its acceptance. Otherwise it continues for a "reasonable time," which may have to be defined by a court.
    b. Lapses because of the expiration of time. (This offer is good until midnight, June 30, 19 .)
    c. Is rejected. (Once rejected, the offeror cannot be forced to accept or sell at the original price.)
    d. Is accepted:
      (1) The acceptance must be definite—an acknowledgement is not an acceptance of an offer.
      (2) The acceptance becomes effective by mail as soon as it is posted. If the offer is made by telephone or telegraph, the acceptance is not effective until it is received by the offeror. Therefore a telegram of rejection reaching the offeror negates a letter of acceptance if the telegram reaches him first.
    e. The offeree may in no way change the terms of the original offer. If he does (as Stevens did, see page 114), he is making a counter-offer, which may or may not be accepted by the original offeror.

Criminal Responsibility—chiefly a matter of libel, which is a violation of a legal duty toward someone.

A. Libel is false and unprivileged (not authorized or requested and therefore unprotected, legally) publication by writing, picture, etc. which reflects upon the character of another.
B. In libel cases, intent to injure must be proved, and this is often hard to do.

Postal Responsibility—the use of the mails to . . .

A. *Defraud*—
  1. Extortion (See *Extortion* below)
  2. Threat—the use of too strong language (see *Extortion, A—*below)
  3. The use of postal cards for confidential matter: duns, collection, etc. (As long as no incriminating words, such as "Past due—please remit," etc. are used, statements such as gas, water, electricity, etc. may be printed and sent on postal cards.)
B. Obscene matter sent through the mail: coarse, vulgar, pornographic, indecent matter may not be sent via mail. Again there is the matter of intent—as with *Playboy, Esquire,* etc. If the intent is not obscene, there is no case.

Application to Collection Letters:

Extortion—defined in the Criminal Code of the United States as . . .

"Whosoever shall, under threat of informing or as a consideration for not informing, against any violation of any law of the United States, demand or receive any money or other valuable thing, shall be fined not more than two thousand dollars, or imprisoned not more than one year, or both."

A. As long as the writer confines his threats to civil action which may be taken to recover the unpaid amount, he is safe.
B. When letters take on the threat of criminal prosecution, the person mailing them enters upon dangerous ground: EXTORTION!

Libel—Whenever a collection letter contains information which might be injurious to the credit or character of the debtor, there arises the possibility of libel.

A. Libel consists of the publication of a written or printed statement about a person's character or reputation which tends to defame or injure him in his business, professional, or personal life, or which subjects him to public ridicule or scorn.
B. One guilty of libel may be subjected to both civil and criminal prosecution.
C. The two defenses against the charge of libel are truth and good faith.
   1. In criminal cases, the absence of any malicious intent is usually a good defense.
   2. The truth of a statement is no defense if it is made with malicious intent.
   3. Whenever both truth and good intent are found, the sender of a defamatory letter is never found guilty of libel.
   4. In civil cases, most states hold that truth is a good defense even though the statement is made with malicious intent. However, a small group hold that even in civil cases, truth must be accompanied by good motive.
   5. In civil action for libel, good motive alone is not a good defense.
D. The essence of libel consists in making known (publishing) the libelous material or information to a third person or persons:
   1. If the sender of a libelous letter has no reason to believe his letter will be opened by a third person (secretary, wife, etc.), no libel is committed.
   2. If he knows that a third person will open the mail, he is liable, for "publication" has taken place.
   3. If an unsealed envelope is used and it is proved that a third person has opened and read the letter, liability results.
   4. If the recipient becomes angry and shows the letter to a third party, no liability results.
   5. Mailing "dunning statements" on postal cards or post cards constitutes libel.

Application to Credit Letters

Deceit—If the credit information given to the person requesting it is unduly favorable, the recipient may under certain conditions recover damages in a tort (a civil wrong) action of deceit.

A. The action of deceit is based upon intentional misrepresentation, or one recklessly made without regard to its truth or falsity—made for the purpose of inducing another to rely upon it.
   1. If a person relies upon this information to his detriment, he may recover for damages sustained.
   2. If the one supplying the information is honest in his opinions and has taken reasonable pains to find out the truth of his statements made, no liability results.
   3. Most of the time the person supplying the information is giving only his personal opinion. If an honest opinion is fairly given, no cause for action arises.
   4. Persons who share credit information do well to make it clear that the statements given are matters of opinion only.

Libel—the publication of defamatory credit information.

A. To a civil action of libel, truth is always a good defense.
B. In criminal cases, good faith may be used as a defense.

Privilege—If the information is requested by one who has a definite interest to protect, the one supplying this information is privileged. (This applies also to information about job applicants.)

A. Because of privilege, one giving credit information at the request of one who expects to use this information as a basis for extending or denying credit is not guilty of libel even though the information is untrue.
B. If the facts or statements are volunteered when not requested, or if from the character of the letter malice is apparent, privilege is denied.
C. The communications of business agencies are probably privileged, although the law is somewhat vague about this matter.
   1. If the information is sent only to persons having a present interest in it, no liability results.
   2. When the information is sent to all who subscribe to a service, including those who have no immediate interest, untrue statements are probably libelous although made in good faith.
D. The law is still uncertain about a group of competitors who agree not to extend credit to certain individuals as long as they are on the delinquent list of any member of the association—in short, who form a "blacklist."
   1. If the debtor is denied the right to purchase either for cash or on credit from these merchants, privilege is probably lost.

2. If the list is used merely to stop further extensions of credit by members of the organization, the one giving the information probably can set up privilege as an effective defense.

Legal Rights in Business Letters

1. The receiver may retain the letter once he has received it, for the paper on which the letter has been written is his, and he may sue to recover it.
2. However, the receiver has no right to publish the contents of the letter without the consent of the writer.
3. Thus the use to which the receiver may put the letter is limited, and the sender is protected from unfavorable publicity.

The Moral

1. Watch what you say, how you say it, and on what you say it.
2. Don't use a letter without the written permission of the writer or else . . .

Word Pests That Infest Business Letters

A talk given before the annual meeting of the Pest Control Operators of California, Inc., December, 1958, at the Pomona Campus of California State Polytechnic College.

There are all kinds of pests. Human pests like barflies, braggarts, Milquetoasts, know-it-alls, wolves, party dolls, blabber mouths, etc. Then there are radio and TV commercials—pests that scream at you, bawl you out, shake their finger in your face, wave a roll of . . . uh. . . er . . . blow your nose, bathe you, expose your innards for everyone to see, etc. Then, of course there are termites, fleas, bedbugs, mosquitos, cockroaches, rats (two legged as well as four), bats (in and out of belfries), gnats, and a host of other flying, crawling, biting, squirming, lying, cheating, backbiting pests.

But the pests I'd like to talk about now are known under the generic name of *pestifori wordii*, more popularly known as simply word pests—the kind that infest and poison so many modern business letters.

Pestifori wordii can be further classified or subdivided into eight major groups: 1. *pestifori vagii*, or vague words: 2. *pestifori inaccuratii*, or inaccurate words; 3. *pestifori supercillii*, or snooty words; 4. *pestifori triteii*, or stale, hackneyed expressions; 5. *pestifori verbasii*, or wordiness; 6. *pestifori frigidii*, or cold, unfriendly words; 7. *pestifori pompousii*, or pompous, bombastic words; and, to draw this nauseating classification to a revolting closing, 8. *pestifori antiquatii*, or old-fashioned language.

Now if you don't like my Latin, you're in good company. I don't like it either. But, like the Immortal Bard, who bragged that he has "little Latin and less Greek," TIME MARCHES ON! And if you find that hard to figure out, just wait until you read some examples taken from modern business letters. And those writers weren't even trying to be funny!

With your kind permission, let us pause a moment to peruse a sample of strictly modern (1890 variety, that is) business writing—a spacious tent crammed full of more word monsters than Gracie Allen can spawn in a dozen TV programs—more, perhaps, than you will even use in doing your daily dictation tomorrow.

> Pursuant to yours of the 20th inst., which valued communication has been brought to the writer's personal attention, beg to state that the undersigned is deeply cognizant and aware of the prime urgency of the situation relative to the unfortunate and unavoidable delay in processing shipment of the parts for your Model AB-3. However, under the prevailing and existing circumstances, and due to the fact that there has been an unfortunate and unavoidable delay in requisitioning the requisite steel necessary for the complete and satisfactory completion of your order, it will, in all probability, require the expenditure of an additional amount of time in the amount of seven days, more or less, before we can hope to be in a position to initiate your shipment. Trusting that this will explain clearly to your complete and utter satisfaction our present position in this matter and assuring you of our sincere and earnest desire to be of whatever assistance and aid we may be under the aforementioned unfortunate and unavoidable circumstances, we beg to remain,

See what I mean?

Translated into simple nickel-and-dime words, this pish-pash means:

> You may be sure that we, too, are disturbed by our inability to ship you the parts you need so badly for your model AB-3. It may not comfort you much to hear that the steel shortage is the sole villain— but it's the truth, Mr. Doe.
>
> Perhaps we can ship some of these parts within a week, but I won't promise. You have our assurance that they *will* be sent as soon as possible.

Wallowing in a welter of wasted words, it took that pompous old stuffed shirt 173 words to say what Conversational Charlie did in only 75—almost 100 fewer! And at the cost of business letters today, that's a clear saving of at least $1.50. But we won't have time to go into that now!

And all it took to fumigate the original and drive out all the *pestifori wordii* was one generous squirt of good old H. T.—*The Human Touch*—guaranteed to kill in one spraying all word pests in your business letters.

Let's take a closer look at each of the eight major species of most noxious and nauseating pests—

LETTER WRITING

Pestifori Vagii

Fuzzy wording results from fuzzy thinking. You can't hope to draw a single fine thread of thought out of a wadded ball of cotton. And many a business writer has a great big ball of wadded cotton where his brain ought to be. *Ergo*—more Latin!—fuzzy thinking; *ergo ergo*—fuzzy wording, or wooliness. This writer is truly an intellectual nudist; you can't pin a thing on him. He persists in using expressions like these:

at your earliest convenience—who knows, it may never be "convenient!" Especially if I am asked to pay some money!

by return mail—there just ain't no such animal! Back in the days of the Pony Express, yes, for then the rider usually betook himself to the local bistro to wash down the dust, etc., and you had plenty of time to pen your reply and actually send it "by return mail" or "by return post." Today? Hogwash! Say what you mean: *immediately, promptly, soon, within five days,* or *by December 20.*

sign the enclosed and return to us immediately—who does what to whom, and who's going to get stuck with the bill? Add the word "it" and I'll buy this expression.

your letter of recent date—don't you know the date of his letter? Better get it out and see what you're answering.

your letter of even date—today? If so, in this area of California, how in heaven's name could that be possible—mail a letter one day and have it delivered that same day! IMPOSSIBLE! Be specific.

Come to us for *dignified credit*—what's dignified about having to borrow money? This certainly is sugar coating the pill!

to initiate your shipment—egads! No wonder there is so much breakage!

Pestifori Inaccuratii

A highfalutin' way of saying just plain "inaccurate!" Closely akin to *pestifori vagii*, this pest differs more in species than in genus. Carelessness is its father, indifference its mother. From such inauspicious parents come such offspring as—

enclosed please find—why make the poor sucker . . . er, I mean "reader" . . . hunt? Why not simply *attach* or *enclose* the material so that it can easily be seen?

your kind order at hand—how in Heaven's name can an order be either "kind" or "unkind?" And does this mean that he has your order clutched in his hot little fist? Simply thank him for his order. That's the natural way.

kindly sign on the dotted line—don't you dare do it *roughly,* or *gruffly,* or *toughly!* One can sign his name legibly or illegibly, yes—but *kindly?* Never. Say *Please.*

Thank you kindly for your patronage—shades of the Immortal Bard again! He lived in a day when artists and writers had to have "patrons"—wealthy noblemen to whom they servilly dedicated their works in return for enough money to keep their VW's in gas. Today we do not need "patrons," and we have "patronage" only in politics. Business is business, not politics.

we are not in a position to—you don't have to screw yourself into a pretzel-shape just to say simply "we cannot."

the enclosed self-addressed stamped envelope is for your convenience in replying—Bushwa! In the first place, it's for your payment. In the second place, if your reader is smart enough to read your letter he can see that it is stamped. And in the third place, did you ever see an envelope address itself? How else can it be *self*-addressed?

thank you in advance—a sneaky way of putting your reader under obligation to do what you ask, even if he doesn't want to. You've already thanked him for doing it; so he's a cad if he doesn't. And who wants to be a cad? Either say you'll appreciate his doing this, or wait until he actually does it. Then thank him.

kindly command me—go ahead and do it—I DARE YOU!

we are contemplating adding—still up on Cloud 9 thinking things over, eh?

your valued communication—would you call a complaint or a collection letter a "valued communication?" Don't go overboard. Plain people are the salt of the earth. Most readers like 'em plain, simple, natural, friendly.

we beg to remain—begging's undignified and unmanly. DON'T! Remain? Where?

convenient monthly payments—what idiot thought that one up? Who ever heard of any payments being "convenient?" But we best not pursue this further.

my personal attention—what other kind is there? Ever give anything your impersonal attention?

Pestifori Supercillii

Which is just another way of saying snooty words —the kind that makes you feel the writer is disdainfully looking down his nose and sneering at you as he writes them:

we have your letter and contents noted—don't brag about having read a business letter. It's all in a day's work. Instead, thank him for his letter. He'll like that, you may be sure.

in due course of time—just keep your shirt on, Buster. We'll get around to you when we're good and ready, not before! This is a good way NOT to win new friends and influence more favorably old and valued customers.

kindly permit me to say—that pompous old billygoat! How I'd like to puncture his inflated ego! Why ask permission? He's going to say it anyway. So go ahead and do it; you're just a-wasting good words and valuable time.

for your perusal, kindly peruse—perfectly acceptable expressions when Grandpa wore rompers. But today, no one goes around "perusing" anything. Say it simply: "Read carefully." Even a low-grade moron can understand that.

with your kind permission—how can "permission" be kind or unkind? Only living things, particularly human beings, can be kind.

we trust same is satisfactory—here the word "trust" implies ill-concealed arrogance or scorn. But if you use "hope" and substitute "this" for "same," you are using a great BIG dash of good old H.T. Do it more often, please.

the undersigned, the writer, yours truly—call a spade a spade here. Don't have I-trouble, or WE-writis, either. But don't go to these silly lengths to avoid using these good old standard pronouns. Personal pronouns are some of our most intimate words.

Pestifori Triteii

Call them trite, hackneyed, stale, moth-eaten, moss covered, or what you will, they are really dead as the dodo. They have outlived their usefulness and have long since died. Why not bury them and sweeten the atmosphere of your business letters?

above-mentioned orders, above listed parts numbers—say either "these," or exactly what you mean. But if you MUST use "above," for Pete's sake put it where it belongs: *after* mentioned or listed: "orders mentioned above;" "parts listed above."

aforementioned, aforesaid—Ho hum. More business gobbledegook of the Gay Nineties! Use "these." Or you might say "mentioned previously."

herein, hereto, herewith—unnecessary fat, like that spare tire I'm wearing around my middle! Get rid of them PRONTO!

our stock is depleted (or *exhausted*)—poor old stock, just plain tuckered out! Avoid the unpleasant implication by saying:: "We are out of ... ."

at the present writing—now? If so, then SAY SO!

a party is interested in—one person? two? how many? Call a person a person in a letter. Only in legal documents can you use "party" correctly: "Party of the first part . . .", etc.

inst.—like *prox.* (for *proximo*) and *ult.* (for *ultimo*), *instanto—inst.* for short—went out with bustles and bows. Unfortunately, some business letter writers haven't found that out!

Pestifori Verbasii

Probably the most annoying pest is wordiness—verbosity—garrulousness—circumlocution — beating around the bush and never coming to the point directly—using five words when one or two would do the job—being prodigal with words. After all, they are in the dictionary, like money in the bank. And what are words and money for if not to spend? But extra words take your reader's precious time—and his patience, too. So save him time and money by avoiding:

inasmuch as—which means "since" or "because."

in the amount of $15—a roundabout way of saying "for $15."

at all times—does it ever mean anything other than ALWAYS?

relative to—this means "about."

at an early date—windy for "soon."

at this time, at the present time, at the present writing—all mean NOW!

costs the sum of—strike the last three words and what do we have left? COSTS!

due to the fact that, in view of the fact that—roundabout ways of saying "because" or "since."

under separate cover, by separate cover—either eliminate entirely or say "separately."

in the neighborhood of—this means "about" in any man's language.

thank you again—once is enough. Don't be a modern Uriah Heep!

to your complete satisfaction—you probably won't be satisfied if it isn't "complete."

in the event that—wordy for "if."

I wish to say that, May I say that, Permit me to say that—not only pompous and supercilious, but downright unnecessary. Start with whatever follows the word "that."

consensus of opinion—in its definition, "consensus" includes the word "opinion." Therefore say simply: "The consensus is that we should . . ."

we are today in receipt of—a sneaky, roundabout way of saying "today we received."

first of all—of what else, pray? Strike "of all."

the requisite steel necessary—needless doubling. "Requisite" means "necessary."

conclude and end, cognizant and aware, prime urgency, first and foremost, sincere and earnest—some people can't say a thing once and have done with it. They have to shake it as a dog shakes a bone. More needless doubling. Use either word, but not both!

Pestifori Frigidii

Cold, unfriendly formality, whether it was intentional or not, has done more to kill off the fruits of business than any single other verbal pest. And the cure for this pest is a generous spraying of good old H.T. (the Human Touch) to help you avoid—

this will acknowledge your request for—brrr! How cold and unfriendly can a letter opening be? Warm it up 100 degrees by thanking him for his request.

you claim that we shipped you some defective...—put up your dukes, Buster. Them's fightin' words. Call me a liar, will you?

your complaint has been received—and I had good reason to complain, too! *This* time DON'T call a spade a spade. Call a complaint a "suggestion," a "request," a "request for adjustment," or some thing that won't make your reader blow up in your face.

Please acknowledge!—written this way, the pronunciation of "please" becomes puh-LEEZ! Soften the shock with a "will you?" at the end.

your postal card inquiry—you bloomin' cheapskate! NO! Thank him for his inquiry, no matter what it was written on. Treat all inquiries first class.

according to our records—sounds as if you're calling him a liar in no unmistakable terms. These are dangerous, sandpaper words. Use them rarely, if ever.

we hope this information will satisfy you—take that and don't bother me any more! Another good way of how NOT to win new friends.

Pestifori Pompousii

A business letter's a poor place for florid, bombastic, oratorical language—

be good enough to send me—if you don't send him something, you're not good enough!

your esteemed communication—oh slush, get your rubbers. Cut out the sentimentality.

feel free to—we *are* free to do what we want here in America in 1958, as long as it doesn't infringe on the rights of others. Instead, say "please" or "just."

for your perusal—sounds familiar. Haven't we taken a crack at this one earlier?

upon investigation we find that your account is...—your real thought begins with YOUR.

I feel you will be able to—keep your cotton-picking paws to yourself! Say "think."

pursuant to yours of the 20th inst.—shades of the dear, dead past. *In pace requiscat!*

Pestifori Antiquatii

In short, OLD FASHIONED! Hangovers from Great-Grandpappy's day. Use some bright new conversational pieces to take the place of these old chestnuts—

as per your letter of—say "in your letter of."

in compliance with your request of—this means, simply, "as you requested." SAY IT!

I have before me your letter—who gives a hoot *where* you have it? Thank him for it.

I beg to remain—one of the weakest closings you can use. Eliminate it entirely.

thanking you for your kind attention, hoping to hear from you soon, trusting you will favor us with your order—all weak, spineless closings. Avoid the participle at the beginning of your letter and also at the ending. Use strong, active verbs: "Thank you for...," "We hope to hear...," "We'd like to fill your order, Mr. Blow." End with your reader's name. He'll love you for that.

* * *

Well, my friends, the time has come when we must part. And as old Willie said, "Parting is such sweet sorrow." But you won't have any sorrow if you will go back over the last dozen letters you have dictated and eliminate all the word pests you have become acquainted with today. And when you do, resolve never again to let these word pests creep into your business letters and upset the delicate balance of friendly human relations that you and your salesmen have built up between you and your customer-friend.

Remember, what was good enough for Great-Granddaddy ISN'T GOOD ENOUGH FOR US TODAY! We live in another world—a world in which the language of the dear dead past has no place. May it forever rest in peace and preserve us from any and all word pests!

John P. Riebel

APPENDIX

SELECTED READINGS

Suggestions for the Preparation of Technical Papers

By ROBERT T. HAMLETT

Summary—The value and purpose of technical papers is presented, followed by generalized suggestions for their preparation. Separate sections deal with the *introduction, main body,* and *conclusion.* Throughout is interspersed information on illustrations, value of good logic and grammatical correctness, along with other data for the writing of a paper from its conception through ultimate delivery and publication.

I. INTRODUCTION

THE ENGINEER RARELY FACES a more clean-cut opportunity for accomplishment than that presented to him when he is chosen to prepare a technical paper. The direct benefits of successful accomplishment are three-fold: the author's professional prestige is enhanced, the reputation of the organization he represents is maintained or improved, and last but by no means unimportant, the standing of the engineering profession in general is raised. With these inviting benefits, it is unfortunate that they are only occasionally realized because of poor preparation and even poorer presentation of the technical paper.

The engineer has always labored under the stigma that "Engineers cannot write." It is questionable whether engineers as a class write any more poorly than doctors or lawyers or salesmen. Perhaps the subjects we write about are more complex and require more specific knowledge of the reader. Whether this poor reputation is justified or not, the only logical course for engineers is one of continual self-improvement until this undesirable *class distinction* disappears.

Courses in technical writing are given in many of the better schools but unfortunately the student seldom appreciates at that time the importance of effective writing, and even worse he retains little of what he learned because in the years immediately following graduation there are few opportunities for him to prepare a technical paper. His knowledge of ordinary rules of grammar, rhetoric, and logical presentation become rusty from inactivity and he finds that writing clearly, and keeping in mind these rules is like reading a foreign language taken in high school; the rules tend to confuse rather than simplify his task.

To attempt to lay down in this article a complete and final set of rules for preparation of the perfect technical paper would be an impossible task. There are many variables entering into the preparation of a particular technical paper to be presented under certain circumstances at a specific meeting. Further, the complete skills involved in preparation of a paper encompass the entire education and experience of the engineer. However, there are certain accepted qualities which any successful technical paper must possess. It is the purpose of this article to refresh the engineer's mind on some of these fundamentals and to stress other factors which can make his paper more effective.

The material for this article is derived from the author's avid interest and attendance at technical meetings, from the instruction pamphlets of prominent technical societies, from a number of excellent textbooks on technical writing (see bibliography), and from the helpful suggestions of Sperry's Directors of Engineering.

II. THE PRINCIPAL ELEMENTS

A. The Outline

It is well to recognize at the beginning that writing a technical paper is hard, and sometimes very boring, work. There is certainly no royal road to perfect technical exposition. One must be willing to write and rewrite many times. The successful writer often tears up his copy and starts over again when he finds that the logical development of the paper is blocked by the existing approach.

Most authorities agree that the best way to start is by setting down an outline of the paper, i.e., writing down the principal topics to be covered. Carry the outline as far as possible the first time, let it rest for a few days and then try again. Missing blocks in the outline will begin to appear with increasing ease. The major and minor topics will form a basis for the start of actual writing. Do not worry about organization of the paper until a large portion of the text matter has been written. Preparing an outline, a first draft, and a final copy may appear to involve an unnecessary amount of work, but it is usually true that such a routine actually saves time.

When the basic technical material has been developed, it is time to look at the paper from the reader's viewpoint. The reader's requirements are simple but definite: he must be carefully introduced to the subject of the paper, the subject must be adequately covered, and finally the subject must be concluded. It is alarming how often technical papers violate these three simple rules.

The development of a good technical paper may be compared to the preparation of a good dinner. First there must be an appetizer (introduction) which whets the reader's interest in what is to follow, second the main course (body of text) must be well balanced and full of meat, and third the dessert (conclusion) must be satisfying and should leave a pleasant effect on the reader. While many other courses (soup, salad or spinach!) may be added to round out the technical meal, these three basic elements remain the same for any paper, and must be blended together carefully to accomplish the writer's purpose.

I am indebted to one of my Navy Publication friends for an apt phrase in this connection. He says every effective piece of technical writing requires "that first you tell them what you are going to tell them; then you tell them; and then you tell them what you have told them"—this simplified expression repeats again the basic requirement in any technical paper for *introduction, main body* of information, and *conclusion*.

B. The Introduction

Without question the *introduction* is the most important part of the paper—from the reader's viewpoint. Whether the reader will continue with the paper at all depends largely upon the impression created by the *introduction*. Because of the tremendous growth in variety and complexity of technical subjects, there is an increasing demand from readers that the first page or two of a technical paper should provide a comprehensive idea of the whole paper. The average writer is likely to write too long an introduction or none at all.

It should be recognized that while the *introduction* is read first, it should be written last—after the main body and conclusion are completed, for it must include in an abbreviated form some of the material from each. Do not hesitate to spend a large amount of time in the preparation of the *introduction* for it will pay attractive dividends in number of readers.

C. The Main Body of Text

This portion of the paper contains the technical facts which justify the paper itself. This part of the paper offers the least difficulty to the engineer. He is on more familiar ground where technical grasp of the subject is the primary requisite. If an outline has been prepared the writing should proceed satisfactorily. The first rough draft should be written rapidly without regard for literary style. Too much attention at this time to grammar and spelling will slow down the development of basic material.

A search of contemporary literature on the subject should be made so that the material to be presented will not unknowingly duplicate or contradict existing literature. If the paper does differ in important conclusions with any previously accepted literature, the differences should be pointed out and substantiated by the author. The author should make use of the facilities offered by his Engineering Library for a search of contemporary literature on his subject. The preparation of a satisfactory bibliography is covered in another portion of this article.

Accuracy of data in the paper hardly needs mentioning. The engineer by nature and training is careful in the weighing and analyzing of data and is seldom tempted to distort facts to gain a temporary advantage. However, he cannot exercise too much care in being correct and honest in all of his statements.

Be constructive and positive in presenting the material, never antagonistic, pessimistic or negative. Tearing down some other engineer's reputation will seldom add to the author's professional standing. Direct criticism of competitor companies by name is particularly unwise. In fact the shortest route to the listener's good graces is by paying tribute to others whether they are competitors or associates.

While it is essential that the text cover the subject adequately it is also important that it be neither too detailed nor too complex for the intended reader. After the main body is prepared, go over it several times to cut out material not absolutely necessary for clarity. Almost any technical paper can be boiled down considerably with little loss to the reader. It is an old story around Sperry that our former president, Mr. Reginald Gillmor, was a stickler not only for good written material but also for concise writing. Many times he would return copy to the writer with a notation "cut it in half." After sweating it out the writer would make the required reduction, but then get another shock when he received a second note from Mr. Gillmor "to cut it in half" again. While this method cannot be applied generally, many technical papers could be cut in half and be more interesting and just as informative.

The writing in technical papers should be impersonal; do not use *I* if it can be avoided; try to keep the language in the third person. It is permissible, however, to use *we* occasionally, if its meaning is clear. For example, following several references to a project in the author's company, it may be more diplomatic to use *we* instead of repeating the company name and be criticized for too much "name advertising."

Sentence length is important in the technical paper. When the draft copy has been completed, it is advisable to go over the sentences again and separate the longer ones into lengths that will not burden the reader's power of concentration. If the paper is to be delivered, short sentences will help the speaker in his breathing; 13 words maximum is a good rule to follow. This is a point often overlooked by the engineer who is not a regular speaker.

Carelessness in spelling, grammar or speaking by the engineer may bespeak carelessness in other elements of the paper and may well lead the audience to question the accuracy of the technical statements. Do not split infinitives when you can avoid doing so. The prejudice against split infinitives is deep-seated and persistent. Usually it is just as easy to write effectively as it is to effectively write. However, if there is real gain in emphasis or clearness through splitting the infinitive, you can do so and be in the company of many excellent writers—but you are likely to be misjudged by some readers.

The use of headings and sub-headings is often neglected by the technical author. The more complex a subject becomes the more necessary it is to break it up into a number of parts which the reader can visualize. More than three degrees of sub-headings are not recommended for a paper. For instance, a good example of main and sub-headings would be:

I. GENERAL DESCRIPTION OF XX RADAR SET
  A. Transmitting System
    1. Purpose and general description
    2. Detailed circuit analysis
       a. Modulator
       b. Pulse forming network
       c. Clipper circuit
       d. _____
       e. _____

  B. Receiving System
    1. Purpose and general description
    2. Detailed circuit analysis
       a. Local oscillator
       b. Receiver mixer circuit
       c. I-F section
       d. _____
       e. _____

Avoid the use of unfamiliar terms unless you have time to define them. This is particularly important in the delivered paper. If necessary, a list of symbols should be provided to clarify the text. Long equations or complicated derivations should be placed in an appendix rather than in the main body of the text. Use footnotes sparingly; from the reader's standpoint it is much better to integrate such material with the text. Bibliographical references are an exception; they are usually carried as footnotes on the same page of the matter to which they apply.

D. The Conclusion

The *conclusion* is another challenge to the writing ability of the engineer. It should sum up the major points made in the text and leave the reader with a feeling that the conclusions are fully justified by the data presented. The normal purpose of the technical paper is to inform and not to sell or arouse to action, but it is difficult to visualize a good paper which does not accomplish these latter purposes to some degree. The *conclusion*, like the *introduction*, requires careful writing and rewriting before it will accomplish the author's purpose. One simple warning: do not state that certain conclusions are "obvious" — nothing irritates the average reader more than the assumption by the writer that his own logic requires no substantiation.

E. Illustrations and Lantern Slides

Illustrations can add much to the readability and conciseness of technical papers. As Lord Kelvin pointed out "a single curve, drawn in the manner of the curve of prices of cotton, describes all that the ear can possibly hear as the result of the most complicated musical performance...." The judicious use of illustrations will improve the paper in many ways. It is well to review the completed text for instances where illustrations can shorten or supplement the written material. Do not try to show too much on *one* illustration; a simple illustration will be instantly valuable to the average reader who may not be inclined to concentrate on more complicated diagrams.

If the technical paper is to be delivered, lantern slides can be used advantageously and here it is particularly important not to include so much on the slide that it is

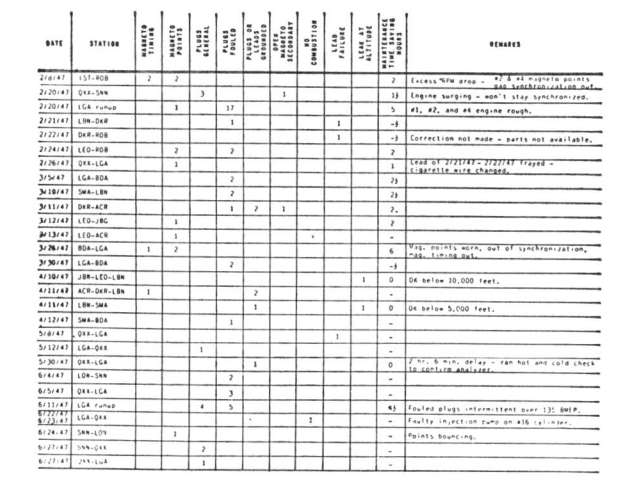

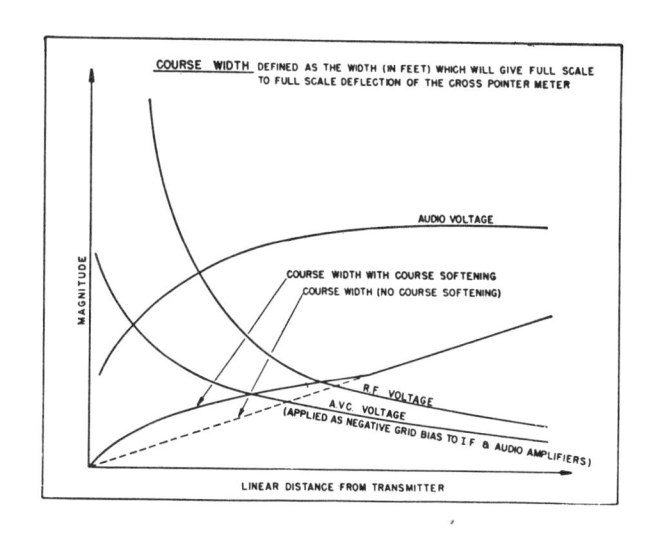

The chart above left is almost unreadable. It is ineffective as a lantern slide and appropriate for a publication only if a large space could be devoted to it. On the right is an excellent example of a good slide or a good diagram for a published paper.

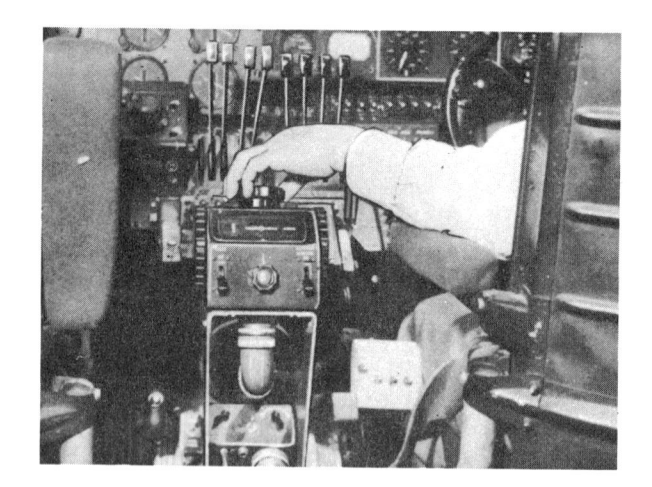

Generally only illustrative material directly concerned with the component under discussion should be included in a lantern slide. Too much background matter often ruins the effect. The photograph (slide) above left is effective to illustrate the complexity of a cockpit but too detailed to permit the pedestal controller of the A-12 Gyropilot to be noticed. The slide on the right, with the co-pilot's hand directed to the controller is far more effective for this purpose.

unreadable by all in the audience. For examples of good and bad slides see the illustrations. The usual lantern slide size is 3¼" x 4"; the original illustration should be about three times this size. Lettering on the original should not be less than ¼" in height; this assures readability in the rear seat of the average-size lecture room.

F. Bibliography

Every good technical paper should have a bibliography of literature related to the subject. This is necessary not only to guide the reader if he has desire to pursue the subject further, but it also indicates that the author is acquainted with the literature in his field and has made use of others' knowledge in the preparation of his paper.

Engineers in preparing their papers frequently and inadvertently offend their readers by using incomplete bibliographical references. In the case of books, the reader may wish to procure for his personal library one or more of those listed. It is appropriate then to include the publisher's name. Page references also are valuable, and page references usually are erroneous unless the edition number of the book also is given. In the case of periodicals, it is helpful to list the volume number as well as the month and year along with page references. Libraries bind their periodicals into volumes and it is helpful both to the reader and the librarian when this number is known. Bibliographies are usually carried as footnotes on appropriate pages of the prepared copy but may be included as a separate section after the *conclusions* section.

The form of bibliographical references may vary but the following are typical and adequate:

For a book —

[1] J. H. Morecroft, *Principles of Radio Communication* (New York: Wiley and Sons, Inc., 1933; 3rd Edition), p. 402.

For a periodical —

[1] P. H. Trickey, "Field Harmonics in Induction Motors," *Electrical Engineering,* L (December 1931), pp. 937-939.

III. Delivery

No matter how excellent the technical paper may be, it loses much of its effectiveness when poorly delivered. One does not have to be a Dale Carnegie graduate to make a creditable appearance before a technical society, but one does have to obey some of the common rules of listener psychology if he hopes to walk off the platform with a feeling of accomplishment instead of confusion and ineffectiveness.

After the paper has been completed, read it out loud several times to get the feel of it. If some of the sentences or paragraphs are too long, cut them into shorter sections which can be read without making the talker puff like a steam engine. If particular words in the text are hard to pronounce, substitute synonyms that are easier to enunciate. Determine the correct reading speed for yourself and stick to it. The average technical lecturer reads about 150 words per minute; if he is speaking without notes this will drop to approximately 100 words per minute. Using the accepted average of 300 words (double-spaced) on the standard sized typewritten sheet, a 10-page article should take about 20 minutes to read or 30 minutes to deliver without notes. Accurate timing of the technical speech will add much to its effectiveness, and will save embarrassment for the author, particularly if the material

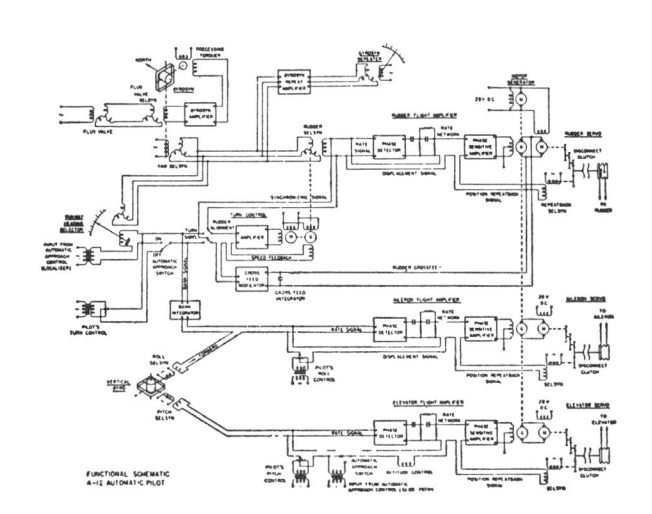

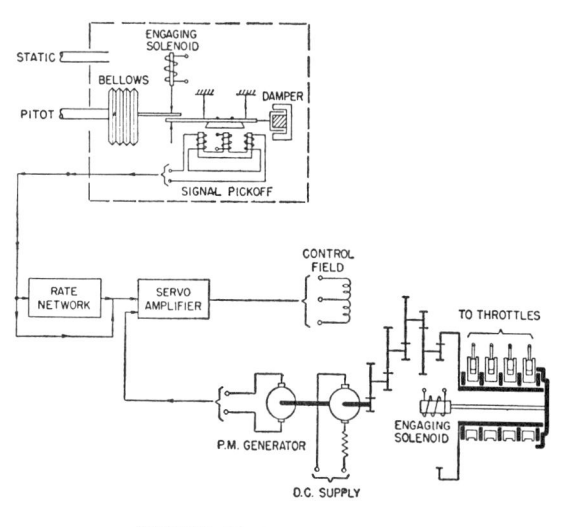

An audience cannot grasp a mass of detail in the moments that a lantern slide is shown on the screen. The diagram on the left above has far too much detail. It might be acceptable for a printed paper if a half page could be allotted. The diagram on the right is well arranged and of the correct content for either a slide or a figure in a paper.

is so long that important conclusions have to be cut short.

Nearly all technical papers are read verbatim by the authors, but there is a growing feeling that engineers should overcome their reticence and not read their papers in a monotonous tone that lulls the audience to sleep. In the opinion of this writer, the most effective technical presentation is partially read, and partially spoken without apparent reference to the written text. The successful talker refers to his notes when necessary, and reads in detail such portions as require exact statements; this dual method gives an atmosphere of authority which is effective and convincing. There is increasing support for the practice of preparing a simplified version of a written paper for oral presentation. Techniques are covered by W. J. Temple in his paper "Preparing the Oral Version of a Technical Paper," published in the March 1948 number of *Proceedings of the I.R.E.*

Above all else, *rehearse* the technical paper several times before its actual delivery. Rehearse it first in front of fellow engineers who are familiar with the subject and who can criticize any apparent technical errors. Rehearse it again in front of someone who is not familiar with your subject (the "better half" is a constructive critic!). This is a tough assignment but it is worth the effort.

IV. CONCLUSION

The preparation of a good technical paper is a real challenge to the engineer. Into its preparation can go the complete range of his abilities—education, experience, and knowledge of human behavior. The technical paper sticks out all over with its good and bad points. No amount of patience and concentration is too great to apply to the task, and the rewards always justify the effort.

The accompanying check list may serve as a "silent" critic of a technical paper.

Good organization, accurate and complete technical material, correct grammar and spelling, suitable illustrations, and effective delivery—these basic points should be kept in mind as the principal factors which will make the technical paper command the interest of its audience, which after all is the only justification for writing it.

V. BIBLIOGRAPHY

A. C. Howell, *A Handbook of English in Engineering Usage* (New York: Wiley & Sons, Inc., 1942; 2nd edition).

Thomas R. Agg and W. L. Foster, *The Preparation of Engineering Reports* (New York: McGraw-Hill Book Co., 1935).

J. R. Wilson, *Writing the Technical Report* (New York: McGraw-Hill Book Co., 1940).

Leslie M. Oliver, *Technical Exposition* (New York: McGraw-Hill Book Co., 1940).

An A.S.M.E. Paper—Its Preparation, Submission and Publication, and Presentation (New York: American Society of Mechanical Engineers, 1947).

Herbert B. Michaelson, "Techniques of Editorial Research," *Journal of the Franklin Institute.* CCXLVII, No. 3 (March 1949), pp. 245.

M. D. Hassialis, "What Constitutes an Acceptable Technical Paper," *Mining and Metals Magazine,* XXIX (September 1948), pp. 456.

W. J. Temple, "Preparing the Oral Version of a Technical Paper," *Proceedings of the I.R.E.,* XXXVI (March 1948), pps. 388-389.

A Manual of Style (Chicago: University of Chicago Press, 1947; 10th edition, 11th impression).

Check List

For the Preparation and Delivery of a Technical Paper

Do—

Recognize the personal and professional opportunities presented in the preparation of a good technical paper.

Prepare an outline before beginning actual writing.

Be willing to write and rewrite every part of the paper.

Be extremely careful with the accuracy of your material.

Consider reader's viewpoint carefully.

Be sure the paper has clearly defined *introduction, main body,* and *conclusion.*

Write the *main body* first, the *conclusion* second, and the *introduction* last.

Keep the main text as concise as possible.

Put long equations and derivations in an appendix.

Use headings and sub-headings for complex material.

Prepare a *conclusion* that sums up the main points made in the body of the text.

Use adequate and suitable illustrations.

Use lantern slides if paper is delivered.

Prepare an adequate bibliography of literature directly related to the subject.

Read paper out loud several times if it is to be delivered orally.

Time your talk so that it fits into allotted period in meeting.

Rehearse talk in front of technical associates.

Rehearse talk in front of non-technical friend.

Try to deliver some portions of the paper without apparent reference to your written material.

Give proper credit to any individuals who inspired or contributed substantially to the paper.

Don't—

Use first person; third person is preferable.

Make mistakes in spelling or grammar.

Split infinitives—unless you are sure it helps!

Employ long and complicated sentences or paragraphs.

Use unfamiliar symbols—if they must be included, define them.

Include too many footnotes; integrate them with the text.

Assume your conclusions are obvious to the reader.

Hesitate to write and rewrite the paper several times.

Use illustrations that have too much in them. Lantern slides should be readable by all in the audience.

Read entire paper in a monotone without once looking at the audience.

Expect your audience to be interested in your paper if you haven't been careful to prepare it with their interests in mind.

Technical Writing Grows into New Profession: Publications Engineering*

By ROBERT T. HAMLETT

Summary — Engineering-level technical writing is described as requiring, foremost, the skills and knowledge of an engineer and, secondly, the ability to write well. For this combination of work the term *publications engineer* is proposed. The technical writers' participation in an engineering project is outlined on a time basis, starting with the sources of information and being completed with delivery of the printed work. Satisfying aspects of the field are discussed and the future is predicted as of growing value to the engineering profession as a whole.

INTRODUCTION

THE TREMENDOUS EXPANSION in the size and productiveness of the engineering profession has been due, in a large measure, to the ability of research and development engineers to enlist other engineers for special tasks or services related to their basic problems. It was not so many years ago that an engineer was *the* engineer—he was charged with responsibility for all engineering work on a project. This was possible because the end result of his engineering work was usually a single unit or instrument which operated without "tie-in" or reference to other equipment. He found time somehow to solve all of the engineering problems that arose in connection with his "brain child."

But the modern era of *systems* rather than *instruments* has changed the engineering approach to a very marked degree. One hears now about systems engineers, product engineers, project engineers, standards engineers, administrative engineers, test engineers, field engineers, production engineers, packaging engineers, industrial engineers, etc., etc. What has happened? Simply that the individual engineer can no longer carry all the burdens of the job of engineering a system or even a single instrument which ties into a system. While a very gifted engineer, possessing high skill in many branches of engineering, may still be able to visualize and guide the work on his project, he is no longer able to carry on the many individual investigations, attend the frequent engineering conferences, plan the fiscal and field testing programs, solve the production and packaging problems, etc.

This ability of the engineer to pass on responsibility to other engineers has given rise to still another field of specialization within the engineering profession—that of *technical writing* (Fig. 1). The products of this new field are instruction books, training manuals, engineering reports, technical data sheets, and many other types of technical information. The workers in this field are variously referred to as technical writers, engineering writers, specification writers, technical report writers, etc. This author prefers to call the workers in this field *publications engineers* in keeping with other well-established titles such as standards engi-

---

* This paper appears essentially in the same form in the October 1952 *Proceedings of the I.R.E.* and is printed simultaneously here with permission of that journal.

Subsequently published in: *Missouri Shamrock, Michigan Technic, Northwestern Engineer, The Georgia Tech Engineer, Kansas Engineer, Minnesota Techno-Log, Illinois Technograph,* and *Rutgers Engineer.*

September-October 1952

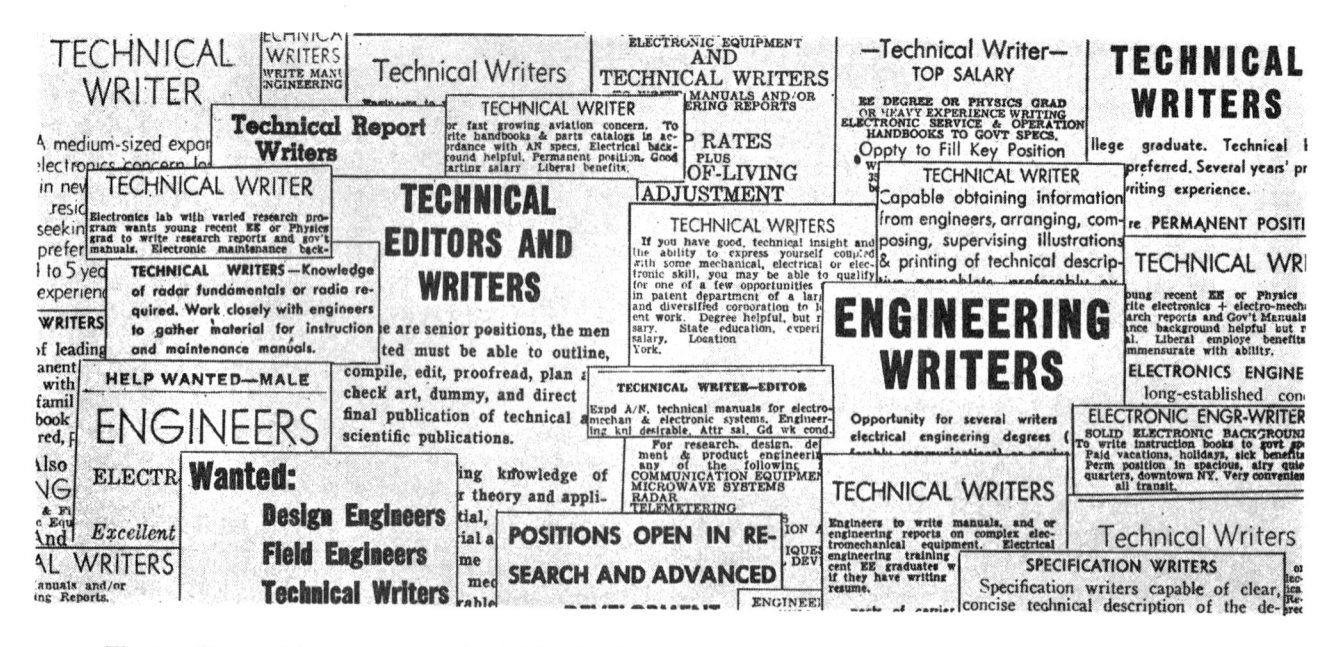

Fig. 1—Demand for engineer-writers, identified herein as publications engineers, is evidenced by these classified advertisements selected at random from employment sections of newspapers and magazines.

neer, test engineer, field service engineer, etc. This new title will be used throughout the article.

WHAT IS A PUBLICATIONS ENGINEER?

The principal reason why this author prefers the new title publications engineer to that of technical writer is that it more clearly designates the duties of such a worker, and also places him in a proper professional status with fellow engineers, where he rightfully belongs. For he is an engineer first and a writer second. The term technical writer, as commonly accepted, refers to a person who writes material on technical subjects to various levels of intelligence but is not usually concerned with the actual publication processes and problems.

The publications engineer is an engineering specialist who relieves other engineers of the major portion of the responsibility for production of all publications required as a result of the engineers' work (Fig. 2). The publications engineer writes technical material, plans and directs preparation of copy, and carries through on all details concerned with actual production of the publication. It is necessary to repeat that he is first an engineer, then a writer, and finally a publications man.

Engineers have always labored under the stigma that they cannot write well. It is a common attitude, even in pre-college education, to assume that because the student is superior in mathematics he must be inferior in English. This affects the student's attitude and he very naturally uses it as an excuse for not seriously studying the subject in which he is prejudged to be inferior. When the "superior" math student goes to engineering school it is a foregone conclusion that there is very little that can be done to help him there. However, he is given one or possibly two courses in English (especially "arranged" for engineers) early in his college work. Usually no further attempts are made to help him overcome a deficiency which will handicap him throughout his entire career.

There is no doubt that some engineers cannot write well —but some lawyers, some accountants, and some doctors cannot write well! Some doctors do not develop a pleasing "bedside" manner, so they become fine surgeons or specialists. So some engineers do not write well, or simply do not have time to write well—and because of this, other engineers now find an interesting and well-paid profession.

The publications engineer must be an engineer who has writing aptitude. This aptitude may have never become very obvious because of the lack of encouragement received during his education. The author has seen many engineers, who felt certain that they were below average in writing aptitude, develop into excellent writers of technical material. No one can doubt that the engineering profession would be in a much better position if there were more effective writers amongst engineers. (The same might be said for effective speakers.)

The publications engineer must be an engineer with unquenchable thirst for learning. If he is a mechanical engineer he must be learning more about electronics; if he is an electrical engineer he must be learning about aerodynamics, hydraulics, etc. He is constantly challenged to describe something about which he knows practically nothing. But with his basic engineering education under his hat, he tackles each unknown with some confidence that he can understand and interpret the facts for others who may know more or less about it than he does. Many fine technical descriptions result when engineers who are educated in one field begin to write on subjects in other engineering fields—they use analogies which greatly aid the reader in applying the description to his own experience.

The publications engineer must have a working knowledge of the advantages and disadvantages of many types of reproduction processes such as spirit duplication, mimeograph, Photostat, blueline and blueprint, Ozalid, offset printing, and letterpress printing. He is familiar with type faces, paper stock, cover materials, binding methods, etc. He understands the problems involved in production of copy by typewriters, Varitypers, typesetting, and Phototype. He has a practical knowledge of the arts of photography and retouching, and he guides technical illustrators in visualizing and rendering special illustrations for use with his written words.

All of his talents and acquired knowledge are combined in the process of preparing a publication that must meet government or commercial specifications covering content, format, practicability, and literary standards. He is at the same time an engineer, a writing specialist, a publications expert, and a student of psychology!

Fig. 2—Publications engineers produce a **variety of matter requiring skills of both engineer and writer.**

VARIETY OF WORK

When the young publications engineer has developed confidence in tackling new writing projects, he finds the variety of writing assignments to be one of the most attractive features of his job. It is a familiar complaint among engineers that they become too specialized and know too little of what is taking place in the scientific world around them. While no scientist can hope to keep abreast of the tremendous evolution of technical achievements now taking place, the publications engineer finds real satisfaction in testing and adding to his knowledge in many different fields. As an example, at Sperry the skilled publications engineer develops a descriptive knowledge in such varied fields as radar, hydraulics, servomechanisms, gyroscopics, computing mechanisms, ballistics, optics, navigation, and aerodynamics. When the occasion demands he becomes, for a time, a writing specialist in one or more of these fields.

In addition to the variety of writing from the product standpoint, there is also much variation in the material to be gathered on any one product or system (Fig. 3). Some of the assignments require the publications engineer to work intimately with the equipment; in some cases he completely disassembles and reassembles the units. In other cases, he accompanies the equipment on trial runs or field tests. These experiences give a "practical" satisfaction to those who like to feel that they are not just "theoretical" writers.

Another attractive feature of the publications engineer's work lies in the variety of contacts which he makes in the course of the development and approval of a publication. A typical life story of an instruction book prepared for

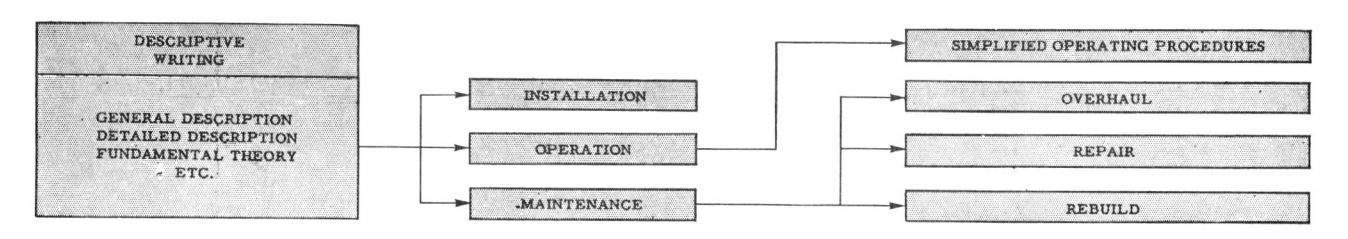

Fig. 3—Publications engineer's writing begins early with a project and follows product into the field.

the Armed Services (Fig. 4), gives an indication of the many individuals concerned in the preparation or approval of the publication prior to its final printing; the publications engineer works constantly with all of those shown.

THE FUTURE FOR PUBLICATIONS ENGINEERS

Young engineers often raise the question as to the future of technical writing or publications engineering. There are several factors which appear to be of importance in attempting to predict the future—but to the author they all look favorable toward increasing opportunity for this new profession. First, the complexity of equipment and systems certainly will continue to increase—automatic control is the ultimate goal of nearly all future instrumentation, and with such control always comes increased technical complexity. With increasing complexity there is greater need for more complete instructional material. As one associate put it: "The equipment becomes more complex but the intelligence of the average user remains the same." Second, granted that complexity will increase, there is the immediate following condition that the equipment will be much more costly and must be repaired rather than replaced. This adds again to the need for publications which will be adequate for the purpose. The funds allocated for publications will necessarily increase but will still be a very small portion of the total cost of the equipment. Third, if the caliber of engineering graduates coming into publications engineering is maintained or raised, there will be a broadening in the scope of their work since they themselves will develop opportunities for using their special skill to supplement the work of other engineers. This is a very important responsibility in any new profession—to develop and broaden particular skills and to offer them to others. If the publications engineer pursues his new profession with a spirit of genuine service to other engineers, there can be little doubt that the engineering profession will welcome and encourage this newcomer to its ranks.

CONCLUSION

Publications engineering is a new profession which has grown rapidly in the past few years because of the increasing complexity of equipment and the inability of the research and development engineers to undertake the extensive writing projects which have become necessary.

The publications engineer must have a sound engineering education and must possess writing aptitude—although it is pointed out that many young engineers possess this aptitude and may not be conscious of it.

The publications engineer has a thorough knowledge of the reproduction and printing processes, and can guide the publication through all of its various stages from rough draft to its printed form.

The variety of work assignments and the personal contacts appeal greatly to certain engineering graduates. Some of the writing assignments cover theoretical aspects, while others are along practical lines where the writer works closely with the equipment in the factory or in the field.

The personal satisfaction factor is quite high for the publications engineer since his assignments are usually of short duration, compared to those of the engineer, and he sees the final results of his labors at more frequent intervals.

Finally, the future of this new addition to the engineering profession looks promising because of the trend towards more complex equipment and the accompanying requirements for more complete handbook and engineering report coverage. The future will also depend upon the efforts which publications engineers make to find new areas of service to the engineering profession.

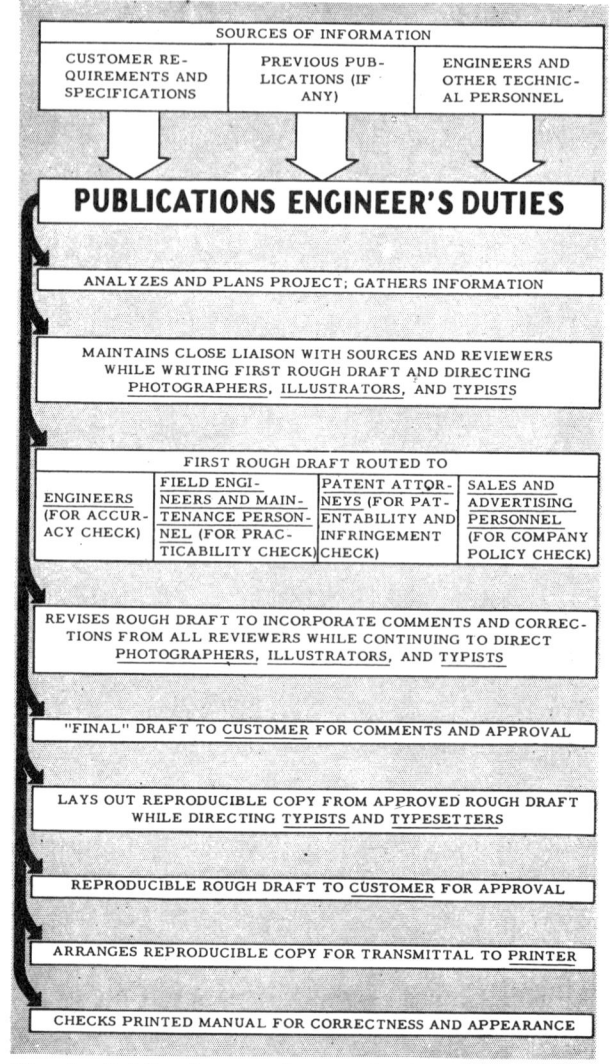

Fig. 4—Publications engineer gains broad knowledge of product: its engineering, manufacture, and application. Persons with whom he consults directly are underscored in this diagram of manual's life cycle.

It is foolish to believe that one's readers will be sure to read a poorly written report or message.

MANAGING WORDS!

by LEON R. HAY

One of the important tasks of any executive's job is to communicate with others through writing. Writing is a necessary part of his regular work, and the ability to write effectively is a valuable asset. To be able to express thoughts clearly and to understand what is expressed by others are prerequisites for successful executive performance. The more effectively the executive can convey ideas and information to others, the more successful he is and will be.

Good writing—whether it be a business report or a novel—does three things: (1) it communicates a thought; (2) it conveys a feeling; and (3) it benefits the reader through added knowledge. To accomplish these three ends, the writer should ask himself these questions:

1. What is the purpose of the report?
2. What information is desired?
3. What does the reader want to know?
4. What attitude should the reader develop toward the report?
5. What action is expected of the reader?
6. How is an idea conveyed from one person to another with the smoothest flow and the fastest way?
7. How are the writer's thoughts brought into concrete form?
8. What are the alternate ways of organizing and designing the report?

These questions are worth thinking about before putting words on paper. When words are put together, they convey not only the purpose of the report, but also the character and mood of the writer, both of which are important to the reader's understanding.

Peter Drucker, writing in *Fortune* magazine, had this to say about business writing:

The ability to express ideas in writing and in speaking heads the list of requirements for success. As soon as you move one step up from the bottom, your effectiveness depends on your ability to reach others through the spoken or written word. And the further away your job is from manual work, the larger the organization of which you are an employee, the more important it will be that you know how to convey your thoughts in writing and speaking. In the very large organizations, whether it is the government, the large business corporation, or the army, this ability to express oneself is perhaps the most important of all the skills a man can possess.

How does one become a better communicator? There are two ways. The one to consider first is the method of getting ideas on paper. The basic skill in most businesses is the ability to organize and to express ideas in writing. Communicating ideas is dependent on a definite plan and design. Some authorities say that organization, not language, is the problem in report writing, and that the important thing is to put the elements of information in the order in which the reader will use that information.

The second way lies in a greater familiarity with the techniques of communication. We think in words. The quality of ideas is determined by the meaning of those words. The use of symbols—words—has a bearing on the productivity or lack of productivity on the job. The symbol world (words) in which we live is taken for granted. The depth, the complexity, and the importance of the symbols of communication for personality and interpersonal relationships are seldom realized.

If the objectives of the report are to be achieved, the report has to be read. Those who read reports know that the way the writer assembles, analyzes, and presents his information determines to a large extent the effectiveness of that report. Those who write reports have an obligation to be intelligible. They are not writing to impress their reader but to express thoughts.

The business of report writing is the business of making choices. In a general sense, it is the business of selecting adequate facts, determining their priority, arranging the material, choosing words, and constructing sentences. The choice of words and the organization of thoughts determine the quality of writing. Having numerous thoughts to convey, the writer surveys them and then shuffles them into the order of their importance.

Organization and Writing Style

A wise report writer works to acquire good organization and writing style. He makes a gross mistake when he tries to cram into his reader's mind a mass of unorganized ideas, facts, and viewpoints. He knows that it is foolish to believe that his readers will be sure to read and understand a poorly written

LEON R. HAY
is Assistant Professor of Business
at San Jose State College,
San Jose, California.
He has a B.A. and an M.A. degree
from Colorado State College
and an Ed.D. degree from the University
of Southern California.

report. He knows also that readers who are interested in the topic of his report may not be receptive to information poorly organized and presented.

Effective communication represents important opportunities to save valuable executive time and to increase company profits. There are four basic objectives in an effective communication process: (1) to secure a reading; (2) to be understood; (3) to be believed; and (4) to induce action.

To secure reading of a written report, the reader must be persuaded to tune in the program—to pick up and read the report, article, or brochure. His attention must be held, and he must be impressed and convinced. Unless his attention has been secured, there is little chance of accomplishing the remaining three objectives.

Qualities to be Kept in Mind

To be understood requires a logical organization of ideas and design of the materials. The reader must know what the writer is talking about and must understand him. When writing a report, the desirable qualities to be kept in mind include clarity, simplicity, completeness, concreteness, conciseness, coherence, good language, and accuracy.

Readers must believe what is said. Many memorandums, letters, and reports fail this point of communication. Readers are skeptical of what they read. They judge material as inadequate, inappropriate, or unsound, and often communication breaks off at this point. They may read, understand, but not believe.

The fourth objective of communication is action. Persons communicated to must act. Those individuals engaged in workaday communication activities seek action as an end result of that communication. The action does not have to be overt. It could be merely acceptance of the report. A message may be read, understood, and believed, but not acted upon.

Words are the writer's tools. Since all writing must start with words which grow into sentences, a command of words is necessary for forceful, convincing writing. Words are like building blocks. To attempt to write without an adequate vocabulary is like trying to build a brick wall without the right kind of bricks. Thoughts are brought into concrete form through the use of words arranged in phrases, clauses, sentences, paragraphs, and whole messages.

The writer needs an extensive vocabulary for variety; active verbs, to keep the action moving; similes, to create pictures in the reader's mind; metaphors, to make meanings clear; and rhythm, to contribute to smooth easy reading.

An effective report writer knows that the strong words are nouns, verbs, adjectives, and adverbs; that the weak words are pronouns, prepositions, and conjunctions. He knows that nouns and verbs are used to present facts in a vigorous manner, and he recognizes that adjectives and adverbs used execssively or indiscriminately have, or may lead to, connotations which may cause the wrong effect. He knows that words have both actual meanings and suggested or implied meanings.

The ease with which the reader understands ideas depends upon the way words are arranged within a sentence. All business decisions must be communicated, and the executive, to be successful, must communicate the meaning of business decisions and policies to personnel at all levels.

Selecting and Rejecting

A good communicator, no matter how confidently he may dash off sentences and paragraphs, is conscious of selecting and rejecting words many times in the course of writing a message or a report. He chooses one word in preference to another; he chooses one arrangement of works in preference to another; and he chooses an arrangement of sentences in preference to another. His choice and arrangement of words determine his technique as a communicator and his success as an executive.

The writer may use his technique to write simply; he may use his technique to be complex. He may choose to be direct and reveal his meaning completely. He may choose to be secretive or to reveal his meaning only partially. His writing is effective when he makes effective choices.

When the writer does not choose his words carefully, he can create problems for his reader. Usually a writer will want to reveal his meaning completely. He will want to write simply, clearly, directly. His problem in writing is not that he intends to be confusing, but that he writes as he does because he does not understand how to choose words or because he doesn't make effective choices.

He Reads Mechanically

When a reader takes up a memorandum, letter, or report, he does not read from idea to idea, even though he may think he does. He reads mechanically, from period to period. He tries to take in all the ideas in a sentence in one gulp. He pauses for a comma or a semicolon, but he does not stop until he comes to a period.

Often the reader gets lost in a sentence. He may find it necessary to return to the beginning, and he may try again to work his way through to the period. Depending on his interest and need for information, he may make the return journey many times. Or, he may abandon the whole thing.

To see how confusion can reign supreme, especially when the writer does not keep the reader in mind, note a 90-word statement on how to file an income tax return.

If instead of purchasing another residence, you begin construction of a new residence either one year before or within one year after the sale of your old residence and use it as your principal residence not later than eighteen months after the sale, none of the gain is taxable if your costs attributable to construction during, plus the cost of the land acquired within, the period beginning one year before the sale and ending eighteen months after the sale equals or exceeds the adjusted sales price of the old residence.

The emphasis of a sentence lies not in its length but in its shortness. A long-spun sentence produces a narcotic effect. Such a sentence demands effort—memorization—on the part of the reader, because he must keep in mind the first phrases or parts of the statement until he reaches the full idea in the final phrase. It is erroneous, however to conclude that simple sentences are always best. The reader must be given variety. Hence, long sentences should be broken by occasional short, sharp ones to revive attention and interest.

Words must be arranged so that important words get the impact. Some method of mechanical emphasis must be used. Among the most important mechanics of a report is punctuation.

Punctuation can reverse the meaning of a sentence. Here is an illustration. "The sales manager said the salesman was brilliant." "The sales manager," said the salesman, "was brilliant." The sales manager said, "The salesman was brilliant."

Punctuation guides the reader through a report and helps him sort out thoughts according to what was intended. Punctuation marks have the effect of making the reader slow down and take notice.

For each type of reporting, there is a specialized vocabulary. These specialized words may come from the whole area in which the writer works; they may be peculiar to that profession or occupational group. Quite often they are simple words which have been given a special **meaning**.

Separated by a Common Language

An old saying holds that Americans and British are two peoples separated by only a common language. Perhaps the quip needs updating: Americans are one people separated by jargons and cants of professions and would-be professions.

The term *jargon* describes two different kinds of language, one much more objectionable than the other. In its broad sense, jargon is any loose, fuzzy, unintelligible talk or writing. Its main drawback is that it is a mysterious language. An engineer doesn't understand the physician's shoptalk any more than the physician understands a bricklayer's shoptalk.

It is this very unusual terminology that makes shoptalk appeal to some persons. One has only to think of the jargon used by some radio amateurs or to sit a few minutes in the dispatching office of the city's police department to become aware of shoptalk. The words used are a form of shorthand and usually carry a precise meaning to the people in each group. For the member of the public, such jargon is meaningless.

A recent newspaper report stated that when the National Council of Juvenile Court Judges met, it advised psychiatrists to cut out the Freudian patter in court appearances. "Use words even the delinquent can understand," said the judges. If psychiatrists did that, perhaps the rest of us could understand their lingo.*

By No Means the Worst Offenders

But psychiatrists are by no means the worst offenders. Their jargon merely mystifies. The lingo of accountants and economists is worse because it bewilders. Worst of all is the cant of educationists. It enrages. It does so because it is spurious and pretentious.

Time was when it seemed necessary to use such jargon and cants to achieve precision of meaning. Experience brought two revelations: (1) confirmed jargoneers talk at, not to or with, one another, and (2) the better a man is in his profession, the simpler his language.

Good report writing needs to be appropriate to the occasion, to the purpose, to the reader, and to the writer. It must not be too pompous for its load or be hesitant about what it seeks to do, or be beneath the intelligence of the reader, or be too arrogant for the writer's position.

The executive who fails to write clearly enough to be understood by his reader is lazy. He's a pretender if he does not know what he is writing about. If he is not thoroughly familiar with his subject and cannot express his ideas clearly, he is incompetent in a major function.

In short, writing a report requires preparation, practice, and participation: preparation through reading, analysis, and study; practice through revising and rewriting; and participation through putting the writer's personality and individuality into what he says.

---

*NOTE: In his article, "Make It Simple," Michael Flagg also uses this information from the *San Francisco Examiner*. Note how these two authors make use of this same material. J.P.R.

SECTION I
THE ELEMENTS OF EFFECTIVE WRITING

STYLE

Style is concerned with perceptive judgement, taste, and choice among equally-correct expressions, rather than with specific formulas. Technical writing frequently falls to the level of merely-correct expression in which ideas are presented in a colorless, boring, unconvincing, and generally ineffectual manner. The development of an interesting and effective style depends upon 2 related activities: (1) The acquiring of a literary background comprehensive enough to provide the writer with criteria for discrimination; and (2) the writer's constant attention to the following details: Originality, Conciseness, Concreteness, Phrasing, Color and Emphasis.

Originality

Originality of expression is a direct reflection of originality of thought, coupled with the ability to recognize trite, worn phrases or clichés. The fact that an idea has been expressed in a certain way on one or more previous occasions or in one or more other publications is no guarantee that it has been well expressed, or even adequately expressed. Originality involves the ability to choose words which point out the special character of the subject under discussion, and which differentiate it from others in the same general category.

Conciseness

Conciseness should not be confused with mere brevity. Conciseness is the expression of ideas in clear and precise, but economical terms. It is the absence of useless components, whether such components be words, phrases or sentences. It is achieved by paying constant attention to the following points:

1. Using only **necessary** words
   a. Avoiding padding, wordiness, useless repetition
   b. Avoiding over-qualification; i.e. *very*, et. al.
2. Using only **precise** words
   a. Avoiding jargon, shop-talk
   b. Avoiding the use of general terms. Be specific!
   c. Avoiding the use of approximations. Be exact!

Concreteness

Abstract words (*right, justice, hot, smooth, fast* for example) have different meanings to different people at different times. Thus, they are subject to individual interpretation and may be more confusing than explanatory. Most word choices are between terms of various degrees of concreteness, rather than simply between abstract and concrete terms. For example, *domestic animal, beast of burden, horse,* and *Percheron* vary in their degree of concreteness, but the last term tells the reader more than the preceding ones.

Concreteness of expression can be achieved in some cases only by expanding an idea to show greater detail, and to relate the idea to something already known by the reader. The words *hum, buzz, black,* etc. are as concrete as single words can be; yet they may not be as definitive as the subject requires. By incorporating such words into descriptive phrases, such as *velvety black, glossy black* or *flat black,* the idea becomes more meaningful to the reader.

Phrasing

Phrasing is the art of constructing sentences and paragraphs so that their sound, in the mind's ear of the reader, is appropriate to the subject, varied rather than monotonous, balanced rather than awkward, and purposeful rather than vague. Like any art, phrasing is the result of various principles applied with taste and judgement. Generally the principles are those of grammar and syntax, applied to achieve a pleasant-sounding rhythm and to enhance meaning.

Since the pursuit of any art consists of disciplined practice rather than slavish adherence to fixed rules, it is impractical to formulate rules for phrasing. However, there are several faults which should be avoided in technical writing. They are:

1. "Run on" sentences. Sentences which consist of far too many ideas, words and phrases for the reader to grasp.
2. A succession of short, periodic sentences.
3. Over-use of passive voice.
4. Over-use of inverted sentence structure.
5. Lack of variety in sentence type and length.
6. Awkward-sounding phrases. Unintentional rhyme.
7. Excessive impersonality.

Color

Color in writing is the quality that gives vividness to description. Its use in technical writing is somewhat limited, but when used appropriately it enhances accuracy and facilitates understanding.

Color is achieved by using concrete words which describe specific sensory stimuli; that is, by using terms which appeal to the senses. It is the kind of writing that is sometimes called "drawing word pictures."

Color may be introduced by the careful choice of modifiers — e.g. *crimson* rather than *red*; *mushy, furry* or *spongy* rather than *soft* — or by the use of figures of speech such as simile and metaphor.

Emphasis

Emphasis is the relative importance given to ideas or facts by the way they are expressed. In speech, emphasis may be indicated by gesture, tone of voice, facial expression and pauses. In writing, however, emphasis cannot be shown effectively by similar methods such as capitalization, italicizing, use of heavy punctuation, or by the use of intensives such as *very, most, quite*, etc. Instead, relative importance is indicated by proper subordination, by position, or by repetition.

Subordination: In technical writing, where precise relationships between facts or ideas must be clearly shown, emphasis is critically important. At the same time, technical writing offers more opportunities for misplacing emphasis than does general or descriptive writing. One fault peculiar to technical writing is that of the "stacked-noun-modifier," sometimes called the problem of the "tossed chef salad," or "half broiled spring chicken." A typical example from the stacked-noun-modifier is the following quotation from the manuscript of an Air Force Technical Order. "Tighten the cadmium plated nozzle area control feedback flexible cable sheave box cover bolts and lockwire." Such complete absence of subordination buries the idea *tighten . . . and lockwire . . . the bolts* under a stack of modifiers so high that the idea is almost completely hidden. Such sentences cannot be read; they must be decoded.

Another cause of faulty subordination is the "run-on" sentence— the sentence that consists of so many elements that it is impossible to relate each to the others. Such run-on sentences are always confusing to the reader, and sometimes even to the writer, as the following quotation demonstrates: "Turbine serration failures usually cause an unbalance in the turbine wheel resulting in severe vibrations and general engine damage such as major damage or destruction of the No. 4 bearing air and oil seals and oil jets, severe shroud ring damage, accessories may break off and pieces enter the compressor resulting in compressor failure, possible turbine shaft failure at the No. 3 or No. 4 bearing area if enough buckets are lost." The cure for this fault is simply to construct sentences containing fewer ideas. However, it should be obvious that short, periodic sentences cannot show relationships at all. "Freddy is our cat. He has 4 legs. His fur is black.", is a series of statements of equal value. However, "Freddy, our 4-legged cat, has black fur," contains more than the sum of its parts; relationship has been added.

Careful choice of connectives between elements of a sentence is important in showing the relationship between the ideas those elements express. For example: "Howard Dean, newly-elected President of the First National Bank, is active in church and civic affairs, and he is a Republican." Substituting other connectives for *and* opens up many interesting possibilities: "Howard Dean . . . is active in church and civic affairs, (nevertheless) (but) (although) (however) he is a Republican."

Position: The most emphatic positions for ideas are at the end and at the beginning of a sentence. Thus, the padded beginning, such as "*There are* two parts of the pump which . . .", or, "*It must be remembered that* all designs have been made . . .", is the weakest kind of sentence; the important ideas have been pushed into a position of unimportance. Judicious inversion or use of unconventional sentence patterns can increase emphasis as shown in the following examples:

UNEMPHATIC: The pump was installed as soon as it came.
MORE EMPHATIC: As soon as it came, the pump was installed.

Repetition: Repetition can either contribute to, or detract from, emphasis. Repetition quickly becomes monotony; hence it must be used with discretion. Sentence patterns, words, phrases and sounds may be repeated for emphasis of an idea or to arouse emotional response in the reader. However, the careless introduction of repetitive syllables, such as "The creation of vibration depends on the duration . . ." is merely distracting.

Other factors: Several other weaknesses of style, most of which have been discussed under other headings, contribute to lack of emphasis or to misplaced emphasis. Among them are the following:

1. Over-use of passive voice
2. Clichés, triteness, worn phrases
3. Abstract words and generalities
4. Padding, jargon, over-qualification
5. Circumlocutions — beating around the bush
6. Euphemisms — calling a sewer worker a *sanitation engineer*
7. Excessive impersonality

ORGANIZATION OF INFORMATION AND OUTLINING

General:

The first step in preparation for writing is deciding how *much* information is required to fulfill the function of the publication. The next step is to analyze the body of information to decide how best to present it in logical order. The structural form of this order is known as the organization. The notes made in planning the details of the structure are known as the outline.

The Outline

Purpose. The process of outlining is the second step in preparation for writing. The outline is a working tool for the writer to use as his work progresses. It serves as a map for the territory to be covered in the publication. Just as it is easier to go from Louisville, Kentucky to Omaha, Nebraska when one has a road map, it is easier to write concisely and comprehensively about a subject when one has an outline of it.

Types of Outlines. The 2 commonly-used types of outlines are: (1) the topic outline, and (2) the sentence outline. The topic outline consists of a series of telegraphic words or phrases which briefly describe the subject to be discussed. The sentence outline often includes information that will remind the writer of the approach he plans to use in discussing the topic; i.e., "A brief description of salient features of the speedometer as they reflect dependability and accuracy."

Forms of Outlines. Outlines are usually set down to show by indentations, the various levels of importance assigned to the topics covered. In addition, the topics are designated by letter, number, or letter-number systems. Specimen outlines showing the various systems follow:

Number Systems
Roman-Arabic

CHAPTER X "CUTTING TOOLS"
  I. WOODWORKING TOOLS
    1. Power
      (1) Saws
      (2) Lathes
      (3) Planers
      (4) Routers and Shapers
    2. Hand
      (1) Saws
      (2) Chisels
      (3) Planes
  II. METAL-WORKING TOOLS
    1. Power
      (1) Saws
      (2) Lathes
      (3) Shapers and Planers
      (4) Milling Machines
      (5) Drills
    2. Hand
      (1) Saws
      (2) Files
      etc....

Decimal

CHAPTER X "CUTTING TOOLS"
10.1 WOODWORKING TOOLS
10.1.1 Power
10.1.1.1 Saws
10.1.1.1.1 Circular
10.1.1.1.2 Band
10.1.1.2 Lathes
10.1.1.3 Routers and Shapers
10.1.1.3.1 Routers
10.1.1.3.2 Shapers
10.1.2 Hand
10.1.2.1 Saws
10.1.2.1.1 Crosscut
10.1.2.1.2 Rip
10.1.2.1.3 Backsaws
10.2 METAL-WORKING TOOLS
10.2.1 Power
10.2.1.1 Saws
10.2.1.2 Lathes
  etc ....

Letter-Number System

CHAPTER X "CUTTING TOOLS"
  I. WOODWORKING TOOLS
    A. Power
      1. Saws
        a. Circular
        b. Band

2. Lathes
3. Routers and Shapers
   a. Routers
   b. Shapers
4. Planers
B. Hand
   1. Saws
      a. Crosscut
      b. Rip
         etc . . .

By comparing the 3 systems illustrated, it can be seen that the decimal system is capable of showing an unlimited number of levels of subordination. The letter-number system is limited to 6 levels: I., A., 1., a., (1), (a); while the all-number system is rarely used because it is limited to only 3 levels: I., 1., (1).

Organization of Information

Analyzing the Information. A body of information can be organized in numerous ways. Some of the factors to be considered in deciding what organization is most appropriate, are as follows:

1. Scope of the publication
   a. What is the reader's background?
      (1) How much new information does he require?
      (2) How much detail does he require?
      (3) What use will he make of the information?
   b. What is the purpose of the publication?
      (1) To increase general familiarity with the subject?
      (2) To instruct in the use or operation of a thing?
      (3) To instruct in the maintenance and repair of a thing?
      (4) To report status?
2. Analysis of the Information
   a. Of what major areas does the information consist?
      (1) Structural
      (2) Functional
      (3) Procedural
      (4) Purposes or uses
      (5) Theory
   b. How are these areas inter-related?
      (1) Structurally
      (2) Functionally
         (a) Cause-and-effect
         (b) Prerequisite but non-causal

I-7

(c) Simultaneous effects
(d) Independent

c. What type of detailed information is required in each area?
   (1) Systems
   (2) Components
   (3) Parts — Composition
   (4) Procedures
      (a) General
      (b) Step-by-step

Planning the Organization. Once the information has been analyzed, one or more plans for the type of organization will become apparent. Usually there is no such thing as one **right** organizational plan, and one or more **wrong** ones; however, there is usually one plan that is more **appropriate** than others.

The making of tentative outlines will point to the most appropriate organization for the information required. Usually several successive outlines must be drawn up before all organizational requirements are fulfilled. To repeat: An outline is a **working tool** designed to fit a particular and specific job. Time spent on developing a workable outline will be paid back many times over during the writing of the text to fit that outline. Nevertheless, the outline is not the end in itself; the text is the final product. When the text demands that the outline be revised — even though most of the text be completed — the outline should be revised.

The following principles must be kept in mind as the organizational plan is developed:

1. All the information included under a heading or topic of a given level of importance, must pertain to that heading.
2. Items of comparable importance or complexity must be on the same level of organization with respect to each other.
3. An item on any level of organization must be sub-divided into *not less than* 2 categories at the next lower level, IF IT REQUIRES SUBDIVIDING AT ALL.

NOTE

Inability to conform to any one of these principles usually indicates that the plan or organization is deficient in some way.

I-8

STRUCTURE

Technical writing depends more upon structure for its effectiveness, than does any other kind of writing except the mystery story — but the structures are different. While the mystery story is constructed to misdirect or deceive, the purpose of technical writing is to inform and explain. Thus, the gross structure of most technical compositions consists of a matrix of general information and description, into which details are fitted, developed, and integrated. Over-all structure of a composition is reflected in the structure of the paragraphs that make up the whole work; hence the discussion of paragraph structure applies equally to the whole.

The Paragraph

Just as the whole publication begins with an Introduction, the paragraph begins with a topic sentence. The topic sentence states the thesis to be developed in the body of the paragraph, and usually is an elaboration of one of the points stated in the outline. In literary writing, the topic sentence is sometimes found near the middle or at the end of a paragraph. This shifting of the topic is a device used to create dramatic or emotional effects that usually are inappropriate in technical writing. The length of a paragraph depends entirely upon the amount of discussion needed to develop the idea contained in the topic sentence, and it is not complete until that purpose has been achieved. The test of a good paragraph is that it conform to 4 requirements: *unity, completeness, order,* and *coherence.*

Unity requires that the discussion contained in a paragraph pertain to the topic stated in the first sentence. Any statement that drifts away from the point, and makes it difficult for him to follow the writer's trend of thought.

Completeness implies that the idea stated in the topic sentence is explained adequately, using enough supporting detail, example and illustrative discussion to drive home the writer's meaning.

Order in a well-constructed paragraph may be based on any one of several patterns which exhibit a logical system of development. The components which make up these patterns may consist of a single sentence or of several sentences, and may be described functionally as follows: a topic sentence, a clarifying or amplifying statement, an example, a causal explanation, comparison or contrast with other examples, an analytical breakdown, a summary or integrating statement. The order in which these components appear in a paragraph is determined in many instances by the nature of the subject, and in others by the method of treating the subject. The types of patterns into which these components can be arranged are: chronological, regional or spatial, cause to effect, effect to cause, general to particular, and particular to general. Variations of these basic patterns include: question to answer, problem to solution, etc.

Coherence or *continuity,* the quality which holds sentences together to form a paragraph, is the result of smooth transition from one sentence to the next within a paragraph. Incoherence or randomness of development usually is a symptom of thinking out one sentence at a time. When a paragraph is thought of as a whole — as a unit in which a single idea is stated and developed — the writer achieves continuity without conscious effort. The details that link thoughts together appear as transitional phrases or sentences in the writing itself. Coherence is just as important in linking paragraphs into a unified composition as it is in linking sentences to form a paragraph. Transitional devices are similar in both cases — the transitional phrase or sentence within a paragraph may become a transitional paragraph within the whole composition.

The Sentence

Clear expression depends on craftsmanship in constructing effective sentences, and craftsmanship is never the result of happy accident or slap-dash performance — it develops from complete familiarity with one's tools, and constant striving for perfection in their use. Neat, economical, clear, accurate sentences may appear in the first draft of a composition by an experienced writer; more often they are the result of studied revision and re-writing.

The words that make up sentences may be classified either by their function (noun, pronoun, verb, adjective, adverb, preposition, etc.) or by their structural relationship to each other (subject, predicate, complement, modifier and connective). The functional names of the words are called "parts of speech," while the structural designations of words or phrases are referred to as "elements". The pattern in which the elements are assembled, determines the kind of sentence constructed. The following examples illustrate the 3 kinds of sentences:

Simple Sentence:

Subject *Predicate*
John writes.
Subject *Predicate* *Complement*
John plays the piano.

In more elaborate sentences, the simple sentence is used as a clause:

Compound Sentence: *Independent Clause* *connective* *Independent Clause*
John writes books and he plays the piano.

In the complex sentence, the second clause contains a subject (relative pronoun) that refers to the complement of the preceding clause; thus relating the two:

Complex Sentence: *Independent Clause*   *Dependent Clause*
                           John writes books   that are hard to understand.

These are the 3 basic types of sentences, although the compound-complex sentence consisting of 2 independent clauses and a dependent clause is sometimes considered a fourth type. Notice that each type consists structurally of the elements: subject, predicate, complement. If we use the initial letters of these elements, plus "M" for modifier and "&" for connective, to label the functions of words or phrases in the following sentences, their relationships become clear.

           M_s S   P   C
1. Three-hundred engines were shipped in May and June.
    S   P M_c C
2. Poets and scientists have many common interests.
   &   S   P   C   S   P   C
3. Although the weather was cold, we were comfortable.
    P M_p &   P M_p
4. Slide to the left, and pull slowly upward.
           A   S   P   C
5. Whatever the cause, we must repair the damage.

Notice the introductory phrase in sentence No. 5. This phrase clearly belongs to the sentence, but has no structural relationship to the rest of it. Such constructions are called "absolutes." Notice also that the position of an element has nothing to do with is function. Each of the sentences above, starts with a different element; in fact, sentence No. 4 has no subject except an implied "you," and no complement except an implied "it."

Examined from the functional viewpoint, it may seem that there is such a variety of acceptable constructions that any sentence must be grammatically and syntactically correct. It is true that there are many ways of expressing ideas — each way indicating a difference of emphasis or subordination from all the others; however, constructing a sentence that is syntactically incorrect as well as unintelligible is quite easy — so easy that it is usually done without trying.

Perhaps grammar and syntax become somewhat easier to deal with when certain qualitative characteristics of effective sentences are kept in mind. *Economy, clarity, consistency,* and *variety,* are qualities that are characteristic of good writing, whether they be applied to sentences, paragraphs or larger units of composition. While these attributes are inter-related, they will be considered separately for purposes of discussion.

Economy is one of the rarest virtues of technical writing. In an effort to define boundaries or to be thoroughly explicit, writers tend to add qualification on qualification instead of choosing an accurate, definitive term in the first place. This kind of wordiness is often defended on the basis that some conceivable reader might not be familiar with the accurate term if it were used. This defense may be valid on rare occasions, such as when describing Heisenberg's uncertainty concept to fifth-graders. More often, wordiness is the result of (1) laziness, or (2) an attempt to sound "technical" or ultra-formal. Economy can be achieved only by conscious intent and an absence of pretension on the part of the writer.

Clarity of expression is a by-product of clear thinking. Hazy, half-formed ideas cannot be expressed in any way that makes them appear clear and complete; however, the clearest idea can be expressed ambiguously. Neglecting the first principle of sentence construction — that a sentence is the expression of a single idea — results in such lapses from clarity as the comma splice, run-on sentences, and lack of unity. The idea expressed may be a complex one, including the subordination and relationship of one or more factors to another; but if the idea is too complex for statement in a conventional sentence, it should be split up into 2 or more sentences adherence to these principles may be found on page I-3, under example.)

One of the most deeply-rooted conventions of English syntax is the one that requires that related elements be kept as close to each other as possible. Thus, a subject-predicate-complement series should not be diffused or wedged apart by the insertion of too many modifying elements. Moreover, modifiers should be placed as close as possible to the word they modify. Some examples of poor adherence to these principles may be found on page I-3, under the discussion of subordination.

Another common fault that detracts from clarity is confused pronoun reference. A pronoun that has no antecedent, or one that has no clear relationship to its antecedent, results in ambiguity. For example: "I saw my first automatic screw machine in their plant *which* I thought was very well designed. *This* was just what I had expected." *Which,* in the first sentence, can refer to 2 antecedents, while *this*, in the second sentence, has no antecedent, and can refer to all or any part of the first sentence.

Consistency is the quality of writing that permits the reader to follow the writer's trend of thought smoothly. The writer may choose whatever pattern he considers appropriate for a particular sentence, but having chosen it, he is obligated to continue with that pattern until the sentence is complete. Two faulty sentence patterns are those that include dangling modifiers and lack of parallelism.

The inconsistent construction called the dangling modifier, is usually the result of "backing into an idea" in a periodic sentence — a sentence in which the main thought is not completed until the end. For example: "Having stopped the machine, the whistle blew." The reader expects the introductory phrase to modify the subject of the main clause, and momentarily thinks that "the whistle" must be that subject — only to discover that this construction makes no sense. The structural inconsistency has caused the reader to stop absorbing ideas so that he can decipher the writer's intended meaning.

Parallelism is a convention that requires 2 or more parts of a sentence, containing ideas of equal importance, to be expressed in similar grammatical form. When a series is begun with nouns, it must continue with nouns; when it is begun with verbs of a certain tense and mode, it must continue with verbs of the same tense and mode. When this convention is not observed, an apparent series degenerates into "bastard enumeration." For example: "The engine was long, cylindrical, and it operated at 1200 rpm." We expect a series of adjectives, since *long* and *cylindrical* are both adjectives; yet the third term is not an adjective but a pronoun.

Any disparity or lack of balance between elements, gives a sentence an awkward sound. The elements may be in pairs, or they may constitute a series; they may be clauses, phrases or single words; they may function as any component of a sentence — nouns, verbs, modifiers or complements. Whatever the elements may be, parallel construction gives them a structural and rhythmic pattern that enhances the consistency of the sentence.

Variety of length and structure prevents sentences from becoming monotonous. The subject-predicate-complement order is the conventional linguistic pattern followed by most English sentences, and it is appropriate and clear for perhaps 80 percent of standard writing. In an effort to sound technical or formal, some writers resort to the use of inverted sentence structure on a large scale. This structure lends itself to such faults as over-use of the passive voice and the formation of dangling modifiers, but even when it is used correctly, inverted sentences become monotonous rather quickly.

A pleasant variety of length and rhythm can be achieved by the deliberate application of technique — a sort of engineering approach to variety; however, the deliberate, studied application of technique usually sounds contrived and stiff. A pleasant, natural-sounding variety is the consequence of long practice and experience which results in a trained ear — a "mind's ear" that constantly tests the writer's phrasing for euphony and balance.

PRESENTATION

The purpose of writing is to convey ideas from one mind to others. To achieve this purpose, the writer must present his ideas in such a way that they cannot be misunderstood or misinterpreted, and so that the reader will accept those ideas as valid. This is seldom as simple a process as it seems; many times obstacles to complete understanding are unwittingly written into a manuscript by its author. Unless the technical writer remains aware of the differences in time, regional background, levels of experience and/or education, linguistic conventions, and psychological traits between him and his readers, he risks their misunderstanding. Thus, the grammatically correct expression of logically organized, accurate information does not necessarily constitute effective communication — it becomes effective only when understood and accepted by the reader.

Many technical writers, knowing that their readers are compelled to make the best of whatever publications they are furnished, are satisfied to place the entire burden of understanding on the reader. However, when the technical publication in question is any kind of instruction on the use, servicing or repair of his company's product; or when it is a report capable of reflecting credit on the writer or his group; intelligent self-interest dictates that the writer make some effort to achieve understanding and acceptance by his readers.

In many ways, the problems of the writer and the salesman are similar — both of them use words to direct the thinking of their readers or prospects toward a favorable decision or action. However, the salesman has one advantage withheld from the writer: in his sales interview, he has the opportunity to observe the effect of his words on the prospect, and to change the emphasis or even the direction of his presentation as circumstances dictate. The feed-back that guides the salesman does not exist for the writer; yet the writer can communicate just as effectively as the salesman. To compensate for the absence of feed-back, the writer must develop his faculty of self-criticism and his attitude of objectivity to a high degree. He must be able to assess the effect of his writing on others as if he were one of them — a difficult feat, since his *intended* meaning is already expressed in his own words. He must studiously examine his writing in the light of its purpose, its persuasiveness or appeal, and its clarity.

Purpose

Purpose is not always easy to determine. Contractual requirements merely reflect purposes; they are not purposes in themselves. Stated purposes are often euphemistic substitutes for intentions, and, frequently, the individual or department that orders a publication written has only a vague idea of the results it should achieve. More often than not, a single publication must be designed to serve several purposes or several classes of readers. Nevertheless, the technical writer must have a rather clear goal before he can begin to write effectively to achieve it. Only with his purpose in mind, can he give his writing direction and selectivity. The terms *direction* and *selectivity* imply —

1. that the writer know what kind of reader he will have,
2. that he have an idea of that reader's level of understanding and interest in the subject,
3. that he know what he wants the reader to gain from his writing, and,
4. that he be able to select appropriate ideas and expressions to guide the reader to a predetermined conclusion.

In the process of determining purpose, it is usually necessary to make certain assumptions. Assumptions are always risky, and assumptions about the type of reader expected can lead the writer into serious difficulties. One such assumption is the present-day myth of the Twelve-Year-Old Mind. This myth, based on a fallacy which in turn was based on an arithmetical average, has probably been responsible for more dull writing than any other assumption. Another assumption that consistently causes trouble, is that an engineering report will be read only by engineers, or a project report only by people familiar with the project. The usual result of such limited vision is managerial disgust or irritation, when the report finds its way to the man who decides on the project's financial support or its continuation.

Persuasion

There is a persistent feeling among technical writers that persuasiveness in writing isn't quite nice — that it detracts from the clear, pure technicality of the craft! Supposedly, the stark beauty of the subject itself should be persuasive enough for any competent reader. This thinking is like that of the salesman who expects his product to sell itself. (Both writers and salesmen of this kind have a characteristic emaciated look.)

Persuasiveness in writing is the quality that brings home to the reader the advantage of accepting the idea under discussion; that is, the reasons why certain decisions, actions, products, or ideas would be beneficial or useful to him. These reasons may be stated explicitly, or they may be implied by a careful choice of words, control of emphasis or subordination, or by the order in which ideas are presented. The things that every individual considers beneficial to himself or his group, include the following:

1. Financial advantage — profit making or cost saving
2. Security or safety
3. Health
4. Comfort, or ease of achievement, operation, etc.
5. Prestige or respect
6. Opportunity for altruism, philanthropy

Even in purely informative writing, one or more of these appeals is almost always pertinent. No one will take much of his time to read any technical writing unless he expects to be benefited in some way by the information that he can obtain from it. If the benefits are stated either explicitly or implicitly, the reader's interest is heightened, and the probability of his understanding and accepting the ideas it contains is increased.

Clarity

Clarity in the presentation of ideas depends as much upon the psychological rapport between writer and reader as it does upon the writer's adherence to linguistic conventions. The definition of every word has 2 aspects: denotation and connotation. Denotation is the formal, objective, "dictionary" definition of a word, while connotation is the suggestive, subjective aspect of its meaning, apart from its explicit, formal definition. To some extent, there is general agreement among people regarding both denotation and connotation; however, a part of any word's connotation to a particular individual is based on that individual's experience, his age, sex, station of life, education, and every other influence that relates him to that word. To varying degrees, it is what that word means *to him*. For example, consider the relationship of the following people to the word *cancer*: a person who has never been sick a day in his life, a person whose father died of cancer, an astrologer, a scientist engaged in cancer research, the statistician for an insurance company, and a cancer victim who knows that he has 2 months to live. None of the six is affected by the word in the same way; yet the word has the same denotation for all.

The study of the relationship of words, or signs and symbols, to human behavior is called *semantics*. Semantic considerations are present in the expression of every idea.; they are inescapable. A writer who is familiar with the principles of semantics is in a better position to evaluate his writing in terms of its effect on the reader. A detailed discussion of semantics is beyond the scope of this book; however, the titles of several books on the subject will be found in the Bibliography at the end of this section.

Clarity also depends on an orderly, logical presentation of ideas. For the technical writer, a thorough familiarity with the processes of cause and effect, inductive and deductive reasoning, analogy, and the fallacies in improper reasoning, are valuable aids to clear thinking and the clear expression of thought.

Important as semantics and logic are to the technical writer, they can do nothing for him unless he develops the ability to look at his writing, or examine his thoughts, critically. Self-criticism is psychologically contrary to normal, human inclination. Everyone has a tendency to approve of what he himself has done, and to evaluate his actions in terms of their effect on him rather than on others. Such complete egocentricity is found only in children and mental defectives, but it exists to some degree in all people. Thus, only by deliberately suppressing his natural feelings of self-approval can the writer attain the objectivity to see his work as it will appear to the reader, and to revise it until it is not merely understandable, but impossible to misunderstand.

BIBLIOGRAPHY

General Reference

BIRK, NEWMAN P. and GENEVIEVE B. *Understanding and Using English*, [Third Edition] New York: The Odyssey Press, Inc. (1958)

MCCRIMMON, JAMES M. *Writing with a Purpose*, [Second Edition] Cambridge, Mass.: Houghton Mifflin Co. (1957)

Handbooks

A Manual of Style, [Eleventh Edition] The University of Chicago Press. (1949)

GPO Style Manual, U.S. Government Printing Office.

PERRIN, PORTER G. *Writer's Guide and Index to English*, [Revised Edition] Chicago: Scott, Foresman & Co. (1950)

Linguistics

BODMER, FREDERICK *The Loom of Language*, (LAUNCELOT HOGBEN, Ed.) New York: Norton (1944)

PARTRIDGE, ERIC *The World of Words*, New York: Scribner (1939)

Presentation

KAPP, REGINALD O. *The Presentation of Technical Information*, New York: Macmillan (1957)

ULLMAN, JOSEPH N. *Technical Reporting*, New York: Holt (1952)

Semantics

HAYAKAWA, S.I. *Language in Thought and Action*, New York: Harcourt, Brace (1949)

KORZYBSKI, Count ALFRED, *Science and Sanity*, [Third Edition] Lakeville, Conn.: Non-Aristotelian Library Publishing Co. (1948)

OGDEN, CHARLES K. and RICHARDS, I.A. *The Meaning of Meaning*, New York: Harcourt, Brace (1956)

Structure

JESPERSEN, OTTO and BLACKWELL, BASIL, *Growth and Structure of the English Language*, New York: Oxford University Press (1959)

JESPERSEN, OTTO, *Logic and Grammar*, Oxford: The Clarendon Press (1924)

Style

FLESCH, RUDOLF, *The Art of Plain Talk*, New York: Harper & Brothers (1946)

QUILLER-COUCH, Sir ARTHUR, *On the Art of Writing*, New York: G.P. Putnam's Sons (1943)

STRUNK, WILLIAM, JR. and WHITE, E.B. *The Elements of Style*, New York: The Macmillan Company (1959)

Usage

DEAN, LEONARD F. and WILSON, KENNETH (ed) *Essays on Language and Usage*, New York: Oxford Press (1959)

FOWLER, H. W. *Modern English Usage*, Oxford: The Clarendon Press (1954)

PARTRIDGE, ERIC, *Usage and Abusage—a Guide to Good English*, New York: Harper & Brothers (1942)

Miscellaneous

BAUDIN, MAURICE, JR. and PFEIFFER, KARL G. *Essays for Study*, New York: McGraw-Hill (1960)

DRACH, HARVEY E. *American Business Writing*, New York: American Book Company (1959)

LLOYD, DONALD J. and WARFEL, HARRY R. *American English in its Cultural Setting*, New York: Alfred A. Knopf (1956)

Preparation and Evaluation of an Industrial Report

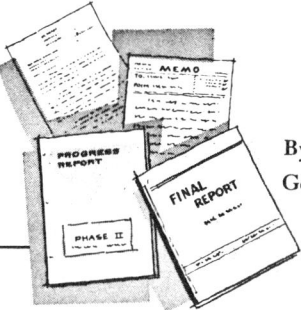

By CHARLES L. TUTT, JR.
General Motors Institute

Industrial reports assist management in making policy and operating decisions by presenting factual information about current or future operating and product design problems. Because of their importance it is essential that such reports be prepared in a uniform manner and be complete, concise, and accurate. Since 1945 General Motors Institute has supervised the preparation of over 2,000 industrial reports required as part of the Fifth-Year program leading to a Baccalaureate degree in either engineering or business administration. Experience gained with the wide range of material covered in these reports has led to the development of specifications which maintain organizational uniformity in their preparation and final make-up. A set of guiding questions also has been developed which serves to evaluate the report as to its technical content and logical presentation of this content.

Report value: a matter of presentation as well as material content

INDUSTRIAL reports are a tool of management. They act as a guide to policy or operating decisions by presenting factual information about current or future operating and product problems. Subjects of industrial reports vary from non-engineering areas, such as accounting, traffic, and personnel management, to technical areas of manufacturing operations and product engineering.

Industrial reports supply management with information such as whether it is feasible to apply automatic data processing methods in an accounting department, whether a proposed change in a manufacturing process will prove economical, or whether a proposed change in the design of a product is feasible.

Because of the broad nature of information supplied management by the industrial report any engineer or non-engineer member of an industrial organization may be required at one time or another to prepare and write a report. The reports may vary in length from a single typewritten page to hundreds of pages bound in book form. Each report, no matter the length, serves an important purpose.

Value of Report Depends on a Clear Objective and Writer's Ability to Find, Analyze, and Appraise Data

Industrial reports are prepared with a specific objective in mind. The objective should:

- Define clearly the problem and indicate its scope
- Indicate the purpose and/or need of the report.

Once the objective of a report is set it then becomes the responsibility of the writer to determine how and where to obtain data necessary to prepare the report and to substantiate findings, recommendations, or problem solution. Experience has shown that there are two types of data:

(a) Data resulting from studies, analyses, and reports which have been completed prior to the report assignment
(b) Data which must be obtained to indicate the existing situation as accurately as possible.

Few industrial reports are based on data obtained from published material found in periodicals, books, or manufacturer's catalogs. The writer must depend, therefore, on locating information pertinent to the assigned report in the industrial organization of which he is a part.

Members of an industrial organization

Fig. 1—Current data used in the preparation of an industrial report to indicate accurately an existing situation may be obtained from test reports, mathematical analyses, or observations of a device under controlled conditions, such as shown here.

REPRINT from the GENERAL MOTORS ENGINEERING JOURNAL
Volume 4   April-May-June 1957   Number 2
for educators in the fields of engineering and allied sciences

JULY-AUGUST-SEPTEMBER 1957

© 1957 by General Motors Corporation. All rights reserved under the International and Pan-American Copyright Conventions. Requests for permission to reproduce any part or parts of this publication may be directed to Joseph Karshner.

constantly make studies and collect data to assist in meeting daily responsibilities and in making decisions. Thus, a great amount of data in the form of memos; research, test, and departmental reports; and an individual's memory of how similar problems have been handled in the past provide a good background as to where to find and how to collect the necessary data.

Current data can be obtained in many ways. In a technical report, data can come from such sources as test reports, observations of a device under controlled conditions (Fig. 1), or a mathematical analysis. Non-technical reports must depend on such devices as surveys, questionnaires, or statistical analyses.

The value of an industrial report depends upon the validity, accuracy, and soundness of the data which supports any conclusions, findings, or problem solutions. The value of the data, in turn, is dependent upon the time spent in preparing and setting specifications as to how it must be obtained. It is essential, therefore, that the writer of an industrial report have:

- Knowledge of how similar problems have been handled in the past
- Ability to acquire and appraise data
- Knowledge of informational sources both within and outside the organization
- Ability to subject the problem to critical and analytical thinking
- Ability to put together fact and reasoning into readable and understandable English.

Over 2,000 Industrial Reports Prepared by G.M.I. Graduates

During the past 12 years, General Motors Institute has been working with GM Divisions and Staffs in the preparation of a wide range of industrial reports written by graduates of the 4-year co-operative programs. Before being awarded an appropriate Baccalaureate degree in either engineering or business administration a graduate of a 4-year co-operative program must submit evidence to G.M.I. that he can apply the knowledge and experience gained during his program studies and work experience. This is achieved through a Fifth-Year Project Study Report program in which a student is assigned to solve a problem which is of current or future interest to the sponsoring Division or Staff and acceptable to G.M.I. The graduate is guided while solving the assigned problem by both an Institute faculty member and a technical advisor appointed by the sponsoring Division or Staff. A Baccalaureate degree is awarded when the graduate meets the objectives of the assigned problem and the written Project Study Report is accepted by both the sponsoring Division or Staff and G.M.I.

During the period that the Project Study Report program has been in operation over 2,000 industrial reports have been written. Of these, over 60 per cent have concerned manufacturing line or staff operations and approximately 20 per cent have been in the product engineering areas of design, development, testing, and research. The remaining reports have dealt with areas of sales and service, personnel management, accounting, traffic, purchasing, and material control.

Specifications Developed for Each Part of Report Assure Uniform Presentation

Over the 12-year period that the Fifth-Year Project Study Report program has been in operation, G.M.I. has found it necessary to develop specifications which not only cover the wide range of subject matter but also maintain a uniformity in the preparation of these reports. These specifications, based on experience, recognize that the industrial report should have four basic parts presented in the following order: (a) introduction, (b) conclusions (recommendations or findings), (c) main discussion, and (d) appendix.

A preface should be included if required. Also, the use of a table of contents and list of illustrations aids in quick and efficient use of the report.

The following is a discussion of G.M.I. specifications as applied to each part of an industrial report.

The Preface

A preface should include pertinent information concerning the situation that led to the report assignment and necessary acknowledgements. The industrial plant situation is explained first so that the significance of the report will be more apparent to the readers. Acknowledgements should be made to those who contributed substantially to the report or success of the problem solution. The nature of each contribution should be explained.

Fig. 2—The author of an industrial report should use a style of writing which is objective, impersonal, unemotional, and unbiased and should present information in an orderly and accurate manner.

The Introduction

The introduction of an industrial report should clearly and immediately state the problem which existed, as well as the exact purpose or objective of the report in relation to the problem. Background material necessary to understand the report and investigation may be included, but should be held to a minimum.

The procedure of investigation is part of the introduction and should give a clear and concise picture of the method used. This enables the reader to judge the validity of the report. In reports where there is no step-by-step procedure of conducting the investigation, the introduction should end with a statement indicating the order of discussion in the remainder of the report.

Background information included in the introduction should be limited to that needed to orientate the reader. This includes necessary definitions, history, or other such pertinent information.

The Conclusions (Recommendations or Findings)

The introduction should be followed by the conclusions and/or recommendations, if any are to be made. Where no conclusions or recommendations are made, a summary of findings is desirable.

General conclusions or recommendations should precede those which are specific. Each specific conclusion, recommendation, or finding should be keyed to the substantiating data in the main discussion of the report. Page references may be made or the conclusions, recommendations, or findings may be grouped under headings corresponding to the sections making up the main discussion of the report. In any case, a listing of the conclusions, recommendations, or findings is recommended.

GENERAL MOTORS ENGINEERING JOURNAL

The Main Discussion

The sections of the report which make up the main discussion should be organized to read independently. The opening sentence of each section should make clear that part of the report to which the section is related. If a section deals with only one phase of the investigation, a detailed procedure can be described either immediately following the opening sentence or at the most appropriate point in the discussion. Also, the opening of each section should explain the organization of data which are to be included.

Data must be complete, accurate, specific, and conclusive. The conclusions, recommendations, or findings, are valid only to the extent that they are supported by data obtained through a logical procedure of investigation. The data and procedure used should be presented so that the reader arrives at the same conclusions as the writer. The discussion of the data should be concluded with a summary of the conclusions, recommendations, or findings of the section.

In cases where a section is primarily informational, its organization necessarily will vary from one which is investigational. For example, if a section reports an analysis of a method used in a manufacturing plant, the opening should indicate the purpose of the section, present briefly the necessary background material, and give the order of discussion of data. At the end of the section, the data should be summarized.

The Appendix

An appendix is often needed to present detailed data, background, or other information not required for the development of the main discussion of the report. Material included in the appendix is required to give added support to the conclusions, recommendations, or findings through such means as photographs, drawings, graphical presentations, calculations, or tabulations.

The above specifications allow the writer considerable freedom as to style of writing and use of illustrative material (Fig. 2). The style of an industrial report, however, should be objective, impersonal, unemotional, and unbiased. Report content should be written so that it is direct, sound, accurate, orderly, and precise. The language should be that of the writer, as he is personally responsible for the report.

Evaluation of the Report

Technical Evaluation	Report Evaluation
Total Report	
Does total report: • Fulfill original objectives? • Cover all points essential to the main purpose of the assigned report? Is each part of the report in proportion to the complexity or significance of the corresponding parts of the assigned report?	Does total report have: • Information arranged and presented in a sound and effective manner? • A suitable title page giving essential information? • A table of contents and list of illustrations which are complete, accurate, and easy to understand?
Preface	
Does preface: • Explain the assigned report accurately? • Explain any change from the original objective during the development of the report? • Give an accurate account of the work experience related to the assigned report? • Acknowledge the help of those who contributed to the preparation of the report?	Does preface: • Explain the reasons which gave rise to the selection of the report assignment? • Give a clear account of work experience relating to the assigned report? • Make acknowledgements in proper form: name, title and type of aid?
Introduction	
Does the introduction: • State the problem so that it corresponds with the objectives? • Give the main steps of the procedure accurately?	Does the introduction: • Give enough background information so that the nature of the report is easily understood? • State the problem clearly and without ambiguity; • Make clear the main steps in the procedure? • State the specific purpose of the report? • Present the order of discussion for the remainder of the report?
Conclusions	
Are conclusions: • Significant, pertinent, and valid? • Substantiated by the data presented in the report? • Appropriate to the assigned report? • Supplemented by a summary of findings and recommendations when necessary?	Are conclusions: • Identified by an opening statement? • Grouped with general before specific conclusions? • Presented by including page numbers of substantiating text or grouped according to sections of the text so that the reader can locate substantiating data for any statement? • Accurately grouped and labeled as conclusions, recommendations, or findings? • Presented in lists, charts, graphs, or other suitable means of summarizing?

Table I—These guidelines for the evaluation of a report were developed at General Motors Institute. The guidelines are designed to assure uniform evaluation and to maintain a high uniform standard of quality.

Evaluation of the Report (Continued)

Technical Evaluation	Report Evaluation
Main Discussion	
Does main discussion: • Describe any tests, equipment, or procedures used with sufficient completeness and accuracy so that the reader could use the information as a guide to a similar problem? • Give specific sources of all information? • Give complete and exact figures for all results and omit inexact information such as "many," "few," and "more?" • Use technical terminology accurately?	Does main discussion: • Identify the area to be considered? • Indicate the order in which each section is arranged? • Explain clearly how data were gathered, processed, and interpreted? • Relate data clearly to the conclusions reached? • Give exact source of information in proper form, including footnotes and bibliography when needed? • Use precise language? • Develop the discussion in a logical and clear order so that the material is easily usable? • End with a summary or grouping of conclusions developed in the section?
Illustrations	
Are illustrations: • Provided when necessary as determined by the nature of the data or discussion? • Consistent in quality with the text discussion? • Accurate in their interpretation? • Sound in the techniques used?	Are illustrations: • Referred to in the text? • Placed near text reference? • Reproduced properly? • Clearly numbered and labeled? • Used when desirable as a summary device?
Appendix	
Does the appendix: • Contain essential supporting or supplementary material? • Contain all material which belongs there?	Does the appendix: • Contain appropriate material? • Have a usable arrangement?
English	
	Is the English: • Accurate in following the conventions of language? • Clear, precise, and readable?

Guidelines Established to Evaluate the Industrial Report

Once an industrial report is completed, the important job of evaluating it begins. An evaluation should be made to determine first the completeness and accuracy of the content and then to evaluate the report as a clearly and logically organized presentation of the development of the content.

At General Motors Institute, obtaining uniformity in evaluating some 300 reports a year by 90 faculty members became a major problem when attempting to maintain a consistently high level of quality in all reports. It was necessary, therefore, to establish guidelines to assist the readers in obtaining a uniform evaluation of these reports (Table I). These guidelines, in the form of questions, cover each part of the report and are designed to evaluate the report as to content, preparation, and organization.

Nature of Report Determines Reproduction Method to Use

Experience has indicated that the nature of the report determines the number to be reproduced. In turn, the number required generally determines the method used for reproduction.

A typewritten original with carbon copies will meet the need when four or less copies are required. This method, however, does not allow for additional copies if required later. Typed vellum masters with a carbon backing will produce an unlimited number of copies by any one of the ammonia blueprint processes but are not economical for runs of more than eight or ten copies. Additional, individual copies, however, can be reproduced from the vellum masters whenever required. The most favored process for reproducing G.M.I. reports at the present time is to prepare paper plate masters and reproduce them by the multilith process. Runs of from 10 to 100 copies are economical by this method. Additional copies are reproduced easily from the masters.

To increase the use of industrial reports within an organization, a subject listing of report titles with a brief abstract of each report is of value. The abstract should be short (50 to 100 words) and should enable a person to determine whether reading the full report will be of value. The abstract should give a clear indication of the objective and scope of the report, mention the procedure, and indicate the results achieved.

Conclusion

The industrial report is used not only to increase available information on a subject or problem but also to communicate that information to management and personnel involved. Today, increasing emphasis is placed upon the use, recording, and availability of industrial reports. Their value increases still further as their availability increases within an organization. It has been the experience of General Motors Institute that uniformity of organization and quality of preparation gives a systematic approach to industrial report writing and results in their greater use.

What Price Verbal Incompetence?

by EDWIN A. LOCKE, JR.

It seems to me that I have never heard so much misuse and abuse of the English language by people occupying responsible positions as in recent years. And my question is: What ought we to do about verbal incompetence—about the carelessness in speaking and writing which is so prevalent among us?

It is not exaggerating to say that America's international position depends in some degree on our ability as a people to use words effectively and grasp their actual meanings. We have entered a period of greatly increased competition from other countries. Our qualifications as leader of the free world are being tested as never before. Our diplomats are constantly in the spotlight. Every word that they utter or write is exposed to hard critical judgment. Our government must compete in propaganda with other nations to influence the world's peoples, and our success or failure in this department can profoundly affect our destiny. If we are to maintain leadership, we will have to show great skill in the arts of communication. Those who do not understand us may well turn against us.

I shall never forget one incident of the days when I was working for our government in a diplomatic capacity. There was a meeting in London where a very high official of our government had to explain our position on a touchy matter to the ministers of several other countries. I think all of the Americans present, including myself, were embarrassed for him and for the United States. He rambled, he stumbled, he used words that distorted his meaning. He not only failed to make his point but he confused the issue. It literally took weeks of patient effort to correct the false impressions that he created at that meeting, and we never did win the agreement that we sought.

I have heard a Congressman shock a group of Asiatic visitors by saying proudly that Americans are an "aggressive" people. I suppose he meant to say that we are a courageous, vigorous people. But his audience understood him to mean that we are a warlike people, and their worst fears were confirmed. I hate to think of how many times in our recent history similar episodes must have occurred—meetings where our spokesmen used the wrong words, or failed to use the right ones that would have made their meaning clear. There are days when, as I read the newspapers, I find myself repeating the closing lines of Kipling's *Recessional:*

> For frantic boast and foolish word
> Have mercy on thy people, Lord!

We are told, and I think we can all agree, that verbal incompetence is often a symptom of deeper problems of the mind and spirit. But there are surely many instances when it results from loose and undisciplined mental habits, from a lack of respect for words. Unless we take action to correct the trend, verbal incompetence may become a national calamity.

Lately I have come to think that the sector of our society that suffers most seriously from verbal incompetence is business. There, too, the national interest is involved. The misleading use of words is a major source of inefficiency and waste motion in business. It is all the more serious because it is hard to measure. I venture to say that all the thefts and embezzlements that corporations suffer every year do not cost our economy as much as verbal incompetence.

The waste created by misunderstanding is one that America can ill afford. Our industry is now compelled to meet concentrated competition, not only from the Communist countries, but even more important, from nations friendly to us. High prices—and waste means high prices—can keep us out of markets all over the world. And if our foreign trade falls away—or even if it fails to grow—our political influence and strategic alliances could be jeopardized.

All of us, in whatever walks of life, have a big stake in the efficiency of American business. And for that reason, we must take a serious view of the continuous economic losses due to verbal incompetence.

I have seen more than one business shaken by a single letter or memorandum in which words were used loosely or wildly. A story was recently told to me by the head of an important company. Call him Mr. Brown. He was at the time trying to establish friendly relations with an executive of another company, a Mr. Slade, who was an important potential customer for Brown, and Brown had given a good deal of thought to the best way of cultivating him.

One day, a letter from Slade arrived at Brown's office. Slade said that he was reviewing his requirements for the year ahead, and that if Brown would like to talk with him, he would make himself available.

Now it happened that Brown just then was away on a trip. In his absence, Slade's letter went to one of his young assistants for reply—call him Harvey. This is what Harvey wrote to Slade, "Dear Mr. Slade: In Mr. Brown's absence, I am writing to say that your request for an appointment will be brought to his attention immediately on his return."

When Brown got back a few days later, he telephoned Slade at once. Slade shocked him by saying that he was no longer interested in pursuing the matter. He said that he judged companies by the tone of their correspondence, and after receiving Harvey's note he had got in touch with another company, a competitor of Brown's, and had concluded a deal with them. He added that he had been surprised to find that his letter to Brown was regarded as a request for an appointment.

When Brown hung up the phone, he sent for Harvey. Now the point that interested me most is that Harvey could not see that there was anything wrong with the letter he had written. He said, "But Mr. Brown, that letter from Mr. Slade *did* ask for an appointment."

Brown said, "You don't seem to understand. Slade wrote that if I wanted to see him, he would make himself available. He wasn't requesting an appointment. He was giving *me* a chance to request one."

And then young Harvey said, "But after all, it's practically the same thing, isn't it?"

Business is full of Harveys—young men whose minds have never been trained to pinpoint the meaning of the words they use, and whose careers suffer accordingly. That little anecdote is characteristic of what goes on all the time.. A man can have many virtues and abilities, but if he does not use language accurately and carefully, he can be a positive menace to a business enterprise.

This is a country where each year hundreds of thousands of young men go into business with their hearts set on executive careers. Yet it is relatively rare to find a young business man who recognizes how much his chances for an executive post depend on his ability to use words effectively. Many companies, including the one with which I am connected, today give increasing weight to the ability to communicate effectively as a test of executive potential.

Of course, there are plenty of young people who have a bright surface and glib tongues—who look at first glance as if they might be of executive caliber. But when they begin to talk seriously, or to express themselves in writing, they too often reveal serious verbal limitations. Sometimes, listening to a hopeful young man, or reading something he has written, I have been reminded of the way a child uses finger paint—a dab here and a smear there. The child hopes that father will recognize his painting and say, "Oh, yes, that's a cat." Many otherwise intelligent people, when they talk or write, similarly seem to feel that they have done all that can be expected of them if the other fellow just gets the general idea. They may not know it, but they are intellectually crippled.

The heads of several other companies have told me that they, too, are deeply concerned over this problem. They have all had experience with young executives who seem almost indifferent to the meaning of words. I have been told of a memorandum written by one such young man, and which caused a good deal of trouble. His company specializes in issuing reports on the steel industry. One day the editor of these reports received a memo from one of his assistants. It said, "I talked with Anderson, and he predicts a price rise before April." Anderson was an important steel man.

The report for that week was going to press, the editor was in a hurry, and he did not stop to check with Anderson. In a few days the item appeared in print, and then Anderson telephoned in a state of rage. He demanded an apology and a retraction. He had made no prediction, he said. All he had told the young man was that if certain things happened—which had not yet happened—prices could be expected to rise. Since when was that a prediction? If that was the kind of intelligence the editor was relying on, said Anderson, he would never trust him again.

Now the young assistant who had written that memo knew in general what the word "predict" means. But he did not distinguish between a prediction and a qualified statement of possibilities. He was content to use a word that merely approximated his meaning. As a result, he did serious damage to the reputation of his firm.

If verbal incompetence were confined to the use of the wrong word, it would be bad enough. But equally dangerous is the frequent inability of business men to sense the effect of their words on the persons who will hear them or read them.

I have known a single word, used insensitively, to touch off a costly labor dispute. A large company was negotiating a new contract with a labor union. Both sides had presented their views in writing. The negotiation was progressing in a somewhat tense but reasonable atmosphere. At this point, the union leadership presented a letter raising a new condition. The letter hinted that if the new condition was not accepted by the company a strike might result. This was, of course, a familiar bargaining tactic.

The union's letter was given for reply to a young man in the company. By current standards, he is well educated—a graduate of a great university—with a good academic record, and a lively mind. The letter he composed was for the most part sensible. But at one point he said, "It would be criminal to call a strike for such a reason." None of his superiors who read the letter saw anything wrong with it, and it went out.

Now it was true that a strike under those circumstances would have been illegal. The young man knew the difference between "illegal" and "criminal." To do him justice, he used the word "criminal" only in its figurative sense, to show indignation. Unfortunately, the union took it literally. The word "criminal" was like a slap in the face to them. One of them, in fact, had a jail record. They reacted violently to what they felt was a gratuitous insult. "Who is he calling criminals?" was their reaction. From that point on, they became hostile, the situation deteriorated, and a useless strike followed at great cost both to the union members and to the company.

Another costly aspect of verbal incompetence in business is what might be called the careless cliche. Please understand that I am not objecting too much to cliches as a whole. They may be despised by poets, but as we all know a cliche accurately used can on occasion be a time saver and a boon to the weary mind. The trouble arises when the cliche is wrongly used.

I know about a letter written by the sales manager of a well-known company to a customer. The letter explained why a certain salesman had left the company. The sales manager was angry at the salesman for quitting and in his letter he said, "It's just a case of a rat leaving the ship."

He failed to remember that it is the *sinking* ship that rats desert. But this thought came to his customer, and he mentioned it to others. Soon people were gossiping that the company was in trouble. It took an investigation to unearth the source of the rumor, and a good deal of effort to undo the damage that had been done. The head of that company told me that he figured the cost of that one little misused cliche at about $10,000.

Then there was a memorandum issued by an officer in another company, with this apparently innocent sentence in it: "Let's apply this new credit policy with discretion right across the board."

The writer of that memo meant that the new policy should be applied in all appropriate cases, but that there would be some cases in which it was not applicable, and care should be taken to handle such cases discreetly. That was not the impression that was created in the minds of the men who received the memo. As they understood the order, the new credit policy was to be applied to all of the company's customers, "right across the board," and the words "with discretion" merely meant that they were to be polite about it.

It took just two days for the earthquake to develop. Then complaint began to come in from outraged customers, demanding to know what the company meant by refusing to extend the usual credit terms. Tempers were lost. Orders were canceled. The company's top management became alarmed. Before the tangle was straightened out, I was told, the company had lost $50,000 worth of business.

To me, one of the most irritating forms of verbal incompetence is wordiness. It is of course hard to be concise. I have a good deal of sympathy with the man who said, "If I'd had more time, I would have written you a shorter letter." We all know what he meant. But a great deal of the unnecessary verbiage in business, I am convinced, results not so much from lack of time as from mental laziness or confusion.

More than once I have seen executives spend valuable hours and brain energy trying to grasp the meaning of a ten-page report, when a single page of accurate writing would have served the purpose. I have seen the employees of a plant bewildered and disturbed by a long, incomprehensible instruction from the home office, until it was reduced to a few brief sentences that told them clearly what to do.

Business does not want wordy men, but it urgently needs men who respect words. I hate to suggest that our overburdened schools take on more responsibilities than they already have, yet I cannot help wondering if this is not essentially a problem of education.

People are most responsive to the discipline of language when they are young. In several instances I have tried to get mature business associates to sharpen their use of words, but the results have been a good deal less than spectacular. Once a young man has left school, if he has not already been imbued with respect for words and given the mental training necessary to distinguish shades of meaning, the chances are that he will always be weak in this department.

People who cannot use words accurately are likely to be people who cannot grasp meanings successfully. And much may depend on the ability of the American people to understand the actual meanings of the propagandistic words that are being hurled at them today. Why are so many people everywhere carried away by demagogues and fanatics? In part, I think it is because they have never been exposed to the least semantic discipline. They do not really understand the words that they hear or read. It is only the emotional overtones that reach them. And this unthinking emotionalism can in the long run make them dangerous to their countrymen, to themselves, and to the world.

I would go so far as to say that verbal incompetence is threatening to become a chronic disease of the American intellect. It needs to be dealt with by an all-out effort by the qualified men, dealt with as we deal with polio or muscular dystrophy. The literate people of this country, as I see it, have a responsibility to restore respect for the word, to reduce the proportion of verbal incompetents in the population.

I believe from my heart that if the schools and colleges of this country would boldly decide to meet this problem head-on they would have the support not only of business, but of serious-minded citizens from every walk of life. The American people already stand in heavy debt to the teachers and school administrators of the country, but if education can strengthen the use of language in our time, the next generation will have even more to be grateful for.

"Mr. Edwin A. Locke, Jr., '32, an Overseer of Harvard College, is president of the Union Tank Car Company. This article [in the *Harvard Alumni Bulletin,* February 17, 1962] is adapted from an address delivered to a joint meeting of the Howland Club of Chicago Principals and the Superintendents' Round Table of Northern Illinois." Permission to use this excellent and significant article was graciously granted by the *Harvard Alumni Review.*

JPR

My attention was drawn to this illuminating article by Mrs. Helen Myrick LaFleur's condensation in the Ginn and Company's WHAT THE COLLEGES ARE DOING for Fall, 1962. Had Mrs. LaFleur not reprinted it in part, I probably would never have had an opportunity of seeing it. For so doing, Mrs. LaFleur has earned my sincere thanks.

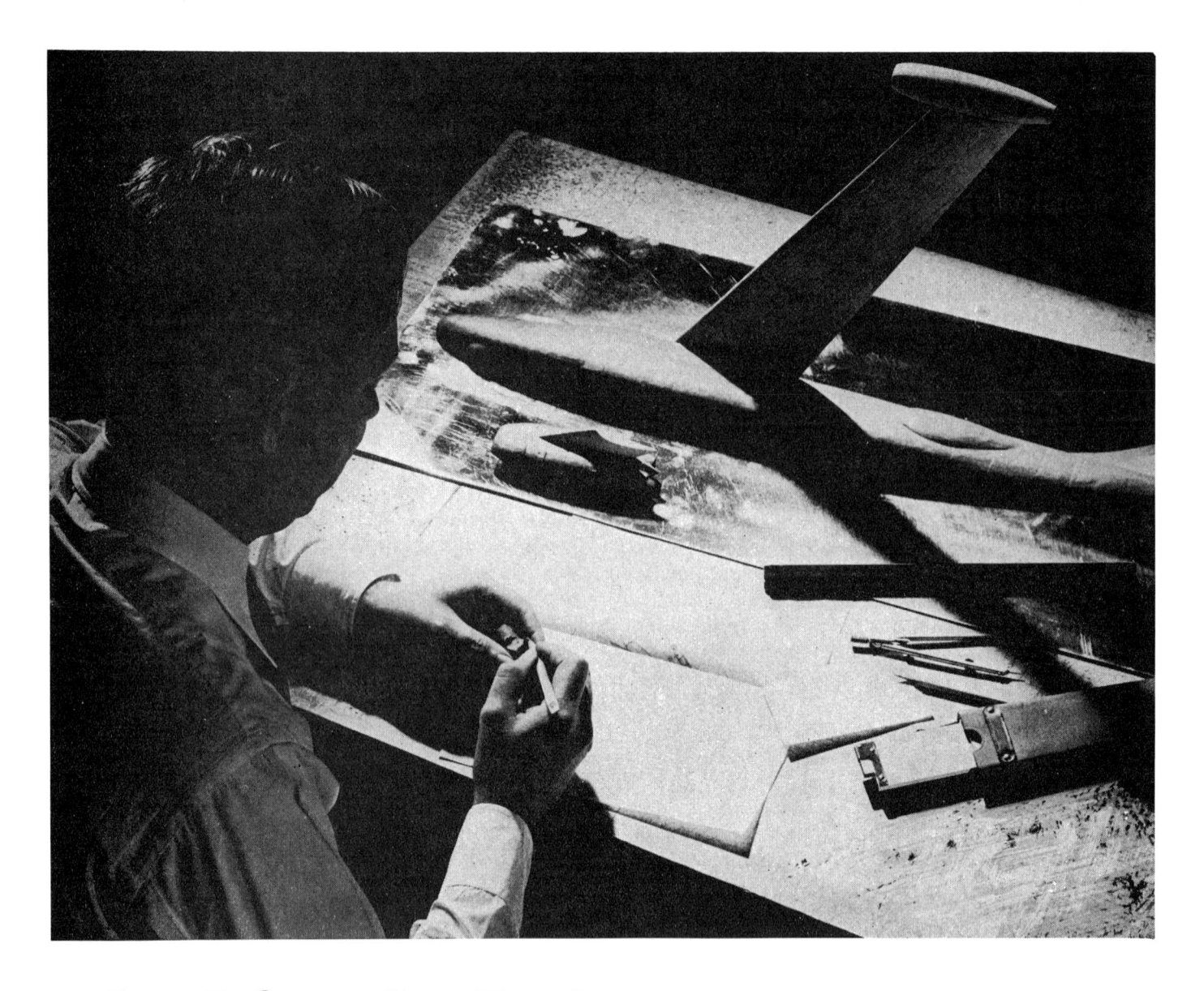

Applying the Engineering Method to
REPORT WRITING

by JAMES W. SOUTHER
University of Washington, Seattle, Washington

The secret of effective report writing is to be found in the application of the engineering method to the solution of writing problems. An analysis of technical reports indicates that, in general, writers face two main difficulties: (1) the problem of designing their reports to do a specific job in a particular technical situation and (2) the problem of knowing where to start and what steps to follow in the writing of a report. Unfortunately, most suggestions regarding reports so often deal with only the finished product, describing it in detail but ignoring completely the process by which it is evolved. Yet, this phase of writing is the one with which most writers have the greatest difficulty.

In writing as in design, quality products depend upon accurate and complete analysis, detailed and purposeful planning, and careful and select application. Every element of the problem must be taken into consideration and a knowledge of the available tools and devices brought to bear on the solution. Usually able to solve design problems within their own technical areas, engineers need only apply the same method to their writing problems in order to achieve more effective results.

Check List for Effective Report Writing

1. **ANALYZING THE PROBLEM**—determining the elements of the problem and the relationships existing between them.

2. **PLANNING THE TREATMENT OF THE PROBLEM**—determining some tentative order of investigation.

3. **INVESTIGATING THE PROBLEM**—gathering and evaluating data and material and drawing conclusions.

4. **DESIGNING THE PRODUCT**—arranging the material so that it accomplishes its purpose.

5. **CONSTRUCTING THE PRODUCT**—applying the design.

6. **CHECKING THE RESULTS**—determining if the product actually accomplishes its purpose.

7. **MODIFYING THE PRODUCT**—changing the product in light of evidence provided by the check.

8. **PREPARING THE FINAL PRODUCT**—turning out the finished product.

I. Analyzing the writing problem
A. Who will read the report?
B. What is the purpose of the report?
C. What industrial action is desired?
D. What is the scope of the report?
E. What specifically has been asked for?
F. How much time is allotted for the completion of the report?
G. What special directives or orders must be considered?

II. Planning the treatment of the problem
A. What kind of information must be included: facts, information, results, conclusions, recommendations, or a combination of these?
B. What is known; what is unknown?
C. Which elements are of major importance, which of minor importance?
D. What previous studies or reports can be of aid?
E. Who can be of aid?
F. What tentative order of investigation should be followed?

III. Investigating the problem
A. Are the data accurate?
B. Are the data complete?
C. Are there enough data for the proposed paper?
D. Have all the important phases been covered?
E. Which are the most important facts and results?
F. Do the conclusions actually grow out of the data?
G. Should the emphasis be placed on the data, the method, the results, or the conclusions?
H. Does the nature of the report require that all phases be presented in great detail?

IV. Designing the report
A. What organization will make the material best fulfill its purpose?
B. What level of technical usage can be understood by the reader?
C. How can the material be organized so as to be most useful and to save the reader time?
D. What particular form will best support the use to be made of the report?
E. Is a statement of authorization, purpose and scope required?
F. Does the complexity of the report require a table of contents, an index, or an abstract?
G. What specific data, examples, details, and illustrations are required for clarity of meaning?
H. What facts must be interpreted?
I. What parts of the report must be emphasized?

V. Constructing the report
A. Follow the determined organization.
B. Do not waste time trying to get started; come back to the beginning later.
C. Write as rapidly as possible, leaving exact wording and mechanics to be checked over at a later date, in order to have life and continuity in the report.
D. Work in stages if the report is long and complex.
E. Include everything of importance; the report can be cut later.

VI. Checking the report
A. Organization
 1. Is the identity of the subject clear from the beginning?
 2. Is space wasted at the beginning of the report?
 3. Is the subject advanced by clear-cut stages?
 4. Is the relationship between one stage and the next clear?
 5. Does the conclusion leave the reader with the desired point of view?
B. Content
 1. Is the material complete enough to accomplish the purpose of the report?
 2. Are more examples, details, facts or illustrations needed?
 3. Do the facts require more interpretation?
 4. Are the major points emphasized enough?
C. Form
 1. Does the form make the parts easily accessible?
 2. Is the beginning and the end of each section indicated by the use of titles and proper spacing?
 3. Does the form of the report represent the co-ordination and subordination of the material?
 4. Are organizational devices needed: tables of contents, indexes, abstracts, etc.?
D. Style
 1. Does the style facilitate rapid reading?
 2. Is the exact meaning conveyed?
 3. Is the report clear for later reference?
 4. Is there any deadwood to be removed?
 5. Are the sentences direct and effective?
 6. Are the mechanics correct?

VII. Modifying the report
A. Make the necessary changes, additions, or deletions in the content of the report.
B. Make the necessary alterations in the organization of the report.
C. Make the necessary mechanical and stylistic alterations.
D. Make necessary changes in form.

VIII. Preparing the final report
A. Use standard materials.
B. Be neat and accurate.
C. Make only small changes on the finished manuscript.

The eight basic steps of the engineering method (above), are applicable to writing problems and, as in engineering, each is important. The particular items to be considered in solving writing problems, however, need further explanation, for they may represent unfamiliar material to some engineers.

Analyzing the Problem
- What is the purpose of the product?
- How will it be used?
- Who will use it?

The point of attack in report writing as well as in engineering is the analysis of the problem—determining the purpose, the industrial role, the audience of the report.

A report directed toward a stricter observance of recommended engineering practices in a particular section will differ from one which is merely a survey of adherence to present recommended practices. Both will differ from one which aims at improvement and extension of the recommended procedures themselves. The difference in the reports arises from their different purposes. The first stipulates clearly and concisely what is to be done in the future; little mention of old practices is needed. In the second, a statement of past procedures and of the adherence to them makes up the report. In the last, a statement of recommended modifications and additions to past rules is the essence of the report. Each differs as its purpose differs.

For example, if a report is to be used for reference, its engineering role requires that it be complete in all details since the material will probably be unfamiliar to the reader when the report is used—at least the immediate context from which the report sprang will have long disappeared. Moreover, in this kind of a report, the organization must provide easy access to all parts of the report, for its content, scope and data must be clearly identified if it is to be useful, if it is to fulfill its industrial role.

In addition to the purpose and industrial role of the report, the writer must determine, as best he can, who will use it and what the reader specifically desires. He must consider the education and experience of the reader, for these factors will determine the amount of detail and the level of technical language and usage which the writer can safely incorporate in his report. For example, a report describing a new home appliance to a mechanical engineer will obviously differ from one for the average consumer.

Examination of only a few engineering reports will reveal what happens when the writer fails to analyze the writing problem. Such reports no more satisfy their requirements than does a mechanical design which has not grown out of a study of the design problem.

Planning the Treatment of the Problem
- What elements are of major importance?
- What aid is available?
- What tentative plan should be followed?

If the report is to be successful, the writer must determine what is of most importance to his reader and to the purpose of his report. He should determine whether facts, results, conclusions or recommendations are most vital to the industrial action he is striving to accomplish.

Competent engineers frequently fail to determine what is essential to the report which they must write. They fail to distinguish between the *important* and the *related*. Then, playing safe, they cover all phases of the problem. Although the most important material is included in the report, it is so hidden in related but less important material that the report becomes useless. It becomes ineffective because it has lost direction.

Once the writer has distinguished between the elements of major importance and those of lesser importance, he is in a position to consider in proper perspective the task facing him. He can then form a tentative plan of attack based on a thorough analysis of the problem he faces. He knows what he is attempting to do in his report; he knows what is of major importance to his task; he knows what he must do in order to complete the report. With this knowledge he can plan his program for solving the problem and writing the report.

Investigating the Problem
- Are the data accurate and complete?
- What are the results?
- What conclusions can be drawn?

Investigation of the problem is the stage of report writing where the engineer has least difficulty; here he is quite at home. He is particularly adept at gathering material, and accuracy and completeness of data are generally the rule. Yet, the results achieved, or the conclusions drawn, are often of much greater importance to the industrial function of the report. For example, a report which is to determine whether or not money is to be invested in a new product line must emphasize results and conclusions, for it is on them that the financial decisions will be based. If a report is a weekly progress report, however, the data are of prime importance and conclusions are not usually included.

Since the engineer is trained in the techniques of gathering his technical material, little need be said of them. It is important, however, that he be warned of the unnecessary work that often results from failing to realize what is basic to the study. Often, much time and labor are spent gathering information which would obviously prove not germane to the project had proper consideration been given it.

Designing the Product

- What design will make the data best fulfill its purpose?
- What design will make the data most useful?
- What design will emphasize the important parts?

After the material is gathered and evaluated, the writer faces the all-important task of organizing his material, or *designing* the report he is to write. From the many possible ways of organizing his material, the writer must choose the particular one which he feels is best. Such a choice, to be effective, must be based on a realistic analysis of the problem. Success or failure depends on the ability of the report to satisfy its industrial function. The material must be organized so that it accomplishes its purpose of clearly communicating to others the exact information intended, whether it be a recommendation to a board of control, a financial statement of the quarter, a statement of project progress, a result of a laboratory test, or a procedure for soldering electrical connections. Each statement must look both backward and forward; each must be a bridge over which the reader can easily move in his efforts to understand the report.

In addition to being clear and understandable, the material must be organized so as to be most useful to the reader, and the writer must constantly keep the needs of the reader in mind if his report is to be effective. The growing demand for abstracts and summaries in industrial reports stems from their usefulness to the people who use the reports. The effective report writer will place the material which is of greatest interest to the reader at the beginning of the report, for very often the order in which the writer gathered his material, or the order in which the test was conducted, is not the most satisfactory arrangement for the report which covers them. The results and conclusions, in most cases, are far too important to be placed at the end of the report, and the efficient report writer places them in a position of emphasis, near the beginning.

Good report form is more than attractive; it is functional as well. Effectively designed reports save the reader time by having all parts clearly identified through proper use of titles and subtitles. Sections of equal importance are given identical physical arrangements, and relationships of subordinate sections are made obvious at first glance by the manner in which they are placed on the page. Good form is an extension of the basic organization of the material within the report. The format is a pleasing graphic expression of the structural development of the material contained.

Constructing the Product

- Has the determined organization been followed?

Once the report has been designed, the writer should write as rapidly as possible in order to give life and sparkle to his phrasing, as well as to save the continuity of ideas which is often destroyed by constant rework and polishing. In the first draft, he should pay little attention to the mechanics of writing, for these can be corrected before rewriting. Moreover, when he is in doubt about including any information, he should remember that it is much easier to cut than to expand. If the report is long and complex, the writer will often find his work easier if he writes each stage of it separately, finishing one part before moving to the next.

Although the report should follow the determined organization, the writer, however, should not make himself a slave to his plan. Any new ideas which occur during the writing should be added. The writer will also find it is much easier to rewrite his own material effectively if he will wait a day or two before reworking it.

Such items as abstracts and summaries should not be written until the report is finished, for reading and outlining the report will provide the writer with the essential information for his abstract or summary.

Checking the Product

- Is the product complete?
- Are the proper elements given importance?
- Does the product accomplish its purpose?

Upon completion of the first draft, preferably after some time has elapsed, the writer should thoroughly check his report for organization, content, form and style. Often he will find it quite helpful to have someone else check the report to see whether it is clear and achieves its intended purpose. Then, trying to place himself in the position of the reader, the writer should determine whether or not the subject is clear at the beginning, for there most space is wasted. He should make certain that the direction of movement within the report is logical and clear—that the relationship between facts and their interpretation, between data and conclusions, is made obvious both by the arrangement of material in the sections and by the arrangements of the sections in the report. The data must be interpreted for the reader, for contrary to a popular notion, facts do not speak for themselves. The efficient report writer interprets them so that his reader cannot misunderstand. Most important of all, however, he should determine whether or not the report will leave the reader with the desired point of view—whether or not it does what it was meant to do.

The report should be checked for clear identification and easy accessibility of all parts. The form, supplementing and supporting the organization of the contents of the report, should make all titles clear—headings, capitalization, and spacing should be consistent. Identical format should apply to sections of equivalent status; headings or position on the page should differentiate major and minor sections. In addition, consideration should be given to organizational devices such as a table of contents, an index and an abstract.

In matters of style, the writer should carefully check his report to see if the exact meaning is conveyed and whether or not "deadwood" can be removed. He should make every effort to be as direct and as concise as full understanding will allow. Finally, he should check his report for mechanical errors in spelling, punctuation, and grammatical construction.

One word of warning should be offered at this point: the writer should make every effort to take a detached attitude toward his report. He should not become so *ego-involved* that he resents any criticism of his report. The detached viewpoint is necessary to both comfortable working relationships with others and effective report writing.

Modifying the Product

- Have the required changes been made?

After the report has been thoroughly checked, it should then be modified and corrected. The weaknesses indicated by the check should be overcome and the errors removed. Both the check and the modification should be made with the reader and the purpose of the report clearly in mind, for they govern both.

Preparing the Final Product

- Have standard materials been used?
- Is the product accurate?
- Have only small alterations been made on the finished product?

In preparing the final copy of his report, the writer should make certain that standard materials are used and that the copy is neat and accurate. Once it is finished, only minor changes should be made, for both its appearance and it effectiveness influence the writer's reputation.

Application of the engineering method to the solution of writing problems is certain to produce more effective reports, for it is a realistic approach to the problem of designing reports to meet their particular roles. Reports, like all engineering products, must be designed to satisfy a particular function which presents its own specific set of requirements. Since success in report writing depends on the ability to communicate, the report's purpose, use and readers must always be its main guiding principles. Application of the eight basic steps of the engineering method, with attention to the details included in the accompanying check list, should produce reports that will better fulfill their intended functions.

MAKE IT SIMPLE! — Or You Won't Get Your Message Across!

by MICHAEL FLAGG,
Editor, *California Safety News*

Volumes have been said and written about communication in general—and communication of course includes *both* the written and spoken word.

We hear and read much, for instance, about *vertical* communication, and about *horizontal* or *lateral* communication. But far too little is said or written about *clear* communication.

And of course *clearness is the most vital ingredient of any communication,* if we assume that the main purpose of language is to *reveal* thought—and *not* (as too often seems to be the case) to conceal it.

It is, therefore, refreshing to see more and more authorities in various fields emphasize the need for clearness in communication in any and every field.

The *San Francisco Examiner* recently carried a splendid editorial entitled *"Use English"* which follows. (The italics are ours.)

An old jest holds that Americans and English are two people separated by a common language.

The jest needs updating.

Americans are becoming one people separated by the jargons, cants, and argots of the several professions and would-be professions.

When the National Council of Juvenile Court Judges met in conference here, it advised psychiatrists to cut out the Freudian patter in court appearances.

Said the judges: *Use words even the delinquent can understand. If they did that, perhaps the rest of us could understand too.*

Psychiatrists are by no means the worst offenders. Their jargon merely mystifies.

The labored lingo of economists and accountants is worse because it bewilders.

Worst of all is the cant of educationists. It enrages. It does so because it is spurious, pretentious and curiously akin to carny con talk.

Time was when, in our innocence, we thought use of such jargons necessary to achieve precision of meaning. (The precise word is still to be treasured when no simple equivalent is available.)

But gradually experience brought to us two revelations:

(1) Confirmed jargoneers talk *at,* not *to,* one another;

(2) *The better a man is in his profession, the simpler his language.*

Conclusion: It is easier to learn an occupational cant than the occupation itself.

Too, cant is contagious. Overexposed to it, people who know better—and sadly we include our own craft—find themselves sliding helplessly into its maw.

So it is not enough to admonish: When in doubt, use English.

There must be the further admonition: Stay doubtful.

Professor Claude Coleman, a professor of English and director of a special honors curriculum for gifted undergraduates at Southern Illinois University, is of the same opinion.

"*Our foolish society has confounded itself with its tools of communication,*" he says.

He derides those who "*have constructed vocabularies so involved and complex they can talk only to other splinters from the same wood as themselves.*"

There is no doubt that *we must make is simple, or we won't get our message across*—a fact that cannot be overemphasized.

For this reason we reprint an article that appeared in the *CSN* a few years ago.

Many safety messages might just as well be sent to the dead letter office. They are unwept, unhonored, and un-understood—because their authors don't make them simple.

They forget, or do not know, that *the ABC's of good writing* (and good speaking, too, for that matter) *are three in number.*

    Be *A*ccurate.
    Be *B*rief.
    Be *C*lear.

That you should be *accurate* goes without saying. If you are inaccurate, everything you write will be distrusted, and no one will pay any attention to what you write.

And you should be *brief*, but smooth. You *can* be brief without being abrupt or terse or jerky. What you write should be like the old gag about the proper length of a woman's skirt—long enough to cover the subject, and short enough to be interesting.

It isn't easy to be brief. It means going over your work again and again; and then, if possible, leaving it alone for at least a few days before making the final revision. It takes time.

Pascal, the famous French philosopher and mathematician, expressed the thought well in a note to a friend: "I have made this letter rather long only because I have not had time to make it shorter."

Above all, you should *be clear.* You may be accurate, and you may be brief; but if you are not clear you might just as well throw what you write into the wastepaper basket. (It'll save others the trouble.)

It is particularly important to be clear in a safety message, for a clear safety message may mean the difference between life and death.

Remember this. *You are seldom clear unless you make it simple.*

The trouble is that, unless we control ourselves, we become infatuated with the sound of our own words. And if that happens, we can kiss the message goodbye.

Ask a man "How does this work?"—and nine times out of ten he'll answer you briefly and simply Ask him to put it in writing, however, and he too often begins to think in terms that he believes, *wrongly,* will impress you.

(And once you try to impress, you might as well quit writing.)

The better you know your subject, the clearer it is in your own mind, the more simply can you express it. And simplicity pays off, a truth that is more and more evident.

Most banks today publish financial statements in language that almost anyone can understand—a far cry from thirty years ago. They know that however imposing their figures may be, they are useless if they are not understood.

The instructions for filing federal income tax—instructions that are probably read by more persons than anything else—are written simply. They *have* to be simple, or they would be valueless.

We could cite a hundred other cases, but they would show the same thing: *if something isn't written simply, it's hardly worth writing.*

There is no room for argument on this point: *there is virtue in simplicity* (in any sphere).

It is only the layman and amateur who tries to be "journalistic." The top writers and journalists of today are usually models of simple, straight-forward English.

Say What You Mean

Be specific. *Say what you mean.*

Have it crystal clear in your own mind, and then write as you would talk to an old friend.

You will probably have to go over it and make changes, of course; for many faults which can be covered by a speaker's personality lie bare in cold merciless print.

A classic example of the right and wrong way of writing something was given some years ago by a famous medical journal:

Fifteen people fell ill with vomiting an hour after eating lizard soup. Skin tests showed they were hypersensitive to lizard.	A series of cases of f o o d poisoning is reported and their causation discussed.

Is there any question which is the right way? Is there any question which report was reproduced and translated all over the world?

Make it Simple

Write simply. This does *not* mean writing down.

If you will be yourself, and be friendly, you'll be surprised to find how simply you will write.

One important rule is this—*avoid jargon.*

Don't Say	Say
prior to 1949	before 1949
of a blue coloration	blue (or bluish)
to a large extent	largely
relative to	about
approximately 400 (unless you mean, say, 399.8)	about 400
he made a motion to the chair	he moved
to some extent	somewhat
aetiological factor	cause
considerable	much, large, huge
it is believed by him	he believes
pursuant to	following, or according to

The "Don't Say" column gives just a few of the hundreds of words and phrases that are commonly misused and overworked and that, what is far worse, hamper clearness.

My particular aversion is the phrase *relative to*. Instead of saying "I spoke to him about the accident," too many persons prefer to say "I spoke to him relative to the accident."

Relative to has its proper uses, but *rarely* in sentences like the one quoted.

Verbs Tell the Story

Remember, simplicity is not drabness or dullness, but good taste—like a well-dressed woman, to bring the fair sex in again.

The power in your writing depends largely on your choice of verbs. They tell the story. So *choose your verbs well!*

Instead of trying to find a longer word for a shorter, spend the time selecting the verb that is precisely right.

Take, for instance the simple verbs *walk, stride, saunter, trudge*. They have differences in meaning, and each presents a different picture.

Walk is the general term for moving along on foot. You can walk fast or slow; leisurely or rapidly; smoothly or bouncily; and so on.

Stride is to move along by long and somewhat measured steps.

Saunter is to walk in a leisurely, lazy, or aimless way.

Trudge is to walk or march on foot steadily, wearily or without spirit, and usually with effort.

Yes, you should choose your verbs well.

Don't be Pedantic

Don't be affected in your writing. Don't stick too closely to old-fashioned rules that make for stilted expression.

It is perfectly all right, for instance, to end a sentence with a preposition. It is much smoother, stronger, and clearer to say *a safe place to work in* rather than *a safe place in which to work*.

We say that *America is a wonderful country to live in*. Rephrase it in the old pedantic way and see how weak and stilted it sounds.

Winston Churchill, told that he shouldn't end a sentence with a preposition, ridiculed the advice by his reply: *"That is a pedantry up with which I will not put!"*

The good writer of today will split infinitives when it makes for smoother and clearer expression. In many cases, a phrase is awkward, artificial, or unclear unless the infinitive is split. Take the sentence, *It is difficult to always tell the truth*. Place the *always* anywhere else in the sentence and see what I mean.

It Isn't Easy!

Don't think it's easy to write simply. It isn't.

You must first know your subject well, you must know exactly what you want to say, and then you must write, write, and re-write.

But the results are worth it—in the help and value to the reader, and in the satisfaction from anything well done.

It CAN Be Simple

One of the most absorbing and most simply written books I have ever read is a book with a most forbidding title—"Lectures on Psychoanalytic Psychiatry," by A. A. Brill, the father of psychoanalysis in this country.

It is a thin volume consisting of ten or twelve *lectures to doctors,* and covering the entire range of human behavior from birth to death.

And yet, except for necessary technical terms, the language is so simple and clear that anyone can enjoy it (and profit from it) at first reading.

The author knew his subject so well (and was so sure of himself) that he had no need to puff it up or try to impress.

The book is perfect proof that you *can* write simply, regardless of the subject, if you remember the ABC's of writing.

Truth and Beauty Are Simple

The more we mature, the more do we realize that truth and beauty are simple.

Recall the lines of poetry, the passages in the Bible, the safety slogans and safety messages, that moved you. Are they not all simple?

8 *steps to better engineering writing*

RICHARD M. KOFF, senior associate editor

Reprinted from
Product Engineering
Copyright 1959 by McGraw-Hill Publishing Co., Inc.
In its weekly issues

Product Engineering

HORIZONS

YOU, TOO, CAN WRITE / *or can you?*

Back in the black days of 1932, "consulting engineer" was a pseudonym for an engineer out of a job. One very competent "consultant" took on a pay-out-of-savings job—his income was to be a percentage of what he saved his new employer. As is so often true with the unsentimental outsider, he found a number of places where substantial savings could be made. But, three erudite reports-to-the-president later, there was no evidence that any of his ideas had even gotten a hearing, let alone been implemented.

A growling stomach is quite an incentive, so he went to the president. He was right; all of his reports had been put aside until the president "had time." Why? The reports all followed standard form, stating the objective, the procedure, the method of investigation, and finally the conclusions. The president had started each one, but finding no initial money-saving content, had put each aside in turn.

"But," the idea man protested (as he told me later). "The first report alone concludes with savings of $100,000!"

"Good Lord, Man," exclaimed his boss, "Why didn't you say so at the beginning?"

The report maker was afflicted with a familiar ailment—he wrote logical, well-thought-out reports that matched his orderly mind, but were deadly dull. He had failed to realize that he was writing for an audience of one—a busy, sales-minded executive who inherently hated to read. The president could be caught and held only by prose that told him in the first few words how much money it would save him.

That engineer recast his reports to suit his audience. He dropped the fancy words that proved how smart he was, the tedious explanations that proved how long he'd worked and how profoundly he'd thought, and told a busy man how to save a buck. He's now the president himself.

This problem is in our minds as we begin a series of eight short articles on how to write a report. The idea came from a reader who liked our series on how to read (Jan 5, 12, 19, 26, Feb 2 '59). We've read enough engineering reports, articles and papers to see the need. The fact that more than 7,000 readers have asked for reprints of the earlier series suggested rather pointedly the need and treatment. The experts and laymen who've seen the series like it. So here it is.

Author Dick Koff has no illusions—he has probably violated most of his own rules in the articles proposing them. He has not been exhaustive. He hasn't followed the traditional format. He hasn't provided the unbeatable formula for a report. But he *has* been terse and to the point. He has tried to deal with today's problems, as you face them.

These eight quick lessons will not make you a Lincoln or a Shakespeare; you can guarantee *that* only by proper selection of grandparents and proper development of all your years up to now. You, in short, must have the mind and heart of a genius to write for the ages.

But that isn't your immediate problem—or ours. We've got to write so the desired audience reads and profits *now*. So do you.

8 steps to better engineering writing...

RICHARD M. KOFF, *senior associate editor*

1..	VANITY AND LAZINESS, BE SIMPLE
2..	BE POSITIVE, BE BRAVE
3..	BE PERSONAL, BE SPECIFIC
4..	BE CONCISE, DON'T OVERSTATE
5..	VOCABULARY, GRAMMAR, PUNCTUATION
6..	TABLES, FIGURES, CAPTIONS
7..	WHERE TO PUT WHAT
8..	SIT DOWN AND WRITE

Lesson.. 1

Vanity and laziness, in that order, are to blame for most bad writing. For some reason, anyone who has learned to read assumes he has learned to write as well. Criticism or revisions are therefore felt to be direct attacks on the author's education or intelligence.

In industry, writing ability is assumed to improve automatically with authority and salary. The president's letters and reports are corrected by no one; the junior engineer's by everyone.

So... your first and most important step in learning to write is to swallow some pride. Your golden words will be improved by your boss, by your assistant, even by your secretary. If you really want to learn to write, you must learn to evaluate their criticisms objectively—not react like a wounded bull.

Laziness is a factor, because most people feel that writing a report or a letter is a necessary evil, not an end in itself. Anyone can do it, so it should take no time or effort.

Actually writing is as much thinking work as it is the use of grammar, or spelling, or punctuation. You need imagination (What is my reader interested in?... How well does he know the subject?), logic (What ideas shall I present first?... What is the next step?), and perseverance (How can I get my point across faster?). But it is boring to have to go over old territory again, and it can be disconcerting if the mental review reveals gaps in your own knowledge.

So laziness combines with pride to say, "It's enough. It's right. I wrote it and understand it, so will the reader. Thank you, Miss Jones; that will be all."

To break this train of reasoning (or emotion, really) you must recognize that writing is time-consuming, productive work. It is respectable and demanding, and good writing can have almost as much influence on customers, suppliers, associates, and prospects as your company's service or product itself.

HOW TO REVISE

It is usually easier to edit than it is to write; hindsight is better than foresight. In editing you take an involved or complex sentence and reduce it to its bare essentials. You then add complexities, but only if they are necessary to meaning.

In its simplest form, the English sentence consists of subject and predicate; or subject, verb and object. For clarity, positive statements in this form can't be beat. Furthermore, subjects and predicates are nouns and verbs. The English language is so rich that good nouns and verbs need few modifiers. Adjectives and adverbs are often used to make up for poor selection of words in the first place.

Here is an example of a complex sentence and its revision step by step:

The field of stress analysis is one in which model studies have often been used successfully. (Understandable, but backwards somehow.)

Models have often been used successfully in the field of stress analysis. (Gets the subject up front. Eliminates "one in which.")

Models have been used for stress analysis. (Reduced to bare essentials. Are "often" and "successfully" necessary modifiers?)

At this point editing stops. The author must determine his exact shade of meaning. How about:

Models are useful for stress analysis.

NOW YOU TRY

The following five sentences were written by engineers in letters or reports. Note that you have to read some of them two or three times before you understand what is happening to what. By changing the order of the words or splitting a complex sentence into two or more simple sentences, can you edit them into better writing? Our versions (by no means the only way they could be written) will be found below.

1.. Familiarity with the method whereby arithmetic operations can be performed is highly desirable.

2.. The cutting of tubes that will have practically no burr has posed quite a problem to manufacturers for years.

3.. To obtain the best possible results in the application of induction heating it is sometimes necessary to modify the design of the part to suit the characteristics and practical requirements of this method of heating.

4.. The choice of the correct alloy is of prime importance and it will be found that a great deal of trouble can be prevented if all details are taken into consideration and if any doubt should arise, one should submit his questions to the Technical Department.

5.. The base metal of an ornament may very well be an inexpensive imitation even when the surface is highly reflective and of a rich-looking finish.

1.. Know how to do arithmetic.

2.. It is difficult to cut tubes without leaving burrs.

3.. Modify the part for induction heating.

4.. Alloy choice is critical. When in trouble ask an expert.

5.. (This is a sleeper.) All that glitters is not gold.

8 steps to better engineering writing...

1.. VANITY AND LAZINESS, BE SIMPLE
2.. BE POSITIVE, BE BRAVE
3.. BE PERSONAL, BE SPECIFIC
4.. BE CONCISE, DON'T OVERSTATE
5.. VOCABULARY, GRAMMAR, PUNCTUATION
6.. TABLES, FIGURES, CAPTIONS
7.. WHERE TO PUT WHAT
8.. SIT DOWN AND WRITE

Lesson..2

Good writing is rarely achieved in the first draft. This is true for a good business letter or engineering report as much as for a famous play or novel. But, in industry, revision is out of fashion. The current image of a big business executive is a man who can dictate to four secretaries simultaneously and close a couple of million-dollar deals on the telephone between paragraphs.

When executives try to live up to this image, their letters are bad because they are stereotyped, ("We are in receipt of yours of the 10th inst..."), if not rambling and incoherent. An acceptable dictated letter takes careful planning (expert letter writers often make extensive notes before calling for the secretary). You will need a stock of graceful phrases to help tide you over the inevitable awkward places as well.

Our first rule about simple sentences (subject, verb, object) and unadorned nouns and verbs will cover you in most short (one-page) letters. But longer reports and letters simply cannot be dashed off in this way—not even by professionals. When you have to communicate more than just yes or no, or "Why don't we have lunch together some day?", then standard phrases and dictation from notes won't get you off first base. You can dictate the first draft, but that's all it ever will be—a rough draft—needing revision after revision before it will say what you want it to, economically and understandably.

So this is a plea for the brutal art of rewrite. We started last week by editing a few complex, inverted sentences into shorter, more-logical form. Even the best writers produce sentences of that kind in their first drafts. Impatience, laziness, the press of other demands on your time, will tempt you to stop there. The result is poor writing, poor reader impressions, and misunderstanding.

THE SECOND RULE

A close corollary to the "be simple" rule is a second which says, "Be positive, be brave." Sounds like a Middle Ages injunction for knights-errant, doesn't it? But it applies to modern-day writing—particularly to that written by engineers and scientists who, in their written communications, are the worst cowards of our generation. For example:

Under certain conditions of temperature and relative humidity, the moisture content of the air seems to tend to increase the likelihood of oxidation of iron and certain iron compounds when exposed to these atmospheres.
Iron will rust in damp atmospheres.

In an attempt to answer all possible critics the scientific writer modifies his words with "almost, very, maybe, tends to, etc." until the nouns and verbs are covered with a meringue of modifiers.

Nothing in life is absolutely so. You don't have to make this point in every sentence you write. The reader has lived; he knows the risks in crossing busy intersections. Give him your ideas bravely and let later paragraphs, or his own experience, supply the modifiers.

Bravery also implies a positive attitude toward life. Avoid statements which are intended to describe by exclusion or to damn by faint praise. If you wish to damn, damn in so many words. If you think a theory or a person has disadvantages, say so. Don't dwell on the lack of virtue.

Long bearing life cannot be expected in dust-laden environments.
Dust destroys bearings.
Weather predictions are not likely to be as reliable as one might wish.
Weather predictions are unreliable.

Here are five cowardly, negative statements made by engineers. Can you rewrite them in shorter, braver statements without altering the meanings?

1.. We do not think the proposed gear-tooth design can carry the specified load.

2.. An inspection of the production run seems to indicate there is a not very careful lathe hand somewhere in the shop.

3.. We don't have much hope for the mathematical model proposed by Mr Smith.

4.. The coating can hardly be expected to stand up under salt-water spray.

5.. No invention resides in adding means to make a device movable when, without such means, the device would not be movable.

1.. The gear teeth are too weak.
2.. A sloppy lathe hand is messing up the production run.
3.. Mr Smith's mathematical model won't work.
4.. Salt spray will destroy the coating.
5.. Making an immovable object movable is not invention.

8 steps to better engineering writing...

1.. VANITY AND LAZINESS, BE SIMPLE
2.. BE POSITIVE, BE BRAVE
3.. **BE PERSONAL, BE SPECIFIC**
4.. BE CONCISE, DON'T OVERSTATE
5.. VOCABULARY, GRAMMAR, PUNCTUATION
6.. TABLES, FIGURES, CAPTIONS
7.. WHERE TO PUT WHAT
8.. SIT DOWN AND WRITE

Lesson..3

Most of us have been taught in grade school never to begin a paragraph with "I," that it's probably wise never to use that personal pronoun at all. Engineers and scientists have that lesson reinforced in their college years by instruction in the "scientific method" in which objective truth is supposed to be its own best salesman — the colder and harder the better.

Once out of school and faced with some of the market-place atmosphere of industry, we realize that objective truth by itself has only a very small voice to attract the attention of a distracted reader. The argument here is not with "truth," but with excessive objectivity, which freezes all the humanity and interest out of most technical writing.

The man who writes for a larger public, even those who are engineers and scientists, knows better. Thor Heyerdahl, archeologist and explorer, starts his best-selling book:

"I had no *aku-aku*.
"Nor did I know what an *aku-aku* was, so I could hardly have used one if I had had it."

These sentences couldn't be more personal and it's almost impossible to stop reading the book once you start.

They also demonstrate a second, related rule: Be specific. It would be far more logical for Heyerdahl to start with generalities. What were his theories, how were they formed? Instead you are told about an *aku-aku*. No definition of terms, no generalities, but a very specific thing which you are curious to know more about.

To be specific means to talk about trees, not forests; murder and arson and theft, not crime; valves and pumps and reservoirs, not hydraulics; steam and boilers and turbines, not thermodynamics. Steam and turbines make pictures in your reader's mind while thermodynamics is the name of the only course he nearly flunked.

HOW TO BE YOURSELF

At first it will seem difficult, immodest even, to inject yourself into a letter or report. The temptation to generalize (and pontificate) will be almost irresistible. But to the reader the personal note will not seem immodest and the specific reference will add drama. For example, here is a memo written by an engineer to his immediate superior:

This is in reference to Engineering Department equipment and the efficiency thereof. In general, the newest additions have been behaving reasonably well. A ballistics problem awaiting solution for some time has finally been solved. The Structures Department has also been making good use of the equipment. However, there are still certain mechanical and design difficulties to be ironed out. The Human Engineering aspects need some attention to make the unit easier to operate and control. The input-output devices have caused certain delays in handling. Maintenance and repair work will be required...

But it also could have been written

You asked for my opinions about the new engineering department computer. Well, we've had pretty good results so far. The trajectory integration problem was solved in 15 minutes. The structures men are happy as clams now that the iterative strut has been programmed. But there are still some bugs. The signal lights occasionally start flashing like a pinball machine, and they really panic you if you've never seen it before. The tape reader jammed last Tuesday and spilled a couple of thousand feet of tape into the control cubby. It took us an hour to clear a path to Sam Jarvis who was running his stress-analysis problem at the time...

NOW YOU TRY

Here is a paragraph from the introductory chapter of a well-known engineering reference text. Use a little imagination—place yourself in the shoes of the author for a moment—and try writing the paragraph more personally and more specifically to give it some life and interest. Our version (by no means the only one, or the best) appears below.

Before a new idea or process in any branch of engineering or natural science can be utilized, it must be embodied in a suitable physical form. For this reason, a knowledge of the principles of mechanical design is a necessary part of an engineer's training, even though the student may not expect to become a professional designer...

Engineering is hardware—screws and nuts and bolts, castings and resistors, pilot lights, bearings, gears and IC engines. No matter how theoretical your research, no matter how high up the ivory tower you'd like to work, you must be able to make airplanes out of aerodynamics, radios and TV sets out of solid-state physics.

8 steps to better engineering writing...

1.. VANITY AND LAZINESS, BE SIMPLE
2.. BE POSITIVE, BE BRAVE
3.. BE PERSONAL, BE SPECIFIC
4.. BE CONCISE, DON'T OVERSTATE
5.. VOCABULARY, GRAMMAR, PUNCTUATION
6.. TABLES, FIGURES, CAPTIONS
7.. WHERE TO PUT WHAT
8.. SIT DOWN AND WRITE

Lesson..4

Never "tell all."

This simple rule is one of the most difficult for engineers to follow, yet it makes good sense. The reader isn't interested in knowing everything you do about a subject—not by a long shot. Give him what he needs to know; nothing more. It's good psychology, too—you won't have to say "I don't know" to the questions an executive will always ask.

Careful omission of extraneous facts is half the battle. It cuts reports down to manageable size and makes concise writing at least possible. The other half is to omit needless words from the facts you decide are essential. William Strunk Jr., in *The Elements of Style*, wrote:

"Vigorous writing is concise. A sentence should contain no unnecessary words, a paragraph no unnecessary sentences, for the same reason that a drawing should have no unnecessary lines and a machine no unnecessary parts. This requires not that the writer make all his sentences short, or that he avoid all detail and treat his subjects only in outline, but that every word tell."

No one can produce lean writing on the first try. It is difficult enough to get complex thoughts on paper at all. But once you have a sentence before you, it should be relatively simple to weed out the needless words, leaving the thought all by itself and in a form that every reader later will think is the only natural way to express it.

Much of what we have said in previous lessons will result in leaner writing. Be simple, be positive, be brave, be specific—all of these rules will contribute to more concise prose. In addition, there are some standard phrases editors have been trained to blue-pencil almost without thinking:

the fact that (because)
he is a man who (he is)
in the case of
from the point of view of
in regard to (about)
in order to (for, or to)
check up (check)
drop down (drop)
very
at the present time (now)
this is a picture of (in captions)

And then add to this list those useless modifiers: entirely satisfactory, completely full, slightly pregnant.

At the bottom of this page you will find a letter liberally sprinkled with these phrases and how it might be pared. Is anything lost in the translation?

You respect the shorter-letter writer for several reasons: He writes (and therefore thinks) clearly and concisely. He does not burden the reader with unnecessary information. Also he does not "protest too much." No one could honestly be as apologetic as the first man pretends for three bad castings.

This rule, "don't overstate," means don't sell too hard, don't excuse with more reasons than necessary, don't explain too much. One or two excuses is enough—additional ones cast doubt. When the teacher asked Johnny why he was late for school, he answered, "Mommy's car had a flat tire, the bus didn't stop when I waved, and anyhow I got a splinter in my finger."

The splinter would convince you, the entire story wouldn't.

NOW YOU TRY

The best way to practice concise writing is to read with attention. Look for needless phrases, irrelevant information and overstatements in newspaper reports, technical articles and advertisements. Practice rewriting, mentally, the particularly bad examples. It's not hard, and it can reveal much faulty thinking by the author.

Dear Mr ------- :
It has been brought to our attention that this company's most recent shipment of sand cast pump housings was not up to our usual high standard. As a matter of fact, three housings were unsatisfactory by reason of the fact that dimensions in more than one case exceeded the allowable tolerances as given on your blueprints.
We are very sorry that so unfortunate and inconvenient an occurrence should have taken place and are ready and willing to rectify the situation as soon as possible. As in all such cases we will be happy to replace any and all such unacceptable castings with new ones. Please pack them up and ship them to us so that we can correct our molds and make new housings according to your drawings.
Apologetically yours,

Dear Mr ------- :
I'm told our latest shipment of pump housings includes three out-of-tolerance housings.

We're sorry this happened and if you'll return the defective housings they will be replaced.
Yours truly,

8 steps to better engineering writing...

1.. VANITY AND LAZINESS, BE SIMPLE
2.. BE POSITIVE, BE BRAVE
3.. BE PERSONAL, BE SPECIFIC
4.. BE CONCISE, DON'T OVERSTATE
5.. VOCABULARY, GRAMMAR, PUNCTUATION
6.. TABLES, FIGURES, CAPTIONS
7.. WHERE TO PUT WHAT
8.. SIT DOWN AND WRITE

Lesson .. 5

Up to now, we've been studying rules about **what** to write rather than **how**. Vocabulary, grammar, punctuation — these are the mechanics, the tools. And, frankly, you don't have the time or interest to go back and study them in detail.

But you've been speaking, thinking and reading the English language for decades. You can rely on your ear for words and phrases, and with the few hints given below, get away without a review of formal "book learning" in most of your writing.

This means you must rely on what sounds right to YOU—not what you think will sound right to your boss, customer or colleague. Don't try to write "down" to a serviceman in a manual, or "up" to an executive. Anything that sounds unnatural to you—any unfamiliar word, phrase or sentence structure will sound ten times stranger to the man who really knows how to use it.

Most good style manuals or writing texts cover these subjects far better than we can here. The serious student is referred to the bibliography at the end of Lesson 8.

VOCABULARY

Get a good desk dictionary and keep it within reach. If you don't know how to spell a word, look it up. And read the definitions while you're at it—you may be surprised.

To build a bigger vocabulary, read, but a $25 word should not be used if a 10¢ one can be found.

Watch out for: allusion-illusion, being that, between-among, case-instance, comprise, data, different than-from, due to, effect-affect, can't hardly, imply-infer, irregardless, lay and lie, like-as, literally, phase, principle-principal, regard, shall-will, that-which, type, unique, utilize, virtually, very, while, who-whom, you and I.

Here are five examples from the above list. Which are correct usage?

1 .. The higher temperatures will not effect steel hardness.
2 .. Are you inferring that our lathe screws are inaccurate?
3 .. It went together easily like a slip fit should.
4 .. This machine has a fairly unique joy-stick control.
5 .. The tests were virtually finished when we found the trouble.*

GRAMMAR

Again the best bet is to rely on your ear. What sounds right is most likely to be right. Your written English, with proper allowance for more careful phrasing, should be modeled from your spoken style. The most common offenders are:

The split infinitive. An infinitive, for these purposes, is a verb preceded by *to* (to go, to run, to design). The rule is: don't put an adverb modifier after the *to* and before the verb (to quickly go, to breathlessly run, to elegantly design). In each instance the modifier should precede or follow the infinitive. There are exceptions to this rule, but they're rare.

The dangling participle. A present participle (the usual offender) is a verb with an -ing ending. When a participial phrase starts a sentence, you must be very careful that the subject of the phrase is also the subject of the rest of the sentence.

Testing the bearing, race wear appeared at 1000 rpm.
Testing the bearing, I found race wear at 1000 rpm.
Being badly worn, I had the handle replated.
Finding the finish worn, I had the handle replated.

PUNCTUATION

In descending order of difficulty, commas, semicolons and colons cause most punctuation problems. Here's a rundown on these three, plus some comments on hyphens.

*All are wrong.

Commas. Parenthetical words and phrases should be separated by commas. (The oldest drill press, shaky and dangerous, was finally replaced.)

Independent clauses joined by a conjunction (and, but, for) should be separated by a comma. (I ordered the replacement parts, but I doubt that they will arrive on time.)

A series of items should be separated by commas. There is a difference in opinion about whether a comma should precede the "and." Decide for yourself and then be consistent. (Lines number one, two, and three will be shut down for repairs.)

For the rest, read a sentence aloud. Place a comma where you pause for emphasis or to make the meaning clear (assuming colons or semicolons do not apply).

Semicolons should separate independent clauses having no conjunction. In other words, two short, complete sentences which you feel belong together may be joined by a semicolon. (Take a short break; that gearbox is heavy.) The semicolon also separates major portions of a series separated internally by commas. (A short, small drill; a heavy, long bushing; . . .)

Colons usually introduce a list, a restatement or an example. (Standard screw threads will be: #4, 6, 8, and 10.)

Hyphens. Look up all compound words unless you are absolutely sure. Most compound modifiers of nouns and verbs take hyphens unless the first modifier ends in -ly. (A four-inch pipe, a fluid-power control, caught red-handed, *but:* an elegantly solved problem).

If you've got the time, dip into H. W. Fowler's *Modern English Usage* now and then. It's not always modern American, but it's a delight to read and includes more examples of good and bad prose than you'll find anywhere else.

8 steps to better engineering writing...

1. VANITY AND LAZINESS, BE SIMPLE
2. BE POSITIVE, BE BRAVE
3. BE PERSONAL, BE SPECIFIC
4. BE CONCISE, DON'T OVERSTATE
5. VOCABULARY, GRAMMAR, PUNCTUATION
6. TABLES, FIGURES, CAPTIONS
7. WHERE TO PUT WHAT
8. SIT DOWN AND WRITE

Lesson..6

How long is a letter, a report, an article? You can count the number of words or pages for an objective total, which might satisfy your engineering instincts—but it will be worthless. The length of a report is measured by your reader's first quick glance. He estimates how long it will take him to read, weighs this against the value or pleasure the subject seems likely to give, and decides whether to read, scan, or ignore.

Good appearance is the best persuader (right after subject matter). Clean typing and well-thought-out illustrations should not need mentioning here, but some common-sense pointers will bear repeating.

TYPED COPY

Only letters should be single spaced. One page of closely typed information, generously bordered in white space, will seem to be only a couple of minutes' reading, and a personally addressed letter is difficult to resist. But be very cautious about running over to a second page. How many such letters have you started to skip through, or hesitated even to start, just because the mass of words was discouraging?

In longer reports, paper economy never justifies single spacing. If the shear weight of a double-spaced report becomes a factor, you've probably written too much. Circulate the conclusions and file the rest.

TABLES

One problem with tables is that they force you to be logical. If you've skimped on an experiment or you don't like the way your product shows up in comparison with the competitor's, it will be difficult to cover up in a table. However, engineers are wild for tables; they collect them the way squirrels save nuts. So it may pay to do a little more research just to have a good table in your report.

Use tables whenever you have four or more sets of data. Even qualitative and descriptive matter can be put in tabular form to advantage.

Use summary tables in the body of a report, details in the appendix.

All tables need title and number (usually roman).

Identify all columns and rows, indicating units where applicable. Note that "inches x 10^{-2}" may be misleading. Should you multiply the listed figure by 10^{-2} or divide? Make sure the reader knows what you mean.

Use the same units for comparable quantities.

Align columns on the decimal point for similar units. Do not align for different units.

Number footnotes across a row, then down and across the next row.

Similar tables should have similar format.

Do not use ditto marks; repeat the figure.

Use a 0 before the decimal point on numbers less than 1 (0.435). Add a comma after the third zero in decimals (0.000,34).

FIGURES

Time and effort spent on good illustrations are as much or more important than time spent on writing. Most people, engineers included, look at the pictures first.

Graphs are better than tables to show trends. The danger here is excessive detail (limit ordinates and abscissas to about half-inch spacing if possible), or too many curves per graph. Curves should be several line weights heavier than the ordinate lines. Use different colors for a one-copy report, different line styles (dashed, dotted, etc.) for reports to be reproduced.

Charts, like bar charts, pie charts and the like, are a bit unsophisticated for an engineer reader, but management and advertising men tend to be impressed. If you must, go whole hog. Use color bars of pressure-sensitive tape or other gimmicks available from your local art-supply store.

Diagrams, cutaways, perspectives, isometrics, even cartoons are all lovely because they transmit a lot of information quickly or a little information powerfully. Keep them simple.

Photographs, the picture-in-a-minute variety particularly, spark up a dull report and make reading a pleasure instead of a chore—if they show something important.

Illustrations must be edited too! The first sketch is just as unsatisfactory as a first draft of a manuscript. Take the time to pare it down to the essentials (retake the picture if necessary). Does the most important information dominate the page?

Any flipping to and from the text should be avoided if possible. Paste the figure right where it belongs in the text or paste it on the right-hand edge so that it can be folded out clear of the report.

Don't get carried away by illustrations. A picture may be worth 1000 words, but 10 pictures are not worth 10,000 words.

CAPTIONS

To be of any use at all, illustrations must be self-explanatory. Captions can do this for you. Here are some pointers:

Never start with "A photograph of ..." or "A drawing of ..." The reader can figure that out for himself.

Make the caption something more than a tag or label. Point out what is significant about the figure. Account for every important element, and tell where it is, too (top, right, left).

Be concise. A long caption competes with its illustration, particularly when it repeats the text.

8 steps to better engineering writing...

1. VANITY AND LAZINESS, BE SIMPLE
2. BE POSITIVE, BE BRAVE
3. BE PERSONAL, BE SPECIFIC
4. BE CONCISE, DON'T OVERSTATE
5. VOCABULARY, GRAMMAR, PUNCTUATION
6. TABLES, FIGURES, CAPTIONS
7. **WHERE TO PUT WHAT**
8. SIT DOWN AND WRITE

Lesson..7

Who reads engineering reports and letters? Our guess would be:

- 65% are industrial executives,
- 15% are engineering colleagues,
- 15% are students or assistants,
- 5% are public relations people and the general public.

What is your purpose in writing? A letter may suggest a project and express your interest in doing the R & D. A progress report may show encouraging results but show that costs are over the budget. An article may outline a new design technique developed under your supervision.

In each case your overt purpose is to inform; your ulterior purpose is to influence. You can do neither without the conscious or unconscious cooperation of the reader.

WHERE TO PUT WHAT

Your reader is busy, harried—and lazy. To get his attention, see the suggestions in Lesson 6 about making reports and letters more attractive looking. **To save him from work, predigest the information; put the conclusions up front.**

This is the single most difficult thing to teach engineers. All our training is of the object-procedure-results-conclusions school. We approach the writing task as if it were a problem in geometry: Given . . .

Most of your readers know better than you do what has been "given."

When the doctor returns from the operating room, you ask, "How's my wife? How's the baby? When can I see them?" Sex, weight, time, and blood pressure can wait. Similarly the chief engineer, the research director, the president, want your recommendations first. The why's and wherefore's can come later.

Here's one approach to the technical report based on these principles:

Title page. Make your title short and use an active verb rather than a label. "The proposed 10-gpm pump" becomes, "Will a 10-gpm pump pay its way?"

If necessary, a paragraph of two or three short sentences may amplify the title, but make sure they generate interest rather than destroy it.

"The 5-gpm model is losing sales, but development and tooling costs of a 10-gpm pump will be high. Here are Engineering and Production cost estimates plus a Sales forecast. Net profit should be $20,000 in five years."

The reader *could* stop here, and that's a sign of good report writing, but he's more likely to go on.

Add your name, the date and what other information necessary for the record.

This is enough for the first page of a more-than-10-page report. Shorter reports can combine title with abstract.

Abstract. A much-too-formal word for the most important part of your report. This page (never more than one) has a synopsis of the problem, conclusions (if any), and recommendations. You can give reasons (without proof), tabulate values (without derivations) even photograph a final model (a recommendation in picture form). The combination of title and abstract on one page makes an ideal "short" report.

Contents page. This is really the index. Its primary purpose is for finding specific information. Its secondary purpose: to show the structure of a report, the plan of treatment.

Introduction. Set the stage. Why was the report written? Where did your information come from? How has it been presented?

Body. Here you prove what you said up front. List the "given" and its derivations. The order of presented material should be logical rather than chronological. Make use of subheadings, underlining, capital letters to divide your information into chewable "bites." Leave detail proof for the appendix. Headings must show the structure of the report—they'll be repeated on the contents page.

Conclusions. Recapitulate the reasoning with references to the page where each point is proved.

Appendix. Includes charts, graphs, tabled data, and tangential studies whose conclusions were used in the body of the report.

Bibliography. This may be limited to other reports or it may include technical books, handbooks and the like.

There's nothing sacred in this arrangement. Its greatest value lies in the emphasis placed on the reader—his wandering attention and peculiar interests. Don't be bound by convention or college training. Most likely the ideas that appeal to you will appeal to others. Note carefully the reports you read and admire. What makes them readable? Can you apply the same techniques in your own?

8 steps to better engineering writing...

1. VANITY AND LAZINESS, BE SIMPLE
2. BE POSITIVE, BE BRAVE
3. BE PERSONAL, BE SPECIFIC
4. BE CONCISE, DON'T OVERSTATE
5. VOCABULARY, GRAMMAR, PUNCTUATION
6. TABLES, FIGURES, CAPTIONS
7. WHERE TO PUT WHAT
8. SIT DOWN AND WRITE

Lesson .. 8

That first sentence is almost impossible to get on paper. You doodle, hem and haw, take a coffee break, look up a reference, and pretty soon it's time for lunch.

You're in good company. There isn't a writer in the world who gets up in the morning eager to rush to work.

The problem is that writing requires a frontal attack—you can't sneak up on it. Engineering problems are surrounded by so many small mechanical tasks—a report to read, a specification to check, availability of components or materials—that you drift deeper and deeper into the heart of a problem by slow stages. By the time you're ready to wrestle with the core, you're saturated with information, the mental engine is all warmed up, and momentum alone can carry you through.

You should try to create the same atmosphere for writing. Reports are based on tremendous amounts of information, most of which must be chewed over several times before a pattern appears. Hurry this chewing process and you'll wind up with poor reasoning, serious gaps, and plain bad writing in the report.

Every report should have a message—one that can be expressed in a sentence or two. What are you really trying to accomplish? What is the best way to set out your ideas and data for this purpose?

The moment of clarity, the perception of a plan or design, finally comes; then the writing can follow your mental design just as an assembly drawing follows a layout.

OUTLINES AND FIRST DRAFTS

Some people can't work without outlines; others can't work with them. Some writers like the erasability of a pencil draft; others can't read their own handwriting. You must choose for yourself. However, a few techniques apply for everyone.

Once started, write the first draft quickly. If you're writing fluently don't let interruptions break the chain of thought. The boss who wants good reports must give you the privacy to write them; don't be afraid to tell him so.

Don't worry too much about grammar, phraseology, or punctuation in the first draft. Get your ideas on paper in logical order and leave the polishing for later drafts.

Opening paragraphs tend to be pretty dull. When you're ready for the first revision, try tearing off the first paragraph or two and begin with paragraph three.

Start unfamiliar ideas well back in familiar territory. The reader is not insulted when he reads what he already knows—he's flattered. This applies only to technical derivations or the explanation of a technical discovery.

Watch for your own boredom. It makes you skip essential links in the chain of reasoning. Writing is slow work and takes more patience than most people believe. Cut off a small slice of subject and give it the works. Continue only if your interest and energy are strong.

It's a rare individual who can write well for more than an hour or two at a time. Take a break, go look out the window, think about something else for a while—and you'll come back refreshed.

When you revise, put off the role of author and imagine yourself in the audience. Each paragraph, each sentence is new. It is clear? What does the author want to say? Could it be said more simply, more directly?

As for the rest, the best teacher of writing is your pencil.

A FINAL TEST

The following paragraphs contain 24 errors. Some are purely mechanical (punctuation, grammar, vocabulary), others are errors in expression. Nine professional editors caught 20 or more of the 24 errors. Can you do as well?

The corrected copy is on the next page.

```
The four bar linkage has a
nearly, but not quite, hypnotic
affect on some engineers. Being
that the elements are so simple
the many different functions
they can perform are very sur-
prising. Four bar linkages are
utilized in automobiles, fold-
ing beds printing presses, and
steam engines. They may be de-
signed to closely follow a pro-
scribed path in space to transmit
a measured force, or to accu-
rately solve a complex algebraic
function.
    Four links pivoted at their
ends are the principle elements
of a four bar linkage. Consider-
ing one of the four fixed in
space the motions of the others
are measured relative to the
fixed, unmoving link. Between
the changing lengths of the four
links an almost infinite number
of speeds, and paths are pos-
sible for the two moving pivots.
```

This is the corrected version...
of the test on the previous page. Your grammar, vocabulary, and punctuation are above average if you can find 20 of the 24 errors.

① The four-bar linkage has ~~a~~ an almost ② ~~nearly, but not quite,~~ hypnotic ③ ёffect on some engineers. ~~Being~~ Since ④ ~~that~~ ⁁the elements are so simple, ⑤ the many different functions they can perform are ~~very~~ sur-⑥ prising. Four-bar linkages are used ⑧ ~~utilized~~ in automobiles, fold-⑨ ing beds, printing presses, and steam engines. They may be de-⑩ ⑪ e signed to |closely| |follow| a pr⁄o-⑫ scribed path in space, to transmit a measured force, or to |accu-⑬ rately |solve| a complex algebraic function. ⑭ Four links, pivoted at their ⑮ al ⑯ ends, are the princip~~le~~ elements ⑰ of a four-bar linkage. ~~Consider-~~ is considered ~~ing~~ ⑱ Öne of the four, fixed in ⑲ and space, ⁁the motions of the others are measured relative to the ⑳ fixed, ~~unmoving~~ link. ~~Between~~ By ⁁the |changing| lengths of the four ㉑ ㉒ ㉓ links, an ~~almost~~ infinite number ㉔ of speeds,⁄ and paths are pos-sible for the two moving pivots.

References for further reading:

Fowler, H. W. *Dictionary of Modern English Usage.* Oxford University Press, 1937. 742 p. $3.75

Hicks, Tyler G. *Successful Technical Writing.* McGraw-Hill Book Co, 1959. 294 p. $5.50

Perrin, Porter G. *Writer's Guide and Index to English.* Scott, Foresman and Co, 1950. 833 p. $2.75

Strunk, William Jr, and E. B. White. *The Elements of Style.* Macmillan, 1959. 71 p. $2.50

Style manuals or guides are available from most publishers. Style, in this sense, refers to the use of commas, capitals, spelling, and typefaces standardized for a magazine or book. If you are writing for publication, the editor should be able to supply you with the manual he follows.

"The Engineer's Bookshelf," *Product Engineering,* Mar 30, '59, p 45, lists a dozen general references for the engineer's deskside library. Almost 600 best references in 22 specialized fields of engineering make up the bulk of this guide. Copies are still available. Send 25¢ to Readers Service Dept, *Product Engineering,* 330 West 42nd St, NY 36, NY.

A LESSON FOR THE TEACHER

the 9th step to better engineering writing

Our recent series of writing lessons brought a sprinkling of brickbats amid the shower of requests for extra copies. We are much chastened, as you will see below.

RICHARD M KOFF, *senior associate editor*

■ Careful, careful. Each word must be weighed and measured, each construction examined from all angles, each sentence read and reread by trained editors. But we goofed anyway, as sharp-eyed readers of our "8 Steps to Better Engineering Writing" series were quick to point out.

So here are their comments. Some refer to clearcut and indefensible errors. Others are less certain and we discuss them a bit.

Lesson . . 3   (Sep 21 p 29)

One sentence was so bad it still makes us blush. We wrote:

The man who writes for a larger public, even those who are engineers and scientists, know better.

A high school senior was quick to note that the verb (*know*) should agree with the subject (*man*). We caught the error in the reprinted series and made the sentence:

The man who writes for a larger public, even those who are engineers and scientists, knows better.

But this is wrong too! The parenthetical phrase ("even . . . scientists") should also agree with the subject. Correctly, then, the sentence would be:

Men who write for a larger public, even those who are engineers and scientists, know better.

Lesson . . 5   (Oct 5 p 47)

A reader writes, "May I take issue with your stand on the split infinitive . . . you indicate that split infinitives are bad usage. This is incorrect . . . most college English teachers accept them as perfectly good usage."

Not to reopen an old debate, we still feel (as do most editors and grammarians—see the references at the end of Lesson 8) that the split infinitive is undesirable and to be avoided except when absolutely necessary.

In this same lesson we wrote, "Don't try to write 'down' to a serviceman in a manual . . ." An experienced technical writer says, "Unless you write to his level . . . you will not get the message across." Quite true, and a professional writer must be very sensitive to the needs of his reader. But if an engineer tries to write in the vernacular of servicemen, or if his descriptions are condescending, he will irritate the reader far more than if he is natural—even if over their heads sometimes.

Lesson . . 7   (Oct 9 p 43)

"It upset me a great deal to see apostrophes used incorrectly."

We wrote, "why's and wherefore's"; should have written, "whys and wherefores."

Apostrophes are for possessive rather than plural forms, but certain plurals can cause trouble. You would mind your p's and q's (not ps and qs).

Lesson . . 8   (Oct 26 p 43)

The sample paragraphs containing 24 errors actually had several we overlooked. The second sentence was corrected to read, "Since the elements . . ." Should it have been, "Because the elements . . ."?

Our reference (Perrin's *Writer's Guide and Index to English*) says, "*Since* and *as* can be used in such clauses, but they are less definite, more casual, and more characteristic of easy speech than of writing."

Sentence four reads ". . . to solve a complex algebraic function." You may solve an equation or evaluate a function. You can't solve a function.

The last sentence reads, "By changing the lengths of the four links, an infinite number of speeds and paths are possible . . ."

The participial phrase opening this sentence is a dangler. The subject of the sentence (*number*) should be the subject of the phrase (*you*).

In this same sentence, should the verb (*are*) be singular rather than plural to agree with the subject (*number*)? Perrin says, "When a writer means the group as a whole, a collective noun takes a singular verb and singular pronoun; when he means the individuals of the group, the noun takes a plural verb or plural pronoun."

In this case the verb should be plural. But a complete rewrite of the sentence might be more to the point.

And last, here's a letter both angry and sad. Our question is, can it possibly be representative?

To the Editor:

About your series of articles on "How to Write." It's getting so I can't pick up an engineering or technical magazine without thinking I've gotten hold of a textbook on freshman English—Phooey!

Didn't your article writers go to school? Don't they realize that the average engineer has had to write short, terse, dynamic, interesting essays for several years, in grade school, then for four years of high-school English has written short, terse, dynamic, interesting essays and then for two or three years in college English courses has had to turn in short, terse, dynamic, interesting essays? When, as a newly graduated engineer, I wrote up my first short, terse, dynamic, interesting engineering report, my boss, a kindly man, merely blue-penciled all the terse, dynamic, verbs and wrote in the acceptable passive verbs such as "was done," "was performed," "would be appreciated," etc.

In short, you can write tersely and use the first person in intracompany memos, but readability cannot be tolerated in writing that goes to the customer (and especially so when your customer is the US Government!).

PS—Better withhold my name if you are rash enough to print this. I have enough troubles!

WHAT IS TECHNICAL WRITING?

by ROBERT HAYS
Southern Technical Institute

[By permission. From *Word Study,* copyright 1961 by G. & C. Merriam Co., Publishers of the Merriam-Webster Dictionaries.]

One of the many omens of creeping specialization has been something called "technical writing," "report writing," "engineering English," or "the technical style." And although a dean from a technical school recently remarked that there is no such animal as "technical writing," evidence shows that engineers, technicians, and their teachers and college administrators feel certain that "technical writing" exists. Courses called by the various names given to technical writing appear in many if not a preponderance of the curricula of engineering colleges and technical institutes.

Nor are course titles the only proof that technical writing is a lively subject indeed. *The National Union Catalog* lists at least 47 books since 1950 concerned with the subject. A recent research project carried out by Encyclopædia Britannica easily located 27 articles dealing with technical writing; this research project was by no means definitive. A recent study sponsored by the Carnegie Corporation found that from eight to eleven percent of the curricula in technical institutes is devoted to communication courses.

What then is technical writing? What are the characteristics peculiar to the technical style? What distinguishes it—aside from content and subject matter—from prose written for lay readers or from journalese?

First, technical writing is not a new language, however much a new language might be desired. The technical style preserves the basic Teutonic word order, perhaps maintaining the subject-verb-object sequence more consistently than does prose sculptured by the literary craftsman.

Second, technical writing is probably more conservative, more the slave of the rule, than is the style of popular fiction or even such publications as *The English Journal.* A survey of company-produced publications will reveal industry and engineering devoting much time and energy to teaching their fledglings how to write *correctly.* Gideon Bibles may appear more frequently in hotel rooms; but the book beside the organization manual on the junior executive's desk will be a dictionary, and his secretary will probably have a secretarial handbook plus a dictionary. Research in linguistics may have cast serious doubt on the meaning of "correct English," but Lockheed Aircraft Corporation, General Motors Corporation, Shell Oil Company (to mention only three at random) and many other industrial giants have published guides to *correct usage.*

Third, technical writing shares much of the "common" English vocabulary. The verbs heard on trolleys and at tennis matches are also used in managerial conferences and over drawing boards; and these verbs are conjugated the same in technical writing as in other prose styles. The workhorse articles "a," "an," and "the" appear in reports just as they appear on the front page of the daily paper.

The question is, how does the technical style differ from other prose? There are two fundamental differences, one perhaps psychological and the other linguistic.

The psychological difference lies in the writer's attitude toward his subject. This is predominantly an attitude of utter seriousness. Technical reports avoid exaggeration, for exaggeration might cause misinterpretation of a specification or erection of a structure on the wrong side of a property line. After five o'clock engineers and technicians may be like people. But during working hours decisions often involve lives, reputations, property, the future of organizations. On the job the engineer or technician writing his report must dedicate himself to facts. The appropriate attitude is one of objectivity (if humanly possible), respect for data and their limitations, and caution.

But the greatest difference, at least for teachers and students of technical writing, is linguistic. Technical style demands a specialized vocabulary, especially in its adjectives and nouns. This difference alone would justify the study of technical writing. Only the rare course in English composition would cover these usages. The dean who thinks that engineers and technicians need only another course in English composition instead of a course in technical writing has forgotten that students are not born with a knowledge of many technical words.

At least seven types of words bother readers and writers of technical English:

1. Words demanding a specificity of technical meaning
2. Words in the general vocabulary which are often confused with technical words
3. Pairs or triads of words with similar meanings but differences in spelling
4. Pairs or larger groups of words with similarity in pronunciation but differences in spelling, part of speech, or meaning—including homonyms
5. Words in the general vocabulary demanding a specificity of meaning—words which vex trolley riders as well as technicians
6. Words confused because of metathesis
7. Sets of words causing special problems, problems often technical in nature

The first category is the largest. Naturally, this is the category which has given technical writing its name. For instance, there are *absorb* and *adsorb,* two terms (verbs this time) which have first cousinship of meaning. A blotter will *absorb,* but a glass beaker will *adsorb.* To the trolley rider *acceleration* and *velocity* both mean his bus is moving fast; not so to the technician, who insists that *"acceleration* is calculated as change in *velocity* per unit of time, whereas *velocity* is a measurement of the time spent in traveling a certain distance in a given direction." Or, "*acceleration* is a measure involving time squared, whereas *velocity* is a vector."

To the trolley rider, bugs have "feelers." Press him and he may remember that certain little creatures have *antennae,* or maybe it is *antennas.* The biological scientist will insist that the creatures have *antennae*; an electronics technician writes about the *antennas* of a microwave installation.

When the trolley rider drives to work on a rainy day, he walks to his automobile along a *cement* walkway or a *concrete* walkway. Perhaps the material in his walkway depends on how hard it is raining or something less direct. Architects and building-construction technicians know that *cement* comes in 94-pound bags. *Concrete* is something the contractor makes on the job by mixing *cement* with sand, crushed stone, and water.

The fact that American scientists and technicians develop a split personality when they learn basic units accounts for many peculiarities of technical style. Nowadays people practicing engineering and technical professions must learn both British and metric units. Thus *centi (centimeter), kilo (kilocycle, kilogram, kiloton,* etc.), *mega, (megacycle, megaton),* and *milli (milliamperes, millimeter)* add bulk to the technical style. Many industrial concerns (Eastman Kodak Company, for one) are now labeling products in both systems; perhaps one day Johnny will learn to read and write in the vastly more convenient metric system.

The units needed in calculating the application of energy embrace a squad of terms which the trolley rider considers synonyms. To start with, there is *energy,* which comes in two kinds of packages: kinetic and potential, and which is equated to mass (more about this in a moment) times a constant. *Work* is something else. *Power* and *torque* the layman has heard, but he probably considers that *torque* is just a harder way to spell *power.* Or perhaps *torque* is used because it looks more appealing in Detroit's ads. Not so, says the technician, for *torque* means *force* (another one) times distance. *Power* means *work* per unit of time. Whatever the trolley rider may think, *force* and *pressure* are not synonyms; otherwise, no one could lift an automobile with his hydraulic jack.

To a layman, *mass* and *weight* may seem interchangeable, unless he is on a reducing diet—in which case he always "loses *weight.*" To the lab technician or physicist, *weight* varies with the location at which he makes the measurement. *Mass* is a dependable quantity. The *mass* of a bucket, no—make it a liter, of water will be the same on Chesapeake Bay Ferry, on the top of Mount Everest, and on the plant Uranus. The *weight,* however, depends on the attraction of the celestial body on which the observer takes the measurement. Fortunately, there is yet no urgency to weigh a liter of water on Uranus; in fact, for many practical purposes, *mass* and *weight* are interchangeable.

And finally, in this class are those two fraternal twins *flammable* and *inflammable. The prefix in,* as all know, so often is the linguistic equivalent of a minus sign: in (−) plus efficient (+) equals inefficient (−). But butane, nethane, and many other hydrocarbons are both *flammable* (+) and *inflammable* (+); that is, a bystander should go elsewhere to light his cigarette. Fearful of the consequences of combining ignorance of combustion with knowledge of language, safety engineers are now urging that *flammable* be used exclusively. This change comes slowly, for the owner might wait until his propane truck needs a new coat of paint.

A few words in the common vocabulary cause confusion when placed alongside technical words. *Capacity* and *rating* would certainly rank as useful words in the lay vocabulary, and the distinction may not be clear. Yet a motor has a *rating* which is lower than its *capacity.* For that matter, in electrical work *capacity* (or *capacitance*) has a highly specialized meaning. *Complimentary,* the common word, might seem to be the identical twin—with a dash of misspelling—of *complementary:* but *complementary* in mathematics refers to related angles. And *integration* for the social sciences means one thing but for the mathematician quite another.

Like the common vocabulary technical writing has twins, triplets, or even quadruplets of confusion. For example, certain words have similar meanings but differences in spelling or punctuation or both. *Aid* and *aide* are closely related; so, often, are *adapt* and *adopt.* And the triplets of confusion *accent, ascent,* and *assent* appear in reports as do *decent, dissent* and *descent.*

Some twins or triplets have similar pronunciation and meaning but differences in spelling or part of speech as most often used: *ascent* and *ascend; advice* and *advise; material* and *materiel;* and *vertex* and *vortex. Parameter* and *perimeter* almost earn a place in this category.

Trolley riders, engineers, scientists, and technicians —all may have to reach for the dictionary to *differentiate* (the trolley rider's and not the mathematician's term here) good old *principal* and *principle* or *affect* and *effect.* The second word in each pair appears often in technical writing, as in *Archimedes' Principle* and the *Doppler Effect.*

Sometimes words perplex technicians and laymen too because of an apparent metathesis. These include *casual* and *causal; bare* and *bear; perform* and *preform; stake* and *steak; break* and *brake; great* and *grate;* and *discreet* and *discrete.* With some "twins" the addition or deletion of a letter makes all the difference. Builders use *lath,* whereas machinists use a *lathe;* wire may be specified in *mils* to be installed in newly constructed *mills.* Other confusions result from *ordinance* and *ordnance; dyeing* and *dying; envelop* and *envelope;* and the college student's dilemma of *moral* and *morale.*

Finally (not finely, as in *finely divided particles*), a special class of words haunts the engineering writer.

The comparison of adjectives makes some sort of sense in English. But in technical English some oft-used words have no logical comparative or superlative degrees. For example, angle A is 89° 59′ 59″, and angle B is 89° 59′ 58″. Is angle A *squarer* than angle B? Not really, for neither one is square within the tolerances of many measuring instruments. Similar words for which logical comparisons do not exist might be *complete, cylindrical, cubic, hexaganol, perfect, perpendicular, rectangular, saturated, true,* and *unique*. Use of the phrase "more nearly" before the positive degree is technically sound, but carpenters are not accustomed to talking about one board being *"more nearly square"* than another.

Technical writing requires, of course, more than skill in using words. The technical writer must know his subject, be able to record data and manipulate formulas, and have skill in constructing graphs. However, technical writing seems here to stay as one of the subdisciplines of language study.

NOTES

Arbitrary Signs and Symbols

MUSIC

staff with notes—whole note, half note, quarter, eighth, sixteenth, thirty-second; a dot after a note adds to it half the length of the note without the dot; to extend the compass of the staff, *ledger lines* are added above or below

breve; double whole note

rests—whole, half, quarter, eighth, etc.

brace—used to connect two or more staffs indicating that the parts on these staffs are to be performed simultaneously

bar—a vertical line across the staff, dividing it into equal measures of time; a double bar marks the end of a division, movement, or composition, while a single heavy bar is used (as in a hymn tune) to mark the end of a verse or period

G clef; treble clef—used to indicate that the second line represents the first G above middle C

F clef; bass clef—used to indicate that the fourth line represents the first F below middle C

C clefs—used to indicate that any line or space on which they are placed represents middle C

♯ sharp
♭ flat
♮ natural—used to annul the effect of a previous ♯ or ♭; the *sharps* or *flats* placed at the beginning of a composition or section are called collectively the *key signature*

× or ✕ double sharp—used to raise a note two half steps
♭♭ double flat—used to lower a note two half steps

♯ single sharp—used after a double sharp
♭ single flat—used after a double flat

repeat—used to indicate the beginning and end respectively of a passage to be played or sung twice

𝄋 or :𝄋: segno; sign—used to mark the beginning or end of a passage to be repeated

:𝄋:, +, ※ presa—used to indicate where successive voice parts take up the theme

common time 4/4

alla breve—used to indicate 4/2 or 2/2 time

♪ or ♩ long appoggiatura—used as an embellishing note a degree above or below the principal note

♫ acciaccatura; short appoggiatura—used to indicate that the note is to be performed very quickly

∼ ∞ turn—a grace consisting of four tones: 1) the one above the principal tone; 2) the principal tone; 3) the one below the principal tone; 4) the principal tone

⋰ 2 inverted turn—a grace of four tones like the turn but beginning with the *tone below* instead of the *tone above*

⋏⋏ mordent

𝆖 trill; shake

𝄔 arpeggio

8va all' ottava; at the octave—used above the staff to indicate that the tone or tones are to be sounded an octave higher than written; used below the staff to indicate that they are to be an octave lower

⌢ or ⌣ fermata; hold—used over or under a note; when placed over a double bar denotes the conclusion of the piece
< crescendo
> decrescendo; diminuendo
<> swell
> < ∧ accent marks—used to indicate that a tone or chord is to be given additional stress
▬ tenuto mark—used to indicate that a note is to be held to its full value
' or . staccato—placed over or under a note
⌢ or ⌣ slur; tie
⊔ ⊓ ∧ down-bow } used in music for
∨ up-bow } stringed instruments

PHYSICS

$Å$ angstrom unit
A mass number
$α$ alpha particle
$β$ beta ray
C capacitance
c velocity of light
e electronic charge
g acceleration due to gravity
k susceptibility to magnetism
L inductance
$λ$ wavelength
$μ$ micron or microns; permeability; modulus (used with a specifying subscript); index of refraction
$mμ$ millimicron
$μμ$ micromicron
m_0 rest mass of a particle
n neutron
$ν$ frequency
p proton
R resistance
$ρ$ density
T kinetic energy
V potential energy
X reactance
Z impedance

PUNCTUATION
see page 1193

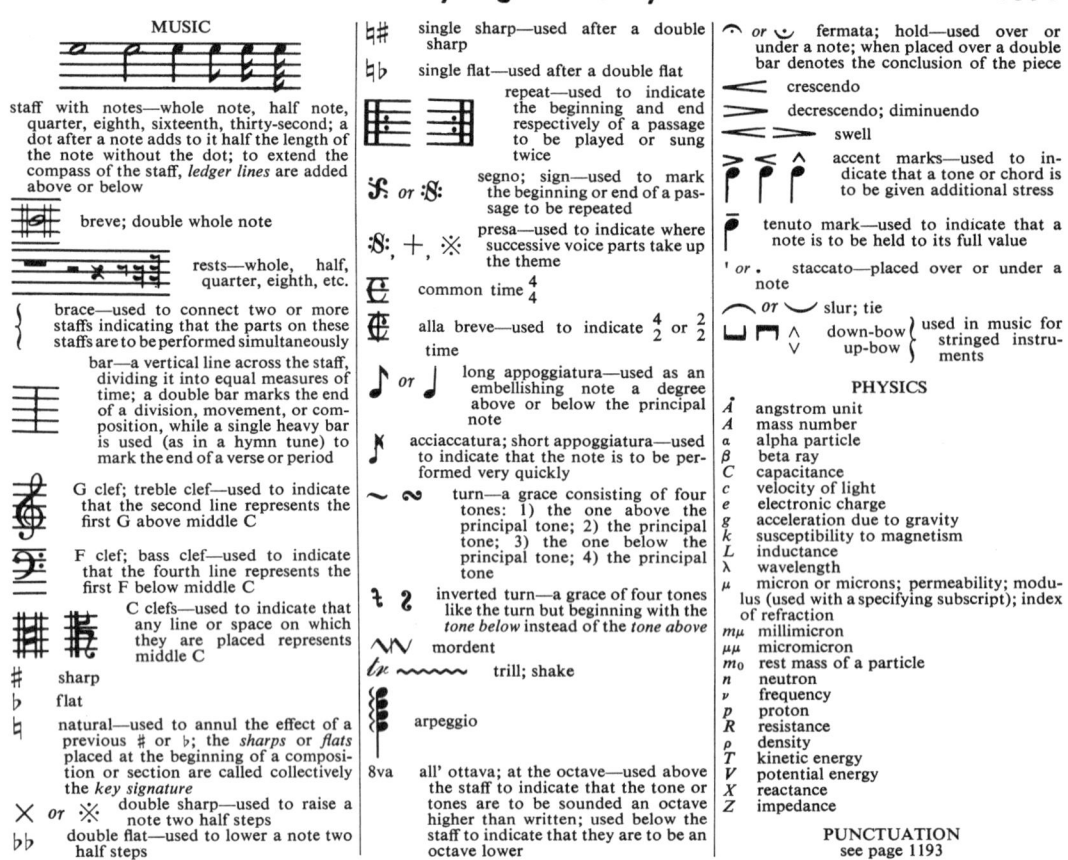

PROOFREADERS' MARKS

𝓈 or 𝓎 or 𝒿 (L *dele*) dele *or* delete; take out or expunge
𝓈 take out a letter and close up
⌢ print as a ligature; thus, a͡e (i. e., print æ); also, close up
∨ or ⌣ less space
◡ close up entirely; no space
𝟿 turn a reversed letter
∧ or > caret; insert at this point the marginal addition
or ♯ space or more space
Eq # space evenly—used in the margin
⌊ or ⌐ or [carry farther to the left
⌋ or ¬ or] carry farther to the right
⊓ elevate a letter or word
⊔ sink or depress a letter or word
☐ em quad space; or indent one em
1/m, |—|, 1/em or |¹| or ᵉᵐ one-em dash
‖ straighten ends of lines
≡ or /// or \\\ straighten a crooked line or lines
⊥ or ⊤ push down a space which prints as a mark
× or + or ⊗ broken or imperfect type—used in the margin
¶ make a new paragraph

○ (a ring drawn around an abbreviation, figure, etc.) spell out—used in the text
ⓢⓟ spell out—used in the margin
⊙ period
⌃ or ,/ comma
:/ or :⊙ colon
;/ semicolon
⩒ apostrophe or single closing quotation mark
⩔ double closing quotation mark
⩒ inverted comma or single opening quotation mark
⩔ double opening quotation mark
=/ or -/ hyphen
[/] brackets
(/) parentheses
wf wrong font—used when a character is of a wrong size or style
ital put in italic type—used in the margin with ____ under text matter
rom put in roman type—used in the margin with ____ under text matter

bf put in boldface type—used in the margin with ____ under text matter
⌐ ¬ transpose
tr transpose—used in the margin
lc lowercase—used in the margin with a slanting line drawn through the letter in the text
= or sc or sm caps put in small capitals—the double lines drawn under the letters or word
≡ or caps put in capitals—the triple lines drawn under the letters or word
ld insert a lead between lines
stet restore words crossed out—usually written in the margin (with dots under the words to be kept)
∨ set as a superscript; thus, ₃⌄ (i. e., print ³)—used in the margin
∧ set as a subscript; thus, ⌃₃ (i. e., print ₃)—used in the margin
? is this correct as set?—used in the margin

see following page for illustration of the application of these marks

By permission. From *Webster's Seventh New Collegiate Dictionary* © 1971 by G. & C. Merriam Co., Publishers of the Merriam-Webster Dictionaries.

PROOFS OF LINCOLN'S GETTYSBURG ADDRESS WITH CORRECTIONS
MARKED (above) AND MADE (below)

"Fourscore and seven years ago our fathers brought forth on this continent a new nation, conceived in liberty, and dedicated to the proposition that all men are created equal. Now we are engaged in a great civil war, testing whether that nation, or any nation so conceived and so dedicated, can long endure. We are met on a great battlefield of that war. We have come to dedicate a portion of that field, as a final resting place for those who here gave their lives that that nation might live. It is altogether fitting and proper that we should do this. But, in a larger sense, we cannot dedicate—we cannot consecrate—we cannot hallow—this ground. The brave men, living and dead, who struggled here, have consecrated it, far above our poor power to add or detract. The world will little note, nor long remember, what we say here, but it can never forget what they did here. It is for us the living, rather, to be dedicated here to the unfinished work which they who fought here have thus far so nobly advanced. It is rather for us to be here dedicated to the great task remaining before us,—that from these honored dead we take increased devotion to that cause for which they gave the last full measure of devotion—that we here highly resolve that these dead shall not have died in vain—that this nation, under God, shall have a new birth of freedom—and that government of the people, by the people, for the people, shall not perish from the earth."

By permission. From *Webster's Seventh New Collegiate Dictionary* © 1971 by G. & C. Merriam Co., Publishers of the Merriam-Webster Dictionaries.

NOTES